Programming in Standard
FORTRAN 77

Programming in Standard
FORTRAN 77

A. Balfour
Director, Marketing Support, Europe—Africa Division, Burroughs

D. H. Marwick
Lecturer in Computer Science, Heriot-Watt University

HEINEMANN EDUCATIONAL BOOKS

Heinemann Educational Books Ltd
22 Bedford Square, London WC1B 3HH

LONDON EDINBURGH MELBOURNE AUCKLAND
SINGAPORE KUALA LUMPUR NEW DELHI
IBADAN NAIROBI JOHANNESBURG
PORTSMOUTH (NH) KINGSTON

ISBN 0 435 77486 7

First published 1979
Reprinted 1981, 1983, 1985, 1986, 1987, 1988

British Library Cataloguing in Publication Data
Balfour, Alexander
    Programming in Standard Fortran '77.
    1. FORTRAN (Computer program language)
    I. Title II. Marwick, D H
    001.6'424   QA76.73.F25
ISBN 0-435-77486-7

Typeset by Preface Ltd, 1–3 The Malverns,
Cherry Orchard Lane, Salisbury, Wilts
and printed in Great Britain by
Richard Clay Ltd, Bungay, Suffolk

Preface

In writing this book the authors have attempted to provide a *comprehensive* coverage of FORTRAN 77, as defined in the new Standard, for experienced FORTRAN users. At the same time, the text is equally suitable for those with no previous knowledge of FORTRAN, but who possess some familiarity with elementary programming techniques.

Structured programming and design techniques have been emphasized wherever possible, bearing in mind the limitations of FORTRAN 77 for this purpose. The authors hold the highly pragmatic view that, since FORTRAN is so widely used as a scientific programming language, its existence should be accepted, despite its blemishes, and every effort made to encourage its devotees to write *good* FORTRAN programs, and to adopt FORTRAN 77.

Adherence to the Standard in the interests of program *portability* has also been emphasized, since it is by no means uncommon nowadays for FORTRAN-based programs and packages to be moved from machine to machine. Throughout the text, problem areas with regard to program portability have been highlighted, and an attempt has been made to gather together various aspects of program portability in Chapter 21.

The book is aimed at three categories of reader:

(a) current FORTRAN users;
(b) undergraduate students, postgraduate students, and staff in universities, technical colleges, colleges of education, etc.;
(c) scientists, engineers, and technologists in industry.

Care has been taken to provide many worked examples and exercises throughout the text, and solutions to most exercises have been provided.

It is appropriate to note here the achievement of the FORTRAN Standards Committee X3J3 in the production of FORTRAN 77. While it is inevitable that the resultant language will not please everyone, the effort involved in revising FORTRAN in the face of often conflicting views and advice should not be underestimated. The authors gratefully acknowledge the work of the committee.

The authors also acknowledge the efforts of Arthur Bloch in collecting together well-known laws, theorems, postulates, etc., which explain why many projects are unsuccessful. The quotations at the beginning of each chapter are taken from his book *Murphy's Law and Other Reasons Why Things Go Wrong* (Price, Stern, and Sloan). The one exception is the quotation for Chapter 18 which is one of Ted Glaser's many quotable quotes.

In the course of writing the book, the authors have received assistance and advice from a number of people. In particular, thanks are due to Ian Aitchison, Hunter Davis, and Allen McTernan of the Department of Computer Science, Heriot-Watt University, with an especially large thanks to Anne Alexander who not only typed the manuscript but suffered, with infinite patience, the retyping required by both the large and small alterations inevitable in the production of a book.

A. Balfour

August 1979

D. H. Marwick

Contents

1 FORTRAN: History and Overview

Smile ... tomorrow will be worse. *(The Murphy Philosophy)*

FORTRAN is a programming language designed originally for the solution of problems involving *numerical computation*. Today it is the most widely used programming language within the scientific programming world, and indeed many scientists and engineers regard it as an indispensable tool. At the same time, programming language experts point to its glaring deficiencies which discourage good programming practice, and lament the continued widespread use of FORTRAN to the detriment of other more modern programming languages. To understand why FORTRAN is both highly popular and highly criticized, some appreciation of the history of FORTRAN is necessary.

The development of FORTRAN goes back to the early 1950s. Sammet (1969), for example, cites the IBM document *PRELIMINARY REPORT, Specifications for the IBM Mathematical FORmula TRANslating System, FORTRAN* (1954) which formed the basis for the release in 1957 of a FORTRAN system for the IBM 704. In June 1958 FORTRAN II for the IBM 704 was released, a new version of FORTRAN containing a number of significant enhancements to the original, for example the subprogram concept. Between 1958 and 1960 similar FORTRAN systems were released for the IBM 709, 650, 1620, and 7070 systems.

In the early 1960s implementations of FORTRAN proliferated rapidly as other manufacturers sought to combat the challenge of IBM in the scientific programming world by providing FORTRAN compilers for their own computer systems. Each implementation not only incorporated minor differences of interpretation of facilities in IBM FORTRAN, which was by no means itself well defined, but also, in most cases, significant extensions to the language. In addition IBM developments of FORTRAN were continuing, a major event being the release of FORTRAN IV for the IBM 7090. FORTRAN IV added many new facilities (e.g. complex and double precision arithmetic) to FORTRAN II, and also dropped some of its machine-dependent statements, a welcome innovation.

The 1966 Standard

The need to control and standardize the multiplicity of FORTRAN systems was therefore apparent by the early 1960s, and in May 1962 a committee was established by the then 'American Standards Association' to formulate proposals for standardization. *Two* standards (American National Standards Institute, 1966a,b) were eventually published in 1966, one for FORTRAN and one for a subset of FORTRAN known as *basic* FORTRAN. In historical terms, FORTRAN corresponded roughly to FORTRAN IV, and basic FORTRAN to FORTRAN II. By 1966, however, most computer manufacturers and FORTRAN users were sufficiently forward-looking not to be interested in FORTRAN II, with the result that the Standard evolved for basic FORTRAN received relatively little attention.

In retrospect the 1966 Standard for FORTRAN is a disappointing document for two main reasons. Firstly it enshrined in FORTRAN a significant number of minor quirks and illogical restrictions dating back to early FORTRAN compilers and the primitive hardware on which these compilers had been implemented. Barron (1977), for example, states that the Standard has been described as 'a loving compilation of all the bugs in the early FORTRAN compilers', a point of view which is grossly unfair but does contain a germ of truth.

Secondly the 1966 Standard did not use a *formalized notation* for describing FORTRAN, despite the success of such an approach several years earlier in defining the syntax of Algol 60. Instead English prose was used, with all its associated opportunities for ambiguity and misinterpretation. As a result the 1966 Standard does not give a precise, clear definition of FORTRAN, and any compiler writer using it as a guide encounters many areas of difficulty. Indeed, complete books have been written since 1966 attempting to clarify the Standard. *Standard FORTRAN Programming Manual* (National Computer Centre, 1970) is particularly noteworthy. About it, Barron says 'it will probably tell you more about FORTRAN than you wish to know'.

The 1977 Standard

In 1970 the X3J3 Technical Committee of the American National Standards Institute commenced work on the formulation of a new FORTRAN standard, using the following principal development criteria:

(a) program portability;
(b) compatibility with existing standards and practices;
(c) addition of desirable new features;
(d) consistency and simplicity to the user;
(e) capability for efficient implementation;
(f) allowance for future growth;
(g) acceptability to users.

The efforts of this committee culminated in 1977 with the agreement of a new Standard (American National Standards Institute, 1978) for FORTRAN 77, describing once again a *full* language and a *subset* language.†

The full language FORTRAN 77 contains some significant features not available in 1966 Standard FORTRAN, and also liberates programmers from some of the

†Only the full language is considered in this book.

illogical restrictions of the 1966 Standard, regrettably not always in a logical fashion. It is also interesting to note that the new Standard specifies the rules that must be adhered to by *Standard conforming programs* rather than *Standard conforming compilers*. It is the programmer's responsibility to write Standard conforming programs and, if he or she does not adhere to the Standard, the effect of presenting that program to a FORTRAN 77 compiler is *undefined*. In other words, a standard conforming FORTRAN 77 compiler must accept standard conforming programs and process them correctly; what it does with a FORTRAN 77 program containing non-standard features and enhancements is compiler-dependent, and unpredictable in terms of the specifications in the Standard.

It is important to bear the above point in mind when reading other chapters in this book. For example, whenever it is stated that a particular entity is 'invalid', it implies that it should not be used in a standard conforming program. It does *not* imply that a standard conforming FORTRAN 77 compiler will signal an error when the entity is encountered. Some may, and others may not.

Conclusions

FORTRAN is the most widely used language for scientific programming purposes, and will continue to be so in the foreseeable future for the following reasons:

(a) FORTRAN compilers are widely available. It is unusual to discover even a minicomputer system which does not have a FORTRAN compiler.

(b) Practitioners in other disciplines who already use FORTRAN are reluctant to expend time and effort learning a better, more modern programming language. In addition, 'state of the art' languages do not always provide the facilities required by some scientists and engineers, e.g. complex and double precision arithmetic.

(c) During the past twenty years there has been a considerable investment in the development of scientific and engineering programs using FORTRAN. Many such programs are still in operation, having been substantially patched and moved from machine to machine over the years. Rewriting such programs on a large scale is a formidable, and expensive, undertaking.

(d) Major libraries of numerical and statistical software now form a crucial part of any scientific computing environment, enabling users to take advantage of high quality routines which may have required many man-years of effort to produce. Most major libraries are written in FORTRAN, a persuasive force against change.

(e) Although problems do exist (see Chapter 21), FORTRAN programs tend to be more easily portable from machine to machine than programs written in many other languages.

The fact, however, that FORTRAN dominates the scientific computing world should not be used to deduce that FORTRAN is an *ideal* programming language. On the contrary, when examined using modern criteria for a good programming language, FORTRAN has serious short-comings, some of which are:

(a) The language does not have a simple, coherent, logical structure. This is not surprising when it is remembered that, over the years, significant additional facilities have been grafted onto FORTRAN yet at the same time compatibility with earlier versions has been maintained.

(b) FORTRAN is not an ideal vehicle for structured design and structured programming (see Chapter 2).

(c) FORTRAN contains too many special cases, too many irritating restrictions, and too many ways of doing the same thing. These contribute greatly to the occurrence of errors when developing FORTRAN programs. Perhaps the best way to sum up FORTRAN is to quote Barron (1977), who states that 'The remarkable and depressing fact is that it has survived so long with so little alteration, like some hardy weed'.

While FORTRAN 77 retains many of the deficiencies of earlier versions of FORTRAN, the new language is a substantial improvement over FORTRAN 66 in a number of significant respects. The introduction of improved control structures, for example, makes FORTRAN 77 a better vehicle for structured programming than FORTRAN 66. The more elaborate character handling facilities available in FORTRAN 77, and also the introduction of list directed input/output, are two other examples of welcome innovations.

The FORTRAN 77 Standard is therefore a noteworthy step along the road to providing FORTRAN with some of the features considered necessary in a modern programming language. Since this is the case, it is important that those who wish to program in FORTRAN should adopt the new Standard as quickly as possible, and adhere to it under normal circumstances.

2 Program design

A carelessly planned project takes three times longer to complete than expected; a carefully planned project takes only twice as long. (*Golub's Second Law of Computerdom*)

Before discussing the programming language FORTRAN 77 it is useful to consider in general terms what is involved in solving a problem using a computer. Although the use of a computer should not in itself alter the basic approach to problem solving, the thought and care required to design a satisfactory computer program are often underestimated. Therefore in this chapter the steps involved in designing a program from initial problem specification are discussed.

There are five phases involved in designing a program:

(a) Specify the problem.
(b) Analyse the problem.
(c) Design a method of solution (an algorithm) for the problem.
(d) Code the algorithm into a suitable programming language.
(e) Test the program.

In practice, these phases are rarely independent and it is often necessary to return to previous phases for further investigation before reaching a satisfactory result.

Carelessness or lack of attention to any of these phases can lead to a significant amount of unexpected and unnecessary extra work. In particular, it is important to have designed a suitable algorithm before starting the coding phase. Otherwise, the final program may well be far from suitable. The reason for this is simply that the two phases (c) and (d) require different thought processes, one in the design of a method of solution to the problem and the other in implementing this algorithm on a computer. Doing both simultaneously often leads to one taking precedence over the other, which as a consequence is deficient in some respects.

Problem specification
It should be self-evident that if a problem is not well specified the resulting program may be unsatisfactory. Since the problem often originates from a person without computer expertise (the customer), the onus is on the programmer to ensure that he or she has sufficient information on the problem before the design is too far advanced. This may require several discussions with the customer, including one or two *during* the design phase. The end result must, of course, satisfy the customer and not simply gratify the programmer.

A simple example of the kind of assumption that is made but which can lead to frustration occurs in the specification:

'Print a table of squares of numbers from 1 to 100.'

The assumption (which is probably reasonable in this case) is that the numbers involved are the integers $1, 2, 3, \ldots, 99, 100$. However, in a particular application the natural progression may be $1, 1.5, 2, 2.5, \ldots$, or $1, 3, 5, \ldots$, or even $1, 2, 3, \ldots, 9, 10, 15, 20, \ldots, 45, 50, 60, 70, \ldots, 90, 100$. It is 'natural' for the customer to think in his own terms (and indeed he should be *encouraged* to do so), and hence the programmer must determine what these 'natural' terms of reference are before proceeding.

Problem analysis
The analysis of the problem is really the first phase of the algorithm design. It includes the determination, in general terms, of what is involved in the solution, how it splits into a number of smaller sub-problems, and whether or not it is really a special case of a more general problem which can be solved using an existing program. Do not 're-invent the wheel'. If there is an adequate program in existence, take advantage of the fact.

Algorithm design
This is the most difficult phase. To design an algorithm which will work for all sets of data presented to it in a reasonably efficient manner and to the satisfaction of the customer is seldom an easy task. Note that 'satisfaction' includes not only the correct results presented in the appropriate form, but also the cost of running the program. Hence a good algorithm ought to be an optimum one in terms of the computer resources used.

The program coded from the algorithm will process *data*. The manner in which these data are held may influence significantly the efficiency of the program. Thus during the design phase thought should be given to how the data involved are best held and structured. Detailed consideration of this aspect is beyond the scope of this book.

The language chosen to describe the algorithm being designed is of some importance. There are many popular description languages including flowcharts and English language statements. However, the structure of the algorithm should be clear from the description in order to minimize the misunderstandings that can so easily arise in the design process. Therefore a structured description language using pseudo-English language statements has been chosen to represent algorithms in this book. This is introduced later in the chapter.

Coding
This phase, while requiring great care, should be relatively simple. Since the method of solution has been determined at the previous phase the programmer can concentrate on the problems involved in implementing the algorithm and making the best use of the computing resources available. As shall be seen, there are very few *types* of instruction in designing algorithms, so that, with experience, it is a fairly straight-

forward task for a programmer to convert an algorithmic description into the programming language to be used.

Different programming languages have different characteristics. If a choice of language is available consideration should be given to which is the best for the application in hand.

Testing

If the previous phases have been executed with thought and care, testing should reveal few deficiencies. However, remembering that the program must be able to deal satisfactorily with all data presented to it, *appropriate* test data must be devised in an attempt to ensure that all situations are handled correctly.

The time-consuming part of this phase is the finding and correcting of an error in the program. Thus again it is emphasized that, if the problem is understood and the algorithm has been designed with care, the majority of errors should be those introduced at the *coding* phase and hence not too difficult to find.

Maintenance

Unless the program is written as a 'one-off' exercise, it will become a production program which will be used again and again. Three problems may arise:

(a)   an error is found;
(b)   the customer wishes some amendment to be made;
(c)   the customer wishes to expand the task, and hence program enhancements are required.

Thus the program must be *maintained*. Whether or not the original programmer does the maintenance, it is essential that sufficient documentation exists to enable all the above problems to be solved with the minimum of effort. It is surprising how quickly the originator will forget the details of programs for which he or she has been responsible.

Maintenance is often an underrated part of programming, probably because it is an unattractive aspect. Nevertheless it is a vital part, and the more carefully the groundwork has been laid in the implementation stages, the simpler maintenance will be. Further, if a good programming style is developed, the code is more easily read and hence changed. Some pointers to a good programming style are considered in Chapter 22.

Conclusions

Programming is more than simply writing programs in a favourite computer language (Dijkstra, 1972). The design process is the most important and the most challenging phase and, unless it is treated as such, the resultant program may well not do what is required, execute efficiently, or be easy to maintain. *When programming concentrate on the design phase.*

The design phase

There are many approaches to designing algorithms, but one of the most successful is known as 'top-down' design (Yourdon, 1975).

Top-down design

This approach requires the programmer to consider the whole problem (i.e. the specification) as the top level and then to split this into its logical parts. Each of these parts is considered independently and is further split into its logical parts. This *refining process* continues until the level of coding is reached. It will be noticed that at each level there is an algorithm for the solution of the problem.

By checking carefully at each level that the algorithm will solve the problem correctly, the programmer can be confident that he has a valid program as the final level. There may of course be small errors, such as transcription errors, but the overall structure should be correct and, with care, logical errors should be localized and simple to find.

The care taken to produce a correct program gives a confidence in the end result that is often lacking in other approaches to programming.

Example 2.1   For many team games, competition is organized into leagues with the position of each team in the league being recorded in a table. This league table is updated after every match between two teams.

Given a league table and set of match results as data, design an algorithm to update the league table and print it. For simplicity, assume that all data input is correct. Further steps would be required if the input data were to be validated.

First refinement

(a)   The current league table must be read in and should be printed so that the updated table can be checked manually from the current table and the results. (During the development of a program, it is good practice to print out data which are read, since they can be of assistance during the testing phase.)

(b)   For each match result the table entries for *both* teams must be updated.

(c)   The match results may have caused some teams to change their position in the table and so the table must be sorted before being printed.

This leads to the algorithm:

(1)   Read the current league table.

(2)   Print it.

(3)   Read the match results and update the entries for both teams in the table.

(4)   Sort the updated table.

(5)   Print it.

Second refinement

Each part is examined separately and further refined if necessary.

(a)   Reading the table involves discovering (or deciding on) the format of the information in the table and also how to store it for simple access during updating and sorting.

(b)   Printing the table involves deciding on the layout of the printed table.

(c)   Again a decision on the format of the match results input, whether they should be printed and how, will be made. An aspect of efficiency at this stage is how the match results are stored. If it is assumed that each result will be read, printed, and processed separately, there is no need to store all the results together: only one result at a time.

(d)   The position of a team in the league depends on the points accumulated by the team during the competition. Where two or more teams have an equal number of points, there is often a method of differentiating between them, which depends on the sport concerned. For example, in Association Football, goal difference is used.

(e)   This part is the same as (b) above.

This leads to a new algorithm:
(1)   Read the current table.
(2)   Print it.
(3)   For each match result
    (a)   read the result,
    (b)   print it,
    (c)   update the first (home) team entry in the table,
    (d)   update the second (visiting) team entry in the table.
(4)   Sort the updated table.
(5)   Print it.

Modularity

The top-down design approach produces a number of 'logical parts' or *modules*. Each module is independent of all other modules in that it is expected to process specified input data and produce specified output data without affecting any other module or data. It is of no significance at this stage how a module achieves its objectives and indeed it may be replaced by another module which is functionally equivalent (i.e. one that accepts the same input data and produces the same output data).

By retaining this modularity down to the level of the program, the program is simpler to follow and understand, which in itself aids the maintenance of the program. There are a number of ways to retain modularity, for example by making each module a *procedure* (see Chapter 12). Clearly some modules may be applicable to a number of parts of the program (e.g. a sort module, a module to solve a set of simultaneous equations), in which case the module appears only once in the program but is used in a number of different places.

Example 2.2   Consideration of the league table problem above (Example 2.1) will show that modules 2 and 5 are identical. Note that they are not printing identical information but they are printing a table in a specific format. This module lends itself to being converted into a procedure *within* the program.

Modules 3c and 3d likewise are identical in that they are required to update the league table with information on a given team from the match result.

Style

By not taking sufficient care in the design stage a programmer can end up with a highly complex program. There are programmers who consider this to be a virtue, adding to the excitement of the challenge of program maintenance.

When in doubt, keep the program simple; it is easy to make it complex. There are occasions, however, when, for reasons of computer efficiency, it may be necessary to write a complex module (Knuth, 1974). This will be a conscious decision say, to speed up a portion of the program after having gained confidence with a simple version, i.e. it is a further refinement to a lower level.

Good programming style comes with experience and from good, simple, modular design (Kernighan and Plauger, 1974).

Algorithmic description language

There are many different ways of writing down an algorithm but there are two qualities that any given method must have, namely:

(a)   it must be unambiguous;
(b)   it should cater easily with the top-down, modular design approach.

Further, it is generally recognized that three basic building blocks are required:

(i)   a processing statement;
(ii)   a decision structure;
(iii)   a looping structure.

These three statement-types can be used at all stages of the design process.

The algorithmic language detailed below has these characteristics and is used throughout the rest of the book.

The processing statement

The processing statement is a 'black box' statement indicating some unit of processing. Depending on the level of design, it may describe a complex operation (such as 'design a bridge to cross the river') or a simple operation (such as 'square the number'). A processing statement is written as a simple (clear) English sentence or as a pseudo-statement from a programming language.

At a further stage of refinement, a processing statement may be expanded to include several processing statements, decision and looping structures.

The decision structure

Decisions are taken on the current values of given data in the calculation (e.g. whether or not a number is zero). There are two forms of the decision structure:

(a)   The **if-then** statement, where a single operation is either executed or it is not, e.g.
     if the customer's bank balance is negative **then** notify the manager.
(b)   the **if-then-else** statement, where there is a choice between two operations, e.g.

if dinner at the restaurant costs less than £5 **then** dine at the restaurant
else dine at home.

Note that the decision is made up of a comparison (a *logical expression* — see
Chapters 9 and 16) and one or two processing statements, thus:

(a)   **if** *logical expression* **then** *processing statement;*

(b)   **if** *logical expression* **then** *processing statement A*
      else *processing statement B*

Obviously sufficient information must be available prior to the decision being taken
to ensure that the logical expression can be evaluated.

At a further stage of refinement, any part of a decision structure may be
expanded to include processing statements, decision and looping structures.

The looping structure

The solutions to many problems require a sequence of steps to be repeated a number
of times, e.g. scanning a table of names requires the examination of each entry in the
table *in turn*. Such a sequence is known as a *loop* and there are two main looping
structures:

(a)   the **loop while** statement, where the sequence of steps is repeated until
       some condition becomes true, e.g.
       loop while there is at least one more course **do** eat the next course.

(b)   the **loop for** statement where the sequence of steps is repeated a fixed
       number of times, e.g. processing a list of 50 entries in a table would be
       written
       loop for $i = 1, 2, \ldots, 50$ **do** process the ith entry.

Note that:

(a)   a **loop while** statement is made up of a logical expression and a process-
       ing statement thus:
       loop while logical expression **do** processing statement.

(b)   a **loop for** statement is made up of a loop index, together with the values
       it will take, and a processing statement thus:
       loop for *index* = *values* **do** *processing statement.*

       The list of values must indicate clearly which values the index will take.
       Examples of the **loop for** statement are:
       loop for $i = 1, 2, \ldots, n$ **do** processing statement;
       loop for $j = 2, 4, 6, \ldots, 2n$ **do** processing statement;
       loop for $k = 1, 2, \ldots, 10, 15, 20, \ldots, 50, 60, 70, \ldots, 100$ **do**
       processing statement.

Obviously sufficient information must be available prior to entering the loop to
ensure that in the **loop while** statement the logical expression can be evaluated and
in the **loop for** statement the values to be taken by the index are defined. It is also
important that the loop *terminates*, that is, the sequence of steps is not repeated
indefinitely.

At a further stage of refinement, any part of a looping structure may be expanded to include processing statements, decision and looping structures.

Example 2.3   The algorithm obtained at the second refinement of the league table problem above (Example 2.1) can now be written:

$$
\left.
\begin{array}{l}
\text{read the current table} \\
\text{print it}
\end{array}
\right\} \begin{array}{l} \textit{processing} \\ \text{statements} \end{array}
$$

loop while there is a match result to process **do**
$$
\left.
\begin{array}{l}
\{\text{read a result} \\
\quad \text{print it} \\
\quad \text{update the home team entry} \\
\quad \text{update the visiting team entry} \}
\end{array}
\right\} \begin{array}{l} \textbf{loop while} \\ \text{statement} \end{array}
$$

$$
\left.
\begin{array}{l}
\text{sort the updated table} \\
\text{print it}
\end{array}
\right\} \begin{array}{l} \textit{processing} \\ \text{statements} \end{array}
$$

(Notice the bracketing of several processing statements within the **loop while** statement.)

Third refinement

The only modules requiring further refinement before coding are the update module and the sort module. Typically, each entry in the league table consists of the team name, the number of matches played, won, drawn, and lost, the total number of points awarded and various statistics accumulated from past matches (e.g. In Association Football, the total number of goals scored for and the total number of goals scored against). In addition, a match result consists of the names of the two teams together with some indication of the result (e.g. the number of goals scored by each team). Therefore the information presented to the update module will be the team name and the result of the match. The algorithm is:

search the league table for this team
update the number of matches played
if the team won this match **then** update the number of matches won
     else if the team drew this match
       then update the number of matches drawn
        else update the number of matches lost
calculate the points awarded for this match
update the points total
update the accumulated statistics

Note the use of an **if-then-else** statement within another **if-then-else** statement.

The refinement of the sort module is left as an exercise for the reader.

Layout

It will be noticed from the algorithms in Example 2.3 that some statements (or parts of statements) are indented on the page and/or bracketed together. The reason for this is to make the algorithm clear and easy to read. Good design requires algorithms and programs that are easily read. As a result, program maintenance is simplified.

The layout of algorithms (and, later, programs) is largely a matter of common sense. Thus if a looping or a decision structure operates on several statements, the statements should be bracketed together *and* indented to make the intention clear. For example:

> **loop while** there is match result to process **do**
> >   {read the result
> >   print it
> >   update the home team entry
> >   update the visiting team entry }

A decision structure can be very obscure especially where there are a number of nested **if-then-else** statements. Careful use of indentation is necessary to aid clarity, e.g.

> **if** the team won this match **then** update the number of matches won
> >   **else if** the team drew this match
> >   **then** update the number of matches drawn
> >   **else** update the number of matches lost

Exercise 2

1 The league table algorithms (Examples 2.1, 2.2, and 2.3) were developed without any particular game being used. Choose a game where league tables are used and adapt the algorithms given in Example 2.3 for this game.

2 Using the game chosen in question 1 design an algorithm for the sort of module in Example 2.3.

3 Given the valid date of a day in the twentieth century in the form: day number, month number, year number, design an algorithm to print out the date of the following day. (E.g.

> 15, 3, 42 leads to 16, 3, 42;
> 28, 2, 76 leads to 29, 2, 76;
> 31, 12, 29 leads to 1, 1, 30.)

4 Design an algorithm to validate a date supposed to lie between 1st January 1950 and 31st December 2050 inclusive. Assume the date is given in the form: day number, month number, year number.

5 A is a vector of m numbers and B is a vector of n numbers. Both are sorted into numerically ascending order prior to input. Assuming that there are no duplicate values within any one vector, design an algorithm to merge A and B into a new vector C such that C is sorted into numerically ascending order and contains no duplicate values. (For example, if $A = \{1, 2, 4, 5, 10\}$ and $B = \{2, 6, 10, 12\}$ then the resultant vector $C = \{1, 2, 4, 5, 6, 10, 12\}$.)

3 What does a FORTRAN 77 program look like?

The sooner and in more detail you announce the bad news, the better.
(*White's Chappaquidick Theorem*)

The presentation of FORTRAN 77 adopted in this book is essentially one of *synthesis*, i.e. the simplest 'building blocks' which can occur in FORTRAN 77 are described, it is then explained how to combine these 'building blocks' into more complicated entities, and so on, until complete FORTRAN 77 programs emerge. Unfortunately, although this approach is logically attractive in many ways, it does mean that the reader has no feel for what a typical FORTRAN 77 program looks like until about one-third of the text has been studied.

In order to remedy this a complete FORTRAN 77 program will be presented and described in this chapter. It must be emphasized that the reason for doing this is to give the reader an *over-all* impression of a typical FORTRAN 77 program. It is hoped that a broad picture of FORTRAN 77 will be created into which the detailed syntax and semantics of FORTRAN 77 described in later chapters can be inserted in context.

The FORTRAN 77 program to be discussed is given on page 15. Its purpose is to read in the lengths of the three sides of a triangle, and to evaluate and output (a) the area of the triangle, and (b) the sizes of the angles. The line numbers given in the left-hand column are purely for explanatory purposes, and have no connection with the actual program.

The complete FORTRAN program is called an *executable* program and consists of, in this case, two *program units*. One program unit is the *main program* running from line 1 to line 17, and the other is a *function subprogram* running from line 18 to line 22. The main program is called 'TRIANG' (line 1), and the subprogram 'ANGVAL' (line 18).

Each program unit consists of a sequence of *statements*, one per line in the example program, with the exception of one output statement which requires *two* lines. Some statements are *executable* statements, whereas other statements are *non-executable* statements. Roughly speaking a non-executable statement provides information to the FORTRAN 77 compiler, but is not actually compiled into executable machine code. An executable statement, on the other hand, is compiled into executable machine code. The statement

PROGRAM TRIANG

Line No.

```
1       PROGRAM TRIANG

2       LOGICAL FLAG

3       READ *, A, B, C

4       PRINT *, ' THE LENGTHS OF THE SIDES OF THE TRIANGLE ARE', A, B, C

5       FLAG = (A+B).GT.C .AND. (B+C).GT.A .AND. (C+A).GT.B

6       IF (FLAG) THEN

7            S=0.5*(A+B+C)

8            AREA=SQRT(S*(S-A)*(S-B)*(S-C))

9            ANGA = ANGVAL(B,C,A)

10           ANGB = ANGVAL(C,A,B)

11           ANGC=180-(ANGA+ANGB)

12           PRINT *, ' AREA OF TRIANGLE IS', AREA,

13      +              ' ANGLES OF TRIANGLE ARE', ANGA,ANGB,ANGC

14              ELSE

15           PRINT *, ' INVALID INPUT DATA'

16      END IF

17      END

18      FUNCTION ANGVAL(X,Y,Z)

19      PI = 3.14159265

20      TEMP = (X*X+Y*Y-Z*Z)/(2*X*Y)

21      ANGVAL = (180/PI)*ACOS(TEMP)

22      END
```

PROGRAM TO CALCULATE AREA AND ANGLES OF A TRIANGLE

for example, is a non-executable statement, whereas the statement

$$ANGC = 180 - (ANGA+ANGB)$$

is an executable statement.

Within the statements occur *constants* and the *names* of *variables*. For example, 0.5 (line 7) and 180 (line 11) are two constants, the first of which is a number with a decimal fraction part and the second of which is an integer. B and ANGB, on the other hand, are the names of two variables, representing respectively the side *b* and the angle *B* of the triangle. Note how, because FORTRAN 77 does not allow lower-case letters, B has been used for the side *b* of the triangle, and a different name, ANGB, created for the opposite angle. The following diagram may prove helpful:

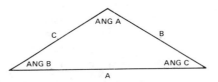

The program may now be explained on a line by line basis thus:

Line 1 specifies the name of the main program to be TRIANG.

Line 2 is a *type* statement and indicates that the variable named FLAG is to assume 'logical values'. Since this is the only type statement in the program it is assumed that the other variable names which occur represent variables which will assume 'normal arithmetic values'.

Line 3 is an *input* statement, and indicates that three numbers are to be read in, and their values given to the variables with names A,B,C. In other words, the lengths of the three sides of the triangle are to be read in.

Line 4 is an *output* statement, and indicates that the message THE LENGTHS OF THE SIDES OF THE TRIANGLE ARE and the values of the variables with names A, B, and C are to be printed out. This provides a useful check that the values read in were the intended ones!

Line 5 is a *logical assignment statement* which gives the logical variable FLAG the value **true** if $a + b > c$ and $b + c > a$ and $c + a > b$, and the value **false** otherwise. In other words, FLAG is given the value **true** if the values read in are the sides of a genuine triangle, in which the sum of any two sides always exceeds the third side. Note how .AND. is written for 'and', and the rather peculiar .GT. for 'greater than'.

Line 6 is a *BLOCK IF statement* indicating that in this case, if the value of the logical variable FLAG is **true**, lines 7 to 13 are to be executed, and if the value of the logical variable FLAG is **false**, line 15 is to be executed. Note how the BLOCK IF statement acts in conjunction with the *ELSE statement* (line 14) and the *END IF statement* (line 16) to select one of two groups of statements for execution, depending on the truth value of the logical variable FLAG. The combined effect is obviously similar to an **if-then-else** statement as described in Chapter 2.

Lines 7 and 8 evaluate the area of the triangle, the value being assigned to the variable named AREA, using the well known formula

$$\text{Area} = \sqrt{s(s-a)(s-b)(s-c)} \text{ where } s = \tfrac{1}{2}(a+b+c)$$

Note how '*' is the multiplication operator† in FORTRAN 77, and how a 'special function' SQRT has been used to obtain the square-root.

Line 9 is a statement which calls into action the subprogram ANGVAL. Its effect, without going into detail, is to evaluate the angle opposite the side *a* of the triangle and to give this value to the variable called ANGA.

Line 10 similarly references the subprogram ANGVAL to evaluate the angle opposite the side *b* of the triangle and to give this value to the variable called ANGB.

† * is also used for other purposes in FORTRAN 77.

Line 11 is an *arithmetic assignment statement* which gives to the variable ANGC the value of 180 — (ANGA+ANGB). Fairly obviously, line 11 is the FORTRAN 77 equivalent of the mathematical formula

$$C = 180 - (A + B)$$

for the angles of a triangle.

Lines 12 and 13 contain an *output statement* which prints out

(a)   the message AREA OF TRIANGLE IS followed by the value of AREA;
(b)   the message ANGLES OF TRIANGLE ARE followed by the values of ANGA, ANGB, and ANGC.

Since the statement spreads over two lines, a *continuation character* '+' has been used on the second line.

Line 15 is an *output statement* which prints out a message indicating the occurrence of invalid input data. Depending on the input data either line 15 or lines 7 to 13 will be executed.

Line 17 is an *END statement*. When the END statement in a *main program* is executed, program execution is terminated.

Line 18 is a *FUNCTION statement* specifying the name of a function sub-program, in this case ANGVAL, and the names of 'parameters' used by the sub-program. When the subprogram is referenced (as in line 9) these 'parameters' are replaced by actual variables from the main program.

Line 19 is an *arithmetic assignment statement* giving the variable PI the value 3.14159265, a fairly good approximation to π.

Line 20 is an *arithmetic assignment statement* giving the variable TEMP the value of $(x^2 + y^2 - z^2)/(2xy)$. This expression is the right-hand side of the well known cosine rule

$$\cos \theta = \frac{x^2 + y^2 - z^2}{2xy}$$

for finding the angle θ in the triangle

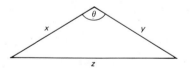

Line 21 is an *arithmetic assignment statement* which associates the value of

$$\frac{180}{\pi} \cos^{-1} (\text{TEMP})$$

with the name of the function. Like SQRT, ACOS is a 'special function' producing in this case the angle (in radians), the cosine of which is given by its argument. Multiplying by $180/\pi$ converts the angle to degrees.

Line 22 is an *END statement*. When the END statement in the *subprogram* is executed, control is returned to the appropriate point in the main program.

The reader will find it instructive to simulate the effect of, say, the first subprogram call (line 9) by reconsidering the effect of lines 19, 20, and 21 when X, Y, and Z are replaced respectively by B, C, and A.

Do not worry if some of the fine detail of this example is confusing at this stage. All the programming concepts involved will be examined and carefully described in subsequent chapters.

Exercise 3

1 With reference to the example program, answer the following questions.
   (a)   Which arithmetic operators occur?
   (b)   List the names of all variables occurring (i) in the main program, and (ii) in the subprogram.
   (c)   List the words which are part of FORTRAN 77, e.g. PROGRAM.
   (d)   What would be the effect of omitting the ELSE statement (line 14)?
   (e)   Could line 11 be replaced by a statement similar to line 9 or line 10?
   (f)   What do you think are the FORTRAN 77 equivalents of 'less than', 'not equal' and 'or'?
   (g)   Can you eliminate the need for a subprogram by replacing lines 9 and 10 by several arithmetic assignment statements?

4 Data types and constants

Regardless of the units used by either the supplier or the customer, the manufacturer shall use his own arbitrary units convertible to those of either the supplier or the customer only by means of weird and unnatural conversion factors. (*Wyszkowski's Theorem*)

FORTRAN 77 permits data of *six* different types to occur in a program, namely INTEGER, REAL, DOUBLE PRECISION, COMPLEX, LOGICAL, and CHARACTER. The purpose of this chapter is to consider how *constants* of these six different types are written.

Constants of types INTEGER, REAL, DOUBLE PRECISION, and COMPLEX are called *arithmetic constants*, so that any constant in a FORTRAN 77 program is either an arithmetic constant, a logical constant, or a character constant. Blank characters occurring in an arithmetic or logical constant have no effect on the value of the constant, although the practice is not to be recommended.

Integer constants

An *integer constant* is merely a whole number written without a decimal point; more precisely, it is an optional sign followed by a non-empty string of digits.

Example 4.1　The following are permissible integer constants in FORTRAN 77:

$$2153$$
$$-36$$
$$0$$
$$123456$$
$$-999$$

Example 4.2　The following are not acceptable as integer constants in FORTRAN 77:

Constant	Reason
3.14159	decimal point is not permitted
−36,320	embedded comma is not permitted
10^3	exponentiation is not permitted

Integer constants are always held *with complete accuracy* within the memory of a computer system. On the other hand, every implementation of FORTRAN 77 imposes some size restriction on integer constants, and it is important to ascertain the range of values within which integer constants must lie for the system being used to run FORTRAN 77 programs. By way of illustration, in Burroughs B6700 FORTRAN all integer constants must be in the range −549755813887 to +549755813887.

Example 4.3 It is certain that most implementations of FORTRAN 77 would find the integer constant

$$1000000000000$$

unacceptably large.

Real constants

In order to define how *real constants* are written in FORTRAN 77 two preliminary definitions must first be made:

(a) A *basic real constant* consists of an optional sign followed by an *integer part*, a *decimal point*, and a *fractional part*. Both the integer and fractional parts are strings of digits, one of which may be empty but not both.

(b) A *real exponent* consists of the letter E followed by an (optionally signed) integer constant, and represents a power of 10. For example, E5 indicates 10^5.

Example 4.4 The following are valid basic real constants:

$$21.632$$
$$-9.4605$$
$$0.0$$
$$.00263$$
$$-37.$$

Example 4.5 The following are valid real exponents:

$$E7$$
$$E+10$$
$$E-5$$
$$E0$$

The valid forms of a real constant are then

(a) a basic real constant;
(b) a basic real constant followed by a real exponent; or
(c) an integer constant followed by a real exponent.

Example 4.6   The following are valid real constants in FORTRAN 77:

Constant	Interpretation
21.632	
−9.4605	
0.0	
.00263	
−37.	
−3.5E4	-3.5×10^4
0.2634E−6	0.2634×10^{-6}
5E+12	5×10^{12}
1E−8	10^{-8}

Note how the presence of a real exponent indicates multiplication by a power of 10.

Example 4.7   The following are not acceptable as real constants in FORTRAN 77:

Constant	Reason
25	This is an *integer* constant
−2,312.4	Embedded comma is not permitted
E5	Real exponent must not stand by itself
5xE−4	Multiplication sign is not permitted
−2.86E−1.4	E must be followed by an integer constant

Unlike integer constants, which are held within the memory of a computer system with complete accuracy, real constants are held to a *certain precision* which depends on the computer system being used. An IBM 370 system, for example, holds real constants with a precision of 24 bits (about 7 decimal digits), whereas a CDC Cyber 70 system holds real constants with a precision of 48 bits (about 14 decimal digits).

The fact that the precision, with which real quantities are held, varies considerably from machine to machine has significant implications for the portability of FORTRAN 77 programs. A FORTRAN program, for example, transferred from a CDC Cyber 70 system to an IBM 370 system may no longer produce adequately accurate results if the arithmetic involved requires a precision of more than 7 decimal digits.

Like integer constants, real constants are restricted to lie within some finite range by every implementation of FORTRAN 77. In addition, constants which are smaller in magnitude than some small positive quantity cannot be distinguished from zero. Once again the precise limits vary from implementation to implementation. On a Burroughs B6700 system, for example, all real constants must lie in the range -4.31359×10^{68} to $+4.31359 \times 10^{68}$, and any real constant with magnitude smaller than 8.75812×10^{-47} cannot be distinguished from zero.

Double precision constants

A *double precision constant* is a decimal number held internally with greater precision than that used for real constants. It may be written in one of two ways:

(a)   as a basic real constant followed by a double precision exponent; or
(b)   as an integer constant followed by a double precision exponent;

where in each case a *double precision exponent* is defined to be the letter D followed by an (optionally signed) integer constant, and represents a power of 10.

Example 4.8   The following are valid double precision constants in FORTRAN 77:

Constant	Interpretation
2.5D−6	2.5×10^{-6}
−8D20	-8×10^{20}
0.1234D+3	0.1234×10^{3}
3.141592653589793D0	3.141592653589793

The letter D in a double precision constant is interpreted in exactly the same way as the letter E in a real constant, the essential difference being that a double precision constant is held internally in computer memory with *greater* precision than the corresponding real constant. As the name suggests, most implementations of FORTRAN 77 hold double precision constants with about *twice* the precision of real constants, although the FORTRAN 77 Standard merely requires them to be held with *greater* precision. By way of illustration, a Burroughs B1700 system holds real constants with a precision of 24 bits (about 7 decimal digits) and double precision constants with a precision of 60 bits (about 18 decimal digits).

Note that the 'D0' in the last constant in Example 4.8 must be present for the 16-digit approximation to π to be converted and held internally in double precision form.

The reader is referred to Chapter 17 for a detailed account of the use of double precision facilities in FORTRAN 77 programs.

Complex constants

A *complex constant* is written as two real or integer constants separated by a comma and surrounded by parentheses. The first of the two constants in the parentheses represents the *real* part of the complex number, and the second the *imaginary* part.

Example 4.9   The following are acceptable complex constants:

Constant	Interpretation
(2,3)	$2+3i$
(−1.6,3.75)	$-1.6+3.75i$
(0,1)	i
(3.0,−1.5E4)	$3.0-1.5 \times 10^{4} i$

Example 4.10   The following are not acceptable as complex constants:

$$(X,Y)$$
$$(2,3.5D-6)$$

The reader is referred to Chapter 18 for a detailed account of the use of complex facilities in FORTRAN 77 programs.

Logical constants

The two *logical constants* in FORTRAN 77 are written .TRUE. and .FALSE.. Note that each logical constant starts and finishes with a decimal point.

The reader is referred to Chapter 16 for a detailed account of the use of logical facilities in FORTRAN 77 programs.

Character constants

A character constant is *written* as any non-empty string of characters preceded and followed by an apostrophe. Unlike other forms of constant, blank characters occurring within a character constant are regarded as significant. In addition, if the character string contains an apostrophe as one of its characters, *two consecutive* apostrophes are used, instead of one, when the corresponding character constant is written in a FORTRAN 77 program. It is particularly important with regard to character constants to distinguish between *the way a constant is written in FORTRAN 77* and its *value*.

Example 4.11   The following are valid character constants in FORTRAN 77:

```
'DONALD KNUTH'
'TEMPERATURE VALUES ARE'
'MAZDA RX2'
'+ — * /'
'XYZ'
'X     Y     Z'
'ROD "THE ROCKET" LAVER'
```

Note that the character constants 'XYZ' and 'X   Y   Z' are different because blanks are significant. In addition, the *value* of the first character constant is DONALD KNUTH, and the value of the last character constant is ROD 'THE ROCKET' LAVER.

According to the FORTRAN 77 Standard any character acceptable to the implementation of FORTRAN 77 being used may occur in a character constant. In the interests of portability, however, it is advisable to adhere to characters in the FORTRAN 77 character set, namely the letters A to Z, the digits 0 to 9, and the thirteen special characters = + — * / ( ) , . $ ' : and blank.

The *length* of a character constant is defined to be the number of characters (including blanks) between, but not including, the delimiting apostrophes, except that each pair of consecutive apostrophes is counted as a *single* character. Since a character constant always contains a *non-empty* string of characters, the length of a character constant is greater than zero.

Example 4.12   The lengths of the character constants

'FRED'
'TEMPERATURE VALUES ARE'
'ROD "THE ROCKET" LAVER'

are respectively 4, 22 and 22.

The reader is referred to Chapter 15 for a detailed account of the use of character facilities in FORTRAN 77 programs.

Exercise 4

1 For each of the constants listed below, place a tick (√) in the appropriate column:

	Integer	Real	Double precision	Complex	Logical	Character	Invalid
21.5							
−0.0							
123321							
1.5734E+6							
−1,000,000							
−.216E−10							
3.612E+N							
.FALSE.							
.TR U E.							
−9.D−20							
−0.0D0							
(1.6,−2.5E4)							
5D4							
−1.624E−1.8							
'TRUE'							
'EVE"S PUDDING'							
'4+3=6'							
TRUE							
'BROTHERS"							
(2.5D0,−6)							
(0,0)							
'2.25D−1.6'							

2 Write down the lengths of the valid character constants in the above table.

3 For the FORTRAN 77 implementation you are currently using, ascertain the following information:
   (a) range of valid integer values;
   (b) magnitude of largest real value;
   (c) magnitude of smallest, positive, non-zero, real value;
   (d) precision of real arithmetic;
   (e) magnitude of largest double precision value;
   (f) magnitude of smallest, positive, non-zero, double precision value;
   (g) precision of double precision arithmetic;
   (h) limitations, if any, on the lengths of character constants.

4 List any points made in Chapter 4 which are worth remembering when writing *portable* FORTRAN 77 programs.

5 Variables

Variables won't; constants aren't. (*Osborn's Law*)

A *variable* in a FORTRAN 77 program is an entity possessing both a *name* and a *type*. To create a name for a variable a programmer may use any combination of not more than *six* letters, A to Z, and digits, 0 to 9, which commences with a *letter*.

Example 5.1   The following are acceptable variable names:

X	VW1600	VOLUME	P25Z
I	H2SO4	TIME	TEMP
ALPHA	X23	FRED	USER

Example 5.2   The following are invalid variable names:

Name	Reason
BBC–2	Hyphen is not allowed
3XY	Must begin with a letter
X4.9	Decimal point is not allowed
AB"	Apostrophes are not allowed
CONDENSER	More than six characters

It is important, in the interests of program clarity and maintainability, to make the names created for variables as meaningful as possible although the 6-character restriction is not always helpful in this respect. Names such as X2P15 and QZUTW almost guarantee the occurrence of errors during the writing of a FORTRAN 77 program, and are certain to lead to confusion and bewilderment if the program has to be amended six months later! It should always be remembered that there is a very great difference between what is acceptable to a FORTRAN 77 compiler and what it is sensible to use in a FORTRAN 77 program.

Variables in a FORTRAN 77 program may assume values of type INTEGER, REAL, DOUBLE PRECISION, COMPLEX, LOGICAL, or CHARACTER. Since this is the case it is necessary to indicate to the compiler whether a particular variable name is the name of a variable which will assume integer values, or the name of a variable which will assume real values, etc. There are essentially two methods of conveying this information in a FORTRAN 77 program:

(a)   by *explicit* type-statements;
(b)   by *implicit* methods.

Type-statements

A typical type-statement for variables which will assume integer values has the form

INTEGER   P, FLAG, COUNT, A1, A2

and indicates, in a fairly obvious manner, that the variables with names P, FLAG, COUNT, A1, and A2 will assume integer values within the 'program unit' in which the type-statement occurs. Precisely what is meant by a 'program unit' will become apparent later. For the moment regard 'program unit' as being synonymous with 'program'. Strictly speaking, however, a FORTRAN 77 'program unit' is either a 'main program' or a 'subprogram', and neither entity has yet been fully described.

Note that in the type-statement

INTEGER   P, FLAG, COUNT, A1, A2

the variable names P, FLAG, COUNT, A1, and A2 have been created by the person writing the FORTRAN 77 program in which the type-statement occurs. INTEGER, however, is different in that it is a sequence of letters built into the definition of FORTRAN 77, and as such is known as a *keyword*.

Type-statements for variables of types real, double precision, complex, and logical are constructed in an analogous manner using the keywords REAL, DOUBLE PRECISION, COMPLEX, and LOGICAL. For example, a FORTRAN 77 program unit may contain the following type-statements:

```
INTEGER      P,Q
REAL         X,VOL,MASS,U,V
DOUBLE PRECISION  XLONG
COMPLEX      Z1,Z2
LOGICAL      FLAG,MARKER
```

indicating that, in the program unit in which the type-statements occur

(a)   the variables named P and Q are of type INTEGER;
(b)   the variables named X, VOL, MASS, U, and V are of type REAL;
(c)   the variable named XLONG is of type DOUBLE PRECISION;
(d)   the variables named Z1 and Z2 are of type COMPLEX;
(e)   the variables named FLAG and MARKER are of type LOGICAL.

Note that, in each case, a type-statement consists of one of the key-words INTEGER, REAL, DOUBLE PRECISION, COMPLEX or LOGICAL followed by one or more variable names separated by commas.

Example 5.3   The following type-statements may appear in a FORTRAN 77 program unit:

COMPLEX	W,Z
LOGICAL	TEST
INTEGER	COUNT, SUM, F,X,N
COMPLEX	Z1, Z2

Note that the order in which type-statements occur in a program unit is unimportant, and that more than one type-statement for, for example, complex variables may occur. On the other hand, the same *variable name* must not occur more than *once* in type-statements in a program unit.

Type-statements for variables of type CHARACTER have a more complicated syntax, and will not be considered in complete detail until Chapter 15. A typical example, however, of a CHARACTER type-statement is:

CHARACTER   P*4, Q*12, R*2, S*6

This indicates that the variables with names P, Q, R, and S are character variables of lengths 4, 12, 2, and 6 respectively, e.g. the variable P can assume character values containing not more than 4 characters. Alternatively, the keyword CHARACTER may be followed by a *length specification* thus:

CHARACTER *6   L*4, M, N, S*8, T

and this length specification is applied to any character variable in the type-statement which does not have its own length specification, in the above case the variables M, N, and T.

Example 5.4   The CHARACTER type-statement

CHARACTER *4   P, Q*6, R*8, NOTE1, NOTE2

indicates that the variables with names P, Q, R, NOTE1, and NOTE2 are character variables of lengths 4, 6, 8, 4, and 4 respectively.

Note that, if a character variable is not given an explicit length in one of the ways described above, it is assigned a length of 1 by default.

Example 5.5   The CHARACTER type-statement

CHARACTER   L, M, N*4, R*6, S, T

indicates that the variables with names L, M, N, R, S, and T are character variables of lengths 1, 1, 4, 6, 1, and 1 respectively.

Implicit naming conventions

If a variable name is used in a program unit in FORTRAN 77 *and it has not occurred in a type-statement in that program unit*, the corresponding variable is assigned a type *by default* according to the following conventions:

(a) if the variable name begins with one of the letters I, J, K, L, M, or N it is assumed to be of type INTEGER;

(b) if the variable name begins with any other letter it is assumed to be of type REAL.

Thus variables of types REAL or INTEGER need not occur explicitly in type-statements, provided that their names begin with appropriate letters. This is the traditional, conventional method of naming real or integer variables in a FORTRAN program, and many programmers will deliberately distort the names of variables (e.g. use XMASS instead of MASS) in order to avoid various type-statements. This practice is not to be encouraged.

Example 5.6 A FORTRAN 77 program unit is to contain variables with the following names and types:

Names	Type
X1,Y,MASS,LENGTH	REAL
COUNT,I,J,KOUNT	INTEGER
D1,D2	DOUBLE PRECISION

Then only the following type-statements are strictly necessary in that program unit:

REAL   MASS,LENGTH
INTEGER   COUNT
DOUBLE PRECISION   D1,D2

I, J, and KOUNT need not occur in an INTEGER type-statement since they begin with letters chosen from I, J, K, L, M, and N. Similarly X1 and Y need not occur in a REAL type-statement since they begin with letters *other than* I, J, K, L, M, and N.

Exercise 5

1 Which of the following are valid variable names in FORTRAN 77?

FVALUE	$\bar{X}$	ART.53	COLOUR
APT26	XBAR	A(25)	FORTRAN77
T'	π	P+Q	EMC2
2PQ	PI	FRED	X15P26

2 In a FORTRAN 77 program unit the variable names X5, WEIGHT, and COUNT are to represent variables of type INTEGER, the variable names L and KAPPA are to represent variables of type REAL, and the variable names Z1, Z2, and Z3 are to represent variables of type COMPLEX. Write type-statements to achieve this.

3 The implicit naming convention could be used to remove some of the variable names from the following type-statements:

REAL	VOL,X,Y,MASS,LIMIT
INTEGER	KAPPA,LEVEL,P,QUANT
COMPLEX	Z1,ZVAL
DOUBLE PRECISION	A,B,C,D1,D2
LOGICAL	FLAG
CHARACTER *6	C1,C2,C3,NAME*12

Which ones?

4 What are the lengths of the character variables named in the following CHARAC-TER type-statements?

(a)   CHARACTER   L*2,M*6,N*4
(b)   CHARACTER *8   ANAME,BNAME,X*6,Y*6,VAL
(c)   CHARACTER   CHAR, C1,C2,P*6,Q*8,CNEW

5 Do you think that the values of real variables will be subject to the same range restrictions and precision limitations as real constants? What about integer and double precision variables?

6 It is permissible in a FORTRAN 77 program to use, as the name of a variable, the name of a keyword containing six or fewer characters, e.g. REAL. What do you think is the effect of doing so, and would you regard it as a sensible thing to do?

6 Arithmetic expressions and assignment statements

> In any calculation, any error which can creep in will do so. (*First Law for Naive Engineers*)

An arithmetic assignment statement in FORTRAN 77 has the form

$$v = \text{arithmetic expression}$$

where v is the name of an arithmetic variable†, i.e. a variable of type integer, real, double precision, or complex. When an arithmetic assignment statement is executed the arithmetic expression on the right-hand side is evaluated and the resulting value is assigned to the variable whose name occurs on the left-hand side, after type conversion (see below), if necessary. Several examples will make apparent what is involved, before arithmetic expressions are considered in greater detail.

Example 6.1   The arithmetic assignment statement

$$Y = (A+B)/(X - 3.654)$$

indicates that the variable Y is to be given the value of the arithmetic expression $(A+B)/(X-3.654)$. Note that for this to be meaningful, the variables A, B, and X must have *defined* values when the arithmetic assignment statement is executed. Note also that the last value assigned to Y (if any), before the execution of the assignment statement is 'overwritten' and no longer available after the execution of the assignment statement.

Example 6.2   The arithmetic assignment statement

$$I = (P*T*R)/100$$

indicates that the variable I is to be given the value of the arithmetic expression PTR/100, an asterisk being used to represent a *multiplication sign*. Once again this is meaningful provided that P, T, and R have defined values when the arithmetic assignment statement is executed.

Example 6.3   The arithmetic assignment statement

$$K = K+1$$

† v may also be the name of an arithmetic array element (see Chapter 10).

indicates that the variable K is to be given the value of the arithmetic expression K+1. In other words, the value K has after the execution of the assignment statement will be 1 greater than its value just before the execution of the assignment statement.

It is fairly obvious from the last example that the 'equals sign' in an arithmetic assignment statement is not being employed in the normal mathematical sense, but instead should be read as 'is assigned the value of'.

Arithmetic expressions

In this section arithmetic expressions involving integer and real constants and variables will be considered in some detail. The use of double precision and complex quantities in arithmetic expressions is postponed until Chapters 17 and 18 respectively. Also considered later are arithmetic expressions involving references to arithmetic functions, array elements, and symbolic names of constants.

At this stage an arithmetic expression is either a real or integer variable or constant, or consists of one or more of these entities combined together using

    (a)   parentheses, (and)

    (b)   the *arithmetic operators* +, −, *, / and **, interpreted thus:

Use of Operator	Interpretation
$x_1 + x_2$	Add x_1 and x_2
$+ x_2$	Same as x_2
$x_1 - x_2$	Subtract x_2 from x_1
$- x_2$	Negate x_2
$x_1 * x_2$	Multiply x_1 and x_2
x_1 / x_2	Divide x_1 by x_2
$x_1 ** x_2$	Raise x_1 to the power x_2

In evaluating an arithmetic expression, the following order or precedence is used for the arithmetic operators:

Operator	Precedence
**	Highest
*, /	Intermediate
+, −	Lowest

where operators of equal precedence are applied from *left to right*, except for ** which in expressions like A**B**C is applied from *right to left*. Wherever necessary, of course, sub-expressions in parentheses will be evaluated first, using the above order of precedence for any arithmetic operators involved.

Arithmetic expressions must not contain *consecutive* operators, e.g. A*−B is an invalid arithmetic expression (write instead A*(−B) or −A*B). On the other hand, the multiplication operator * must never be implied, as in algebra. For example, (A+B)(C−D) is an invalid arithmetic expression, the correct form being (A+B)*(C−D).

Parentheses may be freely inserted in arithmetic expressions, even where they are not strictly required. Thus A+(B*C) is perfectly acceptable as an alternative to the arithmetic expression A+B*C. Similarly A**(B**C) may be written instead of A**B**C, and indeed the additional pair of parentheses are strongly recommended in the interests of clarity.

Example 6.4 The following are permissible arithmetic expressions:

Arithmetic Expression	Interpretation
−9.2635	−9.2635
VAL	val
A+B+2.7	$a+b+2.7$
3*(I+J)	$3(i+j)$
B**2+C**3	b^2+c^3
A**(2*R)+1	$a^{2r}+1$
A/B*C	$(a/b)c$
A/(B*C)	$a/(bc)$
((A+B)/C)**2.5	$((a+b)/c)^{2.5}$
(A*Z+B)*Z+C	$(az+b)z+c$
A*(R**N−1)/(R−1)	$a(r^n-1)/(r-1)$
P**Q**2	p^{q^2}

Note the left to right interpretation in the case of A/B*C, and the right to left interpretation in the case of P**Q**2. It is important to appreciate that P**(Q**2)≠ (P**Q)**2, in general. For example, if P=2 and Q=3 then P**(Q**2)=2**(3**2= 2**9=512, whereas (P**Q)**2=(2**3)**2=8**2=64.

Example 6.5 The following are invalid arithmetic expressions in FORTRAN 77:

Invalid Expression	Reason
2**−N	Two consecutive operators, ** and −
P(A+3.6)	Missing multiplication operator
2.75 − PIP*(A+B))	Unmatched parentheses

Evaluation of arithmetic expressions

The FORTRAN 77 Standard specifies various rules for the evaluation of an arithmetic expression involving real and integer quantities (the assumption made in this chapter).

Firstly, any arithmetic operation whose result is not *mathematically defined* is prohibited in the execution of a program. Typical examples are:

(a) A/B when B = 0
(b) A**B when A = 0 and B ⩽ 0
(c) A**B when A < 0 and B is of type REAL.

Secondly, in evaluating expressions of the form

$$x_1 \text{ op } x_2$$

where 'op' is one of the arithmetic operators $+$, $-$, $*$, $/$ and $**$, the nature of the arithmetic carried out depends on the *types* of the operands x_1 and x_2. There are essentially three cases to consider:

(a) x_1, x_2 *both of type REAL*. In this case *real* (decimal) arithmetic is used provided that, as noted above, the operation is meaningful mathematically.

(b) x_1, x_2 *both of type INTEGER*. In this case, *integer* arithmetic is used. In particular x_1/x_2 where x_1 and x_2 are of type INTEGER produces an *integer* result obtained by *truncating* the mathematical quotient, i.e. by discarding its fractional part. Thus $7/3 = 2$, $3/5 = 0$, and $7/(-4)=-1$.

(c)   *One of* x_1, x_2 *of type REAL and the other of type INTEGER*. In this case the integer operand is *converted* to real form and real arithmetic used to produce a real result. There is *one* exception – in the case $x_1 ** x_2$, where x_1 is of type REAL and x_2 is of type INTEGER, x_1 is raised to the power x_2 to produce a real result without converting x_2 to real form.

Some authors deprecate the use of 'mixed mode' arithmetic as in case (c) above, and classify it as poor programming practice on the grounds that the type conversions taking place 'behind the scenes' introduce unnecessary inefficiencies which can often be easily avoided, e.g. by writing X+6.0 instead of X+6. Such inefficiencies, however, are relatively minor and of little importance compared with the need to achieve good programming design and the need to avoid *gross* programming inefficiencies. Mixed mode arithmetic has therefore been freely used throughout this book. It is also interesting to note that, whereas FORTRAN 77 permits the use of mixed mode arithmetic, FORTRAN 66 does not, an indication possibly of changing attitudes towards this aspect of programming practice.

Example 6.6   Assuming the implicit naming convention for real and integer variables, evaluate wherever possible the following arithmetic expressions in FORTRAN 77 using the indicated variable values.

(a)	(I+J)*(K−5)	I=2, J=3, K=7
(b)	(I+J)/(K−5)	I=2, J=3, K=7
(c)	(I+J)/(K−5)	I=2, J=3, K=5
(d)	X+Y*Z	X=2.5, Y=3.0, Z=4.5
(e)	X+Y**Z	X=2.0, Y=9.0, Z=0.5
(f)	X+Y**Z	X=2.0, Y=−9.0, Z=0.5
(g)	X+Y**(I/J)	X=2.0, Y=−9.0, I=1, J=2

(a) $(2+3)*(7-5) = 5*2 = 10$

(b) $(2+3)/(7-5) = 5/2$, and result truncated to 2.

(c) $(2+3)/(5-5) = 5/0$, hence invalid.

(d) $2.5 + 3.0*4.5 = 2.5 + 13.5 = 16.0$.

(e) $2.0 + 9.0**0.5 = 2.0 + 3.0 = 5.0$.

(f) $2.0 + (-9.0)**0.5$, hence invalid.

(g) $2.0 + (-9.0)**(1/2) = 2.0 + (-9.0)**0 = 2.0+1.0=3.0$

Execution of an arithmetic assignment statement

In executing an arithmetic assignment statement of the form

$$v = \text{arithmetic expression}$$

once the arithmetic expression has been evaluated to produce a real or integer result, the resulting value has to be assigned to the variable whose name is specified on the left-hand side of the assignment statement. Precisely how this is done is indicated in the following table:

Type of v	Type of result	Actions performed
INTEGER	INTEGER	Assign result to v
INTEGER	REAL	Truncate result and assign to v
REAL	INTEGER	Convert result to real form and assign to v
REAL	REAL	Assign result to v

Most of the time the arithmetic assignment statements occurring in FORTRAN 77 programs are such that either the first or last line of the table applies and a straight assignment is made. On occasions, however, a truncation or type conversion is required, as the following example illustrates.

Example 6.7   Assuming the implicit naming convention, what are the values assigned to X and I when the following assignment statements are executed using the indicated values?

(a)   X = (I+J)/(K−5)   I = 6, J=5, K=8
(b)   I = X+Y/Z   X = 2.5, Y = 1.0, Z = 3.0

(a)   (I+J)/(K−5) = (6+5)/(8−5) = 11/3, which is truncated to produce 3 as the result of evaluating the arithmetic expression on the right hand side. Hence, according to the table above, X is assigned the value 3.0.

(b)   X+Y/Z = 2.5+1.0/3.0 = 2.5+0.333 .... 3, yielding 2.833 ..... 33 as the result of evaluating the arithmetic expression on the right-hand side. Hence, according to the table above, I is assigned the value 2.

Intrinsic functions

In order to simplify the writing of programs involving standard mathematical functions such as $\sin x$, $\log x$, $\tan^{-1} x$, etc., the FORTRAN 77 Standard specifies that any implementation of FORTRAN 77 must supply certain 'built in' functions known as *intrinsic functions*. A complete list of FORTRAN 77 intrinsic functions is given in Chapter 12. However, at this point it is sufficient merely to consider some of the available intrinsic functions. These are shown in the table on page 35. Only *specific names* for functions have been given. Most intrinsic functions also possess *generic names* which will be considered later (see Chapter 12).

As the following examples indicate, these intrinsic functions may be freely used in arithmetic expressions, in the same manner as integer and real constants and vari-

TABLE 6.1.   A short list of intrinsic functions.

Intrinsic function	Definition	Specific name	Type of argument	Type of function
Exponential	$\exp(x)$	EXP	REAL	REAL
Natural logarithm	$\log_e x$ $(x>0)$	ALOG	REAL	REAL
Common logarithm	$\log_{10} x$ $(x>0)$	ALOG10	REAL	REAL
Sine	$\sin x$ (x in radians)	SIN	REAL	REAL
Cosine	$\cos x$ (x in radians)	COS	REAL	REAL
Tangent	$\tan x$ (x in radians)	TAN	REAL	REAL
Arcsine	princ.value of $\sin^{-1} x$ ($\|x\| \leqslant 1$)	ASIN	REAL	REAL
Arccosine	princ.value of $\cos^{-1} x$ ($\|x\| \leqslant 1$)	ACOS	REAL	REAL
Arctangent	princ.value of $\tan^{-1} x$	ATAN	REAL	REAL
Square root	$+\sqrt{x}$ ($x \geqslant 0$)	SQRT	REAL	REAL
Absolute value	x if $x \geqslant 0$, $-x$ if $x<0$	IABS	INTEGER	INTEGER
		ABS	REAL	REAL
Conversion to integer	truncate x	INT	REAL	INTEGER
Conversion to real	convert to real form	REAL	INTEGER	REAL

ables, by inserting the appropriate argument in parentheses after the specific name of the function. Note that

(a)   The argument may be an arbitrary arithmetic expression, the value of which must be of the type REAL or INTEGER indicated in the penultimate column of the table.

(b)   The value returned by calling a function into action will be of type REAL or INTEGER as specified in the last column of the table.

(c)   The type of the value returned may also be deduced from the *first* letter of the specific name of the function via the implicit naming convention, i.e. if the first letter of any specific function name in the table is I, J, K, L, M, or N it will return a value of type INTEGER; otherwise it will return a value of type REAL.

Example 6.8   Several mathematical formulas are listed with their FORTRAN 77 equivalents:

Mathematical formula	FORTRAN 77 equivalent
$y = (e^{a+b} + 3)(\cos t - t^4)$	Y = (EXP(A+B)+3)*(COS(T)−T**4)
$x = \dfrac{1}{2a}\{-b + \sqrt{b^2 - 4ac}\}$	X = (−B+SQRT(B*B−4*A*C))/(2*A)
$b = (a \sin B)/\sin A$	B = A*SIN(ANGB)/SIN(ANGA)
$\pi = 4 \tan^{-1}(1)$	PI = 4*ATAN(1.0)
$q = \sin(\cos u) - \cos(\sin u)$	Q = SIN(COS(U))−COS(SIN(U))

Example 6.9   The arithmetic assignment statement

$$Y = ALOG(2)$$

is invalid in FORTRAN 77 since the function ALOG requires the provision of a *real* argument. A correct version is

$$Y = ALOG(2.0)$$

Example 6.10   The trigonometric functions SIN, COS, and TAN require *radian* arguments. Thus, given that the value of ANGC is in degrees, the following FORTRAN 77 assignment statement will evaluate, by the cosine rule, the side C of a triangle:

$$C=SQRT(A*A+B*B-2*A*B*COS(3.14159265*ANGC/180))$$

Example 6.11   It is the programmer's responsibility to provide *meaningful* arguments for the various intrinsic functions. Thus, the assignment statement

$$Y = ALOG10(-2.5)$$

is invalid.

Example 6.12   The intrinsic function REAL is often useful for converting an integer argument to real form. Thus, whereas the assignment statement

$$X = SQRT(I*I+J*J)$$

is invalid assuming the implicit naming convention, the assignment statement

$$X = SQRT(REAL(I*I+J*J))$$

will produce the desired effect.

Further comments on the evaluation of arithmetic expressions†

Earlier in this chapter the rules for evaluating an arithmetic expression were described in terms of operator precedence, expressions in parentheses, left to right evaluation when operators of equal precedence (except **) are involved, etc. The FORTRAN 77 Standard, however, extends the 'rules of the game' by stating that a *mathematically equivalent expression may* be evaluated under certain circumstances.

Thus, for example, since the expressions (X+Y)+Z and X+(Y+Z) are mathematically equivalent, when a programmer writes

$$A = X+Y+Z$$

in a FORTRAN 77 program, assuming the implicit naming convention, it may be interpreted as

$$A = X+(Y+Z)$$

despite the rules for left to right evaluation. Unfortunately, although (X+Y)+Z and X+(Y+Z) are mathematically equivalent, they are not *computationally* equivalent, e.g. in the case where X is large and Y and Z very small.

---

†This section may be conveniently omitted at a first reading.

Similarly the arithmetic assignment statement

$$A = X*Y/Z$$

may be interpreted as $A = (X*Y)/Z$ using left to right evaluation, or as $A = X*(Y/Z)$ using a mathematically equivalent expression. In this case, if X, Y, and Z were all large, the first mode of interpretation might produce a result outside the permissible range of real values for a particular computer system, whereas the second mode of interpretation would be unlikely to do so.

Fortunately, in situations where a programmer requires close control over the way in which arithmetic expressions are evaluated, *parentheses* may be used to indicate precisely what is required, and no mathematically equivalent expression may be substituted which over-rides the *'integrity of parentheses'*. Thus if a programmer wishes to ensure that, in the expression X+Y+Z, the values of X and Y are added together and then the value of Z to their total, he may write (X+Y)+Z, and no mathematically equivalent interpretation may be used which violates the presence of the parentheses.

Example 6.13   To control the way in which the expression X*Y/Z is evaluated in the arithmetic assignment statement $A = X*Y/Z$, write either

$$A = (X*Y)/Z \qquad \text{or} \qquad A = X*(Y/Z).$$

The reader is referred to Sections 6.6.3 and 6.6.4 of the FORTRAN 77 Standard (American National Standard Institute, 1978).

Arithmetic constant expressions

In certain parts of FORTRAN 77 (described in later chapters) only *arithmetic constant expressions* or *integer constant expressions* are permitted.

An *arithmetic constant expression* is an arithmetic expression in which each operand is an *arithmetic constant*, or the *symbolic name of an arithmetic constant* (see Chapter 11). In addition, whenever an entity of the form $x_1 ** x_2$ occurs, x_2 must be of type INTEGER, i.e. exponentiation is permitted with integer exponents only.

An *integer constant expression*, on the other hand, is, as the name suggests, an arithmetic constant expression in which each constant or symbolic name of a constant is of type INTEGER.

Example 6.14   The following are examples of arithmetic constant expressions:

(a)   16.352 + 2.745* 13.297
(b)   −3.5326** 5 − 3.624/(8.715−9.204)

Example 6.15   The following are examples of integer constant expressions:

(a)   3 + 917/13 − 3**6
(b)   − 19*(5+7**2) + 11*13*17

Exercise 6

1 Write FORTRAN 77 arithmetic assignment statements for the following mathematical formulas:

(a) $A = P\left(1 + \dfrac{r}{100}\right)^n$

(b) $y = 3.65x^3 - 2.73x^2 + x - 17.5$

(c) $V = \dfrac{4}{3}\pi r^3$

(d) $y = \dfrac{a + b}{c + d(f + g)}$

(e) $\text{eprox} = 1 + x + \dfrac{x^2}{2} + \dfrac{x^3}{6} + \dfrac{x^4}{24}$

(f) $\alpha = ab + c^d - 16x$

(g) $S = ut + \tfrac{1}{2}ft^2$

(h) $y = \left(\dfrac{1}{a}\right)^2 \left(\dfrac{r}{12.3}\right)^3 \left(\dfrac{s}{23.4}\right)^4$

(i) $z = \left(\dfrac{a + b}{c - d}\right)^{-1.73}$

(j) $\text{val} = 2^{2^n}$

2 Indicate the errors in the following FORTRAN 77 arithmetic assignment statements:

(a)   Y = (A+B)*(C−E**(F/G)
(b)   Z= A/(B(C+D))
(c)   WILLY = (A+2)(A+3)
(d)   GAMMA = Q**−2.6
(e)   X = Y = (6.3U−5T)**5
(f)   PRESSURE = RT/V

3 Assuming the implicit naming convention for real and integer variables, what are the values assigned to the variables on the left-hand sides when the following arithmetic assignment statements are executed, using the indicated values?

(a)   X = A+B*C   A = 2.0, B = 3.0, C = 4.5
(b)   I = (J+K)*L   J = −5, K = 7, L = 10
(c)   X = 2*A − 3*B   A = 4.0, B = −5.0
(d)   J = X/Y+7   X = 5.8, Y = 2.0
(e)   Y = I/J + K/L   I = 2, J = 3, K = 4, L = 3
(f)   X = Y*I/J   Y = 5.0, I = 2, J = 3
(g)   X = Y*(I/J)   Y = 5.0, I = 2, J = 3

4 Write FORTRAN 77 arithmetic assignment statements corresponding to the following mathematical formulas:

(a) $r = \sqrt{x^2 + y^2 + z^2}$

(b) $y = \log_e(x + \sqrt{x^2 + a^2})$

(c) $z = \log_{10} \alpha$

(d) $b = \dfrac{\pi}{2} \left\{ \dfrac{(a^2 + b^2)^{3/2}}{ab} \right\}$

(e) $a = 4\pi \log_e \left\{ \dfrac{3(1 + \sqrt{2})}{1 + \sqrt{10}} \right\}$

(f) $x = 2\pi a \cot \theta$

(g) $S = \tan^{-1} \left(\dfrac{x}{y + ax} \right)$

(h) $v = \sqrt{m} + n$, where m and n are integers

(i) $t = \sin \{\sqrt{a^2 + b^2} \cos^5 (2.537yz)\}$

7 Introduction to input and output

> In any collection of data, the figure most obviously correct, beyond all
> need of checking, is the mistake. (*Finagle's Third Law*)

The input/output facilities provided in FORTRAN 77 are powerful and flexible. A programmer may input data stored in a variety of forms and output data in the form most convenient to him/her. Further, the Standard does not attempt to impose restrictions on the way in which an installation organizes its data files.

This chapter is an *introduction* to FORTRAN 77 input/output. A few basic concepts are discussed before considering some of the facilities required to input and output real and integer values. Further input/output facilities are discussed in Chapters 14 to 19.

Basic concepts

Data, which are to be input or which have been output, are stored in *records* in a *file*. Before any data can be transferred to or from a file the file must be *connected* to a *unit*. FORTRAN 77 statements to transfer data are known as *data transfer input/ output statements*.

Records
A *record* is a sequence of values or a sequence of characters. A record may or may not correspond to a physical entity. For example, in most FORTRAN 77 implementations the 80 characters on a conventional punched card will be assumed to be one record.

A *formatted record* is a sequence of characters representing the data. The layout of the data in the record is called its *format*.

Files
A *file* is a sequence of records and so is simply a collection of data which is input to or output from a program.

An *external file* is a file whose contents are contained on an external storage medium, e.g. a deck of cards or a magnetic disc. The two methods of accessing an external file are known as *sequential access* and *direct access*. For example, a file held on a deck of cards will be accessed sequentially, i.e. the cards will be read in strict order. Direct access will be discussed in Chapter 19.

Units

An external file is accessed physically by an *external unit*, e.g. a card file is accessed by a card reader. A file may exist independently of such a unit but, before any input/output can be performed, the file must be formally associated with a unit. This is called *connection*. A file may be *preconnected* to a unit, when the connection is made prior to execution of the program, either by a computer system specified default or by the computer system job control mechanism. The facility for connecting a file to a unit by program will be introduced in Chapter 14.

Thus within a FORTRAN 77 program, an external file is referred to by its connected *external unit identifier*. An external unit identifier has one of the forms:

(a)   *a non-negative integer expression* whose value indicates some unit previously specified by the computer system;

(b)   an *asterisk* identifying a particular unit designated by the computer system to be *preconnected for formatted sequential access*. There will be one such input unit and one such output unit, known throughout the rest of the book as the *designated input unit* and the *designated output unit* respectively. Normally these will be commonly used units such as the card reader and the line printer or a time-sharing terminal (used for both input and output).

Format

A formatted record is a sequence of characters representing the data. When transferring data, each value is converted (or *edited*) to or from the internal computer representation. Thus the layout (or *format*) of the data in the record must be known when an input/output statement is executed. There are two types of editing:

(a)   by fixed format, where the format is specified precisely in a *format specification*;

(b)   by free format, where the format is not specified precisely. This is known as *list-directed formatting*.

The type of editing to be used for a given transfer of data is indicated by the *format identifier* in the input/output statement.

The format identifier can indicate fixed format in several ways, the simplest being to express the format specification as a character constant. The other methods are considered in Chapter 14.

List-directed formatting is indicated by an asterisk as the format identifier.

Format specification

The format specification specifies precisely how each value should appear in the file and in its simplest form is written

(edlist)

where edlist is a list of *edit descriptors* separated by commas. An *edit descriptor* specifies some aspect of the format of the next portion of the file. There are two types of edit descriptor:

(a)   Those which specify the type and the layout of the next data value in the file. They are known as *repeatable* edit descriptors. In this chapter descriptors for integer and real values only will be used.

(b)   Those which specify aspects such as spacing and skipping data which are not required. They are known as *nonrepeatable* edit descriptors.

Field width

In a formatted record, a data item is contained in a *field* and the number of characters in that field is called the field width.

Example 7.1   Consider the record

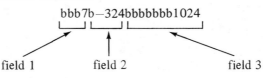

where b indicates a blank character.

This record contains three integers in fields of width 4, 5, and 11 respectively.

Formatted input

The input statement

The input statement is used to read data from a file. It has two forms:

$$\text{READ (cilist) input list}$$
$$\text{READ } f, \text{ input list}$$

where

(a)   cilist is a *control information list* which, in its simplest form, is u, f;
(b) u is a unit identifier;
(c) f is a format identifier;
(d)   input list is, in its simplest form, a list of variable names separated by commas. The input list may be omitted (see Chapter 14).

The execution of an input statement causes values to be read from one or more records in a file connected to the specified unit using the specified format and assigned to the variables in the input list. An input statement always *starts* to read from a *new* record.

The designated input unit is assumed if the second form of the input statement is used or if the first form is used with an asterisk as a unit identifier.

In this chapter a format identifier will be either a character constant containing the format specification or an asterisk indicating list-directed formatting.

Example 7.2   Explain the effect of the following READ statements where *fs* is a format specification:

(a)   READ (7,'*fs*') A, B, C
(b)   READ (*,'*fs*') X, I, Y, J

(c)   READ (IN,'*fs*') TEMP, PRESS, LENGTH
(d)   READ (10,*) INCOME, TAX, OVRTIM
(e)   READ '*fs*', X, I, Y, J
(f)   READ *, PRINC, INTRST, PERIOD

(a)   Three values are read from the file connected to unit 7 using the specified format and assigned to variables A, B, and C respectively.
(b)   Four values are read from the file connected to the designated input unit using the specified format and assigned to X, I, Y, and J respectively.
(c)   Three values are read from the file connected to the unit identified by the value of IN using the specified format and assigned to TEMP, PRESS, and LENGTH respectively.
(d)   Three values are read from the file connected to unit 10 in free format and assigned to INCOME, TAX, and OVRTIM respectively.
(e)   Four values are read from the file connected to the designated input unit using the specified format and assigned to X, I, Y, and J respectively.
(f)   Three values are read from the file connected to the designated input unit in free format and assigned to PRINC, INTRST, and PERIOD respectively.

Note that:
(i)   an asterisk as a unit identifier specifies the designated input unit, and an asterisk as a format identifier specifies list-directed formatting;
(ii)   the format specification *fs* is enclosed in apostrophes to express it as a character constant;
(iii)   statements (b) and (e) have the same effect if the format specification is the same.

Integer editing for input
The repeatable edit descriptor used for reading an integer has the form

$$\mathrm{I}w$$

where
(a)   the character I specifies integer editing;
(b) w is the field width.

This descriptor causes an integer to be read from the next w character positions of the record. This field must contain an integer constant, though a field containing only blank characters represents the value zero. *Leading* blanks in the field are not significant and *other* blanks will either be ignored or represent zero depending on the interpretation specified when the file was connected (see Chapter 14). To reduce the possibility of error it is recommended that the value is right-justified in the field, or in other words, ensure that all blanks are leading blanks.

Example 7.3   The record from Example 7.1 above

bbb7b−324bbbbbbb1024

may be read from the designated input unit using three edit descriptors in the format specification

$$(I4,I5,I11)$$

by the statement

$$\text{READ '}(I4,I5,I11)',I, J, K$$

Note that:

(a)   the format specification is given as a character constant and so is enclosed in apostrophes;

(b)   this statement means 'read the first integer from the first four character positions of a new record and assign it to the variable I, read the second integer from the *next* five character positions and assign it to J, and read the third integer from the next eleven character positions and assign it to K. Thus after executing this statement I will have the value 7, J will have the value −324, and K will have the value 1024;

(c)   each specified input list item must be of type INTEGER.

Example 7.4   Read the values from the following record in the file connected to unit 25 and assign these values to the variables LENGTH, NUMBER, K1,K2, and K3.

$$\text{bb155bbb28bb3bb5bb0}$$

One possible format specification would be

$$(I5,I5,I3,I3,I3)$$

giving the READ statement

$$\text{READ } (25,'(I5,I5,I3,I3,I3)') \text{ LENGTH, NUMBER, K1,K2,K3}$$

Since the edit descriptors I5 and I3 are repeated, FORTRAN 77 permits abbreviation of the format specification by using a *repeat specification*, thus

$$(2I5,3I3)$$

leading to

$$\text{READ } (25,'(2I5,3I3)') \text{ LENGTH, NUMBER, K1,K2,K3}$$

The general form of a repeated integer edit descriptor is

$$rIw$$

where *r* is the repeat specification which, if omitted, is assumed to be one.

Real editing for input
The most common edit descriptor used for reading a real number has the form

$$Fw.d$$

where
(a)   the character F specifies real editing;

(b)   *w* is the field width which has the same meaning as in integer editing;

(c)   *d* specifies the number of digits in the fractional part of the real number.

As in integer editing, the repeat specification may be used. The item in the input list corresponding to a real edit descriptor must be of type REAL.

This descriptor causes a real value to be read from the next *w* character positions of the record. If the field contains a decimal point the *d*-specification has no effect. It is strongly recommended that real values in a record take one of the forms of a real constant containing a decimal point, whereupon *d*, being ignored, may be specified to be zero. Therefore, when reading a real number, the edit descriptor

$$F w.0$$

may be used.

Again blank characters in the field have the same significance as for integers, with a field containing only blanks returning the value zero.

Example 7.5   The following is a list of character strings (representing real values in a record) and real edit descriptors together with their interpretation

Character string	Edit descriptor	Interpretation
bbb7.5	F6.0	7.5
bbb7.5	F6.3	7.5
−1.0E−6	F7.0	-10^{-6}

Example 7.6   Read the values from the following record in the file connected to unit 142 and assign these values to the variables X,Y,Z, and TOL.

$$bbb1.5bb-12.62bb348.75bb1.0E-6$$

One possible format specification would be

$$(F6.0, 3F8.0)$$

giving the read statement

$$READ\ (142,\ '(F6.0,3F8.0)')\ X,Y,Z,TOL$$

Positioning within a file

When reading from a file, a repeatable edit descriptor causes the value to be input from the *next* field. It is often desired to input a value not from the next field but from some other field, that is, it is necessary to *move* from the current position in the file. A number of non-repeatable edit descriptors are used for this purpose, one of which, the slash edit descriptor, is considered here.

Slash editing for input

The *slash edit descriptor*, on input, causes the remainder of the record to be skipped. If no record has been read or if the file is positioned between two records, the whole of the next record is skipped.

The form of the slash edit descriptor is simply the character /.

Example 7.7   Consider the effect of the statement

READ'(2I4/F6.0,2I10/I5,F9.0)',I,KAPPA,VAL,N,K1,K2,TOL

Values will be read in from records in a file connected to the designated input unit as follows:

    (a)   from character positions 1 to 4 and 5 to 8 of a new record and assigned to I and KAPPA respectively;

    (b)   from character positions 1 to 6, 7 to 16, and 17 to 26 of the following record (the remainder of the previous record being skipped) and assigned to VAL, N, and K1 respectively;

    (c)   from character positions 1 to 5 and 6 to 14 of the following record (the remainder of the previous record being skipped) and assigned to K2 and TOL respectively.

Note that:

    (i)   a slash may replace a comma in a format specification;

   (ii)   the portion of a record which is skipped may contain information of any type;

  (iii)   if the designated input unit was the card reader, for example, the information in columns 9 to 80 of the first card read by this statement, and that in columns 27 to 80 of the second card is skipped. In fact, the information in columns 15 to 80 of the third card will also be skipped since an input statement always starts reading from a *new* record.

Format control

The execution of a formatted input statement is said to be under *format control* and depends not only on the next item in the input list but also the next edit descriptor in the format specification. For each item in the input list, there must be a corresponding repeatable edit descriptor in the format specification. However it is quite permissible for the number of repeatable edit descriptors to be different from the number of items in the input list. In fact, the input list may be empty (see Chapter 14), but if it is not, there must be at least one repeatable edit descriptor in the format specification.

If during the execution of an input statement, a repeatable edit descriptor is encountered but there is no further item in the input list, the input statement terminates.

Example 7.8   The statement

READ '(I5,6F10.0)',N,Y,X,Z

causes four values to be read using the edit descriptors I5 and 3F10.0. The other three F10.0 descriptors are not used.

If there is an input list item but no further repeatable edit descriptor, with the simple format specifications met so far, format control goes back to the beginning of the specification *and a new record is read*.

Example 7.9   The statement

$$\text{READ '(I7,I10)', I,J,K1,K2}$$

will cause values to be read in
    (a)   from character positions 1 to 7 and 8 to 17 of a new record and assigned to I and J respectively;
    (b)   from character positions 1 to 7 and 8 to 17 of the *next* record and assigned to K1 and K2 respectively.

In satisfying the above conditions for the execution of the input statement, the input list and the format specification must not require more characters than are contained in a record. If there are insufficient records in the file to satisfy the execution of the input statement, the program terminates. (Programmed action can be taken under such circumstances and this will be considered in Chapter 14.)

Formatted output

The output statement

The output statement is used to write data to records in a file. It has two forms:

$$\text{WRITE (cilist) output list}$$
$$\text{PRINT } f, \text{ output list}$$

where
    (a)   cilist is a *control information list* which, in its simplest form, is u, f;
    (b) u is a unit identifier;
    (c) f is a format identifier;
    (d)   output list is, in its simplest form, a list of variable names or expressions separated by commas. The output list may be omitted.

The execution of an output statement causes the values of the items in the output list to be written using the specified format to one or more records in a file connected to the specified unit. An output statement always *starts* to write a *new* record. Before executing an output statement all items in the output list must have a *defined value*.

A WRITE statement with an asterisk as a unit identifier and the PRINT statement both refer to the designated output unit.

The output of character information

When designing the layout of information to be output, it is often helpful to include text along with the numeric information to make the output more easily understood. The simplest way to output character information is to use the non-repeatable *apostrophe edit descriptor*. It has the form of a character constant and causes the characters of the constant to be output. (The apostrophe edit descriptor cannot be used on input.)

Example 7.10   The statement

$$\text{WRITE (22,'("YOU MUST BE JOKING")')}$$

will output the characters

YOU MUST BE JOKING

to the file connected to unit 22. Note that:

  (a)   there is no output list because it is not required;
  (b)   the format identifier is a character constant containing the format specification. The format specification is

('YOU MUST BE JOKING')

and so the apostrophes in the format specification must be represented by two consecutive apostrophes in the format identifier.

Certain units specified by the computer system will be used for *printing*, for example the line printer or a time-sharing terminal. If a record is written to such a unit, the first character of the record is not printed but is used instead to control the vertical spacing *before* printing the remaining characters in the record.

First character of the record	Vertical spacing
blank	One line
0	Two lines
1	To the first line of the next page
+	No advance

Example 7.11   The statement

WRITE (2,'("1D.H. MARWICK 1ST SEPTEMBER 1978")')

will print the characters

D.H. MARWICK 1ST SEPTEMBER 1978

on the first line of the next page on unit 2, assuming unit 2 can be used for printing.

Example 7.12   The statement

PRINT '("bFORTRAN 77 EXAMPLE 7.12")'

will print the characters

FORTRAN 77 EXAMPLE 7.12

at the start of a new line on the designated output unit.

Notice that a PRINT statement does *not* imply that printing will occur, for example, if the designated output device is not specified for printing. However it will be assumed throughout the rest of the book that the designated output unit is used for printing.

Integer editing for output

The edit descriptor I*w* is used for writing integers as well as reading them. Here *w* specifies the number of characters to be written to the output file. The value of the next item in the output list is written as an integer constant right-justified in a field of width *w*, with the leading zeros replaced by blanks. A sign, where required, will appear immediately before the integer. (For a positive value, the plus sign is optional.) The value in the output list must be of type INTEGER. The repeat specification may be used freely.

Example 7.13   The following is a list of values and edit descriptors together with the resultant output:

Value	Edit descriptor	Output
21	I5	bbb21
−548	I5	b−548
1182795	I10	bbb1182795
−1	I7	bbbbb−1
0	I4	bbb0
250	I2	**

Note that:

(a)   if the value to be output is zero, the digit 0 is written;

(b)   if the value to be output is too large to be contained within the specified field width, the field is filled with asterisks.

Example 7.14   If I=−13652, J=−914, and KAPPA=600210 then the statement

$$\text{WRITE}(92,\text{'("b",2I6,I8)')I,J,KAPPA}$$

will print the following on a new line on unit 92 (assuming it is a printing unit):

```
−13652bb−914bb600210
└────┴────┴────────┘
 w = 6   w = 6   w = 8
```

Notice that the first character in the record is a blank which is used to specify that the output is to start on a new line.

Real editing for output

The edit descriptor F*w.d* may be used for writing real numbers. In this case, the value of the next item in the output list is written as a basic real constant *rounded* to *d* decimal places and right justified in a field of width *w*. The field width specified should be large enough to include the *d* digits after the decimal point, a sign (if required), one digit (at least) to the left of the decimal point, and the decimal point itself. In general, therefore, $w \geqslant d + 3$. The leading zeros are replaced by blanks and the sign, where required, will appear immediately before the real number. (Again, for positive values, the plus sign is optional.) The value in the output list must be of type REAL. The repeat specification may be used freely.

Example 7.15   The following is a list of values and edit descriptors together with the resultant output:

Value		Edit descriptor	Output
(a)	2.5	F6.2	bb2.50
(b)	−48.9	F6.2	−4.80
(c)	3.14159	F8.3	bbb3.142
(d)	−5282.9271	F12.3	bbb−5282.927
(e)	0.0	F6.2	bb0.00
(f)	−324.29	F5.2	*****

Note that:
   (i) where the value is held to more than *d* decimal places the value output is *rounded* (cases (c) and (d));
  (ii) where the magnitude of a value is less than one, the zero before the decimal point may be replaced by a blank. Thus the output for case (e) may be bbb.00;
 (iii) as with integer output, if the value to be output is too large to be contained within the specified field width, the field is filled with asterisks.

Slash editing for output
As for input, the slash edit descriptor signifies the end of a record. If no record has been written, an empty record is output. For units used for printing, an empty record is a blank line.

Example 7.16   If INDX=15, TEMP=−101.2, X=316.2543, and Y=−24.71652 the statement

       PRINT'("bINDEX=",I3//"bTEMPERATUREbIS", F8.2/"b",2F10.4)',

  +   INDX, TEMP, X, Y

will print the following on the designated output unit (assumed to be a printing device):

INDEX=b15

TEMPERATUREbISb−101.20

bb316.2543bb−24.7165

Note that four records are output including the blank line, the first character of each record being used to specify the vertical spacing. (The character + in the second line of the PRINT statement is a continuation character — see Chapter 8.)

Example 7.17   Values for a loan and an annual rate of interest are given as data in fields of width 10. Write FORTRAN 77 statements to print out the first month's interest.

REAL LOAN

READ '(2F10.0)', LOAN, RATE

PRINT '("bLOANbIS",F10.2/"bINTERESTbRATEbIS",F10.2,"bPERbCENT"//

+   "bFIRSTbMONTHSbINTERESTbIS", F10.2)',LOAN,RATE, LOAN*RATE/1200

For example, if the input record is

$$\text{bbbb1000.0bbbbbb11.5}$$

the output would be

LOANbISbbb1000.00

INTERESTbRATEbISbbbbb11.50bPERbCENT

FIRSTbMONTHSbINTERESTbISbbbbbb9.58

Note that the last item in the output list is an arithmetic *expression*.

Format control

As with input, the execution of a formatted output statement depends on both the next item in the output list and the next edit descriptor in the format specification.

If the output statement has an output list there must be at least one repeatable edit descriptor in the format specification, and for each item in the output list there must be a corresponding repeatable edit descriptor in the format specification.

If, during the execution of an output statement, a repeatable edit descriptor is encountered but there is no further item in the output list the output statement terminates.

Example 7.18   The statement

WRITE(10,'(2I3,5F12.5/2I6/10F10.2)')I,J,X1,X2,X3

causes five values to be written to a record in the file connected to unit 10 using the edit descriptors 2I3 and 3F12.5. The other edit descriptors (including the slashes) are not used.

If there is an output list item but no further edit descriptor, with the simple format specifications met so far, format control goes back to the beginning of the specification and *a new record is started.*

Example 7.19   If I=10, J=4, K=12, K1=−5245, K2=1024, L1=−1 and L2=1425978, the statement

PRINT '("b",I5,2I10)',I,K1,K2,J,L1,L2,K

causes values to be printed to the designated output unit as follows:

bbb10bbbbb−5245bbbbbb1024

   4   −1   1425978

   12

Note that:
- (a) each new record starts on a new line since the first character is a blank;
- (b) the last record contains only one value since there are no more items on the output list.

In satisfying these conditions, the output list and the format specification must not output more characters than can be contained in a record.

List-directed input/output

List-directed formatting means that the format of a record is not given explicitly but the data within a record are held in a free format. It is indicated in an input/output statement by an asterisk as a format identifier.

Since there are no edit descriptors, the input/output operation is controlled by the input/output list alone; hence the name list-directed. Obviously, the type of the item in the input/output list must be the same as the type of the corresponding value in the record.

Records in list-directed input/output

List-directed records consist of characters which represent a sequence of values and value separators. A *value* is usually a constant. A *value separator* appears between values in a record and may be a *comma* or a *blank*. (*Additional* blanks may also appear between values.)

Example 7.20   The following are valid list-directed records:

- (a) 5, 23, −6.2, 1.57   (b) 3.1415   27   −32.5
- (c) −14   (d) 10.78, 53.2   78.9

List-directed input

List-directed input is permitted from any file which allows formatted input. The forms of real and integer values to be input are the same as those acceptable under fixed formatting *except* that blank characters must not appear *within* the constants (since a blank is a value separator). Thus an integer constant and a real constant containing a decimal point should be used as integer and real values respectively.

Example 7.21   The statement

$$\text{READ} *, \text{I}, \text{J}, \text{X}, \text{VAL}$$

means 'starting at the next record on the file connected to the designated input unit, read four values and assign them to the variables I, J, X, and VAL respectively'. Thus if the input record is

$$5, 23, -6.2, 1.57$$

the value 5 would be assigned to I, 23 to J, −6.2 to X, and 1.57 to VAL. Note that the first two values are integer constants and the last two values are real constants thus matching the types of the variables in the input list, assuming the implicit naming convention.

Unlike fixed formatting, the input list may contain more items than there are values in the input record. However, if there are insufficient records in the file to satisfy the input list, the program terminates (see also Chapter 14).

Example 7.22   Assume that three consecutive records on a file connected to unit 6 are:

> record 1 : 12, −8, 7.5
> record 2 : 8.2, 12.7, −34, −89
> record 3 : 27, 3.5, −8

and are being read using the two consecutive statements

> READ(6,*) I, J, X, VAL
>
> READ(6,*) MAX, ALPHA, N

The effect is to assign values to variables as follows:

12 to I, −8 to J, 7.5 to X, 8.2 to VAL, 27 to MAX, 3.5 to ALPHA, −8 to N

Note that:

- (a)   There are insufficient values in record 1 to satisfy the input list of the first READ statement. Therefore another record is read and the first value in record 2 is used.
- (b)   On executing the second READ statement, a *new* record is read and so three values are taken from record 3.
- (c)   The unused values of record 2 are unavailable to the program.

List-directed output

List-directed output is permitted to any file which allows formatted output. The precise form of the information output is heavily dependent on the FORTRAN 77 compiler being used (see Section 13.6.2 of the Standard (American National Standards Institute, 1978)). For example,

- (a)   The value separator *may* be *either* a comma *or* a blank (additional blanks may also appear between values).
- (b)   An output statement will always start a new record but *may* create one *or more* records. The first character of each record will be a blank (to give a new line for printed records).
- (c)   An integer constant is output from an integer item in the output list using an Iw edit descriptor '*for some reasonable value of* w' This could mean one value of w for all integers output, for example, I10 will be used, *or* alternatively a separate value of w could be used for each integer, for example −1 will be output using I3, 1258 will be output using I5, etc.
- (d)   A real constant is output from a real item on the output list using *either* F$w.d$ or E$w.dEe$ (see Chapter 14) depending on the magnitude of the

value output *for some reasonable values of w, d, and e* and a reasonable range for the dependent magnitude.

Thus list-directed output could lead to portability problems. Further, if a record written using list-directed formatting is to be read by a FORTRAN 77 program, a list-directed input statement must be used. Unless it is inappropriate to do so, list-directed input and fixed formatted output will be used in the examples in the rest of the book.

In Examples 7.23 and 7.24 the descriptor F17.3 is used for real values, and a blank is used as a value separator.

Example 7.23   Assuming RATE=11.5, the statement

WRITE (*,*) 'INTERESTbRATEbIS', RATE, 'PERbCENT'

will print on the designated output unit

INTERESTbRATEbISbbbbbbbbbbbb11.500bPERbCENT

Note that the blank inserted by the compiler as the first character in the record is used to control vertical spacing as was the case in fixed formatting.

Example 7.24   Rewrite the FORTRAN 77 statements in Example 7.17 using list-directing formatting. That is, values for a loan and interest rate (as a percentage) are given as data in free format. Print out the first month's interest.

```
REAL LOAN
READ *, LOAN, RATE
PRINT *, 'LOANbIS', LOAN
PRINT *, 'INTERESTbRATEbIS', RATE, 'PERbCENT'
PRINT *
PRINT *, 'FIRSTbMONTHSbINTERESTbIS', LOAN*RATE/1200
```

For example, if the input record is

1000.0, 11.5

the output will be

LOANbISbbbbbbbbbb1000.000

INTERESTbRATEbISbbbbbbbbbbbb11.500bPERbCENT

FIRSTbMONTHSbINTERESTbISbbbbbbbbbbbbb9.583

Note that:
(a)   a separate output statement is used for each line of output since it is unlikely that using a single statement the compiler would create new records exactly where they are required in this case;
(b)   the statement PRINT * causes an empty record to be output which when printed gives a blank line.

Exercise 7

1 Which of the following input statements are invalid and why? Assume that *fs* is a valid format specification.
(a) READ(7,'*fs*') I, J, A, B
(b) READ('*fs*') X,Y
(c) READ '*fs*', X,Y
(d) READ (IC,'*fs*') F,G, I—J
(e) READ (12,*fs*) C,D

2 Which of the following output statements are invalid and why? Assume that *fs* is a valid format specification.
(a) WRITE '*fs*', X,Y,Z
(b) WRITE (*,'*fs*') X,Y,Z
(c) WRITE (2,'*fs*') I, J, 2*I+J, A—B, SQRT(C)
(d) PRINT '*fs*'
(e) WRITE ('*fs*') K+L, C*D+SIN(Z+2*X)

3 A record in a file connected to the designated input unit contains

bb3897621.304bb876bb302.9781

What values are assigned to the variables of the input list in the following READ statements which read this record?
(a) READ'(I4,I3,F5.2,I1,I5,F10.4)',I,J,X,K,L,Y
(b) READ'(3I3,F4.3,2I5,F4.3,I1)',I,J,K,FRED,JIM,IAN,HARRY,NUM

4 Assuming that

I=—10, J=5248, X=—1.5, Y=48.996, Z=87296.3751182

write down exactly what is printed on the designated output unit by the following PRINT statements:

(a) PRINT'(2I6/2F7.2/F12.5)', I,J,X,Y,Z

(b) PRINT'("THE NUMBER OF APPLES IN BARREL",I5,"IS",I2/
  +   "THE AVERAGE PER BARREL IS",F6.1,
  +   "WITH STANDARD DEVIATION",F8.3)', J,I,X,Y

5 (a) What values are assigned to X, I, and Z if the record in question 3 is read using the statement

READ *, X,I,Z

(b) What is printed on the designated output unit by the statements

PRINT *, I,J
PRINT *, X,Y,Z

assuming the variabless I,J,X,Y,Z have the values assigned in question 4, integer values being printed using I10 and real values using F12.5?

6 Twelve temperature readings are held in the variables TEMP1, TEMP2, . . . TEMP12. Write format specifications for PRINT statements to print these temperatures on the designated output unit in each of the following ways:

(a) in a single line;

(b) in a single column;

(c) in four lines grouped three readings to a line.

8 Program structure and layout

> Program complexity grows until it exceeds the capability of the programmer who must maintain it. (*Seventh Law of Computer Programming*)

Various basic components of a FORTRAN 77 program have been discussed in Chapters 3, 4, 5, 6, and 7. In these chapters examples of parts of programs were given, although the structure and layout of the programs were not explained in detail. This chapter is concerned with these aspects of FORTRAN 77, and also the additional statements required to turn a sequence of statements into a program.

Programs

In Chapter 2 it was indicated that a program is the final refinement of an algorithm to solve a problem. A FORTRAN 77 program is therefore a sequence of FORTRAN 77 statements setting out a method of solution to the problem, and also unlike the algorithm at other stages of refinement, the program will be acceptable to a FORTRAN 77 compiler for compilation and subsequent execution. In many ways the algorithmic language used in Chapter 2, while hopefully precise, is informal and relies to a certain extent on human intelligence for its interpretation. The specification of the components of a computer program must be *very precise*, in some cases irritatingly so to a programmer, as has been seen in previous chapters. Thus when coding an algorithm in the form of a FORTRAN 77 program great care must be taken to adhere strictly to the Standard.

A FORTRAN 77 program must contain not only *executable statements* reflecting the actions of an algorithm but also *non-executable statements* giving the premises on which all or some of the executable statements are based, e.g. the *data types* of the variables used. These statements, both executable and non-executable, are grouped together into *program units* corresponding to the modular structure of the algorithm.

Program units
A program unit is either a *main program* or a *subprogram*. A FORTRAN 77 *executable program* must consist of one (and only one) main program and any number (including zero) of subprograms. (Subprograms are considered in Chapter 12.)

As the name suggests, the main program is the central program unit of any FORTRAN program. Execution of the program begins with the *first* executable statement of the main program.

The PROGRAM statement

A main program may be given a name by means of the PROGRAM statement which has the form

PROGRAM name

where name is the symbolic name of the main program. This name has the same form as variable names (see Chapter 5) and should not clash with any other name used in the program.

It is not strictly necessary to name the main program, so that the PROGRAM statement is *optional*. However if it does appear, it must be the *first* statement of the main program.

The STOP statement

The STOP statement when executed causes the execution of the program to terminate. It has the form

STOP

The STOP statement is an executable statement and may appear anywhere in a FORTRAN 77 program.

The END statement

The END statement indicates the end of a program unit. That is, it is the *last* statement in a program unit. It has the form

END

If the END statement of the main program is executed, the program terminates. If the END statement of a subprogram is executed, it has the effect of a RETURN statement (see Chapter 12).

Statement order

A statement is either an executable statement or a non-executable statement.

An executable statement specifies some action to be taken. Assignment statements and input/output statements are examples of executable statements. A non-executable statement provides additional information to the compiler to enable it to produce a complete machine code program. Type statements and the PROGRAM statement are examples of non-executable statements.

In general, the non-executable statements must appear *before* the executable statements in a program unit. Thus using the statements discussed so far in the book

a simple main program has the form

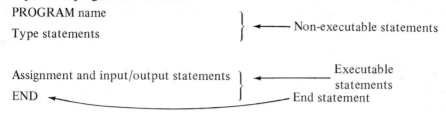

It should be noted that within non-executable statements there is a required order, for example, a PROGRAM statement, if it occurs, must come before the type statements. The precise order will be considered when other non-executable statements have been described (see Appendix 3).

Statement lines

A statement is written in *lines*, the first of which is called an *initial line* and any subsequent lines are called *continuation lines*.

A line is a sequence of 72 characters. The character positions are called *columns* and are numbered consecutively from 1 through 72. Clearly this specification is historically based on punched cards. (The IBM 704 could only read the first 72 columns of an 80 column card.) However, a program may be prepared on any input medium provided no line exceeds 72 characters. On a punched card, the card sequence number is often punched in columns 73 to 80 and is, of course, ignored by the FORTRAN compiler (see Example 8.3).

An initial line is a line containing the character blank or the digit 0 in column 6. Columns 1 through 5 must either be blank or contain a statement label (see Chapter 9).

A continuation line is a line containing any FORTRAN 77 character in column 6 *except* blank or the digit 0. Columns 1 through 5 must be blank.

A FORTRAN 77 statement consists of an initial line and up to 19 continuation lines. The characters comprising the statement must be written in columns 7 through 72. Blank characters in a statement are not significant except in character constants. Therefore considerable freedom exists in laying out a program. Continuation lines (up to 19) should be used not only to contain parts of the statement which will not fit onto the initial line but also to improve layout.

An END statement cannot be continued and so must appear on an initial line only.

Two statements must not be written on the *same* line.

Comments

It often happens that the algorithm as described by a FORTRAN 77 program is not easily understood due, say, to the idiosyncrasies of the language. Thus, it is helpful and good programming practice to annotate the code by inserting explanatory *comment lines*. Comments are used in examples throughout the book unless to do so would obscure the point or points being explained.

A comment line is a line containing the character C or ∗ in column 1. The rest of the line may contain any characters. A comment has no effect on a program, being used solely for documentation purposes, and hence may appear anywhere in the program unit. (If it appears *after* an END statement it is considered to be part of the *next* program unit.)

Example 8.1 For a particular electrical circuit the instantaneous current *i* is given by the formula

$$i = \frac{E}{Z^2} (R \sin \omega t - \omega L \cos \omega t) + \frac{\omega L E}{Z} e^{-R t/L}$$

Using the variables I, E, Z, R, OMEGA, T, L, having declared them as real, the FORTRAN 77 assignment statement to calculate the instantaneous current is shown opposite on page 61.

Note that:

(a) since the expression is a large one, it is more easily followed by writing each part of the expression on a separate line;

(b) on a coding form the letter O is often written Ø, to distinguish it from the digit zero.

Example 8.2 Given as data are the values of the coeffcients *a*, *b*, and *c* of the quadratic equation $ax^2 + bx + c = 0$. Write a FORTRAN 77 program to evaluate and print its roots using the formula

$$x_1, x_2 = \frac{-b \pm \sqrt{b^2 - 4ac}}{2a}$$

Assume that the roots are real and that $a \neq 0$. See page 62.

Note that:

(a) the comment lines are used to provide useful information to a person reading the code, e.g. a maintenance programmer;

(b) to continue a comment, another comment line is used;

(c) liberal use is made of blanks to improve the readability of the program;

(d) layout is improved by using a blank line (QUAD0040) which is treated as a comment line;

(e) columns 73 to 80 contain card sequence numbers.

Example 8.3 A company employee is paid according to hours worked as follows:

(a) at a basic rate between 0800 hours and 1600 hours on Mondays to Fridays;

(b) at one and half times the basic rate between
  (i) 1600 hours and 2400 hours on Mondays to Fridays;
  (ii) 0800 hours and 1600 hours on Saturdays;

(c) at twice the basic rate between
  (i) 0000 hours and 0800 hours on Mondays to Saturdays;
  (ii) 1600 hours and 2400 hours on Saturdays;
  (iii) any time on Sundays.

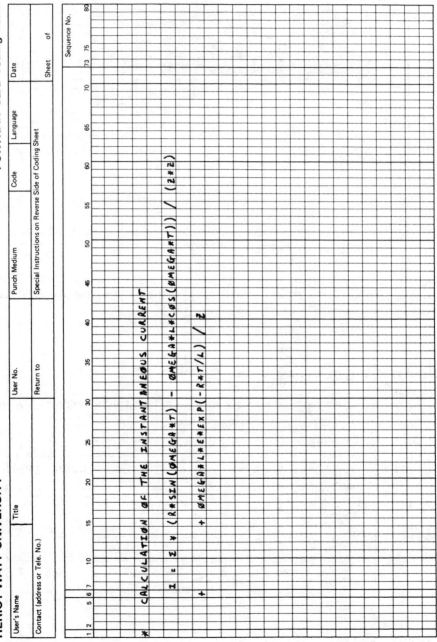

FORTRAN Card Coding Form

HERIOT-WATT UNIVERSITY

```
*  CALCULATION OF THE INSTANTANEOUS CURRENT
   X = E * (R*SIN(OMEGA*T) - OMEGA*L*COS(OMEGA*T)) / (Z**2)
     +   OMEGA*L*E*EXP(-R*T/L) / Z
```

HERIOT-WATT UNIVERSITY

FORTRAN Card Coding Form

| User's Name | | Title | | User No. | | Punch Medium | | Code | | Language | | Date | |
| Contact (address or Tele. No.) | | | | Return to | | Special Instructions on Reverse Side of Coding Sheet | | | | | | Sheet | of |

```
      PROGRAM QUAD                                               QUAD0000
*     THIS PROGRAM EVALUATES THE ROOTS OF A QUADRATIC EQUATION    QUAD0010
*     (THE METHOD USED COULD BE IMPROVED FROM A COMPUTATIONAL VIEWPOINT) QUAD0020
*     WHEN B*B .GE. 4*A*C                                         QUAD0030
      READ A,B,C                                                 QUAD0040
      PRINT *,'THE COEFFICIENTS ARE', A,B,C                      QUAD0050
      TEMP = SQRT(B*B - 4*A*C)                                   QUAD0060
      ROOT1 = (-B+TEMP)/(2*A)                                    QUAD0070
      ROOT2 = (-B-TEMP)/(2*A)                                    QUAD0080
      PRINT *,'THE ROOTS ARE', ROOT1,ROOT2                       QUAD0090
      END                                                        QUAD0100
                                                                 QUAD0110
```

HERIOT-WATT UNIVERSITY

FORTRAN Card Coding Form

User's Name	Title	User No.	Punch Medium	Code	Language	Date
Contact (address or Tele. No.)		Return to	Special Instructions on Reverse Side of Coding Sheet			Sheet of

```
*   THIS PROGRAM CALCULATES ON EMPLOYEE'S GROSS WEEKLY WAGE          WAGES000
     PROGRAM WAGES                                                   WAGES010
     INTEGER EMPNO                                                   WAGES020
     READ *, EMPNO, RATE, TIME, TMHLF1, TMHLF2, DBLTM1, DBLTM2, DBLTM3  WAGES030
     PRINT *, 'EMPLOYEE', EMPNO, 'WORKED'                            WAGES040
     PRINT *, TIME, 'HOURS AT BASIC RATE'                            WAGES050
     TIMHF1 = TMHLF1 + TMHLF2                                        WAGES060
     PRINT *, TIMHF1, 'HOURS AT TIME AND A HALF'                     WAGES070
     DOUBLE = DBLTM1 + DBLTM2 + DBLTM3                               WAGES080
     PRINT *, DOUBLE, 'HOURS AT DOUBLE TIME'                         WAGES090
     GROSS = RATE*TIME + 1.5*RATE*TIMHF + 2*RATE*DOUBLE              WAGES100
     PRINT *, 'AT A BASIC RATE OF ', RATE, 'THE GROSS WAGE IS', GROSS  WAGES110
     END                                                            WAGES120
                                                                    WAGES130
                                                                    WAGES140
```

Given as data are values representing an employee number, the basic rate paid, and the number of hours worked in one week under each of the six categories listed above. Write a FORTRAN 77 program to calculate the employee's gross wage. See page 63.

Exercise 8

1 Write a FORTRAN 77 program to read a temperature in degrees Centigrade and convert it to a temperature in degrees Fahrenheit. Use the formula

$$F = \frac{9C}{5} + 32$$

2 In a very simple income tax system, the first £400 of a person's income is untaxed, the next £300 is taxed at 20 per cent, and the rest is taxed at 30 per cent. Assuming an income of more than £700, write a FORTRAN 77 program to calculate the tax to be paid on a given income.

3 Two FORTRAN 77 intrinsic functions are DIM and MIN which have the following specifications

$$DIM(A1,A2) = \begin{cases} A1-A2 & \text{if } A1>A2 \\ 0 & \text{if } A1 \leqslant A2 \end{cases}$$

$$MIN(B1,B2) = \text{ the minimum of B1 and B2}$$

The arguments and the functions are all of type REAL.
Using the functions, rewrite the program of Exercise 2 assuming any positive income.

4 Given the lengths of two sides X and Y, of a triangle and the enclosed angle, ANGZ, in degrees, write a FORTRAN 77 program to calculate the length of the third side Z and the area of the triangle.

Use the cosine rule, $\cos(ANGZ) = \dfrac{X^2 + Y^2 - Z^2}{2XY}$, to find the length Z and the expression $\frac{1}{2}XY \sin(ANGZ)$, to find the area. (Remember that the argument for both SIN and COS must be in radians.)

5 As a first approximation, a satellite may be assumed to move in a circular orbit round the Earth. The circular velocity V_c, in ft s^{-1}, necessary to maintain the orbit of a satellite at a distance of h feet above the surface of the Earth is

$$V_c = \frac{25830\sqrt{R}}{\sqrt{R+h}}$$

where R is the radius of the Earth (20.904×10^6 ft). The escape velocity, V_e, at any particular altitude is

$$V_e = V_c\sqrt{2}$$

Write a FORTRAN 77 program to read an altitude h, compute the circular velocity and the escape velocity (in miles per hour) and the time taken to complete one orbit (in minutes).

6 The heat required to raise the temperature of a body (in degrees Kelvin) from T_1 to T_2 is

$$a(T_2 - T_1) + \tfrac{1}{2}b(T_2^2 - T_1^2) + \tfrac{1}{3}c(T_2^3 - T_1^3) + \tfrac{1}{4}d(T_2^4 - T_1^4)$$

where a, b, c, and d are constants for the given body. Write a FORTRAN 77 program to read in a, b, c, d, and the temperature limits in $°C$ and calculate the heat required ($K = °C + 273.2$ where K is a temperature in degrees Kelvin.)

9 Control statements

Overdoing things is harmful in all cases, even when it comes to efficiency.

In Chapter 2 it was stated that *three* basic structures are sufficient to describe an algorithm, namely

(a)   a *processing* statement which causes the stated action to be taken;

(b)   a *decision* structure which causes different actions to be taken according to the values of the specified data (there are two types of decision structure: the **if-then** statement and the **if-then-else** statement);

(c)   a *looping* structure which causes a group of statements to be obeyed a number of times (there are two types of looping structure: the **loop-while** statement and the **loop-for** statement).

In moving from the final refinement of an algorithm to the program code it is necessary to use suitable statements from the programming language to implement these basic algorithmic structures. In a given language it is usually possible to adopt a reasonably standard approach to this and so the coding stage should be straightforward. In FORTRAN 77, for example, a processing statement is usually implemented using one or more assignment, input, or output statements (Chapters 6 and 7). Decision and looping structures, on the other hand, require the use of *control statements*.

Control statements are used to control the sequence in which the other program statements are executed. The purpose of this chapter is to examine a number of FORTRAN 77 control statements in some detail. However, since *logical expressions* play such an important role, these will be considered first.

Logical expressions

Logical expressions are used in both decision and looping structures. The full range of logical expressions in FORTRAN 77 is described in Chapter 16. Here only *relational expressions*, which are the most commonly used form of logical expressions, will be considered.

A relational expression is used to compare the values of two arithmetic expressions† and has the form:

$$\text{exp}_1 \text{ relop } \text{exp}_2$$

†Character expressions may also be compared (see Chapter 15).

where $\exp_1$ and $\exp_2$ are arithmetic expressions and relop is one of the following *relational operators*:

Operator	Mathematical equivalent
.LT.	< (less than)
.LE.	≤ (less than or equal to)
.EQ.	= (equal to)
.NE.	≠ (not equal to)
.GT.	> (greater than)
.GE.	≥ (greater than or equal to)

Note that each operator starts and finishes with a decimal point.

Example 9.1   The following are valid relational expressions in FORTRAN 77

Expression	Mathematical equivalent
B*B.LT.4.0*A*C	$b^2 < 4ac$
I.EQ.J	$i = j$
TEMP.GE.100.0	$temp \geqslant 100$
EXP(X+B).LE.(X+1.0)**5	$e^{x+b} \leqslant (x + 1)^5$
A.GT.0.0	$a > 0$
(I+J)*(I+K).NE.L	$(i + j)(i + k) \neq l$

Evaluation of a relational expression produces a result of type **LOGICAL** with a value of **true** or **false**. If the two arithmetic expressions are of different types the value of the relational expression

$$\exp_1 \text{ relop } \exp_2$$

is defined to be the value of the expression

$$((\exp_1) - (\exp_2)) \text{ relop } 0$$

where the appropriate type conversion rules for arithmetic expressions will apply to $((\exp_1) - (\exp_2))$ and the zero is of the corresponding type.

Example 9.2   The relational expression

$$X*X-Y*Y.LT.2*J$$

where X and Y are variables of type REAL and J is a variable of type INTEGER, is evaluated as

$$((X*X-Y*Y)-REAL(2*J)).LT.0.0$$

Comparison of non-integer values

Since *real* values are not held with complete accuracy by a computer system, the relational operators .EQ. and .NE. should not normally be used in arithmetic comparisons involving other than *integer* quantities. To test, for example, whether the real quantities X1 and X2 are (approximately) equal, a relational expression of the form

$$ABS(X1-X2).LT.TOL$$

is recommended where TOL is the 'tolerance'.

If it is known, for example, that the magnitudes of X1 and X2 are *roughly* unity, i.e. neither 'too big' nor 'too small', they may be compared for approximate equality by using a relational expression like

$$ABS(X1-X2).LT.0.5E-4$$

which will have the value **true** if X1 and X2 agree to about 4 decimal places. In this case an *'absolute'* tolerance, $\frac{1}{2} \times 10^{-4}$, is being used.

On the other hand, if X1 and X2 are both very large in magnitude, or very small, it is much more sensible to compare them for approximate equality by using a *'relative'* tolerance in the relational expression, thus:

$$ABS(X1-X2).LE.ABS(X1)*0.5E-4$$

The effect is to make the absolute tolerance much *coarser* if X1 and X2 are both large in magnitude, and much *finer* if X1 and X2 are both small in magnitude. Note, however, that if X2=0 a relational expression involving a relative tolerance is inappropriate since the relational expression above will always have the value **false** unless X1=0.

Example 9.3   Given the following information, write relational expressions for the indicated comparisons:

Comparison	Information
(a) $a + b = c$	a, b, c real and moderate in size. 'Equality' if agreement to about 6 decimal places.
(b) $x = 0$	x real. 'Equality' if magnitude of x is less than $\frac{1}{2} \times 10^{-5}$.
(c) $s = t$	s, t real and large in magnitude. 'Equality' if agreement to about 8 digits.

(a)   ABS(A+B−C).LT.0.5E−6
(b)   ABS(X).LT.0.5E−5
(c)   ABS(S−T).LT.ABS(S)*0.5E−8

Control statements for decisions

The *block IF statement* along with the *END IF statement* and, if necessary, the *ELSE* and *ELSE IF statements* are the control statements used to implement the algorithmic decision structures described in Chapter 2.

The block IF statement
The block IF statement has the form

IF (lexp) THEN

where lexp is a *logical expression*.

A block IF statement always precedes an *IF-block*, which is defined to be all the executable statements after the block IF statement up to, but not including, the corresponding END IF, ELSE, or ELSE IF statement. (The precise meaning of 'corresponding' will be discussed later.)

The effect of a block IF statement is as follows:

(a) if the value of the logical expression, lexp, is **true** the IF-block is executed, after which control is transferred to the corresponding END IF statement;

(b) if the value of lexp is **false** control is transferred to the corresponding END IF, ELSE, or ELSE IF statement.

The END IF statement
The END IF statement has the form

END IF

Execution of the END IF statement has no effect and execution continues with the statement following. For each block IF statement, there must be a corresponding END IF statement.

Example 9.4   The algorithmic decision statement

if the bank balance is overdrawn **then** print it

could be expressed in **FORTRAN 77** as:

IF (BALANC.LT.0) THEN   } block IF statement

PRINT*,BALANC } IF-block

END IF   } END IF statement

In this case, the IF-block consists of *one* statement only. Notice that if BALANCE $\geqslant 0$ then the IF-block is not executed and control passes to the END IF statement.

Example 9.5   The algorithmic statement

if $x > 2$ **then** {assign the value of $(x^4 + x^2 + 1)/(x^3 - 8)$ to y

print x and y}

is coded as

IF(X.GT.2.0) THEN

Y=(X**4+X*X+1)/(X**3−8)
PRINT *,X,Y
END IF

In this case the IF-block consists of *two* statements.

The ELSE statement

The ELSE statement is used when coding an **if-then-else** decision statement. The ELSE statement consists simply of the keyword

ELSE

and it precedes an *ELSE-block*, defined to be all the executable statements after the ELSE statement up to, but not including, the corresponding END IF statement.

Execution of an ELSE statement has no effect and execution continues with the ELSE-block. The ELSE statement is used only in conjunction with the block IF (or ELSE IF) statements. If the value of the logical expression of the block IF (or ELSE IF) statement is **false** the ELSE-block is executed.

Example 9.6 When finding the roots of a quadratic equation $ax^2 + bx + c = 0$ a negative discriminant $b^2 - 4ac$ indicates imaginary roots. Hence code for solving quadratic equations might contain the statements:

```
DISCRM=B*B-4.0*A*C
IF(DISCRM.LT.0) THEN               } block IF statement
     PRINT*,'IMAGINARY ROOTS' ⎫ IF-block
     STOP                      ⎭
                 ELSE               } ELSE statement
     TEMP=SQRT(DISCRM)        ⎫
     X1=(-B+TEMP)/(2.0*A)     ⎬ ELSE-block
     X2=(-B-TEMP)/(2.0*A)     ⎭
END IF                             } END IF statement
```

The decision structure

It should now be clear that the algorithmic decision statements are implemented as follows:

(a) the **if-then** statement has the form

if logical expression then processing statement

and is coded

```
IF(logical expression)THEN
          processing statement
     END IF
```

(b) the **if-then-else** statement has the form

if logical expression then processing statement A
else processing statement B

and is coded

```
IF (logical expression)THEN
          processing statement A
               ELSE
          processing statement B
     END IF
```

Remember that a FORTRAN 77 statement may appear anywhere between columns 7 and 72 of a line. This permits the program to be laid out in a manner similar to the algorithm (see Chapter 2) as shown above.

The ELSE IF statement

Many problems produce a requirement for deciding among three or more processing statements, e.g. in the league table update module in Chapter 2 a decision must be made for each team on whether the match was won, drawn, or lost, that is a 3-way decision.

One way of handling such a structure is as follows:

if *logical expression*$_1$ **then** *processing statement*$_1$

   else if *logical expression*$_2$ **then** *processing statement*$_2$

      else if *logical expression*$_3$ **then** *processing statement*$_3$

         else if

$$\cdots$$

            else if *logical expression*$_{n-1}$ **then** *processing statement*$_{n-1}$

               else *processing statement*$_n$

While this is rather cumbersome, it is, in fact, one of the main mechanisms provided in FORTRAN 77 for handling this structure. The ELSE IF statement has the form

ELSE IF (lexp) THEN

where lexp is a logical expression.

An ELSE IF statement precedes an ELSE IF-block consisting of all the executable statements after the ELSE IF statement up to, but not including, the corresponding END IF (closing the originating block IF statement), ELSE, or ELSE IF statement.

Execution of an ELSE IF statement is similar to the execution of a block IF statement.

Example 9.7   Write FORTRAN 77 statements to set the variable IS to 1 if the value of the variable K is positive, to set IS to 0 if K is zero and to set IS to -1 if K is negative.

```
      IF(K.GT.0)THEN            } block IF statement

          IS=1                  } IF-block

      ELSE IF (K.EQ.0) THEN     } ELSE IF statement

              IS=0              } ELSE IF-block

                      ELSE      } ELSE statement

              IS=-1             } ELSE-block

      END IF                    } END IF statement
```

Using nested block IF statements†

If a program uses a number of block IF statements, some perhaps as part of IF-blocks, ELSE-blocks, and ELSE IF-blocks, it is important to ensure that the various block IF, END IF, ELSE, and ELSE IF statements correspond with each other appropriately. The decision as to which statement corresponds with which can be very confusing even with a relatively simple program.

The FORTRAN 77 Standard assists by defining the *IF-level* of a statement s as $n1-n2$ where

(a) n_1 is the number of block IF statements from the beginning of the program unit up to *and including* the statement s;

(b) n_2 is the number of END IF statements in the program unit up to but *not including* the statement s.

Then the phrase 'corresponding END IF, ELSE, or ELSE IF statement' used when describing the IF-block above should be interpreted as 'the next END IF, ELSE, or ELSE IF statement that has the *same IF-level* as the block IF statement'. A similar interpretation should be given to the word 'corresponding' where it appears in other places in this chapter.

Example 9.8   Consider a program containing (in outline) the following statements:

Line number	Statements	IF-level
1	IF ( ) THEN	1
2	....	1
3	END IF	1
4	....	0
5	IF ( ) THEN	1
6	....	1
7	IF ( ) THEN	2
8	....	2
9	ELSE	2
10	....	2
11	IF ( ) THEN	3
12	....	3
13	END IF	3
14	....	2
15	END IF	2
16	....	1
17	ELSE IF ( ) THEN	1
18	....	1
19	ELSE IF ( ) THEN	1
20	....	1
21	ELSE	1
22	....	1
23	END IF	1

The IF-level of each statement is given in the right-hand column. A line number to aid referencing is given in the left-hand column.

The block IF statement 5 has seven END IF, ELSE, or ELSE IF statements

---

† This section may be conveniently omitted at a first reading.

following it, namely statements 9, 13, 15, 17, 19, 21, and 23.

(a) Statements 9 and 15 have an IF-level of 2 and so correspond to statement 7.

(b) Statement 13 has an IF-level of 3 and so corresponds to statement 11.

(c) Statements 17, 19, 21, and 23 all have an IF-level of 1 and so correspond to statement 5.

(d) The IF-block for statement 5 consists of all the executable statements after statement 5 up to, but not including, the *next* END IF, ELSE, or ELSE IF statement with the same IF-level as statement 5, namely statement 17.

(e) Similarly the ELSE IF-block for statement 17 is statement 18, the ELSE IF-block for statement 19 is statement 20, and the ELSE-block for statement 21 is statement 22.

Thus if the logical expression in statement 5 is **true**, then the following statements are executed: statements 6 to 16 inclusive followed by statement 23. If the logical expression in statement 5 is **false** then control moves from statement 5 to statement 17. If the logical expression in statement 17 is **true** then statement 18 is executed followed by statement 23. The description of the other possibilities is left as an exercise for the reader.

While it may seem complicated as written above, the rules are simply applied common sense. However, without sensible layout the application of the rules to understand a program do become tedious and prone to error. *Therefore pay attention to the layout of the program.* The effort is repaid during the testing and subsequent maintenance of the program.

Control statements for looping

The *block IF statement* in conjunction with the *unconditional GO TO statement* provides the implementation of the algorithmic **loop while** statement.

The same mechanism can be used to implement the algorithmic **loop for** statement, but the *DO statement* is used more often.

Statement labels

A *statement label* is a means of referring to individual statements and is written as a sequence of up to 5 digits at least one of which must be nonzero. The label precedes the statement and is written anywhere in columns 1 to 5 of the initial line of the statement.

Any statement may be labelled but the same label must not be given to more than one statement in a program unit. Although statement labels are numbers, they have no arithmetic significance, that is, they are only a means of identifying statements.

Example 9.9   Consider the following statements

$$I=J+2*K$$

21   READ*,B,COST

$$X=(-B+COST)**2.5$$

$$2 \qquad Z=3.0*X**2-5.7*X+11.6$$

$$17 \qquad \text{PRINT}*,X,Z$$

(a)   The statement

$$\text{READ}*,B,\text{COST}$$

has the label 21.

(b)   The statement

$$Z = 3.0*X**2-5.7*X+11.6$$

has the label 2.

(c)   The statement

$$\text{PRINT}*,X,Z$$

has the label 17.

(d)   The other two statements have no label and so cannot be referred to within the program.

The unconditional GO TO statement

The unconditional GO TO statement has the form:

$$\text{GO TO } s$$

where s is the statement label of an executable statement that appears in the same program unit as the unconditional GO TO statement.

Execution of an unconditional GO TO statement transfers control to the statement identified by the statement label.

Example 9.10   The statement

$$\text{GO TO } 23$$

means 'transfer control to the statement with statement label 23, that is, execute next the statement labelled 23'.

Implementation of the 'loop while' statement

The algorithmic **loop while** statement has the form

loop while *logical expression* **do** *processing statement*

This can be coded as

$$s \qquad \text{IF } (logical\ expression)\ \text{THEN}$$
$$\qquad\qquad processing\ statement$$
$$\qquad\qquad \text{GO TO } s$$
$$\qquad \text{END IF}$$

where s is a statement label.

(Another method of implementing a particular kind of **loop while** statement is given in Chapter 14.)

Example 9.11 Non-negative numbers $x_1, x_2, \ldots, x_n$ are given as data and followed by a negative number. Write instructions to find the sum of the non-negative
numbers.

A suitable algorithm is

> initialize sum to zero
>
> read a number
>
> **loop while** the number is not negative **do**
>
> > {add the number to the sum
> >
> > read another number}

which leads to the code

```
        SUM=0.0
        READ*,X
10      IF (X.GE.0) THEN
            SUM=SUM+X
            READ*,X
            GO TO 10
        END IF
```

Note that:

(a) The processing statements forming the body of the loop must affect at
least one of the variables in the logical expression controlling the loop.
Otherwise, once inside the loop, the program will never come out of it.
Ensure that the loop terminates.

(b) The first READ statement initializes the loop-controlling variable and
then plays no further part in the loop. However, in FORTRAN 77, since
an unconditional GO TO statement must be used to implement the loop,
this READ statement could also be used as the READ statement in the
body of the loop as follows:

```
        SUM=0.0
15      READ*,X
        IF (X.GE.0) THEN
            SUM=SUM+X
            GO TO 15
        END IF
```

While this has the same effect as the original, it destroys the structure of
the loop. Hence this is a *further refinement* which (marginally) increases
the efficiency of the program, and should not be effected until the
original has been thoroughly tested.

(c) The layout of the program should indicate the structure of the loop.

The DO statement

The DO statement specifies a loop, known as a *DO-loop*. The DO statement has the form:

$$\text{DO} \quad s \quad i = \exp_1, \exp_2, \exp_3$$

where

(a) s is a statement label (optionally followed by a comma);

(b) i is the name of an integer, real, or double precision variable called the *DO-variable*;

(c) $\exp_1$, $\exp_2$, and $\exp_3$ are each integer, real, or double precision expressions; $\exp_3$ is optional, and may be omitted together with the preceding comma.

The DO-loop consists of all the executable statements after the specifying DO statement up to and including the statement labelled s which is called the *terminal statement*. In simple terms, the DO-loop is executed firstly with the DO-variable taking the value of $\exp_1$, then the value of $(\exp_1 + \exp_3)$, then the value of $(\exp_1 + 2*\exp_3), \ldots \ldots$ until it passes the value $\exp_2$. Thus a DO statement and its DO-loop have the form

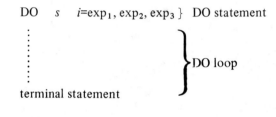

Example 9.12   The statement

$$\text{DO } 10 \text{ I} = 2, 10, 2$$

means 'execute the DO-loop for I taking the values 2, 4, 6, 8, and 10'.

Example 9.13   The statement

$$\text{DO } 112 \text{ KAPPA} = 3, 16, 4$$

means 'execute the DO-loop for KAPPA taking the values 3, 7, 11, and 15.'

Example 9.14   The statement

$$\text{DO } 15 \text{ J} = \text{N}, 1, -1$$

means 'execute the DO-loop for J taking the values N, N-1, N-2, ..., 3, 2, 1'.

The values of $\exp_1$, $\exp_2$, and $\exp_3$ are used as the values of the *initial parameter*, the *final parameter*, and the *incrementation parameter* respectively. The value of $\exp_3$ must not be zero, and if $\exp_3$ and the preceding comma are omitted a value of one is assumed for the incrementation parameter.

Example 9.15   The statements

$$DO\ 12\ K = 1, N, 1$$

and

$$DO\ 12\ K = 1, N$$

are equivalent. In the second statement, exp_3 is missing and therefore the incrementation parameter is given a value of one.

Before execution of a DO-loop, an *iteration count* is initialized for the loop. This value is the number of times the DO-loop will be executed and is obtained from the expression:

$$INT((exp_2 - exp_1 + exp_3)/exp_3)$$

but if the value so obtained is less than zero, the iteration count is set to zero. An iteration count of zero indicates that the DO-loop *will not be executed*. Even if the DO-variable is not of type INTEGER, the initial value of the iteration count defines *exactly* the number of times the DO-loop is to be executed.

Example 9.16   The following table is a list of DO statements with their corresponding iteration counts.

DO statement	Iteration count
DO 10 I=2,10,2	5
DO 112 KAPPA=3,16,4	4
DO 15 J=50,1,−1	50
DO 50 L=27,9,3	0

Since the incrementation parameter may be either positive or negative, the detailed operation of the DO statement and its DO-loop is best explained by the following algorithm:

evaluate the initial, final and incrementation parameters
initialize the DO-variable to the value of the initial parameter
initialize the iteration count (as above)
loop while the iteration count is not zero **do**
  {execute the statements of the DO-loop
  add the value of the incrementation parameter to the DO-variable
  reduce the iteration count by one}

Note that:
(a) a DO-loop will not be executed under the following conditions:
  (i) if, with a positive increment, the value of the initial parameter exceeds that of the final parameter,
  (ii) if, with a negative increment, the value of the final parameter exceeds that of the initial parameter;
(b) the initial, final and incrementation parameters are initialized to the values of exp_1, exp_2, and exp_3 before entering the DO-loop and so *cannot be altered* during the execution of the loop;

(c)   the DO-variable *must not* be redefined by any statement in the DO-loop;
(d)   on leaving the DO-loop, the DO-variable retains its last defined value.

Example 9.17   The following is a list of DO statements with the value of the DO-variable on leaving the DO-loop.

DO statement	Final value of DO-variable
DO 10 I=2,10,2	12
DO 112 KAPPA=3,16,4	19
DO 15 J=N,1,−1	0
DO 12 K=1,N	N+1

The CONTINUE statement
The CONTINUE statement is a dummy statement whose execution has no effect. It is written simply as the keyword

CONTINUE

The terminal statement of a DO-loop (that is the one labelled s) must be an executable statement but must not be, amongst others, an unconditional GO TO, a block IF, a STOP, or a DO statement. To avoid having to remember which statements are permissible and which are not it is recommended that the CONTINUE statement is always used as the terminal statement of a DO-loop.

Example 9.18   Write   a   program   to   tabulate $1^2 + 2^2 + 3^2 + \ldots \ldots + n^2$ for $n = 1, 2, 3, \ldots \ldots, 50$ given that

$$1^2 + 2^2 + 3^2 + \ldots + n^2 = \tfrac{1}{6}n (n + 1)(2n + 1)$$

```
        PROGRAM SUMSQ
        DO 20 N=1,50              } DO statement
          J=N*(N+1)*(2*N+1)/6
          PRINT*,N,J                 } DO-loop
20      CONTINUE
        END
```

Implementation of the 'loop for' statement
The algorithmic **loop for** statement has the form

loop for *index = values* **do** *processing statement*

The loop index, *index = values*, can often be expressed in the form

$$index = exp_1, exp_2, exp_3$$

which means the **loop for** statement may be coded as a DO statement and a DO-loop. For example:

loop for $i = 1, 2, \ldots, n$ **do** *processing statement* may be coded as

DO s I=1,N

processing statement

s CONTINUE

Example 9.19   Given as data are values for $m, x_1, f_1, x_2, f_2, \ldots \ldots, x_m, f_m$ where all values of x are real and all values of f and the value of m are integers. Write a program to calculate the mean, $\bar{x}$, and standard devision σ, of the x values where

$$N = \sum_{i=1}^{m} f_i \tag{1}$$

$$\bar{x} = \frac{1}{N} \sum_{i=1}^{m} f_i x_i \tag{2}$$

$$\sigma^2 = \left(\frac{1}{N} \sum_{i=1}^{m} f_i x_i^2\right) - \bar{x}^2 \tag{3}$$

An algorithm for the solution of this problem is

read m

initialize the sums for the formulas (1),(2), and (3)

loop for $i = 1, 2, \ldots, m$ **do**

{read x and f

accumulate the sums of f, fx, and fx^2 }

calculate and print the mean and standard deviation

leading to the program

```
PROGRAM STATS
INTEGER F
READ *,M
N = 0
FXSUM = 0.0
FX2SUM = 0.0
DO 20 I = 1,M
     READ *,X,F
     N = N + F
     FXSUM = FXSUM + F*X
     FX2SUM = FX2SUM + F*X*X
20   CONTINUE
XMEAN = FXSUM/N
STDEV = SQRT (FX2SUM/N — XMEAN**2)
```

                    PRINT*, XMEAN, STDEV
                    END

Example 9.20   Tabulate values of the expression

$$2 \sin x + 3.165 \, x^2 \, e^x$$

for x ranging from 0 to 3.5 in steps of 0.01.

Algorithm:

            loop for $x = 0, 0.01, \ldots, 3.5$ **do**
                    {assign $2 \sin x + 3.165 x^2 e^x$ to y

                    print x and y}

Program:

                    PROGRAM TABLAT
                    DO 50 X = 0.0, 3.5, 0.01
                        Y = 2*SIN(X) + 3.165*X*X*EXP(X)
                        PRINT *, X, Y
            50   CONTINUE
                    END

While these statements are *valid* FORTRAN 77, they are not *good* FORTRAN 77. The incrementation parameter, for example, has value 0.01, a *real* quantity which may not be held internally with complete accuracy. As a result, X-values obtained by repeatedly adding the incrementation parameter to the initial parameter may be significantly in error. In addition the evaluation of the iteration count involves the application of *real* arithmetic to the expression $(3.5 - 0.0 + 0.01)/0.01$ before truncating the result. The imprecise nature of real arithmetic could conceivably yield 350.99 . . . . . . 99 for the value of the expression, producing an iteration count of 350, rather than the hoped for 351.

It is therefore normally inadvisable to use other than an integer type DO-variable and integer expressions $\exp_1$, $\exp_2$, and $\exp_3$ when constructing a DO-statement. Hence the above FORTRAN 77 statements are better written

                    PROGRAM TABLAT
                    DO 50 I = 0,350
                        X = I/100.0
                        Y = 2*SIN(X)+3.165*X*X*EXP(X)
                        PRINT *,X,Y
            50   CONTINUE
                    END

Notice that the real constant 100.0 must be used in the expression I/100.0. The statement

$$X = I/100$$

would have *disastrous* effects since integer division is used, giving X the value zero for *all* values of I from 0 to 99, and X = 1 for $100 \leqslant I \leqslant 199$, etc.

Nested DO-loops
A DO-loop may contain a DO statement provided that the DO-loop specified by that DO statement is contained within the outer DO-loop, e.g.

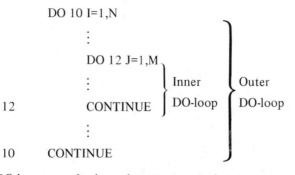

More than one DO-loop may also have the same terminal statement, e.g.

$$\text{DO} \quad 50 \quad K=L,N,3$$

$$\vdots$$

$$\text{DO } 50 \text{ M=J,L,}-4$$

$$\vdots$$

$$50 \qquad \text{CONTINUE}$$

The full power of nested DO-loops will become more obvious in Chapter 10 when the use of arrays and subscripted variables is discussed.

Further restrictions on control statements

Interaction between the DO statement and the block IF, ELSE, and ELSE-IF statements
If an IF-block, ELSE-block, or ELSE IF-block contains a DO statement the DO-loop so specified must be wholly contained within the IF-block, ELSE-block, or ELSE IF-block respectively.

Example 9.21 The following code sequence is valid

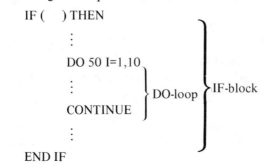

Example 9.22   The following code sequence is invalid:

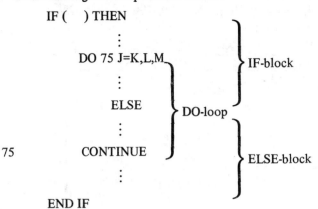

IF ( ) THEN

⋮

DO 75 J=K,L,M

⋮

ELSE

⋮

75   CONTINUE

⋮

END IF

IF-block

DO-loop

ELSE-block

If a DO-loop contains a block IF statement, the corresponding END IF statement must also be contained in the same DO-loop.

Example 9.23   The following code sequence is valid:

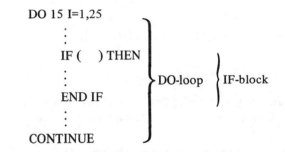

DO 15 I=1,25

⋮

IF ( ) THEN

⋮

END IF

⋮

15   CONTINUE

DO-loop   IF-block

Example 9.24   The following code sequence is invalid:

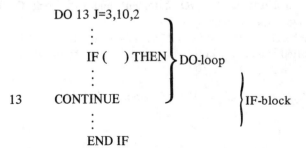

DO 13 J=3,10,2

⋮

IF ( ) THEN   DO-loop

⋮

13   CONTINUE

⋮

END IF

IF-block

As with most restrictions in FORTRAN 77, the reasons for these restrictions are obvious and are unlikely to reduce the programmer's ability to produce a good program.

Restrictions on transferring control

The normal sequential execution of program statements is changed explicitly by using a GO TO statement which causes control to be transferred to another specified executable statement. Such transfer of control is prohibited in the following cases:

(a) into an IF-block, ELSE-block, or ELSE IF-block from outside that IF-block, ELSE-block, or ELSE IF-block respectively;

(b) into a DO-loop from outside that DO-loop;

(c) to an ELSE or an ELSE IF statement.

Exercise 9

1 Assuming the implicit naming convention, write FORTRAN 77 relational expressions to represent the following:

(a) $i = 0$

(b) $j + k \leqslant 2m + n - 12kn$

(c) $a \geqslant b$

(d) $c^2 + d^2 \leqslant g^2$

(e) $\cos(x + y) < \sin(a + b)$

(f) $e^{3u+4w} - \log_e(x - y) > e^{g/f}$

2 Write FORTRAN 77 code for the following decision structures:

(a) **if** repayment period $<$ a year **then** set the interest rate to 20%

(b) **if** income $\leqslant 400$ **then** tax is zero

        else tax is 20% of income over 400

(c) **if** day $\neq 31$ **then** increment day

        else if month $= 12$ **then** {print 'year ends'

                stop}

        else {reset day to 1

            increment month}

3 Consider the following code:

```
IF(YEAR.EQ.2000)THEN
IF(MONTH.NE.2)THEN
PRINT*,'MONTH NOT FEBRUARY'
ELSE IF(DAY.EQ.29)THEN
MONTH=3
DAY=1
ELSE
DAY=DAY+1
END IF
ELSE
PRINT *,'YEAR NOT 2000'
END IF
```

(a) Identify all the IF-blocks, ELSE IF-blocks, and ELSE-blocks.

(b) Write down which statements are executed for all combinations of values of the relational expressions.

(c) Rewrite the code using a sensible layout and attempt (a) and (b) again.

4 Write FORTRAN 77 code for the following loop structures:

  (a)   **loop while** $x > 0$ **do** {accumulate sums of x and x^2

   read x}

  (b)   **loop for** $n = 1, 3, \ldots, 99$ **do** {add $\dfrac{x^2 t}{n(n + 1)}$ to sum}

5 Write down the iteration counts for each of the following DO statements:

  (a)   DO 10 I=1,20
  (b)   DO 11 J=64,29,−7
  (c)   DO 12 K=I−10,2*J+15,M**2

6 Write a FORTRAN 77 program to calculate the square root of a number x using the Newton–Raphson formula for successive approximations to the root y

$$y_{i+1} = \frac{1}{2}\left(y_i + \frac{x}{y_i}\right)$$

until two successive approximations are equal to six decimal places.

7 To convert a temperature from degrees Kelvin (K) to degrees Rankine (R), three formulas may be used.

  (i) $C = K - 273$

  (ii) $F = \dfrac{9C}{5} + 32$

  (iii) $R = F + 460$

Write a FORTRAN 77 program to tabulate the R equivalents to temperatures in K over the range 200 K to 800 K at intervals of 5 K.

10 Arrays and subscripted variables

> Given any problem containing n equations, there will always be $(n + 1)$ unknowns. (*First Snafu Equation*)

The algorithms for solving many problems in science and engineering may be most conveniently and compactly formulated if *array notation* is used. FORTRAN 77 therefore contains facilities for declaring and manipulating arrays of information — the subject of this chapter.

Example 10.1 The matrix

$$P = \begin{bmatrix} p_{1,1} & p_{1,2} & p_{1,3} & \cdots\cdots & p_{1,8} \\ p_{2,1} & p_{2,2} & p_{2,3} & \cdots\cdots & p_{2,8} \\ \vdots & & & & \\ p_{6,1} & p_{6,2} & p_{6,3} & \cdots\cdots & p_{6,8} \end{bmatrix}$$

is an array of 2 dimensions. The lower and upper bounds on the first dimension are 1 and 6 respectively. The lower and upper bounds on the second dimension are 1 and 8 respectively. The commas between subscripts are often omitted (e.g. see Example 10.11) unless so doing introduces ambiguity into the notation.

Array declarators

When using an 'actual' array† in a FORTRAN 77 program unit, information must be provided by the programmer concerning

    (a)   the *name* of the array, created according to the usual rules, i.e. any combination of from one to six letters and digits beginning with a letter;

    (b)   the *type* (INTEGER, REAL, DOUBLE PRECISION, COMPLEX, LOGICAL, or CHARACTER) of the elements of the array (*all* the elements of an array in FORTRAN 77 must be of the *same* type);

---

† As opposed to any array the name of which is a *dummy argument* (see Chapter 13).

(c)   the *number of dimensions* of the array (no array in a FORTRAN 77 program unit may possess more than *seven* dimensions);

(d)   the *lower* and *upper* bounds on each dimension (in FORTRAN 77 no lower bound may be greater in value than the corresponding upper bound).

Essentially this information is conveyed in a program unit by means of an *array declarator* in either a *type statement*, a *DIMENSION statement*, or a *COMMON statement*, the third of which will not be considered until Chapter 13.

An array declarator for an 'actual' array has the form

$$\text{array name } (l_1 : u_1, l_2 : u_2, l_3 : u_3, \ldots\ldots, l_n : u_n)$$

where

(a)   array name is the *name* of the array;

(b) l_i is an *integer constant expression*, the value of which is the lower bound on the *i*th dimension, $i = 1, 2, 3, \ldots\ldots, n$. If l_i and the following colon are omitted for any i, a value of 1 is assumed for that lower bound;

(c) u_i is an *integer constant expression* the value of which is the upper bound on the ith dimension, $i = 1, 2, 3, \ldots, n$.

Example 10.2   Consider the following array declarators:

(a) $A(0:7)$. This specifies a one-dimensional array A with elements $A_0, A_1, A_2, \ldots\ldots, A_7$.

(b) $X(1:20)$. This specifies a one-dimensional array X with elements $X_1, X_2, X_3, \ldots\ldots, X_{20}$.

(c) $X(20)$. This also specifies a one-dimensional array X with elements $X_1, X_2, X_3, \ldots\ldots, X_{20}$ since, if the lower dimension bound and the following colon are omitted, a value of 1 is assumed by default.

(d) $B(0:3, 5)$. This specifies a two-dimensional array B with elements

$$\begin{bmatrix} B_{0,1} & B_{0,2} & B_{0,3} & B_{0,4} & B_{0,5} \\ B_{1,1} & B_{1,2} & B_{1,3} & B_{1,4} & B_{1,5} \\ B_{2,1} & B_{2,2} & B_{2,3} & B_{2,4} & B_{2,5} \\ B_{3,1} & B_{3,2} & B_{3,3} & B_{3,4} & B_{3,5} \end{bmatrix}$$

Once again, 1 is assumed by default for the value of the lower bound on the second dimension.

(e) $C(10,20)$. This specifies a two-dimensional array with elements

$$\begin{bmatrix} C_{1,1} & C_{1,2} & \cdots\cdots\cdots & C_{1,20} \\ C_{2,1} & C_{2,2} & \cdots\cdots\cdots & C_{2,20} \\ \vdots & & & \\ C_{10,1} & C_{10,2} & \cdots\cdots\cdots & C_{10,20} \end{bmatrix}$$

(f) $Y(-2:3*N+1)$. This specifies a one-dimensional array with elements $Y_{-2}, Y_{-1}, Y_0, Y_1, \ldots \ldots \ldots, Y_{3N+1}$. Since any lower or upper bound expression must be an *integer constant expression*, N must be the symbolic name of an integer constant, which has occurred in a PARAMETER statement earlier in the same program unit (see Chapter 11).

Array declarators in type and DIMENSION statements

Type statements may contain array declarators as the following example illustrates.

Example 10.3   A FORTRAN 77 program unit might contain the following type statements:

$$\text{REAL L,M, X(20), Y(-5:5)}$$
$$\text{INTEGER R, FLAG, A(10,10)}$$
$$\text{DOUBLE PRECISION DVALS (0:25)}$$
$$\text{CHARACTER*6 C1,C2,C3, CVALS(30)*8}$$

specifying that

(a)   L and M are the names of two variables of type REAL.
(b) $X_1, X_2, \ldots, X_{20}$ is a one-dimensional array, the elements of which are of type REAL.
(c) $Y_{-5}, Y_{-4}, Y_{-3}, \ldots \ldots \ldots, Y_4, Y_5$ is a one-dimensional array, the elements of which are also of type REAL.
(d)   R,FLAG are the names of two variables of type INTEGER.
(e)   The matrix A

$$\begin{bmatrix} A_{1,1} & A_{1,2} & \cdots\cdots\cdots\cdots & A_{1,10} \\ A_{2,1} & A_{2,2} & \cdots\cdots\cdots\cdots & A_{2,10} \\ \vdots & & & \\ A_{10,1} & A_{10,2} & \cdots\cdots\cdots\cdots & A_{10,10} \end{bmatrix}$$

has elements of type INTEGER.
(f) $DVALS_0, DVALS_1, \ldots \ldots, DVALS_{25}$ is a one-dimensional array, the elements of which are of type DOUBLE PRECISION.
(g)   C1,C2,C3 are the names of character variables each of which is of length 6.
(h) $CVALS_1, CVALS_2, \ldots \ldots, CVALS_{30}$ is a one-dimensional array, the elements of which are of type CHARACTER and of length 8.

Alternatively, *DIMENSION statements* (possibly in conjunction with type statements) may be used to convey the same information. Each DIMENSION statement has the form

$$\text{DIMENSION array declarator 1, array declarator 2,} \ldots \ldots \ldots$$

the *first* letter of each array name indicating the type of the array via the implicit naming convention, *unless* the array name *also occurs* in a type statement in the same program unit.

Example 10.4   The dimension statement

$$\text{DIMENSION A(20), B(0:5), K(5,6)}$$

specifies three arrays, thus

(a) $A_1, A_2, \ldots \ldots, A_{20}$ of type REAL;

(b) $B_0, B_1 \ldots \ldots B_5$ of type REAL;

(c)
$$\begin{bmatrix} K_{1,1} & K_{1,2} & \cdots\cdots & K_{1,6} \\ K_{2,1} & K_{2,2} & \cdots\cdots & K_{2,6} \\ \vdots & & & \\ K_{5,1} & K_{5,2} & \cdots\cdots & K_{5,6} \end{bmatrix}$$
of type INTEGER.

unless the type, indicated by the implicit naming convention in each case, has been altered by the presence of one or more of the names A,B, and K in type statements in the same program unit. For example

INTEGER A
REAL K
DIMENSION A(20), B(0:5), K(5,6)

would specify the type of the elements of the array A to be INTEGER and the type of the elements of the array K to be REAL.

It should therefore be fairly obvious that a programmer has considerable flexibility in terms of specifying array names and associated information within a FORTRAN 77 program unit. Note also that the DIMENSION statement is a *non-executable* statement, and that the order in which DIMENSION and type statements occur within a program unit is of no significance.

Example 10.5   In a FORTRAN 77 program unit a programmer wishes to specify the following arrays

(a) $P_1, P_2, P_3, \ldots \ldots, P_{15}$ of type INTEGER;

(b) $A_{-5}, A_{-4}, A_{-3}, \ldots \ldots \ldots, A_{10}$ of type REAL;

(c)
$$\begin{bmatrix} X_{1,1} & \cdots\cdots & X_{1,20} \\ X_{2,1} & \cdots\cdots & X_{2,20} \\ \vdots & & \\ X_{8,1} & \cdots\cdots & X_{8,20} \end{bmatrix}$$
of type REAL;

(d) $D_0, D_1, D_2, \ldots \ldots, D_{50}$ of type DOUBLE PRECISION;

(e) $L_{-20}, L_{-19}, \ldots \ldots, L_{15}$ of type LOGICAL.

Write appropriate specification statements.

One possible solution is:

```
INTEGER P(15)
REAL A(-5:10), X(8,20)
DOUBLE PRECISION D(0:50)
LOGICAL L(-20:15)
```

Another is:

```
INTEGER P
DOUBLE PRECISION D
LOGICAL L
DIMENSION P(15),A(-5:10),X(8,20),D(0:50),L(-20:15)
```

There are numerous other variations.

Array element names

Like variable names, *array element names* may be freely used in executable state-ments in a FORTRAN 77 program unit. An array element name is of the form

$$\text{array name } (i_1, i_2, \ldots \ldots, i_n)$$

where $(i_1, i_2, \ldots \ldots, i_n)$ is known as a *subscript*†, and consists of a list in rounded parentheses of *subscript expressions*. Each subscript expression is an *integer expres-sion* and the number of subscript expressions in the list must be equal to the number of dimensions of the array in question.

Example 10.6   Given a FORTRAN 77 program unit containing the type statement

$$\text{REAL X(0:20), A(30,40)}$$

the following are valid FORTRAN 77 statements:

Statement(s)	Explanation
S=X(1)+X(3)+X(5)	$S = X_1 + X_3 + X_5$
T=X(I)*A(2,K+1)	$T = X_i A_{2,k+1}$
A(3,4)=(P+Q)**5	$A_{3,4} = (P + Q)^5$
W=5.6*X(I+2*J-K)+21.9	$W = 5.6 X_{i+2j-k} + 21.9$
SUM=0.0	
DO 50 I=0,20	
SUM=SUM+X(I)	$SUM = X_0 + X_1 + X_2 + \ldots \ldots + X_{20}$
50 CONTINUE	
READ*,P,A(1,2),Q	Read in values for $P, A_{1,2}$ and Q

† 'Subscript' usually means something different, each i in $(i_1, i_2, \ldots \ldots, i_n)$ being regarded as a 'subscript' in most programming languages.

Note also that the value of any subscript expression must not lie outside the range specified by the lower and upper bounds on the corresponding array dimension. Thus, for example, in the program unit

$$\text{REAL} \quad X(0:20)$$

$$\vdots$$

$$P=X(I)-17$$

$$\vdots$$

the value of I, when the assignment statement $P=X(I)-17$ is executed, must be in the range $0 \leqslant i \leqslant 20$.

Input and output of array element values

Array element names may occur as items in the input list in a READ statement, or in the output list in a WRITE or PRINT statement. It is therefore straightforward to read in values for specific array elements, and to print out the values of specific array elements.

Example 10.7   REAL   X(20),A(0:10,0:30)

$$\vdots$$

READ*,P,Q,X(14),W,A(I,J+1)

The READ statement will cause 5 values to be read in, using free format, starting at the next record in the file connected to the designated input unit, and these values assigned to P, Q, X_{14}, W, and $A_{i,j+1}$ respectively. Note that I and J must have *defined* values, with I in the range 0 to 10 and J+1 in the range 0 to 30.

Example 10.8   INTEGER   B(20,20)

$$\vdots$$

READ *,I,J,B(I+J,I−J)

The READ statement will cause 3 values to be read in, using free format, starting at the next record in the file connected to the designated input unit and these values assigned to I,J and $B_{i+j,i-j}$. Note that the first two values read in must be integers, and such that I+J and I−J both lie in the range 1 to 20.

Example 10.9   REAL   X(0:15)

                 INTEGER   K(0:10,0:20)

$$\vdots$$

WRITE(*,'("b",2F10.3,I6)')P,X(10),K(2,7)+5

The WRITE statement will cause the values of P,X(10) and K(2,7)+5 to be output on a new line via the designated output unit using the indicated format specification.

   Array names may also occur as items in the input list in a READ statement, or in the output list in a WRITE or PRINT statement. The effect on input is that values are read in and assigned to *all* the elements in the array on a 'one-to-one' basis and the effect on output is that the value of *every* element of the array is printed out.

Example 10.10   REAL   X(15)

$$\vdots$$

READ *,P,Q,X

The READ statement will cause 17 values to be read in, using free format, starting at the next record in the file connected to the designated input unit and these values assigned to P, Q, $X_1, X_2, X_3, \ldots\ldots, X_{15}$ respectively.

Example 10.11   REAL   A(3,4)

$$\vdots$$

READ *,A

The READ statement will cause 12 values to be read in, using free format, starting at the next record in the file connected to the designated input unit and these values assigned to the elements of the matrix

$$\begin{bmatrix} A_{11} & A_{12} & A_{13} & A_{14} \\ A_{21} & A_{22} & A_{23} & A_{24} \\ A_{31} & A_{32} & A_{33} & A_{34} \end{bmatrix}$$

It is obviously important, however, to know *in which order* the 12 values read in are assigned to the 12 array elements, and the FORTRAN 77 Standard specifies '*column order*', i.e. the first value read in is assigned to A_{11}, the second to A_{21}, the third to A_{31}, the fourth to A_{12}, the fifth to A_{22}, etc.

   Note that an alternative to thinking in terms of 'column order' is to observe that the *first* subscript† is allowed to vary more rapidly than the *second*. A similar interpretation is convenient when handling arrays with more than *two* dimensions. In the case of a three-dimensional array, for example, the first *subscript* is allowed to vary more rapidly than the *second*, which in turn is allowed to vary more rapidly than the *third*.

Example 10.12   INTEGER   B(2,3,4)

$$\vdots$$

WRITE (*,'("b",6I10)')B

---

† Here 'subscript' is being used in the conventional manner.

The WRITE statement will cause the values of B_{111}, B_{211}, B_{121}, B_{221}, B_{131}, B_{231}, B_{112}, B_{212}, B_{122}, B_{222}, B_{132}, B_{232}, B_{113}, B_{213}, B_{123}, B_{223}, B_{133}, B_{233}, B_{114}, B_{214}, B_{124}, B_{224}, B_{134}, and B_{234}, to be output in that order via the designated output unit using the indicated format specification, i.e. *six* values to a line.

Implied-DO lists

The forms of input/output list items described so far become rather tedious in situations such as the following:

(a)   input values for the elements X_2, X_3, ... , X_{11} of the one-dimensional array X_0, X_1, X_2, ... , X_{20};

(b)   output the values of the elements in the fourth row of the 6 x 6 matrix A.

One possibility is to write in the case of (a)

    READ*,X(2),X(3),X(4),X(5),X(6),X(7),X(8),X(9),X(10),X(11)

and in the case of (b)

    WRITE(*,'("b",6F10.4)')A(4,1),A(4,2),A(4,3),A(4,4),A(4,5),A(4,6)

both of which are long-winded. Alternatively DO-loops may be used thus:

(a)   DO   100   I=2,11

                  READ*,X(I)

    100   CONTINUE

(b)   DO   200   J=1,6

                  WRITE(*,'("b",6F10.4)')A(4,J)

    200   CONTINUE

However, in case (a) each execution of the READ statement triggers off the reading of a *new* record, i.e. 10 records are required for the 10 values to be input, a rather wasteful situation. Similarly, in case (b) each execution of the WRITE statement triggers off the writing of a *new* record, i.e. 6 records are written, once again a rather wasteful process.

Fortunately these and other difficulties can be avoided by using *implied-DO lists* as items in input and output lists. An implied-DO list has the form

$$(\text{dlist}, i = e1, e2, e3)$$

where

(a)   *dlist* is a list of items each one of which is either (i) a permissible item in an input or output list, or (ii) *another* implied-DO list.

(b)   *i*, the *implied-DO variable*, is a variable of type INTEGER, REAL, or DOUBLE PRECISION. Normally *i* is of type INTEGER, and if dlist occurs in an *input* statement *i* must *not* occur as an *item* in dlist.

(c)   *e1*, *e2* and *e3* are arithmetic expressions of type INTEGER, REAL, or

DOUBLE PRECISION. Normally $e1$, $e2$, and $e3$ are of type INTEGER, and if $e3$ and the preceding comma are omitted a value of 1 is assumed for the incrementation parameter (see below).

The effect of using an implied-DO list in an input or output list is similar to listing the items in dlist with i given the value of $e1$, followed by the items in dlist with i given the value of $e1 + e3$, followed by the items in dlist with i given the value $e1 + 2 \times e3$, etc. More precisely, the controlling mechanism for an implied-DO list in an input or output list is identical to that for a DO-loop, i.e. values for the initial parameter, the terminal parameter, and the incrementation parameter are obtained from $e1$, $e2$, and $e3$, an iteration count is established, etc.

Example 10.13   The READ statement

$$\text{READ*,X,Y,(A(I),I=1,5),Z}$$

is equivalent in effect to the READ statement

$$\text{READ*,X,Y,A(1),A(2),A(3),A(4),A(5),Z}$$

Example 10.14   The WRITE statement

$$\text{WRITE(*,'(''b'',2F12.5)') (X(K),Y(K),K=1,7,2)}$$

is equivalent in effect to the WRITE statement

$$\text{WRITE(*,'(''b'',2F12.5)')X(1),Y(1),X(3),Y(3),X(5),Y(5),X(7),Y(7)}$$

Example 10.15   The WRITE statement

$$\text{WRITE(*,'(''b'',6F10.4)')   (A(4,J),J=1,6)}$$

will output the values of A_{41}, A_{42}, A_{43}, A_{44}, A_{45}, and A_{46} in a single line using the indicated format specification.

Example 10.16   To read in values for all the elements of a 10x15 matrix A, 'row by row', the following input statement may be used:

$$\text{READ*,((A(I,J),J=1,15),I=1,10)}$$

Note how the only list item in the dlist for the implied-DO list with the implied-DO variable I is *another* implied-DO list.

Complete examples involving the use of arrays

In this Section several examples are considered which require the use of arrays. Note, however, that

(a)   references to array elements in a FORTRAN 77 program are significantly *slower* than references to variables;

(b)   large arrays may occupy a significant amount of space in main memory, particularly if virtual memory techniques are not being used.

It therefore follows that the use of arrays should normally be avoided or kept to a minimum, unless doing so will increase algorithm complexity significantly.

Example 10.17 Given as free format data are values for an integer n and the real variables $x_1, x_2, x_3, \ldots\ldots, x_n$. Write a FORTRAN 77 program to output the x-values in the order $x_n, x_{n-1}, x_{n-2}, \ldots\ldots, x_1$. Assume that $n \leqslant 1000$.

```
PROGRAM REVSEQ
REAL X(1000)
READ*,N,(X(I),I=1,N)
WRITE(*,'("b",8F10.4)')(X(I),I=N,1,-1)
END
```

The program is trivial in this case, and requires little explanation. Note, however, that if n is small a considerable amount of space in main memory may be wasted by the type statement

REAL X(1000)

Unfortunately FORTRAN 77 does not permit the 'dynamic' allocation† of storage space for array elements as does, for example, Algol 60.

Example 10.18 Given as input data in free format are *positive* values for $x_1, y_1,$ $x_2, y_2, \ldots\ldots, x_n, y_n$, followed by $-1.0, -1.0$, each input record containing *two* values. Write a FORTRAN 77 program to evaluate S where

$$S = x_1 y_n + x_2 y_{n-1} + x_3 y_{n-2} + \ldots\ldots + x_n y_1$$

Assume that $n \leqslant 500$.

One of the difficulties here is that the number of pairs of x and y values to be input is *not known*. Hence a READ statement containing an implied-DO list as an item cannot be used. An algorithm along the following lines is therefore required:

> read a,b
> assign 0 to n
> **loop while $a > 0.0$ do**
>> {add 1 to n
>> assign value of a to x_n
>> assign value of b to y_n
>> read a, b }
> assign 0.0 to S
> **loop for $i = 1, 2, \ldots, n$ do**
>> {add $x_i y_{n-i+1}$ to S}
> print S

which leads to the FORTRAN 77 program:

```
PROGRAM SUMVAL
REAL X(500),Y(500)
```

---

†That is, the *run-time* allocation of storage space for arrays.

```
                READ *,A,B
                N=0
100             IF (A.GT.0.0) THEN
                    N=N+1
                    X(N)=A
                    Y(N)=B
                    READ *,A,B
                    GO TO 100
                END IF
                S=0.0
                DO 200 I=1,N
                    S=S+X(I)*Y(N−I+1)
200             CONTINUE
                WRITE(*,'("b",F15.5)')S
                END
```

Note that the program would *not* work if each input record contained more than one pair of x and y values. Although in an ideal world it ought to be possible to formulate algorithms independently of the language in which the algorithm will eventually be coded, in practice it is necessary to keep in mind the facilities available in the language and any peculiar restrictions, e.g. that a READ statement in FORTRAN 77 always triggers off the reading of a new input record.

Example 10.19   Given as input data in free format are values for n, the elements of an $n \times n$ matrix **A** row by row, and the elements of an $n \times 1$ vector **x**. Assuming that $n \leqslant 30$, write a FORTRAN 77 program to evaluate **Ax**.
Since

$$\mathbf{Ax} = \begin{bmatrix} a_{11} & a_{12} & \cdots\cdots\cdots & a_{1n} \\ a_{21} & a_{22} & \cdots\cdots\cdots & a_{2n} \\ \vdots & & & \vdots \\ a_{n1} & a_{n2} & \cdots\cdots\cdots & a_{nn} \end{bmatrix} \begin{bmatrix} x_1 \\ x_2 \\ \vdots \\ x_n \end{bmatrix}$$

$$= \begin{bmatrix} a_{11}x_1 + a_{12}x_2 + \cdots\cdots & + a_{1n}x_n \\ a_{21}x_1 + a_{22}x_2 + \cdots\cdots & + a_{2n}x_n \\ \vdots \\ a_{n1}x_1 + a_{n2}x_2 + \cdots\cdots & + a_{nn}x_n \end{bmatrix}$$

it follows that the elements of **Ax** are

$$a_{j1}x_1 + a_{j2}x_2 + \quad \ldots \ldots \quad + a_{jn}x_n$$

for $j = 1, 2, 3, \ldots \ldots, n$. This leads to the following algorithm:

> read n, elements of **A**, elements of **x**
>
> **loop for** $j = 1, 2, \ldots \ldots, n$ **do**
>
> > { assign 0.0 to S
> >
> > **loop for** $k = 1, 2, \ldots \ldots, n$ **do**
> >
> > > { add $a_{jk}x_k$ to S }
> >
> > print S }

and hence the FORTRAN 77 program:

```
                PROGRAM MATVEC
                REAL A(30,30),X(30)
                READ *, N, ((A(I,J),J=1,N),I=1,N),(X(I),I=1,N)
                DO 100 J=1, N
                    S=0.0
                    DO 200 K=1,N
                        S=S+A(J,K)*X(K)
      200           CONTINUE
                    WRITE (*,'("b",F12.4)')S
      100       CONTINUE
                END
```

Other data structures in FORTRAN 77

The variety of data structures 'built in' to FORTRAN 77 is fairly limited, being restricted to

(a) *variables* of types INTEGER, REAL, DOUBLE PRECISION, COMPLEX, LOGICAL, and CHARACTER;

(b) *rectangular arrays* of $1, 2, 3, \ldots, 7$ dimensions, the elements of any array being all of the *same* type – INTEGER, REAL, DOUBLE PRECISION, COMPLEX, LOGICAL, or CHARACTER.

Other data structures such as stacks, queues, doubly linked lists, trees, and records are therefore not directly available in FORTRAN 77, and must be implemented by the programmer creating and manipulating explicit pointers, etc.

Exercise 10

1 Write in FORTRAN 77 array notation the following mathematical formulas:

(a) $d = \sqrt{\{(x_2 - x_1)^2 + (y_2 - y_1)^2 + (z_2 - z_1)^2\}}$

(b) $x = (u_1 + u_3 + u_5 + u_7 + u_9)^3$

(c) $c = a_{1,5} + a_{2,4} + a_{3,3} + a_{4,2} + a_{5,1}$

(d) $w = x_{i+1} y_{j+1} - 2x_i y_j + x_{i-1} y_{j-1}$

(e) $x_{n+2} = x_{n+1} - \dfrac{(x_{n+1} - x_n)^2}{x_{n+1} - 2x_n + x_{n-1}}$

2 (a) Given as input data in free format are *positive* values for an integer n and the real variables $x_1, x_2, x_3, \ldots, x_n$, each input record containing *one* value. Write a FORTRAN 77 program to output the maximum x-value. Assume that $n \leqslant 1000$.

(b) Rewrite the program if input records may contain *more* than one value.

3 Given as input data in free format are *positive* values for $x_1, y_1, x_2, y_2, x_3, y_3, \ldots, x_n, y_n$ followed by $-1.0, -1.0$, each input record containing two values. Write a FORTRAN 77 program to output these values in the order $x_1, x_2, x_3, \ldots, x_n, y_1, y_2, y_3, \ldots, y_n$. Assume that $n \leqslant 500$.

4 Given as input data in free format are values for an integer n and the elements $x_1, x_2, x_3, \ldots, x_n, y_1, y_2, y_3, \ldots, y_n$ of two vectors x and y. Write a FORTRAN 77 program to evaluate and print the scalar product S, where

$$S = x_1 y_1 + x_2 y_2 + x_3 y_3 + \ldots + x_n y_n$$

Assume that $n \leqslant 100$.

5 Given as input data in free format are values for the integers m, n, and p, the elements of the $m \times n$ matrix A row by row, and the elements of the $n \times p$ matrix B also row by row. Write a FORTRAN 77 program to evaluate the matrix product AB. Assume that $m, n, p \leqslant 20$.

6 Assuming that values for the elements of the 10×20 matrix A have already been input, write FORTRAN 77 program statements to find

(a) the *greatest* element of the matrix;
(b) the *number* of elements with negative values;
(c) the sum of the *positive* elements;
(d) the greatest *row* sum.

11 The PARAMETER and DATA statements

> In any formula, constants (especially those obtained from engineering handbooks) are to be treated as variables. (*Third Law for Naive Engineers*)

The purpose of this chapter is to consider two *non-executable* FORTRAN 77 statements: the PARAMETER statement and the DATA statement. Roughly speaking, a PARAMETER statement is used within a program unit to give *names* to *constants* and a DATA statement is used within a program unit to assign *initial values* to certain entities, e.g. variables.

The PARAMETER statement

In many FORTRAN 77 programs it is noticeable that, when *constants* occur within a program unit

(a)   the same constants may occur *several times*;

(b)   some of the constants are *machine dependent*.

In either case, it is desirable that the specification of such constants should be made *once and once only*, preferably near the start of the program unit. If this is done the programmer need only verify that *one* occurrence of a particular constant in a program unit is correct, and any alteration which may be necessary is made in *one* place only. A machine dependent constant, for example, may have to be changed in a program unit run on different machines.

PARAMETER statements are a convenient mechanism for achieving this effect, enabling the programmer to specify a *symbolic name* for any constant in a program unit, a name which can then be used instead of the constant in other later statements in the program unit. The PARAMETER statement has the form:

$$\text{PARAMETER } (\text{name}_1 = \exp_1, \text{name}_2 = \exp_2, \text{name}_3 = \exp_3, \ldots\ldots\ldots\ldots\ldots)$$

where

(a) name_1, name_2, name_3, ... are *symbolic names* created by the programmer in accordance with the usual rules for creating variable names;

(b) $\exp_1$, $\exp_2$, $\exp_3$, ... are *constant expressions*, the values of which 'are associated' with the corresponding symbolic names using the normal rules for assignment statements.

In the examples below, *character* constant expressions and *logical* constant expressions other than simple constants will not be used since constant expressions of these types are not described until Chapters 15 and 16 respectively. Remember also that an *arithmetic* constant expression is an arithmetic expression in which

(a)   each operand is an arithmetic constant or the symbolic name of an arithmetic constant;

(b)   exponentiation is permitted with integer exponents only.

Example 11.1   A FORTRAN 77 program unit might contain the following:

```
LOGICAL    L1,L2
COMPLEX    Z
DOUBLE PRECISION DCONS
CHARACTER*6   NAME, PASSWD
PARAMETER (   LOWLIM=-50,
+             CFAC=5280,
+             XMAX=4.31359E68,
+             PI=3.14159265,
+             ABZERO=-273.2,
+             Z=(2.5,3.7),
+             DCONS=2.12336521728956347D-5,
+             PASSWD='EUREKA',
+             TWOPI=2*PI,
+             PIDIV2=PI/2)
```

Note that:

(a)   Since the PARAMETER statement has been spread over a number of lines, a continuation character must be present in column 6 of each continuation line.

(b)   The *type* associated with each symbolic name is either indicated via the implicit naming convention, or by an appropriate type statement occurring *before* the PARAMETER statement. Thus, for example, CFAC is of type REAL since it has not occurred in an earlier type statement specifying the contrary.

(c)   When the symbolic name of a constant occurs within a constant expression, it must have been defined earlier in the same (or some other) PARAMETER statement in the *same* program unit. Thus, for example, the symbolic constant name PI, which is used in the arithmetic constant expressions 2*PI and PI/2, has already been defined in the line containing PI=3.14159265.

(d)   In associating the value of a constant expression with a symbolic constant name the usual assignment rules apply. Thus, for example, CFAC is the symbolic name of the real constant 5280.0.

The symbolic name of a constant may be used instead of the constant itself in expressions and in DATA statements (see next Section) later in the same program unit. It must not, however, be used within a FORMAT statement (Chapter 14), nor as *part* of another constant, e.g. a constant of type COMPLEX.

It is important also to appreciate that, unlike the name of a variable, the symbolic name of a constant must *not* appear, for example, on the left-hand side of an assignment statement. The symbolic name of a constant is the *name of a constant*, and therefore its value cannot be changed.

Example 11.2 A FORTRAN 77 program unit contains the following statements. List any errors in these statements.

```
        INTEGER   X,Y,Z
        COMPLEX   Z1,Z2
        DOUBLE PRECISION D
        CHARACTER*4   C1,C2
        PARAMETER (   C=2.9978E10 ,
       +              EVAL=2.718281828,
       +              Z1=(3,5),
       +              Z2=(EVAL,1.937),
       +              C1=20,
       +              IMAX=2**23-1,
       +              TWOPI=2*PI,
       +              EPOW5=EVAL**5,
       +              PI=3.14159265,
       +              D=EVAL D-6)
```

Error	Reason
Z2=(EVAL,1.937)	EVAL must not be *part* of another constant
C1=20	C1 is of type CHARACTER
TWOPI=2*PI	PI has yet to be defined
D=EVAL D-6	EVAL must not be *part* of another constant

The DATA statement

The DATA statement is a non-executable statement which can be used to give initial values to *variables, arrays, array elements*, and *substrings* (Chapter 15) in a program unit. DATA statements are especially useful for initializing arrays and for setting up character information. The values of variables, etc., given initial values can, of course, be altered by other statements later in the program unit.

A DATA statement may appear *anywhere* in a program unit *after* the various *specification* statements (see Appendix 3) if any, although it is normally good practice to position all DATA statements *immediately after* the specification statements. It has the following form:

$$\text{DATA nlist}_1 / \text{clist}_1 /, \text{nlist}_2 / \text{clist}_2 /, \text{nlist}_3 / \text{clist}_3 /, \ldots \ldots \ldots \ldots$$

where

(a)   the commas are optional;

(b)   each *nlist* is a list of *variable names, array names, array element names, substring names* (Chapter 15), and *implied-DO lists*;

(c)   each *clist* is a list of *constants* or *symbolic names of constants*, each of which may be preceded by *r*∗, where *r* is a non-zero, unsigned, integer constant or the symbolic name of such a constant, indicating *r* successive occurrences of the constant in the list.

A *one-to-one* correspondence must exist between the items specified in an nlist and the constants specified in the corresponding clist. It is this one-to-one correspondence which is used to give each item in an nlist its appropriate initial value.

Example 11.3   The DATA statement

$$\text{DATA C,Y,I,J/6.7,2.6E4,}-19,42/$$

will initialize the variables C,Y,I, and J to 6.7, 2.6×10^4, -19, and 42, respectively.

Example 11.4   The statements

```
LOGICAL X
REAL A(5,5)
PARAMETER ( PI=3.14159265 )
DATA X,Y,Z,W,A(2,4)/.FALSE.,PI,3*21.6/
```

will initialize the variables X, Y, Z, W, and the array element A(2,4) to **false**, 3.14159265, 21.6, 21.6, and 21.6, respectively.

Example 11.5   The DATA statement

$$\text{DATA I/5/F,G,A(2,5)/3}*-16.4/\text{P,Q/2}*11.3/$$

has the same effect as the DATA statement

$$\text{DATA I,F,G,A(2,5),P,Q/5,3}*-16.4,2*11.3/$$

Note that the two consecutive 'operators' are quite permissible in this DATA statement, since 3∗−16.4 is *not* an arithmetic expression but a specification that the constant −16.4 should be repeated three times in the list.

Example 11.6   The statements

```
REAL A(20,30)
DATA A/600*0.0/
```

will initialize every element of the array A to *zero*.

Example 11.7   The statements

```
CHARACTER*6 X,Y,Z,
DATA X,Y,Z/'BLOGGS','SUTHERLAND','ROBB'/
```

will initialize the character variables X, Y, and Z to BLOGGS, SUTHER, and ROBBbb, respectively. Note how only the first six characters of SUTHERLAND are used, and how ROBB, on the other hand, is padded out to six characters with blanks on the right.

Example 11.8   Assuming the implicit naming convention, the DATA statement

$$\text{DATA I,X/17.8,}-6/$$

will initialize the integer variable I to 17 and the real variable X to -6.0. That is, the usual assignment rules apply when assigning a value to an arithmetic variable.

It is important to remember that a DATA statement is a *non-executable* statement which initializes entities *before* program (not program *unit*) execution. If, for example, a DATA statement occurs in a *main program* it is impossible during execution to transfer control back to the DATA statement. If, on the other hand, a DATA statement occurs in a *subprogram* (see Chapter 12), the position is as follows:

(a)   *first execution of subprogram* — appropriate entities initialized before start of execution;

(b)   *subsequent executions of subprogram* — appropriate entities remain *defined* provided that they are not *redefined*, e.g. by an assignment statement. If any execution of the subprogram, however, redefines such an entity, then that entity is undefined† at the start of all subsequent executions of the subprogram unless a SAVE statement (see Chapter 12) has been used.

The reader is advised to read (b) above carefully. Many FORTRAN 66 compilers preserved the values of entities in DATA statements in subprograms between successive subprogram calls even after the redefinition of such entities.

Use of implied-DO lists

Implied-DO lists, which have already been considered in Chapter 10 in input/output statements, may also occur as items in nlists in a DATA statement. Such an implied-DO list takes the form

$$(\text{dlist}, i = M_1, M_2, M_3)$$

where

(a) i, the *implied-DO variable*, is the name of an *integer* variable;

(b)   *dlist* is a list of *array element names* and *implied-DO lists*, the operands in any subscript expression being restricted to *integer constants*, *symbolic names of integer constants*, and *'meaningful' implied-DO variables*;

(c) M_1, M_2 and M_3 are arithmetic expressions, the operands in which are once again restricted to *integer constants*, *symbolic names of integer constants*, and *'meaningful' implied-DO variables*. As usual, if M_3 and the preceding comma are omitted an incrementation parameter value 1 is assumed. Note, however, that when an implied-DO list occurs in a DATA statement, the corresponding iteration count must be *positive* (i.e. not zero).

† This applies even if the redefinition leaves the initial value unaltered.

The word 'meaningful' in (b) and (c) above requires further explanation. When an implied DO-list occurs as part of a DATA statement, the corresponding implied-DO variable is *local* to the implied-DO list, i.e. *it does not exist outside the implied-DO list*, and it is therefore only *meaningful* to use it *within* the implied-DO list.

Example 11.9   The statements

$$\text{REAL A(6), B(10)}$$
$$\text{DATA X, (A(I),I=3,5),Y,(B(J),J=1,2)/7*0.0/}$$

will initialize X,A(3),A(4),A(5),Y,B(1), and B(2) to 0.0.

Example 11.10   The statements

$$\text{INTEGER L(20),M(0:15)}$$
$$\text{DATA (L(K),M(K),K=1,5,2)/2*0,2*7,2*9/}$$

initializes L(1),M(1),L(3),M(3),L(5), and M(5) to 0,0,7,7,9, and 9, respectively.

Example 11.11   The statements

$$\text{REAL A(20,30)}$$
$$\text{DATA ((A(I,J),I=1,10),J=1,10)/100*10/}$$

will initialize the elements in the 10 x 10 submatrix in the top left-hand corner of A to 10.0. Note that within the inner implied-DO list both I and J are 'meaningful'.

Example 11.12   The statements

$$\text{REAL X(5,5)}$$
$$\text{DATA ((X(I,J),J=1,I),I=1,5)/15*0.0/}$$

will initialize to zero the elements

$$
\begin{array}{lllll}
X_{11} & & & & \\
X_{21} & X_{22} & & & \\
X_{31} & X_{32} & X_{33} & & \\
X_{41} & X_{42} & X_{43} & X_{44} & \\
X_{51} & X_{52} & X_{53} & X_{54} & X_{55}
\end{array}
$$

of the matrix X.

Example 11.13   The statements

$$\text{REAL A(20,30)}$$
$$\text{DATA ((A(I,J),I=(J/2)*2-J+2,20,2),J=1,30),}$$
$$+ \qquad \text{((A(I,J),I=J-(J/2)*2+1,20,2),J=1,30)}$$
$$+ \qquad \text{/300*1.0,300*-1.0/}$$

will initialize all the elements of the matrix A to +1.0 and −1.0 alternately.

Example 11.14   Consider a program unit containing the statements

$$\text{REAL A}(10)$$
$$\text{DATA (A(I),I=1,10)/10*0.0/}$$
$$\text{I=I+1}$$
.
.
.

Then the statement I=I+1 above is *meaningless* since I does not have a defined value at that point in the program unit. This is because the variable I in the statement I=I+1, and the implied-DO variable I in the DATA statement are quite *distinct*†, although they have the *same name*. As mentioned earlier, the implied-DO variable I has no existence outwith the implied-DO list above. An alternative way of viewing the situation is to remember that a DATA statement is *non-executable*, so that, at execution time, the *first* statement to be executed in the above program unit is I=I+1.

Further restrictions on the DATA statement‡

As mentioned earlier, a DATA statement may be used to initialize variables, arrays, array elements, and substrings in a program unit. The following entities, which will be discussed in Chapters 12 and 13, must not occur in an nlist in a DATA statement:

(a)   names of dummy arguments;
(b)   names of functions;
(c)   names of entities in *blank common*, or associated with entities in blank common.

In addition, names of entities in a *named common block* may only occur in an nlist in a DATA statement within a *block data subprogram*.

Exercise 11

1   In a FORTRAN 77 program unit it is required to create the following symbolic names for certain constant values:

Symbolic name	Type of constant	Value of constant
PI	REAL	π
ABZERO	REAL	-273.2
C	REAL	2.9978×10^{10}
DPI	DOUBLE PRECISION	π
FAC	REAL	1760
ZSTART	COMPLEX	$2-3i$
PWORD	CHARACTER*6	KILROY
CSQ	REAL	C^2
PIBY6	REAL	$\pi/6$
IMAX	INTEGER	$2^{39}-1$
OPS	CHARACTER*6	$+-*/**$

Write appropriate type and PARAMETER statements.

†The Standard does, however, specify that the two variables must be of the *same* type, i.e. INTEGER.
‡This Section may be conveniently omitted at a first reading.

2 In a FORTRAN 77 program unit it is required to initialize the following variables and arrays as indicated:

Variable name/Array declarator	Type	Initial value(s)
P	REAL	-1963.57
Q	REAL	2.164×10^{-8}
COUNT	INTEGER	0
D1	DOUBLE PRECISION	-1.57×10^{-4}
D2	DOUBLE PRECISION	-1.57×10^{-4}
Z	COMPLEX	$-5-3i$
L1	LOGICAL	**true**
L2	LOGICAL	**true**
L3	LOGICAL	**true**
X(0:20)	REAL	All elements 0.0
A(10,15)	REAL	All elements 1.0
CVAL	CHARACTER*8	CODEWORD

Write appropriate type and DATA statements.

3 Explain the effects of the following type and DATA statements:

   (a)   REAL X(21)
         DATA (X(I),I=1,21,2),(X(I),I=2,20,2)/11*1.0,10*−1.0/

   (b)   CHARACTER*5 A,B,C
         DATA A,B,C/'DAVID','BOB','FREDERICK'/

   (c)   REAL A(20,20)
         DATA (A(I,I),I=1,20)/20*0.0/

   (d)   INTEGER K(30,30)
         DATA ((K(I,J),J=1,30),I=1,30)/465*−1/

12　Procedures

> The fewer functions any device is required to perform, the more
> perfectly it can perform those functions. (*The Principle
> Concerning Multifunctional Devices*)

In Chapter 2 the concept of modularity was introduced, a module being a logically
distinct operation within an algorithm. By retaining modularity down to the program
level the structure of the algorithm is also retained. Modules will, of course, vary
widely in function and therefore in size. Large modules, however, are often difficult
to understand and should be avoided. In general they can be split into smaller
modules.

The implementation of a module in FORTRAN 77 will vary according to the
function of the module and the personal preferences of the programmer. Two points,
however, should be noted:

(a)　a module should always commence with comment lines containing information about the function of the module and any special methods
used;

(b)　every module should stand out clearly in a listing of the program, thus
emphasizing the structure of the program and making it more easily
understood. This can be achieved by careful layout with liberal use of
comment lines (including blank lines) and indentation.

If a module is sufficiently distinct logically (e.g. the input and validation of data), or
if a module can be used in more than one place in the program (e.g. solving a set of
simultaneous equations), then it is convenient to implement the module as a
procedure. Furthermore a procedure can be copied and used in other programs.

Each procedure is a section of code *referenced* (or called into operation) from
another part of the program. To enable this to be done the procedure is given a
symbolic name. This and the following chapter are concerned with the specification
and operation of procedures written in FORTRAN 77.

There are four categories of procedure:

(a)　intrinsic functions – supplied by the FORTRAN 77 compiler;
(b)　statement functions
(c)　external functions ⎫ – supplied by the programmer.
(d)　subroutines

Statement functions are not covered in this chapter but are described briefly in
Chapter 23.

Functions and subroutines

Functions

Function is the collective name given to intrinsic functions, statement functions, and external functions. The difference between the three categories of function is mainly in their definition, not in their purpose or use. A function is *referenced* from within an expression in another part of the program and its *purpose* is to supply a value to the expression. Therefore a function, when executed, has a *value* and consequently has a *type*.

The general form of a function reference is

$$\text{func(arg)}$$

where

(a) 'func' is the name of the function being referenced;
(b) 'arg' is a list of actual arguments separated by commas. If there are no arguments, *the enclosing parentheses must still appear.*

Example 12.1   Comment on the part played by the functions SIN, SQRT, GPSUM, and AREA in the following statements

(a) $Y = SIN(X)$
(b) $X1 = -B + SQRT(B*B-4*A*C)/(2*A)$
(c) $RESULT = GPSUM(1,R,30) + 3*GPSUM(2,S,20)$
(d) $IF (AREA(X,Y,Z).LT.25) THEN$

(a) SIN is the name of a function which when referenced will supply the value of the sine of X. Thus, on executing the statement, this value will be assigned to the variable Y. Note that X is an *actual argument* and is information processed by the function. Different calls of the same function can have different actual arguments.
(b) The function SQRT is referenced with the expression $B*B-4*A*C$ as its actual argument. The value supplied by SQRT is used in the evaluation of the expression $-B+SQRT(B*B-4*A*C)/(2*A)$.
(c) The function GPSUM requires three actual arguments and is referenced twice in the execution of this statement.
(d) The value of the function AREA is used in the evaluation of the relational expression $AREA(X,Y,Z).LT.25$.

Note that:

(i) the *type* of the value supplied by the above functions depends on a number of factors which are discussed later;
(ii) nothing is stated about the category of the above functions; indeed they may be intrinsic, statement, or external functions. As will be explained later, there are restrictions on the use of the different categories of function, but, in general the *use is independent of the category*.

Subroutines

Unlike a function, a subroutine does not supply a value directly as a result of being referenced, though it may supply values indirectly through its arguments. Its purpose is usually quite different to that of a function. For example, a subroutine might be used to sort entries in a table, validate input data, calculate the eigenvalues of a matrix, etc. Thus a subroutine undertakes a *task* which usually does not produce a single value as a result.

While it is not necessary for a subroutine to have any arguments, information to be passed between the subroutine and the referencing program unit is best done by this means.

A subroutine is *referenced* using a separate statement, the CALL statement.

The CALL statement

The CALL statement has the form

$$\text{CALL subname (arg)}$$

where

(a)   subname is the name of a subroutine (or dummy procedure — see Chapter 13);

(b)   arg is a list of actual arguments separated by commas. If there are no arguments, *the enclosing parentheses are optional.*

Example 12.2   The following algorithm will sort a vector of n numbers into descending order:

assume at least one exchange of values in the vector
loop while at least one exchange occurred during the last loop **do**
          {**loop for** $j = 1, 2, \ldots, n - 1$ **do**
                  { **if** $x_j < x_{j+1}$ **then** exchange the values of x_j and x_{j+1}}}

This can be coded as the following subroutine:

```
          SUBROUTINE SORT(X,N)

 *  THIS SUBROUTINE SORTS THE N VALUES IN THE VECTOR X INTO DESCENDING ORDER

          REAL X(N)

          INTEGER EXCHNG

          EXCHNG = 1

 20       IF(EXCHNG.EQ.1) THEN

 *             INITIALISE THE EXCHANGE MARKER TO -NO EXCHANGE-

              EXCHNG = 0

              DO 10 J = 1, N-1

                  IF (X(J).LT.X(J+1)) THEN

                      TEMP = X(J)

                      X(J) = X(J+1)

                      X(J+1) = TEMP

 *                    SET EXCHANGE MARKER

                      EXCHNG = 1

                  ENDIF
```

```
10          CONTINUE
            GO TO 20
      END IF
      END
```

Note that:

(a)   This example illustrates a typical FORTRAN subroutine. The details of specification and use of such subroutines are examined later. In particular the use of arguments to pass information is covered in Chapter 13.

(b)   A typical reference to the subroutine might be

CALL SORT(A,100)

to sort a vector A of 100 values.

(c)   It would be slightly more meaningful if the variable EXCHNG were of type LOGICAL (see Chapter 16).

(d)   This sorting method is best suited to an almost sorted list, that is, one that will be sorted into descending order after only a few scans.

External procedures

External procedure is the collective name given to external functions and subroutines. An external procedure may be written in FORTRAN 77 or in a language other than FORTRAN 77, e.g. Algol or an assembly language. Clearly procedures written in another language may be machine dependent and, while they are outside the scope of this book (and indeed of the Standard), a program using them is unlikely to be portable.

An external procedure which is written in FORTRAN 77 is called a *procedure subprogram* and hence is a *program unit*. An external function written in FORTRAN 77 is called a *function subprogram*. A subroutine written in FORTRAN 77 is called a *subroutine subprogram*.

Therefore the conversion of a module in an algorithm to a procedure in FORTRAN 77 involves writing a separate program unit — a subprogram. Thereafter it may be referenced from other program units (the main program or other subprograms) of the program. It should be noted that a subprogram may not reference itself either directly or indirectly through another subprogram (that is subprograms may not be recursively defined in FORTRAN 77).

The statements of the subprogram are executed whenever the subprogram is referenced and control reverts back to the referencing unit on execution of a RETURN statement or an END statement (see Chapter 8).

The RETURN statement

The RETURN statement consists of the key word

RETURN

Execution of a RETURN statement terminates the execution of the subprogram and control returns to the referencing program unit. A subprogram may contain any number of RETURN statements. If the END statement of a subprogram is executed it has the same effect as a RETURN statement.

Arguments

The primary means of passing information between a subprogram and another program unit are the *arguments* of the subprogram. A *dummy argument* appears in the argument list of a subprogram. An *actual argument* appears in the argument list of a subprogram *reference*.

Example 12.3　In Example 12.2 the dummy arguments were specified in the statement

SUBROUTINE SORT (X, N)
　　　　　　　　　　dummy arguments

The actual arguments replace the dummies when the subroutine is executed. Thus in the statement

　　　　　　　　　actual arguments
CALL SORT(A,100)

A replaces X and 100 replaces N.

　　Dummy arguments are used to indicate the number and type of the actual arguments which will be passed, and whether each actual argument is a single value, an array of values, or a procedure. During the *execution* of the subprogram the actual arguments in the procedure reference are used in place of the dummy arguments.

　　In a reference to a subprogram the actual arguments must agree in order, number, and type with the corresponding dummy arguments in the referenced subprogram and can include an expression, an array name, an intrinsic function name, or an external procedure name.

　　Actual arguments are used with other categories of procedure in FORTRAN 77. In particular, in an intrinsic function reference, the actual arguments must agree in order, number, and type with the appropriate specification in the list on pages 115–8. More detailed information concerning arguments is given in the next chapter.

Example 12.4　In the sample program in Chapter 3 (page 15) the function ANGVAL(X,Y,Z) calculates the size of the angle (in degrees) opposite the side Z in the triangle with sides X, Y, and Z of known length. The function definition is

```
FUNCTION ANGVAL(X,Y,Z)

PI = 3.14159265

TEMP = (X*X+Y*Y-Z*Z)/(2*X*Y)

ANGVAL = (180/PI)*ACOS(TEMP)

END
```

　　It uses three dummy arguments, all representing real variables, each one corresponding to a side of the triangle. Note that the sizes of the sides are passed to the subroutine via its dummy arguments and the size of the angle is passed back to the referencing program unit through the *function name*.

Typical references to this function are

    (a)   ANGA = ANGVAL(B,C,A)
    (b)   ANGB = ANGVAL(C,A,B)
    (c)   ANGLE = ANGVAL(SQRT(D*D+E*E),2*F,G+H)

Note that:

    (i) the actual arguments agree as to number and type (assuming the implicit naming rule) with the corresponding dummy arguments;

    (ii) in each case, the side opposite the angle to be calculated appears as the third actual argument, hence the difference between (a) and (b);

    (iii) the effect of reference (a) is to replace the dummy argument X in the subroutine by the actual argument B in the subroutine reference, Y by C, and Z by A;

    (iv) the actual arguments in reference (c) are expressions, which will be evaluated before the function is executed.

Summary

The following diagram summarizes the different types of procedures:

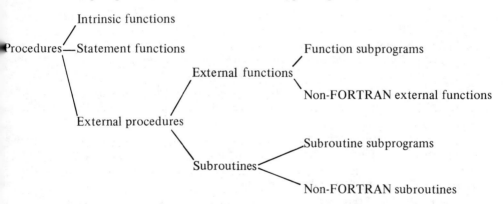

A procedure is accessed by a procedure *reference*. Information may be passed to and from the procedure by means of *arguments*. Dummy arguments appear in the procedure specification and actual arguments appear in the procedure reference. Information is also returned from a function by means of the function name. Control is removed from a subprogram using a RETURN or an END statement.

Intrinsic functions

The FORTRAN 77 Standard specifies that any implementation of FORTRAN 77 must supply certain 'built in' functions known as *intrinsic functions*. Such functions were considered briefly in Chapter 6, and the reader is referred to the appropriate section of that chapter for introductory information.

A complete list of intrinsic functions is given on pages 115–8. Of particular interest is the fact that in FORTRAN 77, unlike FORTRAN 66, many of the intrinsic functions possess not only *specific* names but also *generic* names. The distinction is best explained by example.

Example 12.5   The intrinsic function 'square root' (page 117) has the generic name SQRT and three specific names SQRT, DSQRT, and CSQRT. The specific name DSQRT may only be used with an argument of type DOUBLE PRECISION, and returns a result of the same type. Similarly the specific name CSQRT may only be used with an argument of type COMPLEX, and returns a result of type COMPLEX. The generic name SQRT, on the other hand, may be used with an argument of type REAL, DOUBLE PRECISION, or COMPLEX and returns a value of *identical* type. Note that if the argument is of type REAL, it is immaterial whether the name SQRT is regarded as a generic name or a specific name.

The existence of generic names for intrinsic functions in FORTRAN 77 is therefore of considerable convenience, in that it is no longer necessary to remember a number of different names for the same intrinsic function, one of which had to be chosen depending on the *type* of the actual argument in a particular function reference. Essentially, whenever a generic name is used in a function reference, the *type* of the argument indicates what actions are to be performed to produce the result. Usually the type of the result is the *same* as the type of the argument (or arguments), but there are exceptions to this rule, e.g. the functions for performing type conversion, nearest integer, and absolute value with a complex argument.

In general, therefore, the use of generic names rather than specific names for intrinsic functions is to be strongly recommended. Note, however, that whenever an intrinsic function name is to be used as an *actual argument* in a subprogram reference, the appropriate *specific* name must be used (see Chapter 13).

It should also be noted that it is the programmer's responsibility to use 'sensible' arguments when referencing a particular function. For example, if a function is not mathematically defined for certain arguments, such arguments should not be used in references of that function. Similarly if an argument is such that the desired result of a function reference is outwith the permitted range of real values for a particular implementation of FORTRAN 77, it should not be used.

The remainder of this section consists of a number of examples illustrating aspects of various intrinsic functions. Further information may be found in Chapters 15, 17, and 18 concerning the use of intrinsic functions involving arguments and/or results of type CHARACTER, DOUBLE PRECISION, and COMPLEX respectively

Example 12.6

INT(6)=6
INT(3.6)=3
INT(−2.8)=−2
INT(2.6528D0)=2
INT((−3.6,2.7))=−3

Example 12.7

If I=2, REAL(I)=2.0
If X=−3.6, REAL(X)=−3.6
If Z=(4.8,5.6), REAL(Z)=4.8

Example 12.8	If I=−4, DBLE(I)=−4D0
	If D=2.5D3, DBLE(D)=2.5D3
Example 12.9	CMPLX(2)=2+0*i*
	CMPLX(−1.6,2.5)=−1.6+2.5*i*
	CMPLX((−1.6,2.5))=−1.6+2.5*i*
Example 12.10	AINT(2.6)=2.0
	AINT(−3.9)=−3.0
	AINT(5.73D1)=57.0D0
Example 12.11	ANINT(3.2)=3.0
	ANINT(−5.8)=−6.0
	ANINT(4.2D0)=4.0D0
	NINT(3.2)=3
	NINT(−5.8)=−6
	NINT(4.2D0)=4
Example 12.12	ABS(−7)=7
	ABS(3.623)=3.623
	ABS((3.0,4.0))=$\sqrt{(3.0)^2+(4.0)^2}$=5.0
Example 12.13	If I=5,J=−3, SIGN(I,J)=−5
	If X=−2.6,Y=−4.4, SIGN(X,Y)=−2.6
Example 12.14	DIM(4,3)=4−3=1
	DIM(4,5)=0
	DIM(−3.7,−2.4)=0.0
	DIM(−3.7,−4.8)=−3.7−(−4.8)=1.1
Example 12.15	MAX(3,7,−6,−10,5)=7
Example 12.16	If X=2.5, Y=3.6, Z=−4.8, then
	MIN(X,Y−X,X+Y+Z)=MIN(2.5,1.1,1.3)=1.1
Example 12.17	SQRT(9.0) = 3.0
	SQRT(−5.2) is undefined
Example 12.18	ATAN2(1.0,1.0)=$\dfrac{\pi}{4}$
	ATAN2(SQRT(3.0),−1.0)=$\dfrac{2\pi}{3}$
	ATAN2(−SQRT(3.0),1.0)=$-\dfrac{\pi}{3}$
	ATAN2(−SQRT(3.0),−1.0)=$-\dfrac{2\pi}{3}$
	ATAN2(0.0,1.0)=0
	ATAN2(1.0,0.0)=$\dfrac{\pi}{2}$
	ATAN2(0.0,−1.0)=π
	ATAN2(−1.0,0.0)=$-\dfrac{\pi}{2}$

Table of intrinsic functions

In the following table, x, x_1, and x_2, represent arguments of type INTEGER, REAL, DOUBLE PRECISION, or COMPLEX as appropriate, c_1 and c_2 represent arguments of type CHARACTER, and z represents an argument of type COMPLEX. Note that†.

(a)   INT(x) is obtained by *truncating* x to integer form, the *real part* of x being truncated when x is of type COMPLEX. In addition the FORTRAN 77 Standard advises against the use of IFIX and IDINT, these names having been retained for no other reason than to provide compatibility with FORTRAN 66.

(b)   REAL(x) is obtained by converting x to real form, the *imaginary part* of x being discarded when x is of type COMPLEX. The FORTRAN 77 Standard also advises against the use of FLOAT and SNGL, these names having once again been retained for no other reason than to provide compatibility with FORTRAN 66.

(c)   DBLE(x) converts x to double precision form, the *imaginary part* of x being discarded when x is of type COMPLEX.

(d)   AINT(x) converts x to integer form by *truncation* and then converts the result back to the *same* type (REAL or DOUBLE PRECISION) as the argument.

(e)   ANINT(x) *rounds* x to the nearest integer and then converts the result back to the *same* type (REAL or DOUBLE PRECISION) as the argument.

(f)   NINT(x) *rounds* x to the nearest integer.

(g)   If x is of type INTEGER, REAL, or DOUBLE PRECISION, ABS(x) = magnitude of x. If x is of type COMPLEX, say $x = a + ib$, ABS(x) = $+\sqrt{a^2 + b^2}$.

(h)   MOD(x_1, x_2) returns the 'remainder on dividing x_1 by x_2' More precisely MOD(x_1, x_2) = $x_1 - \mathrm{int}(x_1/x_2) * x_2$, where $\mathrm{int}(x)$ = integer part of x. The result of MOD(x_1, x_2) is *undefined* if $x_2 = 0$.

(i)   The FORTRAN 77 Standard strongly advises against the use of AMAX0, MAX1, AMIN0, and MIN1, i.e. the four functions which return a result different in type from the type of the arguments. Rather than writing, for example, AMAX0(I,J,K) where I,J, and K are of a type INTEGER, it is recommended that REAL(MAX(I,J,K)) should be used.

(j)   Any real or double precision argument x used with SQRT or DSQRT must be *non-negative*. CSQRT(z) is described in Chapter 18.

(k)   Any real or double precision argument x used with LOG, ALOG, DLOG, LOG10, ALOG10, or DLOG10 must be *positive*. CLOG(z) is described in Chapter 18.

(l)   All angles are expressed in radians.

(m)   The result of ATAN2(x_1, x_2) lies in the range $-\pi <$ result $\leqslant \pi$ and indicates the *quadrant* in which the point (x_2, x_1) lies. The arguments x_1 and x_2 must not be both zero.

†Generic names are used whenever possible.

Intrinsic function	Definition	Generic name	Specific name	Number of arguments	Type of argument	Type of function
Type conversion	Conversion to integer (see note (a))	INT	–	1	INTEGER	INTEGER
			INT	1	REAL	INTEGER
			IFIX	1	REAL	INTEGER
			IDINT	1	DOUBLE	INTEGER
			–	1	COMPLEX	INTEGER
	Conversion to real (see note (b))	REAL	REAL	1	INTEGER	REAL
			FLOAT	1	INTEGER	REAL
			–	1	REAL	REAL
			SNGL	1	DOUBLE	REAL
			–	1	COMPLEX	REAL
	Conversion to double precision (see note (c))	DBLE	–	1	INTEGER	DOUBLE
			–	1	REAL	DOUBLE
			–	1	DOUBLE	DOUBLE
			–	1	COMPLEX	DOUBLE
	Conversion to complex (see Chapter 18)	CMPLX	–	1 or 2	INTEGER	COMPLEX
			–	1 or 2	REAL	COMPLEX
			–	1 or 2	DOUBLE	COMPLEX
			–	1	COMPLEX	COMPLEX
	Conversion from character to integer (see Chapter 15)	–	ICHAR	1	CHARACTER	INTEGER
	Conversion from integer to character (see Chapter 15)	–	CHAR	1	INTEGER	CHARACTER
Truncation	int(x) (see note (d))	AINT	AINT	1	REAL	REAL
			DINT	1	DOUBLE	DOUBLE
Nearest whole number	int(x + 0.5) if $x \geqslant 0$ int(x − 0.5) if $x < 0$ (see note (e))	ANINT	ANINT	1	REAL	REAL
			DNINT	1	DOUBLE	DOUBLE

Intrinsic function	Definition	Generic name	Specific name	Number of arguments	Type of argument	Type of function
Nearest integer	$\text{int}(x + 0.5)$ if $x \geqslant 0$ $\text{int}(x - 0.5)$ if $x < 0$ (see note (f))	NINT	NINT IDNINT	1 1	REAL DOUBLE	INTEGER INTEGER
Absolute value	$\lvert x \rvert$ (see note (g))	ABS	IABS ABS DABS CABS	1 1 1 1	INTEGER REAL DOUBLE COMPLEX	INTEGER REAL DOUBLE REAL
Remaindering	$x_1 - \text{int}(x_1/x_2) * x_2$ (see note (h))	MOD	MOD AMOD DMOD	2 2 2	INTEGER REAL DOUBLE	INTEGER REAL DOUBLE
Transfer of sign	$\lvert x_1 \rvert$ if $x_2 \geqslant 0$ $-\lvert x_1 \rvert$ if $x_2 < 0$	SIGN	ISIGN SIGN DSIGN	2 2 2	INTEGER REAL DOUBLE	INTEGER REAL DOUBLE
Positive difference	$x_1 - x_2$ if $x_1 > x_2$ $0 \quad$ if $x_1 \leqslant x_2$	DIM	IDIM DIM DDIM	2 2 2	INTEGER REAL DOUBLE	INTEGER REAL DOUBLE
Double precision product	$x_1 * x_2$ (see Chapter 17)	—	DPROD	2	REAL	DOUBLE
Choosing largest value	$\max(x_1, x_2, \ldots \ldots)$ (see note (i))	MAX	MAX0 AMAX1 DMAX1	$\geqslant 2$ $\geqslant 2$ $\geqslant 2$	INTEGER REAL DOUBLE	INTEGER REAL DOUBLE
		— —	AMAX0 MAX1	$\geqslant 2$ $\geqslant 2$	INTEGER REAL	REAL INTEGER

Description	Definition	Generic	Specific	No. of args	Argument type	Result type
Choosing smallest value	$\min(x_1, x_2, \ldots)$ (see note (i))	MIN	MIN0 AMIN1 DMIN1	≥ 2 ≥ 2 ≥ 2	INTEGER REAL DOUBLE	INTEGER REAL DOUBLE
		— —	AMIN0 MIN1	≥ 2 ≥ 2	INTEGER REAL	REAL INTEGER
Length	Length of character entity (see Chapter 15)	—	LEN	1	CHARACTER	INTEGER
Index of a substring	Location of a substring c_2 in string c_1 (see Chapter 15)	—	INDEX	2	CHARACTER	INTEGER
String comparison	Comparison of character strings according to ASCII collating sequence (see Chapter 15)	— — — —	LGE LGT LLE LLT	2 2 2 2	CHARACTER CHARACTER CHARACTER CHARACTER	LOGICAL LOGICAL LOGICAL LOGICAL
Imaginary part	y where $z = x + iy$	—	AIMAG	1	COMPLEX	REAL
Complex conjugate	$x - iy$ where $z = x + iy$	—	CONJG	1	COMPLEX	COMPLEX
Square root	$x^{\frac{1}{2}}$ (see note (j))	SQRT	SQRT DSQRT CSQRT	1 1 1	REAL DOUBLE COMPLEX	REAL DOUBLE COMPLEX
Exponential	$\exp(x)$	EXP	EXP DEXP CEXP	1 1 1	REAL DOUBLE COMPLEX	REAL DOUBLE COMPLEX
Natural logarithm	$\log_e x$ (see note (k))	LOG	ALOG DLOG CLOG	1 1 1	REAL DOUBLE COMPLEX	REAL DOUBLE COMPLEX
Common logarithm	$\log_{10} x$ (see note (k))	LOG10	ALOG10 DLOG10	1 1	REAL DOUBLE	REAL DOUBLE

Intrinsic function	Definition	Generic name	Specific name	Number of arguments	Type of	
					argument	function
Sine	$\sin x$	SIN	SIN DSIN CSIN	1 1 1	REAL DOUBLE COMPLEX	REAL DOUBLE COMPLEX
Cosine	$\cos x$	COS	COS DCOS CCOS	1 1 1	REAL DOUBLE COMPLEX	REAL DOUBLE COMPLEX
Tangent	$\tan x$	TAN	TAN DTAN	1 1	REAL DOUBLE	REAL DOUBLE
Arcsine	$\sin^{-1} x$ where $-1 \leqslant x \leqslant 1$ result is in the range $-\dfrac{\pi}{2} \leqslant \text{result} \leqslant \dfrac{\pi}{2}$	ASIN	ASIN DASIN	1 1	REAL DOUBLE	REAL DOUBLE
Arccosine	$\cos^{-1} x$ where $-1 \leqslant x \leqslant 1$ result is in the range $0 \leqslant \text{result} \leqslant \pi$	ACOS	ACOS DACOS	1 1	REAL DOUBLE	REAL DOUBLE
Arctangent	$\tan^{-1} x$ result is in the range $-\dfrac{\pi}{2} \leqslant \text{result} \leqslant \dfrac{\pi}{2}$	ATAN	ATAN DATAN	1 1	REAL DOUBLE	REAL DOUBLE
	$\tan^{-1}(x_1/x_2)$ (see note (m))	ATAN2	ATAN2 DATAN2	2 2	REAL DOUBLE	REAL DOUBLE
Hyperbolic sine	$\sinh x$	SINH	SINH DSINH	1 1	REAL DOUBLE	REAL DOUBLE
Hyperbolic cosine	$\cosh x$	COSH	COSH DCOSH	1 1	REAL DOUBLE	REAL DOUBLE
Hyperbolic tangent	$\tanh x$	TANH	TANH DTANH	1 1	REAL DOUBLE	REAL DOUBLE

Function subprograms

A function subprogram is a program unit which has a FUNCTION statement as its first statement. The other statements specify the actions of the function, that is, they are the statements necessary to perform the tasks of the function, including calculating the function value.

The FUNCTION statement
The FUNCTION statement specifies the name of the function, the arguments used by the function, and, possibly, the type of the function value. It has the form

type FUNCTION name (argument list)

where

(a) type is one of INTEGER, REAL, DOUBLE PRECISION, COMPLEX, LOGICAL, or CHARACTER*length and specifies the type of the value of the function. Character functions are described in Chapter 15 but it should be noted here that *length may be omitted. The type also may be omitted under certain circumstances.

(b) name is the symbolic name of the function, created according to the usual rules for names.

(c) argument list is a list of dummy arguments separated by commas. The argument list may be empty *but the enclosing parentheses are still required.*

Example 12.19 The following are valid FUNCTION statements

(a) FUNCTION F(X)
(b) FUNCTION AREA(A,B,C)
(c) INTEGER FUNCTION FAC(N)
(d) REAL FUNCTION LENGTH( )
(e) COMPLEX FUNCTION CADD(X,IX,Y,IY)

Name and type of function subprograms
The value supplied by the function is returned through its name. Consequently, within the function the name is used as a normal variable name which must be assigned a value during the execution of the function. The value of this variable on exit from the function is the value of the function.

Example 12.20 The following function evaluates $n!$ for $n \geqslant 1$:

```
      INTEGER FUNCTION FAC(N)

      FAC=1

      IF(N.GT.1) THEN

            DO 20 I=2,N

                  FAC = FAC*I

20            CONTINUE

      END IF

      END
```

Note that the function name FAC is used within the function as the name of an ordinary variable. In particular, its appearance on the right-hand side of the statement

$$FAC = FAC*I$$

is valid and does *not* constitute a *reference* to the function FAC.

Since a function has a *value*, it follows that it also must have a data *type*. The type of a function can be specified in one of 3 ways as follows:

(a)   in the FUNCTION statement;
(b)   by including the function name in a type statement in the function specification;
(c)   by the implicit naming rule.

If the type is not specified by either of the methods (a) or (b) above, the type is determined in the same manner as for variables and arrays using the implicit naming rule. (The type of a function may also be specified by an IMPLICIT statement (Chapter 23) in the function definition but this is not recommended. Further, the IMPLICIT statement should be used with care in a function as it may affect the type of the function without this fact being realized.)

Example 12.21   The following statements represent valid ways of specifying the type of a function:

(a)   INTEGER FUNCTION FAC(N)

in the FUNCTION statement.

(b)   FUNCTION FAC(N)
      INTEGER FAC

by including the name in a type statement.

(c)   FUNCTION IFAC(N)

by the implicit naming rule (note the name change).

A function name is a *global* name; that is, the function can be referenced by its name from all other program units in the program. Therefore, the name should not be used for any other purpose in the program (except as a variable name in the function itself as described above). However, the *type* of the function is not global and so any program unit referencing the function must specify its type in the same manner as for variables and arrays, namely by the implicit naming rule or by including the name in a type statement. Of course, the type specified in the reference must be the same as the type of the function itself.

Example 12.22   The following skeleton program represents a typical FORTRAN 77 program with a main program and two function subprograms:

                    PROGRAM EX1222
                    REAL MAXIM

INTEGER FAC

$$\vdots$$

X = MAXIM(B,L,K)
TERM = X**M/FAC(M)

$$\vdots$$

END

INTEGER FUNCTION FAC(N)

$$\vdots$$

END
FUNCTION MAXIM(A,M,N)
REAL MAXIM

$$\vdots$$

END

Note that:

(a)   the function FAC is of type INTEGER and so the name FAC must appear in an INTEGER type statement in the main program;

(b)   the function MAXIM is of type REAL and so the name MAXIM must appear in a REAL type statement in the main program.

Execution of a function subprogram

A function subprogram is executed by executing a reference to the function. Where an actual parameter is an expression, it is evaluated and the statements of the function are executed using the actual parameters in place of the dummy parameters.

Example 12.23   Write a function subprogram to calculate the area of a triangle with sides of given length.

The well known formula giving the area of a triangle is:

$$\text{area} = \sqrt{s(s-a)(s-b)(s-c)}$$

where

(a) a, b, and c are the lengths of the sides of the triangle;

(b) $s = \frac{1}{2}(a + b + c)$.

Three arguments are required, namely the lengths of the three sides.

```
FUNCTION AREA(A,B,C)

S = 0.5*(A+B+C)

AREA = SQRT(S*(S-A)*(S-B)*(S-C))

END
```

Example 12.24 Write a function subprogram to calculate the mean of a set of numbers stored in an *n*-element vector.

```
REAL FUNCTION MEAN(X,N)
REAL X(N)
MEAN = 0
DO 10 I=1,N
    MEAN = MEAN+X(I)
10  CONTINUE
MEAN = MEAN/N
END
```

Note that MEAN is used as a REAL variable and so the expression

MEAN/N

uses 'real' division *not* integer division. Remember that integer division produces an integer result, namely the truncation of the real result (see Chapter 6). Thus care should be taken when dividing by an integer. When in doubt use the intrinsic function REAL, e.g. write MEAN/REAL(N).

Example 12.25 Write a function subprogram to calculate the cube root of a number *a*.

Using the Newton–Raphson iterative formula

$$x_{i+1} = \tfrac{1}{3}(2x_i + a/x_i^2)$$

with a first approximation x_0 of $a/3$, a possible algorithm is

> assign $a/3$ to x
> **loop while** abs($x^3 - a$) > abs(a)*10^{-6} **do**
>   assign $\tfrac{1}{3}(2x + a/x^2)$ to x

which leads to the function:

```
      FUNCTION CUBE (A)
******THIS FUNCTION CALCULATES THE CUBE ROOT OF THE VALUE A
******USING THE ITERATIVE FORMULA X= (2X+A/X**2)/3
      CUBE = A/3
1     IF(ABS(CUBE**3-A).GT.ABS(A)*1E-6) THEN
          CUBE = (2* CUBE+A/CUBE**2)/3
          GO TO 1
      END IF
      END
```

Note the use of the relative tolerance in the block IF statement.

Subroutine subprograms

A subroutine subprogram is a program unit which has a SUBROUTINE statement as its first statement. The other statements specify the actions of the subroutine, that is they are the statements necessary to perform the tasks of the subroutine.

The SUBROUTINE statement

The SUBROUTINE statement specifies the name of the subroutine and, when required, the arguments used by the subroutine. It has the form:

$$\text{SUBROUTINE name (argument list)}$$

where

(a)   name is the symbolic name of the subroutine created according to the usual rules for names;

(b)   argument list is a list of dummy arguments separated by commas. The argument list may be empty in which case the enclosing brackets are *optional*.

Example 12.26   The following are valid SUBROUTINE statements

(a)   SUBROUTINE SORT(X, N)
(b)   SUBROUTINE SPEC(VECTOR,N,MEAN,NUMZRO)
(c)   SUBROUTINE CHECK
(d)   SUBROUTINE CHECK(   )

Example 12.27   The following CALL statements may be used to reference the subroutines of Example 12.26, assuming the actual arguments are valid.

(a)   CALL SORT(A,100)
(b)   CALL SPEC(Y,50,AVER,COUNT)
(c)   CALL CHECK
(d)   CALL CHECK(   )

Note that in (c) and (d), since there are no arguments, either statement may be used.

The subroutine name is used purely to identify the subroutine. There is no value and no type associated with it, unlike the name of a function. However the name is global to allow the subroutine to be referenced from all other program units and so the name should not be used for any other purpose in the program. Values calculated in the subroutine may be returned to the referencing program unit through the arguments.

Example 12.28   Write a subroutine to calculate the mean of an n-element vector and to count the number of zero elements

```
SUBROUTINE SPEC(VECTOR,N,MEAN,NUMZRO)

REAL VECTOR(N),  MEAN

MEAN = 0

NUMZRO = 0
```

```
              DO 15 I = 1,N

                 IF(VECTOR(I).NE.0) THEN

                    MEAN = MEAN + VECTOR(I)

                                         ELSE

                 NUMZRO = NUMZRO+1

              END IF
      15      CONTINUE

              MEAN = MEAN/N

              END
```

Note that:

(a)   the dummy argument MEAN is of type REAL and so must appear in a type statement;

(b)   two values are returned through the arguments, namely the mean and the number of zero elements;

(c)   this module could also be written as a function subprogram

REAL FUNCTION MEAN(VECTOR,N,NUMZRO)

with one value returned through the name of the function and one value through the actual argument replacing NUMZRO (see also Example 12.24).

Example 12.29   Example 8.3 (page 60) calculated an employee's gross wage from the basic rate and the number of hours worked under each of six categories, one category being rated at the basic rate, two at 1.5 times the basic rate, and three at double the basic rate. The rules of the company state that no employee should work more than 80 hours in total and not more than 24 hours at 1.5 times basic rate and not more than 16 hours at double the basic rate.

Write a subroutine to read in the employee number, the basic rate, and the number of hours worked in each category, and to check that the information conforms to the above rules. The subroutine should return the employee number, the basic rate and the number of hours worked at each rate. If any of the rules are broken a message should be printed and another employee record read and checked. That is, the records which do not meet the rules are not processed further outside the subroutine. The data are terminated with a negative employee number.

```
          SUBROUTINE CHECK(EMPNO,RATE,TIME,TIMHF,DOUBLE)

   *THIS SUBROUTINE READS AN EMPLOYEES DATA AND CHECKS IT AGAINST

   *               THE RULES

          INTEGER EMPNO

          READ*,EMPNO,RATE,TIME,TMHLF1,TMHLF2,DBLTM1,DBLTM2,DBLTM3
   10     IF(EMPNO.GE.0) THEN

             TIMHF = TMHLF1+TMHLF2

             DOUBLE = DBLTM1+DBLTM2+DBLTM3
```

```
            IF(TIME+TIMHF+DOUBLE.LE.80) THEN

               IF(TIMHF.LE.24) THEN

                  IF(DOUBLE.LE.16) THEN

                     RETURN

                  ENDIF

               ENDIF

            ENDIF

            PRINT 99,EMPNO,TIME+TIMHF+DOUBLE,TIMHF,DOUBLE

    99      FORMAT(' **BROKEN RULES - EMPLOYEE',I8,' WORKED',F7.2,

   +               ' HOURS IN TOTAL'/' ',F7.2,' HOURS AT TIME AND A HALF'

   +             / ' AND',F7.2,' HOURS AT DOUBLE TIME')

            READ *, EMPNO,RATE,TIME,TMHLF1,TMHLF2,DBLTM1,DBLTM2,DBLTM3

            GO TO 10

      END IF

      END
```

Note that a RETURN statement appears in the middle of the coding. The FORMAT statement is used here for convenience and is described in detail in Chapter 14.

Summary of intrinsic functions, function subprograms, and subroutine subprograms

	Intrinsic functions	Function subprograms	Subroutine subprograms
Name	Up to six letters and digits, the first of which must be a letter		
Type	As specified	(a) In FUNCTION statement (b) Type statement (c) Implicit naming rule	No type associated with a subroutine
Definition	As specified in FORTRAN 77	In the statements between the FUNCTION statement and the END statement	In the statements between the SUBROUTINE statement and the END statement
Reference	Writing the name where the function value is required		CALL statement
Number of arguments	One or more as defined	Any number, including zero, as defined. If zero, parentheses must be included	Any number, including zero, as defined
Number of values produced	One	One through the function name, any number through the arguments	Any number through the arguments

Scope of entities in programs

In a FORTRAN 77 program some entities (*global* entities) are able to be referenced from anywhere in the program and some entities (*local* entities) may be referenced only from a restricted part of the program.

Global entities
The global entities in a FORTRAN 77 program are the main program, subprograms, external procedures, and common blocks (see Chapter 13). Obviously the names by which these entities are referenced are *global names* which may be used throughout the program.

Local entities
Local entities are those declared or used within a program unit. Their names are local to that unit cannot be used to refer to the local entity from outside the unit. Such names include variable, array, and constant names. In addition dummy argument names are local to the subprogram concerned. The name of an implied-DO variable in a DATA statement is local to the implied-DO list (see Chapter 11).

If an entity is local to a program unit it does not exist outside that program unit and, if the same name is used in another program unit, that name refers to another entity.

Example 12.30 Consider the skeleton program

```
              PROGRAM EX1230
              REAL X, LENGTH, Y
              INTEGER COUNT, I, J

                  ⋮

              END
              FUNCTION FN(A,B,X,N)
              REAL A,B,Y, X(N)
              INTEGER N,I

                  ⋮

              END
              SUBROUTINE SUB(C,D,I)
              INTEGER C,I,J
              REAL D,X,COUNT

                  ⋮

              END
```

The global names are EX1230, FN, and SUB.
Names local to the main program are X,LENGTH,Y,COUNT,I,J.

Names local to the function FN are A,B,Y,X,N,I.

Names local to the subroutine SUB are C,I,J,D,X,COUNT.

There are a number of name clashes, e.g. X appears in all three program units but refers to three different entitites, namely two distinct real variables (in the main program and SUB) and an array in FN. Also I is used as an integer variable in all three program units but refers to a *different* integer variable in each case.

Definition of local entities

If an entity is local to a subprogram, that entity becomes undefined on exit from the subprogram, that is on execution of a RETURN or an END statement. In other words if that subprogram is referenced again those entities will not have the values they had on the last exit. There are two exceptions to this rule:

(a)   entities initialized by a DATA statement and which have not been redefined (see Chapter 11);

(b)   entities specified in a SAVE statement (see below).

If a reference to a subprogram is executed in a program unit, entities local to that program unit are not available to the subprogram (unless contained in the argument list) but remain defined on return from the subprogram.

Example 12.31   Consider the skeleton program:

```
PROGRAM EX1231
REAL X,LENGTH,Y, G(25)
INTEGER COUNT,I,J
   .
   .
   .
Y = FN(LENGTH,Y,G,25)
   .
   .
   .
END

FUNCTION FN(A,B,X,N)
REAL A,B,Y,X(N)
INTEGER N,I
   .
   .
   .
END
```

The entities local to the main program are variables X,LENGTH,Y,COUNT,I, and J, and the array G. The entities local to the function FN are variables Y, and I, dummy variables A, B, and N, and the dummy array X.

When the reference to FN in the main program is executed the main program local entities LENGTH, Y, and G are made available to FN by being associated with A, B, and X through the argument list. The main program local entities X,COUNT,I, and J remain defined but are unavailable to FN. On exit from FN the entities Y and I local to FN become undefined. That is, they have no defined value on the next reference to FN. (For further information on arguments, see Chapter 13.)

Further facilities available for subprograms

A further three facilities are available for use with FORTRAN 77 subprograms.

(1) *The SAVE statement* causes the values of local entities in a subprogram to be saved for the next reference. That is, they do not become undefined. While apparently useful, the SAVE statement in practice is of limited value since there are very few occasions on which it is useful to save a local entity. Therefore a brief description only is given here.

The SAVE statement is a specification statement, and is, therefore, *nonexecutable.* It has the form

SAVE savelist

where savelist is a list of variable names, array names, and common block names (see Chapter 13) (contained within two slashes) separated by commas. It will be noted that dummy argument names, procedure names, and individual entities in a common block (see Chapter 13) are not permitted. The savelist may be empty in which case it is assumed that all allowable entities in the subprogram are to be saved.

Example 12.32 A subroutine SEARCH(LIST,N,KEY,INDX) searches the *N*-element vector LIST for the item KEY and returns the index of that item in INDX. The method used is a simple linear search, one search starting where the previous one finished. Thus the finishing point must be saved for the next search. (It is assumed that KEY occurs at least once in the vector LIST.)

The following subroutine effects this task:

```
SUBROUTINE SEARCH(LIST,N,KEY,INDX)
INTEGER LIST(N),KEY,INDX,LOOK
SAVE LOOK
DATA LOOK /-1/
IF(LOOK.EQ.-1)THEN
     LOOK = 1
END IF
IF(LIST(LOOK).NE.KEY)THEN
     LOOK=MOD(LOOK,N)+1
END IF
INDX=LOOK
END
```

One of the problems with saving local entities is their initialization and, as can be seen from the above example, this can result in cumbersome and otherwise meaningless code.

The saving of entities in named common blocks is considered in Chapter 13.

(2) *The ENTRY statement* specifies another point of entry to the subprogram. Thus a single subprogram can be written with several entry points.

(3) *The alternate RETURN* facility enables control to be returned to a pre-specified point in the referencing program unit. Thus, in addition to the normal return point, a subprogram may specify several different return points to allow for different conditions met during the execution of the subprogram.

The alternative entry and exit facilities are bad programming practice and should not be used. A well-structured program should be easy to follow and maintain. A module which has several entry points and which also exits to one of several different points is much more difficult to follow than a module with a single entry point and only a normal exit. While the alternate entry and exit facilities may offer a short term advantage, almost certainly they will be detrimental to long term maintenance. In any case, the alternate entry can be implemented using either separate sub-programs or an argument to indicate which entry facility is required. The alternate exit facility can be implemented using an argument to indicate the exit condition. These two facilities are described more fully in Chapter 23.

Exercise 12

1 Write function subprograms

    (a)   DIST(X,Y): to calculate the distance from the origin to a point with co-ordinates (x, y), i.e. the distance is $\sqrt{x^2 + y^2}$.

    (b)   DIST2(X1,Y1,X2,Y2): to calculate the distance between two points with co-ordinates (x_1, y_1) and (x_2, y_2), i.e. the distance is $\sqrt{(x_2 - x_1)^2 + (y_2 - y_1)^2}$.

2 Amend the function subprogram AREA of Example 12.23 to include a check that the three given sides constitute a triangle. If they do not, print an appropriate message on the designated output device and stop.

3 Write a function subprogram SUMGEO(A,R) to calculate the sum of the geo-metric progression

$$a + ar + ar^2 + \ldots + ar^n$$

as n tends to infinity. This sum equals $a/(1 - r)$ provided that $-1 < r < 1$. If r is outside this range print an appropriate message on the designated output device and stop.

4 Write a function subprogram FIB(N) to compute and return the nth Fibonacci number f_n where

    (a) $f_n = f_{n-1} + f_{n-2}$ where $n = 3,4,5. \ldots$;   (b) $f_1 = f_2 = 1$.

5 Write a subroutine subprogram LIMITS(X,N,TOP,BOTTOM) to find the largest and smallest elements in the N-element vector **X**, returning these values in TOP and BOTTOM respectively.

Further exercises on procedures are given at the end of Chapter 13.

13 Program unit inter-communication

The inevitable result of improved and enlarged communication between different levels in a hierarchy is a vastly increased area of misunderstanding. (*Law of Communications*)

As was seen in the last chapter, a module in an algorithm may be implemented in FORTRAN 77 as a procedure, or more commonly, as either a function subprogram or a subroutine subprogram. While a module is a logically distinct operation it is necessary to communicate information between the different modules to enable computations to be made on the appropriate data and results returned. Thus consideration must be given to the communication between the different program units in a program. In the last chapter such communication was introduced informally and it was seen that data could be passed through arguments or, in the case of a function, through the function name. In this chapter, the passing of non-character information between program units is considered in detail. The passing of character information is left until Chapter 15.

Information may be passed between two program units by means of *arguments* or *common blocks*. The common block facility which is considered later in this chapter is a very convenient method of communication. At the same time it severely restricts portability and can produce unexpected side effects leading to obscure errors and difficulties in the maintenance of programs. Hence arguments should be the primary, if not the only, means of communication between a procedure and the program unit referencing it.

Arguments

When a procedure reference is executed an association is established between the *actual* arguments in the reference and the corresponding *dummy* arguments in the referenced procedure.

Example 13.1   In the reference

$$ANGVAL(SQRT(D*D+E*E),2*F,G+H)$$

to the function

$$FUNCTION\ ANGVAL(X,Y,Z)$$

the dummy argument X becomes associated with the actual argument SQRT(D*D+E*E), the dummy argument Y becomes associated with actual argument 2*F, and the dummy argument Z becomes associated with the actual argument G+H.

Each dummy argument is classified as a variable, an array, or a procedure. The rules governing association between dummy and actual arguments will be considered for each of these classifications in turn.

Variables as dummy arguments

A variable as a dummy argument is a local variable within the subprogram concerned and as such must obey the normal rules for the use of variables. In particular the type rules apply and, if necessary, the dummy argument name must appear in a type statement in the subprogram.

The dummy argument may be associated with an actual argument which is a variable, an array element, or an expression (including a constant). However, if information is to be passed back *from* the subprogram using this argument the dummy argument will have a value assigned to it within the subprogram. In this case, the actual argument must not be an expression. Of course, the dummy argument may appear as an actual argument in a reference to another subprogram. That is, the information is passed to more than one subprogram.

Example 13.2   In the subroutine

```
SUBROUTINE SPEC1(VECTOR,N,MEAN)

REAL VECTOR(N)

REAL MEAN

MEAN = 0

DO 10 I=1,N

     MEAN = MEAN+VECTOR(I)

10   CONTINUE

MEAN = MEAN/N

END
```

the mean of the values in the vector VECTOR is left in the argument MEAN. Therefore, the following references to SPEC1 are *invalid* (assuming X is an array):

```
CALL SPEC1(X,50, B+12)
CALL SPEC1(X,100, SQRT(A*A+B*B))
CALL SPEC1(X,M,12)
```

The following references to SPEC1 are valid:

```
CALL SPEC1(X,50,AVER)
CALL SPEC1(X,100,X(101))
CALL SPEC1(X,M,X(M+1))
CALL SPEC1(X,2*L+12,AMEAN)
```

Note that:

(a)   the dummy argument MEAN is a real variable and so appears in a type statement;

(b)   since the dummy argument N represents the number of values to be processed in the vector and is not redefined during the execution of the subroutine, it is valid to associate with it the actual arguments shown, namely a constant, a variable and an expression.

If an argument is used to pass information out from a subprogram, the actual argument need not have a defined value when the reference is executed.

If an actual argument is an expression, the expression is evaluated just *before* the association with the dummy argument takes place. Thus even if, due to redefinition within the subprogram of variables used in the expression, the value of the expression might change, the value of the actual argument will remain constant.

Arrays as dummy arguments

An array as a dummy argument is a local array within the subprogram concerned and is known as *dummy array*. It can be used as a normal array within the subprogram including being passed as an argument to another subprogram. In particular, the dummy array must be specified in an array declarator in the subprogram. An array declarator for a dummy array has the same format as that for an actual array as described in Chapter 10 with a few differences, as follows:

(1) The declarator is permitted in a DIMENSION statement or in a type statement but *not* in a COMMON statement.

(2) The upper and lower bounds on a dimension of the array may be not only integer constant expressions but also expressions containing integer constants and variables. Such dimensions are said to be *adjustable*. A variable contained in an adjustable dimension must be another dummy argument or be in a common block.

(3) The upper bound of the last dimension may be an asterisk in which case the array is said to be an *assumed size array*.

Example 13.3   The following declarators are valid for the dummy arrays X,Y,LENGTH,A,B, and C. M and N are integer variables.

>   DIMENSION X(10), Y(0:20,10)
>   REAL LENGTH(−1:5)
>   DIMENSION A(N,N), B(10,2*N)
>   DIMENSION C(2:M,0:M*N−1,−1:*)

Note that:

(a)   the variables M and N must either be other dummy arguments or appear in a common block;

(b)   A and B are adjustable arrays;

(c)   C is an assumed size array.

Adjustable and assumed size arrays are introduced so that for different references to the subprogram the dummy array may be associated with different actual arrays having different properties (of dimension bounds, number of elements, etc.). When the reference is executed the expressions specifying the adjustable dimensions are evaluated. Hence the properties of the array are fixed for that execution of the subprogram. (Clearly any variable used in an adjustable dimension must have a defined value when the reference is executed.) Similarly, the value of the upper bound of the last dimension of an assumed size array is fixed by the size of the actual array (see 'Array size and subscript values' below).\

Example 13.4   In Example 13.2, the subroutine commencing

SUBROUTINE SPEC1(VECTOR,N,MEAN)

calculates the mean of the values in the one-dimensional N-element array VECTOR. VECTOR is an adjustable array declared in the statement

REAL VECTOR(N), MEAN

Note that N is one of the other dummy arguments.
In the reference

CALL SPEC1(X,50,AVER)

the adjustable dimension is fixed at 50 for this reference.
In the reference

CALL SPEC1(X,M,AMEAN)

the variable M must have a defined value when the reference is executed. The adjustable dimension in the subroutine is fixed at this value for this reference.

Example 13.5   The subroutine commencing

SUBROUTINE PROCES(A,L,LL,M,N)
REAL A(0:10,L:20,LL:N,M−1:M∗N)

illustrates the use of adjustable dimensions through a 4-dimensional array A. Consider the actual arrays defined as follows:

REAL X4(0:10,20,10,20)
REAL Y4(0:10,0:20,−5:5,0:5)

Valid references using these arrays are

CALL PROCES(X4,1,1,2,10)
CALL PROCES(Y4,0,−5,1,5)

It should be noted that the adjustable dimension and assumed size properties are only applicable to dummy arrays. Integer constant expressions must be used when specifying the dimension bounds of 'actual arrays' used in a subprogram.

Restrictions on an assumed size dummy array name are that it must not appear in an input/output list of a data transfer statement, as an internal unit identifier, or as a format identifier (see Chapter 14).

Array size and subscript values†

In order to understand the association between dummy arrays and actual arrays, further consideration must be given to the properties of an array.

The *size of an array* is equal to the number of elements in the array. The size can be calculated from the dimension bounds in the array declarator. If l_i and u_i are the lower and upper bounds respectively of the ith dimension, then *the size of the ith dimension* is $u_i - l_i + 1$ and the size of the array is the product of the sizes of the dimensions.

The *subscript value* of a subscript determines which array element is being identified and is related to the fact that array elements are held in 'column order' as stated in Chapter 10. The subscript value is a function of the subscript expressions, the number of dimensions in the array and the upper and lower bounds of these dimensions as indicated in the following table:

n	Array declarator	Array element	Subscript value
1	$A(l_1 : u_1)$	$A(s_1)$	$1 + (s_1 - l_1)$
2	$A(l_1 : u_1, l_2 : u_2)$	$A(s_1, s_2)$	$1 + (s_1 - l_1) + (s_2 - l_2)*d_1$
$\vdots$	$\vdots$	$\vdots$	$\vdots$
r	$A(l_1 : u_1, l_2 : u_2, \dots, l_r : u_r)$	$A(s_1, s_2, \dots, s_r)$	$1 + (s_1 - l_1)$ $+ (s_2 - l_2)*d_1$ $+ (s_3 - l_3)*d_2*d_1$ $\vdots$ $+ (s_r - l_r)*d_{r-1}*d_{r-2} \dots *d_2*d_1$

where

    (a) n is the number of dimensions $1 \leqslant n \leqslant 7$;

    (b) l_i and u_i are the lower and upper bounds of the ith dimension (if l_i is omitted from the array declarator, then $l_i = 1$);

    (c) s_i is the (integer) value of the ith subscript expression;

    (d) d_i is the size of the ith dimension $d_i = u_i - l_i + 1$.

Example 13.6   The two dimensional array COEFF is declared in the statement

$$\text{REAL COEFF}(3,0:5)$$

The ordered sequence of the elements of COEFF is

$$\text{COEFF}(1,0), \text{COEFF}(2,0), \text{COEFF}(3,0), \text{COEFF}(1,1), \dots.$$

(i.e. 'column order'). The size of COEFF and the subscript value of each element are shown in the following diagram:

Element	1,0 2,0 3,0 1,1 2,1 3,1 1,2 2,2 3,2 1,3 2,3 3,3 1,4 2,4 3,4 1,5 2,5 3,5
Subscript value	1 2 3 4 5 6 7 8 9 10 11 12 13 14 15 16 17 18

$$\text{Size} = 18$$

---

†This section may be skipped on a first reading.

Thus the size is the number of elements in COEFF and is equal to the product of the sizes of each dimension, i.e. $(3 - 1 + 1) \times (5 - 0 + 1) = 3 \times 6 = 18$.

COEFF(1,1) is the fourth element of COEFF in its specified order. Therefore the subscript value specifies which element of the array is being accessed. Using the formula given in the above table, the subscript value of COEFF(1,1) is $1 + (1 - 1) + (1 - 0) \times 3 = 4$.

Association of dummy and actual array arguments†

A dummy argument which is an array may be associated with an actual argument which is an array name or an array element name.

If the actual argument is an array name, an element of the array is associated with the dummy array element with the *same subscript value*. The size of the dummy array must not exceed the size of its associated actual array. If the dummy array is an assumed size array, its size is equal to that of the actual array.

If the actual argument is the name of an array element with a subscript value of p, an element of the dummy array with a subscript value of q is associated with the actual array element with the subscript value of $p + q - 1$. The size of the dummy array must not exceed the size of the actual array less $(p - 1)$. If the dummy array is an assumed size array, its size is equal to the size of the actual array less $(p - 1)$. In other words, the subprogram will use the actual array less the first $p - 1$ elements.

Arguments which are character arrays are considered in Chapter 15.

Example 13.7   Consider the subroutine commencing

        SUBROUTINE SPEC1(VECTOR, N, MEAN)
        REAL VECTOR(N),MEAN

and the actual arrays X1 and Y1 (declared in another program unit)

        REAL X1(50), Y1(−5:5)

The following references are valid

    (a)   CALL SPEC1(X1,50,AVER)
    (b)   CALL SPEC1(X1(26),25,AVER)
    (c)   CALL SPEC1(Y1,11,AVER)
    (d)   CALL SPEC1(Y1(1),5,AVER)

Note that:

    (i) In case (a) the dummy array VECTOR is associated with the whole of the actual array X1 and the association of elements is VECTOR(1) with X1(1), VECTOR(2) with X1(2), . . ., VECTOR(50) with X1(50).
    (ii) In case (b) VECTOR is associated with part of X1 only. The actual argument is an array element X1(26) with subscript value 26. Therefore the association of elements is VECTOR(1) with X1(26), VECTOR(2) with X1(27),. . ., VECTOR(25) with X1(50).

---

†This section may be skipped on a first reading.

(iii) In case (c) the element association is VECTOR(1) with Y1(-5), VECTOR(2) with Y1(-4), ..., VECTOR(6) with Y1(0), ..., VECTOR(11) with Y1(5).

(iv) In case (d) the element association is VECTOR (1) with Y1(1), ..., VECTOR(5) with Y1(5).

It is permissible for the number and size of dimensions in the actual array to be different from those in the dummy array. While this facility is useful on occasions, *it should be used with great care* since, as must be obvious, it can be a source of errors.

Example 13.8   Consider again the subroutine commencing

SUBROUTINE SPEC1(VECTOR,N,MEAN)
REAL VECTOR(N),MEAN

and the actual array X2 (declared in another program unit)

REAL X2(25,50)

The following reference is valid

CALL SPEC1(X2(1,14),25,AVER)

The subscript value of the array element X(1,14) is

$$1+(1-1)+(14-1)*(25-1+1)=326.$$

This element is associated with the dummy array element VECTOR(1). VECTOR(2) to VECTOR(25) are therefore associated with the actual array elements with sub-script values 327 to 350, that is X2(2,14),X2(3,14), ..., X2(25,14) as shown in the diagram.

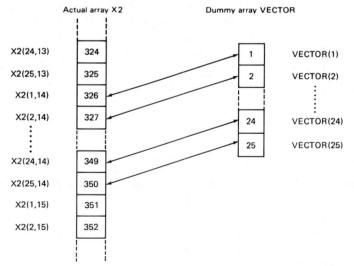

(The numbers in the boxes are the subscript values.)

Hence the effect of this reference to SPEC1 is to calculate the mean of the values in the 14th column of X2.

Note that the two-dimensional array is handled as a one-dimensional array within the subroutine. However, the same 'trick' cannot be used to process a *row* in X2 since its elements are sequenced in *column* order.

Procedures as dummy arguments

A dummy argument that is identified as a procedure is called a *dummy procedure* and may be associated with an actual argument that is a procedure or another dummy procedure. A dummy procedure may be referenced as a function or a subroutine or passed on to another procedure as an actual argument.

If the dummy procedure is to be referenced as a function, the actual procedure must be the name of an intrinsic function, an external function or a dummy procedure. (Statement functions may not be passed as arguments.) The type of a 'dummy function' must be the same as the type of an associated actual function. In the dummy function reference the arguments must agree in number and type with those of an associated actual function. If the name of the dummy function is the same as the name of an intrinsic function, that intrinsic function cannot be referenced in this subprogram.

Example 13.9   The trapezoidal rule for numerical integration is

$$\int_l^u f(x)\,dx = \frac{h}{2}(f_0 + 2f_1 + 2f_2 + \ldots + 2f_{n-1} + f_n)$$

where the area under the curve $y = f(x)$ between the points $x = l$ and $x = u$ is split into n equal panels or trapezoids of equal width h. The value of the function at the ith point $f_i = f(l + ih)$.

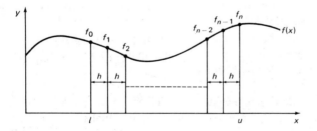

Write a function program

FUNCTION TRAP(FUNX,XLOWER,XUPPER,N)

to integrate a given function FUNX between the points XLOWER and XUPPER.

```
FUNCTION TRAP(FUNX,XLOWER,XUPPER,N)

*THIS PROCEDURE INTEGRATES THE FUNCTION FUNX BETWEEN

*          THE POINTS XLOWER AND XUPPER USING THE TRAPEZOIDAL

******     RULE WITH N PANELS

     WIDTH = (XUPPER-XLOWER)/N

     TRAP = 0
```

```
DO 1 I=1, N-1

    TRAP=TRAP+FUNX(XLOWER+I*WIDTH)

1   CONTINUE
    TRAP = 0.5*WIDTH*(FUNX(XLOWER)+2*TRAP + FUNX(XUPPER))
    END
```

TRAP may be used to integrate numerically SIN(X) from 0.25 to 0.45 using 10 panels as follows

$$Y = TRAP(SIN,0.25,0.45,10)$$

Note that the *name* of the (intrinsic) function SIN is used as an actual parameter.

If the dummy procedure is referenced as a subroutine, the actual subroutine must be the name of a subroutine or dummy procedure. There is, of course, no type associated with a subroutine but in the dummy subroutine reference the arguments must agree in number and type with those of an associated actual subroutine.

In order to pass the name of a procedure as an actual argument, it must be included in either an EXTERNAL statement or an INTRINSIC statement in the program unit containing the reference. In this way the FORTRAN 77 compiler will recognize the name as a procedure name rather than the name of a variable or array.

The EXTERNAL statement

An EXTERNAL statement specifies that a symbolic name is used as the name of an external procedure or a dummy procedure. The form of an EXTERNAL statement is

EXTERNAL list of names

where the list of names consists of the names of external procedures and dummy procedures separated by commas.

If an external procedure name or a dummy procedure name is used as an actual argument in a subprogram reference it must appear in an EXTERNAL statement in the program unit containing the reference.

Example 13.10 Consider the function TRAP of Example 13.9. In referencing TRAP the name of a function is included as an actual parameter. This name must appear in an EXTERNAL statement

        PROGRAM EX1310
        EXTERNAL ERR

        ⋮

        ERF = 1.12838*TRAP(ERR,0,X,N)

        ⋮

        END

```
FUNCTION ERR(T)
ERR = EXP(-T**2)
END
FUNCTION TRAP(FUNX,XLOWER,XUPPER,N)

    ⋮

END
```

It will be noted that in the main program, ERR could not be distinguished from a variable of that name if the EXTERNAL statement were missing.

The INTRINSIC statement

The INTRINSIC statement specifies that a symbolic name is used as the name of an *intrinsic function*. The form of an INTRINSIC statement is

INTRINSIC list of intrinsic function names

If an intrinsic function is used as an actual argument in a subprogram reference its name must appear in an INTRINSIC statement in the program unit containing the reference. It is important to remember that this name should be .the *specific* name not the generic name.

Example 13.11   Consider the function TRAP of Example 13.9. If the function to be integrated is an intrinsic function, its name must appear in an INTRINSIC statement

```
PROGRAM EX1311
INTRINSIC SIN

    ⋮

Y = TRAP(SIN,0.25,0.45,10)

    ⋮

END
FUNCTION TRAP(FUNX,XLOWER,XUPPER,N)

    ⋮

END
```

Again, it will be noted that in the main program SIN could not be distinguished from a variable of that name if the INTRINSIC statement were missing.

Two further points to note about this topic are:

(a)   if the name of an intrinsic function appears in an EXTERNAL statement in a program unit the name becomes the name of some external procedure and the intrinsic function is no longer available to that program unit;

(b) the names of the intrinsic functions for type conversion, string comparison, and for choosing the largest or smallest value must not be used as actual parameters, that is the names INT, IFIX, IDINT, REAL, FLOAT, SNGL, DBLE, CMPLX, ICHAR, CHAR, LGE, LGT, LLE, LLT, MAX, MAX0, AMAX1, DMAX1, AMAX0, MAX1, MIN, MIN0, AMIN1, DMIN1, AMIN0, and MIN1.

Arguments in general

A *dummy* argument in a subprogram may be used as an *actual* argument in a reference to another subprogram.

Example 13.12   The subroutine

```
SUBROUTINE UPDATE(X,M,N,KEY,T)
INTEGER X(M,N),T(N)
      .
      .
      .
END
```

updates a row in the array X with the information in the array T. The actual row to be updated is the Ith where $X(I,1) = KEY$. To find the value of I, UPDATE references a subroutine SEARCH:

```
SUBROUTINE SEARCH(Y,K,L,LOOK,IND)
INTEGER Y(K,L)
      .
      .
      .
END
```

which searches down the first column of Y looking for a value equal to LOOK. When it finds one it returns the appropriate row number in IND.

Thus the reference to SEARCH in UPDATE will be

```
SUBROUTINE UPDATE(X,M,N,KEY,T)
INTEGER X(M,N),T(N)
      .
      .
      .
CALL SEARCH (X,M,N,KEY,I)
      .
      .
      .
END
```

where X, M, N, and KEY are dummy variables in UPDATE being used as actual variables for SEARCH.

Common blocks

A common block is a means whereby a value can be made available to a number of program units in a program. Normally, a value and its symbolic name is available only to the program unit in which it is declared or used. In other words it is *local* to that program unit. Thus to pass information between program units, arguments must be used. However, if a value is stored in a common block it becomes global to those program units which specify that common block. It should be noted that the name used to reference this global value may be different in different program units.

A common block may have a name by which it is known in all program units using it. Therefore that name is global to the program and should not be used for any other purpose in the program. The common block which has no name is called the *blank common block*. There is only one blank common block in a program and it is available to all program units. A common block is specified by a COMMON statement.

The COMMON statement

The form of a COMMON statement is:

$$\text{COMMON /blockname}_1 / \text{ list}_1 \text{,/blockname}_2 / \text{ list}_2 , \ldots \ldots$$

where

(a) The commas are optional.

(b) Each blockname is the name of a common block. If the name is omitted, the blank common block is assumed. (If the *first* blockname is omitted, the two slashes are optional.)

(c) Each list is a list of variable names, array names and array declarators separated by commas. In a subprogram, no dummy argument name may appear in the list. In a function subprogram, the function name must not appear in the list.

The COMMON statement declares that the entitites in list$_i$ are in the common block with name blockname$_i$. If a common block contains an entity of type CHARACTER, all the entities in that common block must be of type CHARACTER.

Example 13.13   The following are valid COMMON statements

(a) COMMON /INFO/I1,I2,COUNT,X,Y

(b) COMMON /DATAI/I4,II,LENGTH,MARKS/DATAR/X1,Y3,A(10)

(c) COMMON /STOCK/PART,SIZE,COST/ /B(0:5),C(20,−1:10)

Statement (a) declares that the entities with names I1,I2,COUNT,X, Y are to be in common block INFO.

Statement (b) declares that I4,II,LENGTH, and MARKS are to be in common block DATAI and that X1,Y3, and the one-dimensional array A are to be in common block DATAR.

Statement (c) declares that PART,SIZE, and COST are to be in common block STOCK and that the one-dimensional array B and the two-dimensional array C are to be in blank common.

Note that:

(i) Arrays may be declared in a COMMON statement (see Chapter 10).

(ii) Entities which are not array declarators may be either variable names or array names. For example, a program unit may contain the statements

```
REAL X(50),Y(-5:5,0:10)
COMMON /INFO/I1,I2,COUNT,X,Y
```

In this case X and Y are array names and I1, I2, and COUNT are variable names (unless they are declared to be arrays in a type statement or another DIMENSION statement).

(iii) Statement (c) may be written

```
COMMON B(0:5),C(20,-1:10)/STOCK/PART,SIZE,COST
```

Since B and C are in blank common and they appear first in the statement the slashes enclosing the name may be omitted.

The name of a common block may appear more than once in a COMMON statement. The lists following successive occurrences of the same common block name are treated as a continuation of the last list.

Example 13.14   The COMMON statement

```
COMMON /DATAI/I4,II,LENGTH,MARKS/DATAR/X1,Y3,A(10)
```

may be written

```
COMMON/DATAI/I4,II/DATAR/X1/DATAI/LENGTH/DATAR/Y3,A(10)
+          /DATAI/MARKS
```

Blank common may be continued similarly. Needless to say, this facility can lead to a confusing program and should be avoided.

Characteristics of a common block

The entities in a common block are held in the *sequence* in which they were declared. This sequence is maintained in all program units specifying this common block. However, the names used to reference these entities in each program unit may be different. Thus the *names* are *local* to the program unit in which the common block is specified while the *entities* themselves are *global*.

Example 13.15   The statements

```
COMMON/INFO/I1,I2,COUNT,X,Y
COMMON/INFO/K(3),A(2)
COMMON/INFO/I,J,KOUNT,X,Y
```

are contained in the main program and the subprograms SUB and FUNC respectively. They all refer to the same common block, INFO, which contains five entities.

INFO					
Names used in main program	I1	I2	COUNT	X	Y
Names used in subprogram SUB	K(1)	K(2)	K(3)	A(1)	A(2)
Names used in subprogram FUNC	I	J	KOUNT	X	Y

That is, for example, the first entity is named I1 by the main program, K(1) by SUB, and I by FUNC; the fifth entity is named Y by the main program and FUNC, and A(2) by SUB.

The type of the entity remains the same for all program units and so *all* references to the entity must assume the same type (except that a complex value in one program unit may be referenced as two *real* values in another (see Chapter 18)). Since using different names can cause confusion, it is strongly recommended that the same names be used for the same entities in different program units.

The *size* of a common block is the sum of the sizes of all the entities declared to be in that block. Common blocks with the same name, except for blank common, must be the same size.

Example 13.16   The statements

COMMON/STOCK/PART(20),SIZE(20),COST(20)
COMMON/STOCK/PARTS(20,2),PRICE(20)
COMMON/STOCK/CONTST(20,3)

appearing in different program units are all valid (assuming all are of the same type) since STOCK is the same size in each.

However, the statement

COMMON/STOCK/PART(30),SIZE(20),COST(20)

appearing in a fourth program unit gives STOCK a different size, thus causing an inconsistency between the declarations of STOCK.

Note that while the names might be different, the entities are the same and so there is an association between the different names used within a common block. Thus the third entity is referred to as PART(3) in the first declaration, PARTS(3,1) in the second, and CONTST(3,1) in the third. When using this facility, it is important to remember that elements in an array are held in 'column' order.

The use of EQUIVALENCE in a common block may affect the size of the common block (see Chapter 23).

Differences between named common and blank common
The use made of common will vary depending on the application being programmed. However, in general, a named common block will probably contain entities which are logically related in some way, with blank common being used for other entities.

Apart from the name and the size rule mentioned above there are a few differences between named common and blank common.

(a)   The entities of a named common block declared in a subprogram will become undefined (that is their values are not saved for the next reference to that common block) on exit from the subprogram unless another program unit currently referencing this subprogram directly or indirectly has also specified this common block, or the common block name appears in a SAVE statement. Since the main program references all subprograms directly or indirectly, the entities in a named common block declared in the main program will never become undefined. Entities in blank common never become undefined.

(b) The entities in a named common block may be initialized using a DATA statement in a BLOCK DATA subprogram. The entities in blank common cannot be so initialized (see below and Chapter 11).

Example 13.17   Consider the following skeleton program

```
            PROGRAM EX1317
            COMMON/INFO/. . . .

            :

            CALL SUB1

            :

            CALL SUB4

            :

            END
            SUBROUTINE SUB1
            COMMON / / . . . ./LOG/ . . . .

            :

            CALL SUB2

            :

            END
            SUBROUTINE SUB2
            COMMON / / . . . ./INFO/ . . .

            :

            CALL SUB3

            :

            END
            SUBROUTINE SUB3
            COMMON /LOG/ . . . .

            :

            END
```

        SUBROUTINE SUB4
        COMMON /LOG/ ... / /...

        :
        :

        END

Assuming that all the common blocks used and all the subroutine references executed are shown, the definition status of the entities in the common blocks is as follows.

| Common block | On exit from subroutine | | | |
	SUB1	SUB2	SUB3	SUB4
INFO	Defined	Defined	Defined	Defined
LOG	Undefined	Defined	Defined	Undefined
Blank	Defined	Defined	Defined	Defined

Note that:

(a)   Entities in blank common are always defined even on exit from SUB1 and SUB4 although blank common is not specified in the main program.

(b)   Entities in the named common block INFO are always defined *because* it is specified in the main program.

(c)   Entities in the named common block LOG remain defined on exit from SUB3 because SUB3 is referenced indirectly by SUB1 which has also specified LOG. However, entities in LOG become undefined on exit from SUB1. Therefore on entering SUB4 the entities in LOG are undefined.

The entities in a named common block can be saved by including the common block name in a SAVE statement (Chapter 12) in each of the subprograms specifying the common block. The names of individual entities in a common block are not permitted in a SAVE statement.

Example 13.18   In Example 13.17, the entities in the common block LOG can be saved by including the statement

                    SAVE /LOG/

in subprograms SUB1, SUB3, and SUB4. The entities therefore remain defined on exit from SUB1 and SUB4.
Note that:

(a)   the name appears between two slashes;

(b)   the statement must appear in each subprogram specifying LOG.

The block data subprogram

A block data subprogram is used solely for the initialization of entities in *named* common blocks using the DATA statement. Thus there are no executable statements in a block data subprogram. It is a program unit and has a BLOCK DATA statement as its first statement.

The form of a BLOCK DATA statement is

BLOCK DATA name

where name is the name of the block data subprogram. The name is global and so should not be used for any other purpose in the program. The name is optional but there may be only one unnamed block data subprogram in a program.

Other statements permitted in a block data subprogram are DATA, PARAMETER, DIMENSION, COMMON, SAVE, END, and type statements. (IMPLICIT and EQUIVALENCE statements (Chapter 23) are also permitted, as are comments.)

It is not necessary to initialize all the entities in a named common block but of course all entities must be declared in the COMMON statement. Further, no individual named common block may be specified in more than one block data subprogram in the same program.

Example 13.19 The following block data subprogram initializes some entities in a common block ACOUNT

```
BLOCK DATA
COMMON/ACOUNT/NUMBER,CREDIT,DEBT,MAXDET
INTEGER SIZE
PARAMETER (SIZE=1000)
INTEGER NUMBER(0:SIZE)
REAL MAXDET(0:SIZE),CREDIT(0:SIZE),DEBT(0:SIZE)
DATA (NUMBER(I),I=0,SIZE)/ SIZE*-1,-1/,
+      (MAXDET(I),I=0,SIZE)/ SIZE*0.0,0.0/
END
```

Note that:
    (a)   the common block is fully specified;
    (b)   not all entities are initialized;
    (c)   the subprogram has no name.

Arguments *versus* common
Procedures assist the programmer to *structure* his program, thus helping it to reflect his algorithm as closely as possible. However, the communication of all the information needed by a procedure can be a frustrating and error-prone exercise, especially if some information is not required by the procedure but is 'passed through' to a second procedure referenced by the first.

It is therefore tempting to use common storage as the primary means of communication between program units. After all, it is global and so all data that may be needed by a subprogram can be placed there and the names used in different program units can be different, giving the flexibility available to arguments. However, experience has shown that common storage is far from ideal (see Gill *et al.*, 1977). For example:

(1) Good programming practice demands that a program be easily understood in

order to simplify both development and maintenance. While much of this under-standing may be achieved through the written documentation and comments within the program, the code itself should be as simple as possible. The understanding of a particular subprogram requires knowledge of all entities used within the subprogram, namely those declared locally and those declared externally and passed to the subprogram. Clarity is enhanced if the external entities are all contained in the argument list. It is seldom practicable to specify a common block to contain only those entities required by this subprogram since the requirements of different subprograms often overlap. Thus by using common storage, there may be entities available in a subprogram but not used.

(2) By using the argument list the subprogram is independent of the environment into which it is placed. This is particularly useful where the subprogram is part of a library and so not necessarily written by the user. If common storage is used, the user is obliged to provide the appropriate common blocks, in itself a source of incon-venience and errors.

(3) Information passed through the argument list is strictly controlled and un-expected side-effects are less likely than when using common storage. A common block in a subprogram may be used quite freely and erroneous variable names which coincide with a variable in the common block, or the use of variable in the common block as a local variable, can cause obscure errors.

(4) Adjustable and assumed size arrays may only be used in a dummy argument list and are not permitted in a common block. Many problems make use of arrays whose characteristics are dependent on a given set of data. While FORTRAN 77 is not as flexible a language as many in its ability to cope with this aspect, it seems sensible to restrict any coding changes to a few statements in, say, the main program (a PARAMETER statement preferably) than to have to change statements in a number of different program units.

(5) When using a program (or subprogram) on a computer other than that on which it was developed the storage capacity may be different, thus necessitating changes in the program, particularly in arrays. The more flexibility that is available the more straightforward such changes will be. The use of common storage provides little, if any, flexibility in this area.

(6) Procedure names can be communicated only through an argument list.

For these reasons of programming practice, flexibility, and portability, it is strongly recommended that the argument list is used in preference to common storage as a means of communication between program units.

Example 13.20   Information on an item consists of the item identity (a positive integer) and seven (integer) values. The information for a number of items is held in a table and when the information on an item changes the appropriate entry in the table must be updated. Given that there are never more than 1000 items, write a FORTRAN 77 program to effect changes in the table. A change consists of the identity of the item to be changed and the seven new values. The table and the list of changes are each terminated by a negative item identity and seven zeros.

Algorithm:

> read the table
> **loop while** there are more changes to be made **do**
>   { read change data
>   update the appropriate table entry }

Algorithm for the update module:

> search the table for the given item
> **if** found **then** update the entry
>   **else** print an error and stop

Two versions of the program are given. The first uses common blocks to pass information between program units and the second uses the argument list only. First program:

```
      PROGRAM UPDTCM
******THIS PROGRAM UPDATES ENTRIES IN A TABLE-USING COMMON
      COMMON TABLE(8,1000),M /ALTER/IDENT,CHANGE(7)
      INTEGER TABLE,CHANGE
******INPUT THE TABLE
      M=1
      READ *,(TABLE(J,M),J=1,8)
1     IF(TABLE(1,M).GE.0) THEN
         M=M+1
         READ *,(TABLE(J,M),J=1,8)
         GO TO 1
      END IF
      M=M-1
      PRINT 50
50    FORMAT('1CURRENT INFORMATION'//)
      PRINT '('' '',8I10)',((TABLE(J,I),J=1,8),I=1,M)
      PRINT 51
51    FORMAT(///' LIST OF CHANGES')
******INPUT THE CHANGES
      READ *,IDENT,(CHANGE(J),J=1,7)
2     IF(IDENT.GE.0)THEN
         PRINT'('' '',8I10)',IDENT,(CHANGE(J),J=1,7)
         CALL UPDATE
         READ *,IDENT,(CHANGE(J),J=1,7)
         GO TO 2
      END IF
      PRINT 52
```

```
52      FORMAT('1UPDATED INFORMATION'//)

        PRINT'('' '',8I10)',((TABLE(J,I),J=1,8),I=1,M)

        END


        SUBROUTINE UPDATE

******THIS SUBROUTINE UPDATES THE APPROPRIATE ITEM ENTRY

        COMMON TABLE(8,1000),M /ALTER/IDENT,CHANGE(7)

        INTEGER TABLE,CHANGE

        CALL SEARCH(INDX)

        DO 10 J=1,7

            TABLE(J+1,INDX) = CHANGE(J)

10      CONTINUE

        END


        SUBROUTINE SEARCH(INDX)

******THIS SUBROUTINE SEARCHES FOR AN ITEM WITH IDENTITY IDENT

        COMMON TABLE(8,1000),M /ALTER/IDENT,CHANGE(7)

        INTEGER TABLE,CHANGE

        DO 50 INDX=1,M

            IF(TABLE(1,INDX).EQ.IDENT) THEN

******             THE ENTRY HAS BEEN FOUND AND HAS INDEX=INDX

                RETURN

            END IF

50      CONTINUE

        PRINT 90,IDENT

90      FORMAT(' ***ERROR,ITEM',I10,' NOT FOUND'/' PROGRAM TERMINATED')

        STOP

        END
```

Second program:

```
        PROGRAM UPDTAR

******THIS PROGRAM UPDATES ENTRIES IN A TABLE-USING ARGUMENTS

        INTEGER TABLE(8,1000),CHANGE(7)

******INPUT THE TABLE

        M=1

        READ *,(TABLE(J,M),J=1,8)

1       IF(TABLE(1,M).GE.0)THEN

            M=M+1

            READ *,(TABLE(J,M),J=1,8)

            GO TO 1
```

```
       END IF
       M=M-1
       PRINT 50
50     FORMAT('1CURRENT INFORMATION'//)
       PRINT'('' '',8I10)',((TABLE(J,I),J=1,8),I=1,M)
       PRINT 51
51     FORMAT(///' LIST OF CHANGES')
******INPUT THE CHANGES
       READ *,IDENT,(CHANGE(J),J=1,7)
2      IF(IDENT.GE.0)THEN
           PRINT'('' '',8I10)',IDENT,(CHANGE(J),J=1,7)
           CALL UPDATE(TABLE,8,M,IDENT,CHANGE)
           READ *,IDENT,(CHANGE(J),J=1,7)
           GO TO 2
       END IF
       PRINT 52
52     FORMAT('1UPDATED INFORMATION'//)
       PRINT'('' '',8I10)',((TABLE(J,I),J=1,8),I=1,M)
       END



       SUBROUTINE UPDATE(X,N,M,KEY,T)
******THIS SUBROUTINE UPDATES THE APPROPRIATE ITEM ENTRY
       INTEGER X(N,M),T(N-1)
       CALL SEARCH(X,N,M,KEY,INDX)
       DO 10 J=1,N-1
           X(J+1,INDX)=T(J)
10     CONTINUE
       END



       SUBROUTINE SEARCH(Y,K,L,LOOK,IND)
******THIS SUBROUTINE SEARCHES FOR AN ITEM WITH IDENTITY LOOK
       INTEGER Y(K,L)
       DO 50 IND=1,L
           IF(Y(1,IND).EQ.LOOK)THEN
******             THE ENTRY HAS BEEN FOUND AND HAS INDEX=IND
                   RETURN
           END IF
50     CONTINUE
```

```
      PRINT 90,LOOK

90    FORMAT(' ***ERROR,ITEM',I10,' NOT FOUND'/' PROGRAM TERMINATED')

      STOP

      END
```

Exercise 13

1 Write a function subprogram TAX(INCOME) to calculate the tax due on a given income. (Both tax and income are, of course, real values). The tax rates to be used are as follows:

Income band	Tax rate(per cent)
0.00 – 2499.99	0
2500.00 – 4999.99	10
5000.00 – 7499.99	20
7500.00 – 9999.99	30
10000.00 and over	40

Note that the tax rates are applied to bands of income. Thus the first £2500 is free of tax; on the next £2500 the tax rate is 10%, and so on. For example, the tax on an income of £6000 is £(2500 x 0 + 2500 x 0.1 + 1000 x 0.2) = £450.

2 Using the subroutine SORT in Example 12.2 (page 108) write a function sub-program MEDIAN(X,N) to calculate and return the median of the N real values in the vector X. Assuming that $N \leqslant 1000$, ensure that the order of values in X does not change. The median is defined to be that value which divides the set of values into two equal groups when the values are sorted. That is, if the n values are sorted, the median is x_r where $r = \text{int}(n/2) + 1$ if n is odd and is $(x_r + x_{r+1})/2$ where $r = \text{int}(n/2)$ if n is even.

3 The mode of a set of values is the value which occurs most often in the set. For example, in the set $\{4,1,7,10,4,8,4,7,9\}$ the mode is 4 since it occurs three times. Write a subroutine subprogram MIDDLE(X,N,MEAN,MEDIAN,MODE) to cal-culate the mean, the median, and the mode of the N real values in the vector X. If more than one value occurs an equal number of times, the first should be returned as the mode. (Remember to choose a suitable tolerance when comparing the real values.)

4 The exam marks in maths, physics, and computer science for a number of students, not exceeding 1000, are held in three vectors MATHS, PHYSIC, and CMPSCI respectively and student identification numbers are held in the vector CANDNO. Thus the marks for a student with an identification number held in CANDNO(I) are held in MATHS(I), PHYSIC(I), and CMPSCI(I). Write two subroutine subprograms to sort the student information into descending order of the computer science mark; one using arguments and the other using common storage. Comment on the differences between the two subroutines. (The sub-routine SORT of Example 12.2 (page 108) may be used as a basis for the two subroutines.)

5 The record concerning hours worked by an employee contains an employee number (integer) followed by seven sets of numbers representing the times at

which the employee started and finished work on each day of the week (Sunday to Saturday) respectively. The starting and finishing times are each given in hours and minutes (i.e. two integers each). If the employee did not work on a given day, the times are given as four zeros. The employee's gross wage is calculated on the following basis:

(a)   at a basic rate between 0800 hours and 1600 hours on Mondays to Fridays;

(b)   at one and a half times the basic rate between
   (i) 1600 hours and 2400 hours on Mondays to Fridays,
   (ii) 0800 hours and 1600 hours on Saturdays;

(c)   at twice the basic rate between
   (i) 0000 hours and 0800 hours on Mondays to Saturdays,
   (ii) 1600 hours and 2400 hours on Saturdays,
   (iii) any time on Sundays.

Write the following subprograms:

(a)   a function TIME(HRS,MINS,HRSF,MINF) to calculate the time (a real value) in hours and fractions of an hour between the start time (HRS,MINS) and the finish time (HRSF,MINF), both given in (integer) hours and minutes.

(b)   three functions BASIC(STHRS,STMIN,FINHRS,FINMIN)
                 BASHLF(STHRS,STMIN,FINHRS,FINMIN)
                 DOUBLE(STHRS,STMIN,FINHRS,FINMIN)

to calculate the total time worked at the basic rate, one and a half times the basic rate, and double the basic rate respectively. The arguments STHRS, STMIN,FINHRS, and FINMIN are each seven-element vectors containing the start and finish times in hours and minutes respectively for each day of the week (Sunday to Saturday).

Given that the employee records have the format (I10,2X,28I2) and are preceded by a record containing the basic rate and the number of employee records to be read in the format (F10.0,I6), write a FORTRAN 77 program using the above subprograms to read the employee records from the designated input unit and to print the gross wage for each employee on the designated output unit.

14 Further input and output

If the input editor has been designed to reject all bad input, an ingenious idiot will discover a method to get bad data past it. (*Troutman's Fifth Programming Postulate*)

Chapter 7 was an introduction to input and output in FORTRAN 77 and in that chapter the basic concepts and the simplest forms of input/output for transferring data were introduced. Building on that foundation, the power and flexibility of the input/output facilities are considered in this chapter. First further aspects of data transfer input/output statements are explored, followed by a discussion of some auxiliary input/output statements.

The facilities for handling data on backing store devices such as magnetic tapes and discs will be discussed in Chapter 19.

Further format

The format of data in a file may be either fixed and specified in an appropriate format specification or free and identified as list-directed. Further consideration is given here to fixed formats and, at the end of the chapter, list-directed formatting is discussed.

A data transfer statement identifies the format specification which may be given as the value of a character constant. Alternatively, the format specification may be given in a FORMAT statement which is identified by means of a statement label. The FORMAT statement must be in the same program unit as the data transfer statement.

Example 14.1   The statement

READ (7,50) A,B,C

means that three values are to be read from the file connected to unit number 7, using the format specified in the statement labelled 50, and assigned to variables A, B, and C respectively. The statement labelled 50 must be a FORMAT statement in the same program unit as the READ statement.

The FORMAT statement

A format specification may be declared in a FORMAT statement, which has the form

FORMAT formspec

where formspec is a *format specification* (see below and Chapter 7). A FORMAT statement is a *non-executable* statement and, since it is meaningful only when used by a data transfer statement, it must be *labelled*.

Example 14.2   The following are valid FORMAT statements:

(a) 50   FORMAT(3F10.0)
(b) 10   FORMAT(I4,I5,I11)
(c) 129   FORMAT(2I4/F6.0,2I10/I5,F9.0)
(d) 4   FORMAT('bINDEX=',I3//'bTEMPERATUREbIS',F8.2/'b',2F10.4)
(e) 25   FORMAT('b',2I6,I8)

Example 14.3   The formats in Example 14.2 may be used by data transfer statements as follows:

(a)   READ(7,50) A,B,C
    50   FORMAT(3F10.0)
(b)   READ 10, I,J,K
    10   FORMAT(I4,I5,I11)
(c)   READ(*,129) I,KAPPA,VAL,N,K1,K2,TOL
    129   FORMAT(2I4/F6.0,2I10/I5,F9.0)
(d)   PRINT 4, INDX,TEMP,X,Y
    4   FORMAT('bINDEX=',I3//'bTEMPERATUREbIS',F8.2/'b',2F10.4)
(e)   WRITE(92,25) I,J KAPPA
    25   FORMAT('b',2I6,I8)

Note that:
　(i) in each data transfer statement, where the format identifier has previously been a character constant, it is now the statement label of the FORMAT statement;
　(ii) since the format specification itself is not expressed as a character constant, character information to be output is contained within a single set of apostrophes (e.g. compare (d) above with Example 7.16, page 50).

Format identifiers
A format identifier may be one of the following:

(a)　the statement label of a FORMAT statement in the same program unit;
(b)　a character expression (including a character constant);
(c)　a character array name;
(d)　an integer variable name that has been assigned the statement label of a FORMAT statement in the same program unit.

The forms other than (a) and a character constant will not be considered further in this book.

Integer editing
There are two edit descriptors which may be used with integer values, namely

$$Iw \qquad Iw.m$$

On input, the effect of both descriptors is the same and is described in detail in Chapter 7. That is, an integer value is read from the next w character positions (i.e. the field of width w).

On output, each descriptor produces a slightly different form for the integer. The use of Iw was covered in Chapter 7. The descriptor I$w.m$ indicates that within the field of width w the integer shall consist of at least m digits. If necessary leading zeros will be included. Of course, m must not be greater than w.

Example 14.4   The following is a list of values and edit descriptors together with the resultant output:

	Value	Edit descriptor	Output
(a)	21	I5	bbb21
(b)	21	I5.2	bbb21
(c)	21	I5.3	bb021
(d)	−548	I5.1	b−548
(e)	−548	I5.4	−0548
(f)	0	I4	bbb0
(g)	0	I4.0	bbbb

Note that:
(i) if m is not greater than the number of digits in the integer the m facility has no effect (cases (b) and (d));
(ii) if $m = 0$ and the value is zero, the output field consists of blank characters only (case(g)) (regardless of the sign control in effect − see 'Sign editing' below).

Real editing
There are six edit descriptors which may be used with real values, namely

$$\text{F}w.d \quad \text{E}w.d \quad \text{E}w.d\text{E}e \quad \text{D}w.d \quad \text{G}w.d \quad \text{G}w.d\text{E}e$$

where w is the width of the field containing the real number, the fractional part of which consists of d digits and the exponent part of which consists of e digits.

On input, the effect of all six descriptors is the same. That is, a real value is read from the next w character positions. The basic form of the real value being read consists of a string of digits optionally containing a decimal point. If the decimal point is included the d-specification has no effect. If the decimal point is omitted the least significant d digits of the string are taken as the fractional part of the value.

Example 14.5   The following is a list of character strings (representing real values in a record) and real edit descriptors together with their interpretation.

	Character string	Edit descriptor	Interpretation
(a) (b)	bbbbbbb7.5	F10.3 E10.3	7.5
(c) (d)	bbbbb12345	F10.3 E10.3	12.345
(e)	bbbbbbbbb1	F10.5	0.00001

Note that:

(i) in cases (a) and (b) the decimal point in the field overrides the d-specification in the descriptor;

(ii) in cases (c) and (d) the least significant d digits in the string are taken as the fractional part and so the effect is to insert a decimal point;

(iii) in case (e) leading zeros are assumed.

This basic form of a real value may be followed by an exponent of one of the forms:

(a)   a signed integer constant;

(b)   the character E (or D) followed by an optionally signed integer constant.

Example 14.6   The following is a list of character strings (representing real values in a record) and real edit descriptors together with their interpretation.

Character string	Edit descriptor	Interpretation
bbb−1.0E−6	F10.0 E10.3 E10.2E2	-10^{-6}
bb12.5−3	F8.2	0.0125
b12.5E−3	E8.0	0.0125
b12.5D−3	E8.1	0.0125
bbb4+5	F6.3	$0.004 \times 10^{5} = 400.0$

Note that:

(a)   the exponent form containing E is interpreted in the same way as that containing D;

(b)   the last case is confusing owing to the fact that there is no decimal point in the input field.

The wide range of forms of real values acceptable as input can in practice be confusing and hence a source of possible errors. Therefore, it is *strongly recommended* that real values in an input record take one of the forms of a real constant containing a decimal point (see Chapter 4).

On output, each of the six descriptors can be used to produce the real value in a different form. The use of F$w.d$ for output was covered in Chapter 7.

When using E$w.d$ or E$w.dEe$, the value of the next item in the output list is written in the form

$$s0. x_1 x_2 \ldots x_d \exp$$

where

(a) s is the sign (a plus sign being *optional* for positive values);

(b)   the leading zero is optional;

(c) $x_1 x_2 \ldots x_d$ are the d most significant digits of the value after rounding,

(d)   exp is a decimal exponent of one of the forms given in the following table:

Edit descriptor	Absolute value of exponent	Output form for exponent
Ew.d	$\begin{cases} \mid \exp \mid \leqslant 99 \\ 99 < \mid \exp \mid \leqslant 999 \end{cases}$	$E \pm y_1 y_2$ or $\pm 0 y_1 y_2$ $\pm y_1 y_2 y_3$
Ew.dEe	$\mid \exp \mid \leqslant 10^e - 1$	$E \pm y_1 y_2 \ldots y_e$

where

(i)   the exponent sign is *not* optional;
(ii) $y_1, y_2, y_3 \ldots y_e$ are digits of the exponent;
(iii) Ew.d must not be used if $\mid \exp \mid > 999$;
(iv) e is the number of digits to be printed in the exponent part.

Example 14.7   The following is a list of values and edit descriptors together with the resultant output:

Value	Edit descriptor	Output
2.5	$\begin{cases} F6.2 \\ E10.2 \\ E10.2E1 \end{cases}$	bb2.50 bb0.25E+01 bbb0.25E+1
−3.14159	$\begin{cases} F8.3 \\ E11.4 \\ E11.3E3 \end{cases}$	bb−3.142 −0.3142E+01 −0.314E+001
0.0005479	$\begin{cases} F10.4 \\ E10.3 \end{cases}$	bbbb0.0005 b0.548E−03
-12.6×10^{140}	$\begin{cases} F11.3 \\ E11.3 \\ E11.3E3 \end{cases}$	********** b−0.126+142 −0.126E+142

Note that:

(a)   using Ew.d, the field width w must be large enough to include the digits of the number, the exponent, the decimal point and its preceding zero, and an optional sign. Therefore, in general, $w \geqslant d + 7$;

(b)   similarly, using Ew.dEe, in general $w \geqslant d + e + 5$.

The effect of using Dw.d on output is identical to the use of Ew.d except that, in the exponent, the character E may be replaced by the character D.

Real values edited by Gw.d or Gw.dEe provide either F-editing or E-editing for output depending on the magnitude of the value concerned. G-editing will not be considered further in this book.

Summary of Numeric Editing Facilities

Type	Descriptors	Effect Input	Effect Output
Integer	Iw	Read integer from field	Write integer in field
	I$w.m$	As Iw	As Iw but value must have at least m characters; if $m = 0$ and value $= 0$ field is blank
Real	F$w.d$	Read real from field; if field contains a decimal point d is ignored	Edit value to have d digits after the decimal point (rounded) $w \geqslant d + 3$
	E$w.d$ D$w.d$	As F$w.d$	Edit value in the form $s0.x_1 x_2 \ldots x_d E \pm y_1 y_2$ $w \geqslant d + 7$
	E$w.dEe$	As F$w.d$	Edit value in the form $s0.x_1 x_2 \ldots x_d E \pm y_1 y_2 \ldots y_e$ $w \geqslant d + e + 5$
	G$w.d$ G$w.dEe$	As F$w.d$	Either F-editing or E-editing depending on the magnitude of the value being output

Note that:

(a) all fields have a width w;

(b) on output, if the edited value cannot fit into w characters the field is filled with asterisks.

Other edit descriptors

Repeatable edit descriptors are used to edit values to and from a file. Non-repeatable edit descriptors are used for all other editing functions such as spacing and skipping data. Such other editing functions considered in Chapter 7 were

> *siash editing* — for indicating the end of a record on both input and output
> *apostrophe editing* — for writing character information

In addition to these functions, FORTRAN 77 offers the following facilities:

(a) *positional editing* (the X,T,TL, and TR edit descriptors) is used to specify the position at which the next character will be transmitted to or from the record (see below);

(b) *blank editing* (the BN and BZ edit descriptors) is used to specify the interpretation of blanks in numeric input fields (see below);

(c) *sign editing* (the S, SP, and SS edit descriptors) is used to control the optional plus sign in numeric output fields (see below);

(d) *colon editing* (the : edit descriptor) is used to terminate format control if there are no more items in the input/output list (the colon edit descriptor has no effect if there *are* more items in the list);

(e)   *scaling* (the P edit descriptor) is used to specify a scale factor for reading and writing real and double precision values (this facility is not considered further in this book);

(f)   *Hollerith editing* (the H descriptor) is an alternative to apostrophe editing to output character strings. (This was the traditional FORTRAN method of writing characters but has been superseded by apostrophe editing. It remains part of FORTRAN 77 for reasons of compatibility.)

Positional editing

The X, T, TL, and TR edit descriptors specify the position at which the next character will be transmitted to or from the record. On input this allows portions of a record to be skipped or read again. On output portions of a record may be skipped or previous characters replaced. When skipping a portion of an output record, a character position which has not been filled will be made blank.

The X edit descriptor has the form

$$nX$$

where

(a) n is a non-zero unsigned integer constant;
(b)   X indicates X editing.

The effect of X editing is to move n character positions forward in the record, that is to skip n characters.

The T edit descriptors have the form

$$Tn \quad TLn \quad TRn$$

where

(a) n is a non-zero unsigned integer constant;
(b)   T, TL, and TR indicate the type of editing described below.

The effect of Tn is to move to character position n in the record. That is, transmission of the next character takes place to or from the nth character position. Note that this could be an effective move backwards from the current position.

The effect of TLn is to move n character positions *backwards* in the record (to the Left). The effect of TRn is to move n character positions *forwards* in the record (to the Right) (and is identical to Xn).

Example 14.8   In a file connected to the designated input unit is the record

bbb1.5bb−12.62bb348.75bb1.0E−6

Consider the effect of reading it using the following input statements

(a)   READ(*,100) A,B,C,D
       100   FORMAT (F6.0, 3F8.0)

The effect of these statements is to assign values as follows:

A = 1.5,   B = − 12.62,   C = 348.75,   D = 10^{-6}

(b)   READ 50, X,I,J,K,Y,Z,R,S
       50   FORMAT (F6.0,TL6,I4,1X,I1,8X,I5,F3.0,T10,F5.0,T17,F6.0,
             +   TR2,F6.0)

The effect of these statements is to assign values as follows:

$$X = 1.5, I = 1, J = 5, K = 348, Y = 0.75, Z = 12.62, R = 348.75, S = 10^{-6}$$

The detailed operation of the statements is as follows

(1) Read a value using F6.0 and assign it to X (X = 1.5). Current position is character 7.

(2) TL6 — move 6 character positions backwards in the record. Current position is 1.

(3) Assign a value to I using I4 (I = 1). Current position is 5.

(4) 1X — skip 1 character (skip the decimal point). Current position is 6.

(5) Assign a value to J using I1 (J = 5). Current position is 7.

(6) 8X — skip 8 characters. Current position is 15.

(7) Assign a value to K using I5 (K = 348). Current position is 20.

(8) Assign a value to Y using F3.0 (Y = 0.75). Current position is 23.

(9) T10 — move to character position 10, i.e. an effective backward move. Current position is 10.

(10) Assign a value to Z using F5.0 (Z = 12.62). Note that the minus sign is character 9 and so is not part of this field. Current position is 15.

(11) T17 — move to character position 17, i.e. an effective forward move. Current position is 17.

(12) Assign a value to R using F6.0 (R = 348.75). Current position is 23.

(13) TR2 — move forward 2 characters. Current position is 25.

(14) Assign a value to S using F6.0 (S = 10^{-6}). Current position is 31.

(15) Read statement terminates.

Pictorially, the editing process appears as shown in the diagram.

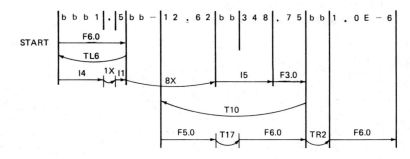

Example 14.9   A program is required to calculate and print an amortization table, each line of which consists of the current balance (LOAN), the next month's interest (INTRST), the monthly repayment (REPAY), and the net balance (BALNCE) at the end of the month. If LOAN = 2000, the annual interest (RATE) = 12, and REPAY = 350, consider the effect of the following statements (all variables are real):

```
         INTRST = LOAN*RATE/1200
         BALNCE = LOAN+INTRST−REPAY
         PRINT 15, LOAN, INTRST, REPAY, BALNCE
15       FORMAT (1X,F9.2,8X,F7.2,8X,F7.2,6X,F9.2)
```

The following record would be printed on the designated output unit:

$$\underbrace{\text{bb2000.00bbbbbbbbb20.00bbbbbbbbb350.00bbbbbbbb1670.00}}$$

    F9.2   8X   F7.2   8X   F7.2   6X   F9.2

Note that:

(a) The first character position in the record is skipped (1X). This is replaced by a blank and, since the record is printed, this character is used to indicate the vertical spacing (see Chapter 7). Thus the record is printed on a new line.

(b) Other FORMAT statements which would have produced the same effect are

  (i) FORMAT (1X, F9.2, TR8, F7.2, TR8, F7.2, TR6, F9.2)

  (ii) FORMAT (1X, F9.2, T19, F7.2, T34, F7.2, T47, F9.2)

Blank editing

The BN and BZ edit descriptors specify the interpretation of blanks *other* than leading blanks in numeric input fields. It should be noted that *leading* blanks are never significant in numeric input fields and that blank editing has no effect on output fields.

The BN edit descriptor has the form

BN

and when it appears in a format specification all blank characters in subsequent numeric input fields are ignored (i.e. Null).

The BZ edit descriptor has the form

BZ

and when it appears in a format specification, all (non-leading) blank characters in subsequent numeric input fields are interpreted as Zeros.

BN and BZ are only operative during the execution of the input statement referring to the format specification containing them. At the beginning of each formatted input statement the interpretation of blanks depends on the value of the blank specifier in the OPEN statement for the unit being used (see below). If this blank specifier is omitted the default interpretation is BN, i.e. blanks are ignored.

Example 14.10   In a file connected to unit 10 is the record:

bbb7b—324bbbbbbb1024

Assuming that the blank specification is null, consider the effect of reading it using the following input statements:

(a) READ(10,'(I4,I5,I11)') I, J, K

    Values are assigned as follows: I=7, J=−324, K=1024. Note that the leading blanks are ignored and there are no other blanks.

(b)   READ(10,'(I5,I7,I8)') I, J, K
Values are assigned as follows: I=7, J=−324, K=1024. Note that all blanks are ignored.

(c)   READ(10,'(BZ,I5,I7,I8)') I, J, K
Values are assigned as follows: I=70, J=−324000, K=1024.

Note that in case (c):

(i) non-leading blanks are interpreted as zeros;

(ii) in the *next* input statement referring to unit 10, blank interpretation reverts to BN until a BZ is met.

Sign editing

The S, SP, and SS edit descriptors control the use of the optional plus sign in numeric output fields. Sign editing has no effect on input fields.

As with BN and BZ, S, SP, and SS are operative only during the execution of the output statement referring to the format specification containing them. Thus at the beginning of each formatted output statement, for all non-negative values, the FORTRAN 77 implementation has the option of writing a plus sign or a blank immediately before the value. (Throughout this book, it is assumed that the option chosen is a blank.)

The SP edit descriptor which has the format

SP

specifies that a Plus sign *must* be written,

The SS edit descriptor which has the format

SS

specifies that a plus sign must *not* be written, i.e. a blank (or Space) is written.

The S edit descriptor which has the format

S

restores the option to the FORTRAN 77 implementation.

It should be noted that, as the production of a plus sign is dependent on the particular implementation, this has an effect on portability. If this aspect is an important feature of the output design, sign editing should be used.

Example 14.11   In Example 14.9 it was assumed that the implementation replaced a plus sign with a blank. Consider the effect of the following statements where LOAN = 2000.00, INTRST = 20.00, REPAY = 350.00, and BALNCE = 1670.00 (all variables are real).

(a)   PRINT 150, LOAN, INTRST, REPAY, BALNCE
    150   FORMAT (1X, SP, F9.2, 8X, F7.2, 8X, F7.2, 6X, F9.2)
             Output produced will be
             b+2000.00bbbbbbbbb+20.00bbbbbbbb+350.00bbbbbbb+1670.00

(b)   PRINT 160, LOAN, INTRST, REPAY, BALNCE
160   FORMAT (1X, F9.2, 8X, SP, F7.2, 8X, SS, F7.2, 6X, S, F9.2)

Output produced will be

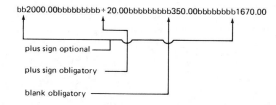

Summary of non-repeatable edit descriptors

		Effect	
Editing	*Descriptor*	*Input*	*Output*
Slash	/	Terminate record	Skip to end of record
Apostrophe	$'h_1h_2\ldots'$	–	**Output character string** $h_1h_2\ldots$
Positional	nX,TRn TLn Tn	Move n character positions forward in the record Move n character positions backward in the record Move to character position n in the record	
Blank	 BN BZ	Non-leading blanks in numeric **fields:** Ignore Interpret as zeros	– – –
Sign	 SP SS S	– – –	Plus sign for positive **values:** Obligatory Replace by blank Optional
Colon	:	Terminate statement if there are no more items in the input/output list	
Scaling	kP	k is the scale factor (not covered in this book)	
Hollerith	nH$h_1h_2\ldots h_n$	–	Output character string $h_1h_2\ldots h_n$

Note that:

(a) n is a non-zero unsigned integer constant;
(b) k is an optionally signed integer constant.

Format specifications

In Chapter 7, it was stated that the simplest form of a format specification is

(edlist)

where edlist is a list of edit descriptors. The full form of a format specification is

(flist)

where flist may be omitted or be a list of one or more of the following items separated by commas:

(a)   a repeatable edit descriptor with an optional repeat specification;
(b)   a non-repeatable edit descriptor;
(c)   an optional repeat specification followed by a format specification with a non-empty list, flist.

If flist is omitted a record is skipped on input and an empty record is written on output (see 'Format Control' below).

The commas separating items in flist may be omitted in the following cases:

(i)   before or after a slash edit descriptor (see Chapter 7);
(ii) before or after a colon edit descriptor;
(iii) between a P edit descriptor (not covered in this book) and an immediately following F, E, D, or G edit descriptor.

Example 14.12   The following are valid format specifications:
(a)   (I4,I5,I11)
(b)   (//I10,3X,F4.2/T50,'INCHES',T30,'FEET')
(c)   (10F10.0/15I5)
(d)   (I4,BZ,(F10.0,4F8.0))
(e)   (1X,SP,I8,F9.2/5(I4,SS,4(E15.3,I6),'PER CENT'))
(f)   (   )

Example 14.13   The following are invalid format specifications:
(a)   (I4, 3(   )) – an empty flist in an inner format specification;
(b)   (10(5F10.0,5I5) – closing parenthesis missing.

Format control
As explained in Chapter 7, for each item in the input/output list of a data transfer statement there must be a corresponding repeatable edit descriptor in the format specification.

If during the execution of a data transfer statement a repeatable edit descriptor is encountered, but there is no further item in the input/output list, the statement terminates.

If, however, there is another item in the input/output list but there is no further repeatable edit descriptor, *a new record is started* and

either control reverts to the beginning of the inner format specification terminated by the last preceding right parenthesis (if a repeat specification exists for that inner format specification, it is reused);

or if there is no such preceding right parenthesis, control reverts to the beginning of the format specification.

The second part of this rule was explained in Chapter 7 ('Format Control'). The first part is best explained by an example.

Example 14.14   The statements

$$READ (7,30) N, (A(I), B(I), I=1,N)$$
$$30 \qquad FORMAT (I4/(2F10.0))$$

will cause to be read from the file connected to unit 7:

(1)   an integer value from a new record using I4 and assigned to N;

(2)   two real values from the next record using 2F10.0, and assigned to A(1) and B(1) respectively;

(3)   two real values from the *next* record, using 2F10.0, and assigned to A(2) and B(2) respectively;

$$\vdots$$

(N+1)   two real values from the next record, using 2F10.0, and assigned to A(N) and B(N) respectively.

Example 14.15   Consider the format specification

$$(2E10.3,2(I2,I3),8X,5(I4,2(F12.4,F12.6)),E16.6)$$

If there are more items in the input/output list after the descriptor E16.6 has been used, control reverts to the inner specification

$$5(I4,2(F12.4,F12.6))$$

Note that:

(a)   this inner specification is repeated 5 times, i.e. the repeat specification is reused;

(b)   if this inner specification is exhausted, the descriptor E16.6 will be used before reverting again to 5(I4,2(F12.4,F12.6)).

If the input/output list is omitted *and* the list, flist, is omitted from the format specification, one record is skipped on input or one blank record is output. It should be noted that flist may be omitted from the format specification *only* if the input/output list is omitted from the data transfer statement.

Example 14.16   The following statement will skip an input record on the file connected to unit 57:

$$READ (57,'(   )')$$

Example 14.17   The following statements will output a blank record to the file connected to unit 33

$$WRITE (33,20)$$
$$20 \qquad FORMAT (   )$$

Records

So far in the book consideration has been given only to *formatted records* which consist of a sequence of characters representing the data. The conversion from characters to internal computer values (and vice versa) is effected by the editing information contained in the format specification. (The specification for list-directed formatting is implicit (see Chapter 7 and below).) The length of a formatted record is measured in characters and is determined by the number of characters placed in the record when it was written.

There are, however, two other kinds of record permissible in FORTRAN 77, namely unformatted records and endfile records.

An *unformatted record* consists of a sequence of values in a machine-readable form only; the precise form being dependent on the computer in use. (Clearly this will be related to the form in which data values are held internally in the computer.) Thus no editing is required when transferring data to and from a record. The length of an unformatted record is measured in computer-dependent units and is determined by the output list used when the record was written, the computer system used, and the external medium on which it is stored. In general, unformatted records are used only on magnetic media such as tapes and discs and, as such, further discussion is left until Chapter 19.

An *endfile record* is the last record in a sequential access file and is written by an *ENDFILE statement* (see below). It has no length property. A direct access file must not contain an endfile record.

Files

File properties

A file has certain properties which to a large extent depend on the media on which it is stored. Thus the properties of a punched card file will be different to those of a disc file. In FORTRAN 77 the set of allowable properties is determined by the computer system. These properties are:

(a)   the file name, the forms of which may be restricted (the file need not be named);

(b)   the access method — either sequential or direct;

(c)   the record type — either formatted or unformatted;

(d)   the record length which may be restricted.

This topic has repercussions for the portability of FORTRAN 77 programs since different installations may choose different sets of allowable properties for the same file. These properties are discussed in more detail in Chapter 19.

External and internal files

A file may be an external file or an internal file.

An *external file* is a file whose contents are contained on an external storage medium (such as a deck of cards) and accessed by an external unit (such as a card reader).

An *internal file* is a file whose contents are stored internally in the main memory of the computer system and therefore must be a character variable, character array, character array element, or character substring. Thus an internal file can be used to transfer and convert information without reference to any external medium. To specify an internal file in a READ or WRITE statement, the name of the character variable, array, array element, or substring is used in place of the external unit identifier.

Since internal files are of limited application, a brief description only is given in this book.

Example 14.18   The statements

CHARACTER*10 INTFIL(100)

⋮

READ(INTFIL,30) A,B,C
30   FORMAT (F10.0)

⋮

would cause three values to be read from the character array INTFIL and assigned to A, B, and C respectively. Of course, sufficient elements of INTFIL must have defined values when the READ statement is obeyed.

In addition to those mentioned above, an internal file has the following *properties*:

(a)   A record of the file is a character variable, array element, or substring. The length of the record is the length of the variable, array element, or substring respectively.

(b)   If the file is a character variable, array element, or substring, it consists of a single record.

(c)   If the file is a character array the records of the file are the elements of the array.

(d)   A record may be read only if the corresponding variable, array element, or substring is defined.

(e)   The variable, array element, or substring that is the record of the file may become defined by writing a record as well as by other conventional means, e.g. an assignment statement or a READ statement.

An internal file has the following *restrictions*:

(a)   an internal file may be used for formatted sequential access only;

(b)   list-directed formatting may not be used;

(c)   an internal file may not be specified in an auxiliary input/output statement (see below). That is, it may be specified in a READ or a WRITE statement only.

Further information on entities of type CHARACTER will be found in Chapter 15.

Input/output statements

In Chapter 7 only the simplest forms of data transfer input/output statements were used, i.e. the READ, WRITE, and PRINT statements with, at most, a simple control information list giving the unit and format to be used. This list may be expanded to include

(a)   the use of key words;
(b)   the ability to deal with end-of-file and error conditions;
(c)   the ability to handle direct access (this aspect is considered in more detail in Chapter 19).

In addition there are auxiliary input/output statements to connect and disconnect a file to and from a unit, to inquire about the properties of the connection, and to manipulate the external storage medium.

Control information list

The control information list is part of READ and WRITE statements as follows:

READ (cilist) input list
WRITE (cilist) output list

where (a) cilist is the control information list, and (b) the input list and the output list are optional (see Chapter 7 and 'Format Control' above).

The control information list provides information on various aspects of the data transfer taking place as listed in the table below. Each item in the list is a specifier consisting of a keyword followed by the character equals (=) followed by a parameter for the specifier.

Specifier	Form	Notes
Unit	UNIT = unit identifier	Obligatory
Format	FMT = format identifier	Omitted for unformatted records
Record	REC = integer expression with a positive value	Used for direct access only (see Chapter 19)
I/O Status	IOSTAT = integer variable or integer array element	Optional
Error	ERR = statement label	Optional
End-of-file	END = statement label	Optional

Note:

(a)   The keyword and the following equals are optional for unit and format. However, if omitted for unit, the unit specifier must be the first item in the list. If omitted for format, the format specifier must be the second item in the list, the first item being the unit specifier without UNIT=.
(b)   The specifiers may appear in any order except as indicated in note (a).
(c)   In the error and end-of-file specifiers the labels must refer to statements in the same program unit as the data transfer statement.

Example 14.19   The following are valid data transfer statements:

(a)   READ(UNIT=7, FMT=50) A,B,C
(b)   WRITE(UNIT=25, FMT=' ("b", 2I6, I8)')I,J,KAPPA
(c)   READ(FMT=129,UNIT=*)I,KAPPA,VAL,N,K1,K2,TOL

(d) WRITE(10,FMT=*) INCOME, TAX, OVRTIM
(e) READ(UNIT=91,FMT=10,REC=2*N−1,IOSTAT=K4,ERR=52,END=99)
  + ((A(I,J),J=1,100),I=1,100)
(f) WRITE(ERR=20,IOSTAT=IFAULT,FMT=51,UNIT=*) X,Y,Z

Error and end-of-file conditions
An error condition is anything recognized by the computer system during the execution of the input/output statement as being a data-transfer error. Thus the set of error conditions may vary from one computer to another.

An end-of-file condition indicates that an attempt is being made to read a record beyond the end of the file. Thus it is meaningful only for READ statements. An end-of-file condition exists if either

(a) an endfile record is encountered while reading a file connected for sequential access (see the OPEN statement below);
(b) an attempt is made to read a record beyond the end of an internal file.

(In addition, an end-of-file condition may exist if an attempt is made to read a record beyond the end of an external file not containing an endfile record if that file has not been created by a FORTRAN 77 program, e.g. a card file.)

The error and end-of-file conditions may be detected by means of the input/output status specifier (IOSTAT) where the variable (or array element) will be defined as follows:

(a) with zero if neither an error condition nor an end-of-file condition occurs during the execution of the statement;
(b) with a positive value if an error condition occurs;
(c) with a negative value if an end-of-file condition occurs, and no error condition occurs.

The actual values used in (b) and (c) depend on the implementation of FORTRAN 77 being used.

If an error occurs during the execution of an input/output statement which does not contain an input/output status specifier or an error specifier, the program will terminate. Similarly, the program will terminate if an end-of-file condition occurs and there is neither an input/output status specifier nor an end-of-file specifier.

Example 14.20 The statement

$$READ(50,FMT='(I4,I5,I11)') I,J,K$$

will read three values from the file connected to unit 50 using the specified format and assign them to I, J, and K respectively. If either an error or an end-of-file condition occurs, the program terminates.

Example 14.21 The statement

$$READ(50,'(I4,I5,I11)',IOSTAT=INFALT) I,J,K$$

will have the same effect as in Example 14.20 if the statement terminates successfully, except that in addition INFALT will be assigned the value zero. However, if an error occurs INFALT will be assigned some positive value, and if an end-of-file condition occurs (without an error) INFALT will be assigned some negative value. In either case the statement will terminate and the program will continue operation with the next executable statement, but the values of I, J, and K will be undefined. After an error the file position is indeterminate.

In general, on detection of an error or an end-of-file condition during execution of a READ statement, the statement terminates and the entities appearing in the input list together with any implied-DO variables become undefined. In addition, after an error the position of the file is indeterminate.

Example 14.22   The statement

$$WRITE(14,92,IOSTAT=IOERR)((X(I,J),J=1,N),I=1,N)$$

will output the values of the elements of the array X to a file connected to unit 14 using the format specified in the statement labelled 92.

If an error occurs, the statement will terminate, IOERR will be assigned some positive value, and the program will continue with the next executable statement. The position of the file will be indeterminate and the values of the implied-DO variables I and J will be undefined. The values of the elements of X are, of course, unchanged.

Note that an end-of-file condition cannot occur during an output statement.

The error specifier
The error specifier enables more direct action to be taken when an input/output error is detected. Thus

    (a)   the input/output statement terminates;
    (b)   the input/output status (if included) is set to some positive value;
    (c)   program execution continues at the statement whose label is given in the error specifier.

Example 14.23   The statement

$$READ(7,20,IOSTAT=K1,ERR=25)(A(I),I=1,N)$$

will cause values to be read from the file connected to unit 7 using the format specified in statement 20 and assigned to the elements of the array A.

If no error or end-of-file condition occurs, K1 will be assigned the value zero and execution will continue with the next executable statement.

If an error occurs, the statement terminates, K1 will be assigned some positive value, and execution will continue with the statement labelled 25. The position of the file is indeterminate and the values of the implied-DO variable I and the elements of the array A are undefined.

If an end-of-file condition occurs (without an error), the statement terminates, K1 will be assigned some negative value, and execution will continue with the next executable statement. Again, the position of the file is indeterminate and the values of I and A are undefined.

Example 14.24   The statement

WRITE(*,FMT=51,ERR=99) PRESS, TEMP, VOL, LEN

will cause values to be printed on the designated output unit according to the format specified in statement 51. If an error occurs, the statement terminates and the program continues with the statement labelled 99.

The end-of-file specifier
The end-of-file specifier enables more direct action to be taken when an end-of-file condition is detected during the execution of a READ statement. Thus

(a)   the statement terminates;
(b)   the input/output status (if included) is set to some negative value;
(c)   program execution continues at the statement whose label is given in the end-of-file specifier.

Note that if an error is also detected it takes precedence and the end-of-file condition is not noted.

Example 14.25   The statement

READ(*,*,END=25)(CAND(I),MATH(I),PHYSIC(I),CHEM(I),I=1,N)

will read a list of values from the designated input unit in free format. If an end-of-file condition occurs the statement terminates and the program continues with the statement labelled 25. The values of I and all the elements of the arrays CAND, MATH, PHYSIC, and CHEM will be undefined.

Auxiliary input/output statements

In addition to the data transfer statements READ, WRITE, and PRINT, FORTRAN 77 provides the six auxiliary input/output statements described below to provide other functions often necessary when handling files of data.

Since a file is a collection of data which is accessed physically by an external unit (e.g. a card reader, a disc unit, etc.) some means is required to indicate which unit will access the file, that is, to which unit the file will be connected. This is done either by

(a) pre-connection through a system specified default (e.g. the designated input and output units) or through operating system control statements or through some other mechanism. The specification of the connection will be predetermined.

or (b) programmed connection using the *OPEN statement* which determines the specification for the connection.

Disconnection is effected by the *CLOSE statement* (note that if a file is connected to a unit, the unit is also connected to that file, that is connection is a property of both the file and the unit).

There are various parameters associated with a file or a unit (e.g. sequential or direct access, formatted or unformatted records, etc.). Using the *INQUIRE statement*, a programmer may determine the values of the parameters which control a given file or unit.

To terminate a sequential access output file, an endfile record should be written using the *ENDFILE statement*.

To provide flexibility in accessing a file, particularly a file stored on a magnetic medium, the *BACKSPACE statement* skips backwards over one record and the *REWIND statement* skips to the beginning of the file. These two statements are considered fully in Chapter 19. (Note that a forward skip over one record may be done using a READ statement without an input list.)

The OPEN statement

The OPEN statement can be used

(a) to connect an existing file to a unit;
(b) to create a new file and connect it to a unit;†
(c) to change certain specifiers of the connection between file and unit.

In executing these functions, certain parameters associated with the file, the unit or this connection of the file to the unit may be defined in the statement.

The OPEN statement has the form:

OPEN (openlist)

where openlist is a list of specifiers as given in the following table.

Specifier	Form	Values permitted in specifier
Unit	UNIT = external unit identifier	A non-negative integer expression (the identifier must not be an asterisk)
I/O status	IOSTAT = integer variable or integer array element	—
Error	ERR = statement label	Label must be in the same program unit as the OPEN statement
File name	FILE = character expression	A valid file name
File status	STATUS = character expression	'OLD', 'NEW', 'SCRATCH' 'UNKNOWN'
Access	ACCESS = character expression	'SEQUENTIAL', 'DIRECT'
Format type	FORM = character expression	'FORMATTED', 'UNFORMATTED'
Record length	RECL = integer expression	>0
Blank	BLANK = character expression	'ZERO', 'NULL'

†The OPEN statement may also be used to create a pre-connected file. Writing to a non-existent file will also create the file.

Note:
- (a) There must be a unit specifier. All other specifiers are optional except that the record length must be specified if the file is being connected for direct access.
- (b) In each character expression the value is that taken after removal of trailing blanks.
- (c) The specifiers may appear in any order except for the unit specifier as indicated below.
- (d) The OPEN statement may appear in any program unit of the program. The consequent connection is valid throughout the whole program and is not limited to that program unit.

The *unit specifier* identifies the external unit being connected. The key word 'UNIT=' is optional, but, if omitted, the unit must be the first item in the list, openlist. Note that neither an internal file nor the designated input/output units may be specified in an auxiliary input/output statement.

The *input/output status specifier* will cause the variable (or array element) to be set to zero if, at the time the OPEN statement is executed, no error condition exists, and to some positive value otherwise.

The *error specifier* allows programmed action to be taken if an error condition exists at the time the OPEN statement is executed. (See also 'The Error Specifier' above.)

The *file name specifier* gives the name of the file being connected to the unit. If this specifier is omitted the file connected to the unit is determined by the computer system, e.g. as directed by a job control statement. Of course, a file need not be named.

The *file status specifier* gives the status 'OLD', 'NEW', 'SCRATCH', or 'UNKNOWN'. If this specifier is omitted, 'UNKNOWN' is assumed. The requirements and effect of each status is as follows:

'OLD' – a file name specifier must be given;
     the file must exist.
'NEW' –a file name specifier must be given;
     the file must not exist;
     the file is created and given the status 'OLD'.
'SCRATCH' – the file must not be named;
     the file will be deleted on execution of a CLOSE statement for this unit or at program termination (this is the method used to provide temporary (scratch) files).
'UNKNOWN' – the status is determined by the computer system, e.g. it may search its directories to see if this file already exists, if it does the status will be 'OLD' but if it does not the status will be 'NEW'.

The *access specifier* indicates the access method to be used for this connection of the file as being either sequential or direct. If this specifier is omitted, sequential access is assumed. It should be noted that the specified access method must be one permitted by the computer system.

The *format type specifier* indicates that this file will be connected for either formatted input/output or unformatted input/output. If this specifier is omitted, formatted input/output is assumed if the file is being connected for sequential access, and unformatted input/output is assumed if the file is being connected for direct access. Note that formatted input/output cannot take place to a file connected for unformatted input/output and vice versa.

The *record length specifier* indicates the length of each record in the file, for this connection. It is only applicable when a file is being connected for direct access, in which case this specifier must appear (see Chapter 19).

The *blank specifier* indicates that the interpretation of blank characters in numeric formatted input fields will be either 'ZERO' or 'NULL'. If this specifier is omitted, the interpretation of 'NULL' is assumed. The effect of each interpretation is as follows:

'ZERO'– all blanks (other than leading blanks) are treated as zeros.
'NULL'–all blanks are ignored, except that an input field containing all blanks has a value of zero.

(See also 'Blank editing' above.)

Example 14.26   The following are valid OPEN statements:

(a)   OPEN(52, FILE='DMDATA',STATUS='OLD')
An existing file, DMDATA, is connected to unit 52 for sequential formatted input/output.

(b)   OPEN(UNIT=37, STATUS='SCRATCH', FORM='UNFORMATTED')
A scratch file is connected to unit 37 for sequential unformatted input/output.

(c)   OPEN(9, FILE='ABFILE', BLANK='ZERO')
ABFILE, a file of unknown status, is connected to unit 9 for sequential formatted input/output where blanks will be interpreted as zeros when reading numeric values. (It is likely, but not certain, that the computer system would use a file named ABFILE if it existed; otherwise a new file would be created.)

(d)   OPEN(104,IOSTAT=K1,ERR=10,FILE='ABDM',BLANK='NULL',
+   ACCESS='DIRECT',RECL=160,FORM='FORMATTED',
+   STATUS='NEW')
A new file, ABDM, is created and connected to unit 104 for direct formatted input/output with records of length 160 characters (see Chapter 19). When reading numeric values blanks will be ignored. If an error condition exists when execuing the OPEN statement, K1 will be assigned some positive value and execution will continue with the statement labelled 10; otherwise K1 is assigned the value zero.

Example 14.27   The following are invalid OPEN statements:

(a)   OPEN(82, FILE='PERSON',STATUS='SCRATCH')
A named file cannot be a scratch file.

(b)   OPEN(98,FILE='WAGES',FORM='FORMATTED',ACCESS='DIRECT')
A file connected for direct access must have its record length specified.

    (c)   OPEN(FORM='UNFORMATTED',25,FILE='CARS',BLANK='ZERO')
        The interpretation of blanks in an unformatted file is meaningless. Also UNIT= is omitted from the unit specifier when it is not the first item in the list.

    (d)   OPEN(FILE='KIDS')
        No unit specifier.

Normally an OPEN statement sets up a connection between a file and a unit both of which are unconnected. However, it is permissible to execute an OPEN statement on a connected file or a connected unit either to connect a different file to the unit or to change the blank specifier value for the current connection. However this is not normally recommended since (a) it is good programming practice to disconnect a unit explicitly before making a new connection, and (b) in a well designed file there will be no need to change the interpretation of blank characters. Note that no other parameter of the connection may be changed in this way.

The CLOSE statement
The CLOSE statement is used to disconnect a file from a unit (and the unit from the file). It has the form:

CLOSE (closelist)

where closelist is a list of specifiers as given in the following table.

Specifier	Form	Notes
Unit	UNIT = external unit identifier	See 'The OPEN statement'
I/O status	IOSTAT = integer variable or integer array element	
Error	ERR = statement label	
File status	STATUS = character expression	The expression may have the value 'KEEP' or 'DELETE'

Note:
    (a)   There must be a unit specifier. The other specifiers are optional.
    (b)   The specifiers may appear in any order except for the unit specifier as indicated in 'The OPEN Statement'.

The *file status specifier* indicates the future status of the file, that is whether or not it has to be kept (or saved). If this specifier is omitted, 'KEEP' is assumed except for scratch files when 'DELETE' is assumed. The requirements and effects of each status value are as follows:

'KEEP'   the file must not be a scratch file;
            the file is not deleted.
'DELETE'   the file is deleted.

Example 14.28 The following are valid CLOSE statements corresponding to the OPEN statements in Example 14.26.

    (a)   CLOSE (52)
          The file is closed and kept.
    (b)   CLOSE (37)
          The file is closed and deleted since it was a scratch file.
    (c)   CLOSE (9, STATUS='KEEP')
    (d)   CLOSE (UNIT=104, STATUS='DELETE')

If a program terminates successfully leaving a file connected to a unit, all such files are closed automatically with the status 'KEEP' except for scratch files which are deleted.

The INQUIRE statement

The INQUIRE statement may be used to investigate properties of a file or of a unit. As it has a somewhat specialized use, for example to determine the permissible file properties on a new installation, only a brief introduction is given.

There are two forms:

    (a)   inquire by file

$$\text{INQUIRE (FILE=filename, inquirelist)}$$

    (b)   inquire by unit

$$\text{INQUIRE (UNIT = extunit, inquirelist)}$$

where
   (i) filename is a character expression yielding the name of a file;
   (ii) extunit is an external unit identifier ('UNIT=' is optional);
   (iii) inquirelist is a list of at most one each of the enquiry specifiers listed below.
Note that
    (a)   the specified file need not exist or be connected to a unit;
    (b)   the specified unit need not exist or be connected to a file.

Specifier	Form	Values assigned to the specifier variable
I/O status Error	IOSTAT = integer* } ERR = statement label }	(as for the OPEN and CLOSE statements)
Existence	EXIST = logical*	if the file (unit) exists **then true** else **false**
Opened	OPENED = logical*	if the file (unit) is connected to a unit (file) **then true** else **false**
Unit number	NUMBER = integer*	if the unit is connected to the file **then the unit number** else **undefined**
Named	NAMED = logical*	if the file has a name **then true** else **false**
Name	NAME = character*	if the file has a name **then the file name** else **undefined**

Specifier	Form	Values assigned to the specifier variable

Access	ACCESS = character*	if there is a connection
		  then either 'SEQUENTIAL' or 'DIRECT'
		  else undefined

Sequential	SEQUENTIAL = character*	if sequential access is permitted on this file
		  then YES
		  else if it is not then 'NO'
		      else 'UNKNOWN'

Direct	DIRECT = character*	if direct access is permitted on this file
		  then 'YES'
		  else if it is not then 'NO'
		      else 'UNKNOWN'

Format	FORM = character*	if there is a connection then either
		  'FORMATTED' or 'UNFORMATTED'
		      else undefined

Formatted	FORMATTED = character*	if formatted records are permitted on this file
		  then 'YES'
		  else if they are not then 'NO'
		      else 'UNKNOWN'

Unformatted	UNFORMATTED = character*	if unformatted records are permitted on this file
		  then 'YES'
		  else if they are not then 'NO'
		      else 'UNKNOWN'

Record length	RECL = integer*	if there is a connection for direct access
		  then the specified record length for the
		  connection
		  else undefined

Next record	NEXTREC = integer*	if there is a connection for direct access
		  then the number of the next record to be
		  transferred
		  else undefined

Blank	BLANK = character*	if there is a connection for formatted I/O
		  then either 'NULL' or 'ZERO'
		  else undefined.

*The specifier variable may be either a variable or array element of the stated type.

The ENDFILE statement

The ENDFILE statement causes an endfile record to be written to the sequential access file connected to the specified unit. It has one of the forms

ENDFILE unit
ENDFILE (eoflist)

where

  (a)   unit is an external unit identifier;

  (b)   eoflist is a list of specifiers as given in the following table.

Specifier	Form
Unit	UNIT = external unit identifier
I/O status	IOSTAT = integer variable or integer array element
Error	ERR = statement label

Note that:

  (a)   there must be a unit specifier (the other specifiers are optional);

(b)   the specifiers may appear in any order except for the unit specifier as indicated in 'The OPEN statement';

(c)   for full details of the specifiers, see 'The OPEN Statement'.

Example 14.29   The following are valid ENDFILE statements

(a)   ENDFILE 10
(b)   ENDFILE (10)
(c)   ENDFILE (UNIT = 52, IOSTAT = IOERR, ERR = 195)
(d)   ENDFILE (64, ERR = 279)

Since an endfile record is the last record in a file, no further data transfer statements may be executed after an ENDFILE statement unless the file has been repositioned by a BACKSPACE or a REWIND statement (Chapter 19).

Example 14.30   Consider a complete program for Example 14.9. It is required to write an amortization table for a loan to the file, TABLE. The columns in the table will comprise the date, the outstanding loan at the start of the month, interest due on that loan, the total due, the total repayment, and the balance at the end of the month. The input data to the program, contained in the file LOAN, will be the date the loan was taken out, the amount of the loan, the annual interest rate, and the desired monthly repayment.

A suitable algorithm would be:

```
read the input data
loop while not end-of-file do
        {write the input data
         calculate the first month's interest
         if the first month's interest ⩾ repayment
                then print a message stating that the repayment is too small
                else
                        {loop while loan > 0 do
                                {increment the date
                                 calculate the total due
                                 if repayment < total due then calculate new balance
                                                           else {set balance to zero
                                                                 set repayment to total due}
                                 calculate total repayment
                                 write a line of the table
                                 calculate next month's interest} }
         read a new set of input data}
```

```
      PROGRAM AMORT

******                AMORTISATION TABLE

*                     ------------- -----

*      A GIVEN SUM OF MONEY IS BORROWED AT A SPECIFIED RATE OF INTEREST WITH
```

```
*       A GIVEN MONTHLY REPAYMENT.  INFORMATION CONCERNING THE INTEREST DUE, THE
******OUTSTANDING BALANCE, ETC. IS TABULATED AT MONTHLY INTERVALS


        REAL LOAN, RATE, REPAY, MRATE, INTRST, TREPAY, TOTDUE, BALNCE
        INTEGER DAY, MONTH, YEAR, IN, OUT
******INPUT AND OUTPUT UNIT NUMBERS ARE GIVEN IN THE PARAMETER STATEMENT
        PARAMETER (IN=7, OUT=2)


10      FORMAT(' DETAILS OF THE LOAN'//
       +        ' DATE ',3I3.2/
       +        ' LOAN ',F9.2/
       +        ' ANNUAL INTEREST RATE ',F6.2,' PER CENT'/
       +        ' REPAYMENT ',F9.2,' PER MONTH'//)
11      FORMAT(' **ERROR - REPAYMENT IS TOO SMALL'/
       +        '               FIRST MONTH''S INTEREST IS ',F7.2)
12      FORMAT(4X,'DATE',8X,'LOAN',3X,'INTEREST',4X,'TOTAL',6X,'REPAID',4X,'BALANCE'/
       +        4X,'----',8X,'----',3X,'--------',4X,'-----',6X,'------',4X,'-------'/)
13      FORMAT(1X,3I3.2,2X,F9.2,2X,F7.2,3(2X,F9.2))


        OPEN(IN,FILE='LOAN',STATUS='OLD')
        OPEN(OUT,FILE='TABLE',STATUS='NEW')
******LOOP WHILE NOT E-O-F DO
1       READ(IN,*,END=99) DAY,MONTH,YEAR,LOAN,RATE,REPAY
            WRITE(OUT,10) DAY,MONTH,YEAR,LOAN,RATE,REPAY
            MRATE=RATE/1200
            INTRST=LOAN*MRATE
            IF(INTRST.GE.REPAY)THEN
                WRITE(OUT,11) INTRST
                                ELSE
                TREPAY=0
                WRITE(OUT,12)
******          LOOP WHILE LOAN.GT.0 DO
2               IF(LOAN.GT.0)THEN
******              INCREMENT DATE
                    IF(MONTH.EQ.12) THEN
                        MONTH=1
                        YEAR=YEAR+1
                                    ELSE
                        MONTH=MONTH+1
```

```
                    END IF

                    TOTDUE = LOAN+INTRST

                    IF(REPAY.LT.TOTDUE)THEN

                            BALNCE  = TOTDUE-REPAY

                                        ELSE

                            BALNCE  = 0

                            REPAY = TOTDUE

                    END IF

                    TREPAY = TREPAY+REPAY

                    WRITE(OUT,13) DAY,MONTH,YEAR,LOAN,INTRST,TOTDUE,TREPAY,BALNCE

                    LOAN = BALNCE

                    INTRST = LOAN * MRATE

                    GO TO 2

******          END OF LOOP WHILE LOAN.GT.0 DO

                    END IF

******          END OF ELSE BLOCK (INTRST.GE.REPAY)

                    END IF

******          READ A NEW SET OF DATA

                    GO TO 1

******END OF LOOP WHILE NOT E-O-F DO

99      CLOSE(IN)

        ENDFILE(OUT)

        CLOSE(OUT)

        END
```

Note that :

(a) the input and output units can be changed by changing the PARA-METER statement;

(b) both the input and output units are opened and closed;

(c) the input uses list-directed formatting;

(d) the use of indentation in the code reflects the structure of the algorithm;

(e) the 'loop while not end-of-file' statement has not been implemented using a block IF statement on this occasion because the end-of-file condition is recognized within the READ statement. Further examples are given in Chapter 19.

Assuming the input file, LOAN, contains the following records:

record 1 : 25 12 73, 1000.0, 12.0, 300.0
record 2 : 15 4 74, 500.0, 12.0, 3.0
record 3 : end-of-file

the output file will contain

DETAILS OF THE LOAN

DATE   25 12 73

LOAN   1000.00

ANNUAL INTEREST RATE   12.00 PER CENT

REPAYMENT   300.00 PER MONTH

DATE	LOAN	INTEREST	TOTAL	REPAID	BALANCE
----	----	--------	-----	------	-------
25 01 74	1000.00	10.00	1010.00	300.00	710.00
25 02 74	710.00	7.10	717.10	600.00	417.10
25 03 74	417.10	4.17	421.27	900.00	121.27
25 04 74	121.27	1.21	122.48	1022.48	0.00

DETAILS OF THE LOAN

DATE   15 04 74

LOAN   500.00

ANNUAL INTEREST RATE   12.00 PER CENT

REPAYMENT   3.00 PER MONTH

**ERROR - REPAYMENT IS TOO SMALL

         FIRST MONTH'S INTEREST IS   5.00

end-of-file.

List-directed formatting

List-directed formatting may be used on a file connected for formatted sequential access and is specified in a data transfer statement by an asterisk as a format identifier.

A list-directed record consists of characters representing a sequence of values and value separators. In addition to a value being a constant, as stated in Chapter 7, it may also be a null value or take one of the forms

$$r*c \qquad r*$$

where

    (a) r is an unsigned non-zero integer constant;

    (b) c is a constant.

These forms represent r successive occurrences of the constant c and r successive null values respectively. This provides a convenient shorthand method of writing values in a file.

A value separator may be a comma, a blank, or a slash. Additional blanks may appear between values.

List-directed input

The valid forms of constants for list-directed input are indicated in the following table:

Type	Form
Integer Real Double precision	As for fixed formatting
Complex	A complex constant (see Chapter 18)
Logical	As for fixed formatting except that the characters slash or comma are not permitted as optional characters (see Chapter 16)
Character	A character constant (see Chapter 15)

Note that:

(a)   blank characters may not appear within a constant except for complex and character constants;

(b)   blanks are never interpreted as zeros;

(c)   if a real or double precision constant *not* containing a decimal point is read, it is assumed to have no fractional digits (i.e. Fw.0).

A null value is specified by no value between successive value separators, no value before the first value separator in a record or the $r*$ form. The null value has no effect on the input list item. That is, if it is defined it retains its previous value and if it is undefined it remains undefined.

A slash used as a value separator causes the input statement to terminate. Any additional items in the input list are unaffected (i.e. null values are assumed).

Example 14.31   Assuming that the variables I, J, X, Y, Z, B, and C are undefined and that A = −1.5 and K = 125, the effect of reading the record

$$10,-14,25.2,-1.0E-6,524,,,24E10/$$

from the file connected to the designated input unit using the statement

$$READ*I,J,X,Y,Z,A,B,C,K$$

is as follows:

I = 10, J=−14, X=25.2, Y=-10^{-6}
Z = 524.0 (no fractional digits are assumed)
A retains the value −1.5 (since the input value is null)
B is undefined (since the input value is null)
C = 24×10^{10} (no fractional digits are assumed)

The READ statement terminates leaving K=125 (a null value is assumed).

List-directed output

The precise form of list-directed output is heavily dependent on the FORTRAN 77 implementation being used. In addition to the points mentioned in Chapter 7, it should be noted that

(a) null values and slashes as value separators are not output;
(b) character constants are not enclosed by apostrophes;
(c) if two or more values are identical, the form $r*c$ may be used.

Since there are so many implementation-dependent factors it is recommended that list-directed output should not normally be used.

Exercise 14

1 (a) What is the output resulting from writing the integer value 1576 using each of the edit descriptors I5,I7.2,I8.5,I3?

   (b) What is the output resulting from writing the real value -0.0162 using each of the edit descriptors F8.4, F6.2, E12.4, E12.3E1, F5.1?

2 In a file connected to the designated input unit is the record

$$bb1234.6bb9.875E3bb-42.57bb83$$

What is the effect of reading this record using the statements

```
        READ (*,15)X,Y,I,Z,J,K,L1,L2,L3,L4,A,K4,M1,M2,M3
   15   FORMAT(F8.0,E9.2,I4,F3.0,BZ,I2,I3,T1,3I2,1X,I2,
   +        BN,TL5,F6.0,T14,I2,TR8,3I2)
```

3 In a file connected to the designated input unit are $(n + 1)$ records the first of which contains the value of n (in a field of width 5) and each of the remaining n records contains a pair of values f_i, x_i (in fields of widths 5 and 12 respectively) where the f_i are integer values and the x_i are real values. Write a FORTRAN 77 program to read the whole file and then print it on the designated output file with the value of n on a separate line and the pairs of values f_i, x_i printed 5 per line. Use one READ statement and one PRINT statement only. Assume $n \leqslant 1000$.

4 In a file connected to unit 24 are the records of telephone calls made by customers. Each record contains the customer identity (an integer in a field of width 10) and three integer values (each in fields of width 5) representing the number of units used in each of the three call periods rated at the peak rate, standard rate and cheap rate respectively. The file is terminated by an endfile record. Write a FORTRAN 77 program to print the file on the designated output unit using suitable headings. Appropriate action should be taken if an error is detected in the file when it is being read.

5 If the file in question 4 has the name PHONE, add appropriate OPEN and CLOSE statements to the program ensuring that the file is saved for future use.

6 Using the file PHONE specified in questions 4 and 5, create a new file to contain the records of those customers who have used more than 25% of their total units at the peak rate.

15 Character handling facilities

Necessity is the mother of strange bedfellows. (Farber's Fourth Law)

Although FORTRAN is primarily intended as a programming language for *numeric, computational* problems, additional character handling facilities were introduced into the language as a result of the 1977 Standard. The purpose of this chapter is to consider these facilities in some detail.

Character constants

Character constants were described in Chapter 4 and the reader is advised to peruse the appropriate section of that chapter before continuing.

Example 15.1 The following table indicates how constants are *written* in FORTRAN 77, and also specifies the *values* and *lengths* of the constants listed:

Representation of constant	Value of constant	Length
'FORTRAN 77'	FORTRAN 77	10
'X∗Y=Y∗X'	X∗Y=Y∗X	7
'ABC'	ABC	3
'A B C'	A B C	5
'C "WISHY-WASHY" BROWN'	C 'WISHY-WASHY' BROWN	21

Character variables, arrays, and type statements

Simple examples of type statements for the specification of *variables* of type CHARACTER have already been given in Chapter 5. For example, the type statement

$$\text{CHARACTER}*6 \quad \text{C1}*4,\text{C2}*8,\text{P},\text{Q},\text{R}*12$$

where C1, C2, P, Q, and R are character variables, indicates that the lengths of these variables are respectively 4, 8, 6, 6, and 12.

More generally, a CHARACTER type statement consists of the keyword CHARACTER followed by

(a)   an *optional* length specification† of the form ∗ *length.*

---

† The Standard uses the term 'length specification' in a slightly different manner.

(b)   an *optional* comma;

(c)   a list of *variable names, symbolic names of constants, function names, array names,* and *array declarators,* each one of which may be followed by an optional length specification of the form * *length.*

Example 15.2   Consider a FORTRAN 77 program unit containing the following specification statements:

        CHARACTER*8 C1,C2*4,A(0:20)*6,B(20,30),C*4,PASSWD
        DIMENSION C(0:5,0:10)
        PARAMETER (PASSWD = 'FRED')

In the program unit:

(a)   C1 is a character variable with length 8, since the length specification *8 is applied to any entity in the list which does not have its own length specification.

(b)   C2 is a character variable with length 4.

(c)   A is the name of a one-dimensional character array, with elements $A_0, A_1, A_2, \ldots, A_{20}$, each one of which is of length 6.

(d)   B is the name of a 20 x 30 character matrix, each element of which is of length 8, since the length specification *8 again applies.

(e)   C, because of the DIMENSION statement, is a character matrix with the indicated dimension bounds, each element of which is of length 4.

(f)   PASSWD is the symbolic name of a constant with value FREDbbbb, the length specification *8 again applying.

Note how the length specification immediately following the keyword CHARACTER is applied to any entity in the subsequent list which does not have its own length specification. If, on the other hand, there is no length specification immediately after the keyword CHARACTER, a length of 1 is applied to any entity in the subsequent list which does not have its own length specification.

Note also that, in the case of an *array*, the length specification applies to each *element* of the array, and not to the whole array.

When a length specification, * *length*, is given, *length* must be one of the following:

(a)   an unsigned, non-zero *integer constant* (as in the examples above);

(b)   an *integer constant expression, enclosed in parentheses* and with a *positive* value;

(c)   an *asterisk* in parenthesis, (*).

A length specification of the form *(*) in a CHARACTER type statement may, however, only be applied to the following entities:

(i)   A *symbolic name of a constant.* In this case the actual length is determined by the length of the *corresponding character constant expression* in the PARAMETER statement.

(ii)   A *dummy argument name.* In this case the length used for the dummy argument is the length of the *associated actual argument*† whenever the subroutine or function subprogram is called into action.

(iii) A *function subprogram name.* In this case the length assumed for the function is that specified in the program unit *referencing* the function (see Example 15.24).

A length specification of the form *(*) may also occur in a CHARACTER FUNCTION statement (see Example 15.24).

Example 15.3   The following specification statements

$$\text{CHARACTER} \quad \text{PVAL}*(*)$$
$$\text{PARAMETER} \quad (\text{PVAL}=\text{'BLACK–CAT'})$$

indicate that PVAL is the name of a symbolic constant with value BLACK–CAT and length 9, the length being determined from the information given in the PARAMETER statement.

Example 15.4   Consider the following FORTRAN 77 program

```
                PROGRAM TCASE
                CHARACTER C (20,30)*8
                    .
                    .
                    .

                CALL SORT(C,20,30)
                    .
                    .
                    .

                END
                SUBROUTINE SORT(A,M,N)
                CHARACTER A(M,N)*(*)
                    .
                    .
                    .

                END
```

When the subroutine SORT is called into action in the main program by the statement

$$\text{CALL SORT(C,20,30)}$$

the actual array C is associated with the dummy array A. As a result, 8 is used as the length of each array element during execution of the subprogram.

Character substrings

When a variable of type CHARACTER or an element of an array of type CHARACTER has a defined value it is convenient to picture that value as being held

†This requires further explanation when the dummy argument is an array name (see page 197).

in a number of consecutive *character storage units*, one character per storage unit. Thus, for example, if the character variable C has the value TODAY IS FRIDAY, its value may be envisaged as being held in character storage units as follows:

T	O	D	A	Y	b	I	S	b	F	R	I	D	A	Y

T being the *first* character in the character string, O the *second,* D the *third*, etc.

In order that contiguous portions of such a character string may be referenced or amended, FORTRAN 77 contains a facility for identifying *substrings* by creating *substring names.* With reference to the above illustration, the substring name C(3:8), for example, refers to the portion of the value of C from character position 3 to character position 8, i.e. the part containing the substring DAY IS. Similarly C(10:15) refers to that part of the value of C from character position 10 to character position 15, i.e. the substring FRIDAY.

In general a substring name has one of the forms

(a) $v(e1:e2)$ where v is the name of a *variable* of type CHARACTER;

(b) $c(i_1, i_2, \ldots, i_m)\,(e1:e2)$ where $c(i_1, i_2, \ldots, i_m)$ is an element of an *array c* of type CHARACTER.

In both cases $e1$ and $e2$, called *substring expressions*, are integer arithmetic expressions, the values of which indicate respectively the *leftmost* character position and the *rightmost* character position of the substring. Note that

(i) The values of $e1$ and $e2$ must be such that $1 \leqslant e1 \leqslant e2 \leqslant L$, where L is the length of v in (a) and the length of an element of c in (b);

(ii) If $e1$ is omitted, 1 is assumed by default; if $e2$ is omitted, L is assumed by default; if both $e1$ and $e2$ are omitted, 1 and L are assumed, by default, for the values of $e1$ and $e2$ respectively.

Example 15.5   If the character variable TEXT has the value

THE BOY STOOD ON THE BURNING DECK

write down the values of TEXT(5:13), TEXT(22:25), TEXT(I–J:I+J) if I=10, J=3, TEXT(:13), TEXT(30:).

Substring name	Substring value
TEXT(5:13)	BOY STOOD
TEXT(22:25)	BURN
TEXT(I–J:I+J)	Y STOOD
TEXT(:13)	THE BOY STOOD
TEXT(30:)	DECK

Example 15.6   If the elements of the character array C_0, C_1, C_2, C_3, C_4 have the following values

$$C_0 \qquad \text{bbGIBSON}$$
$$C_1 \qquad \text{bbbBROWN}$$

$$C_2 \quad \text{MITCHELL}$$
$$C_3 \quad \text{DAVIDSON}$$
$$C_4 \quad \text{bbbCOLES}$$
$$C_5 \quad \text{bbbbbBOW}$$

write down the values of C(0)(6:8), C(2)(1:3), C(4)(6:), C(5)(:5), and C(1)(:).

Substring name	Substring value
C(0)(6:8)	SON
C(2)(1:3)	MIT
C(4)(6:)	LES
C(5)(:5)	bbbbb
C(1)(:)	bbbBROWN

Character expressions and assignment statements

A character assignment statement in FORTRAN 77 has the form

$$v = \text{character expression}$$

where v is the name of a *character variable*, a *character array element*, or a *character substring*. When a character assignment statement is executed, the character expression on the right-hand side is evaluated, and the resulting value is assigned to the entity whose name occurs on the left-hand side.

A character expression is either one of the following:

(i) character constant,
(ii) symbolic name of a character constant,
(iii) character variable name,
(iv) character array element name,
(v) character substring name,
(vi) character function reference,

or is formed by combining together one or more of these entities using parentheses and the *concatenation operator* $//$. The effect of the concatenation operator when used on two character operands thus:

$$x_1 // x_2$$

is to produce a character string whose value is the value of x_1 *concatenated on the right* by the value of x_2.

Example 15.7 The value of 'ABC'//'DE' is ABCDE. The value of 'LINUSbVANb'// 'PELT' is LINUSbVANbPELT.

Note:

(a) The length of the result of applying the concatenation operator $//$ to two operands x_1 and x_2 is the *sum* of the lengths of x_1 and x_2.

(b) Although the Standard specifies a *left to right* evaluation of expressions like $x_1//x_2//x_3$, this is of little significance as far as character expressions are concerned, the order of evaluation and the presence of parentheses having no effect. For example, the values of ('AB'//'C')//'DE' and 'AB'//('C'//'DE') are both ABCDE.

(c) Character expressions may occur in FORTRAN 77 in situations other than on the right-hand sides of character assignment statements, e.g. in *relational expressions* (see below). However, a character dummy argument whose length specification is *(*) must not be used in a character expression as an operand for concatenation, except in a character assignment statement.

Example 15.8   Given a FORTRAN 77 program unit containing the statements

```
        CHARACTER*10 NAME*6,K1*(*),K2*8,C(20,2)*12,X,Y
        PARAMETER (K1='BLOGGS',
       +              K2='SMITH')
        NAME='FARMER'
        C(1,1)='bbbALEXANDER'
        C(1,2)='THOMSON'
        X='Ab'//'Jb'//K1
        Y='NEWb'//NAME//'JIM'
        C(2,1)='bbbb'//NAME(1:3)//'QUHAR'
        NAME(4:6)='SON'
        C(2,2)=C(1,1)(8:11)//NAME(3:6)
```

then

(a) K1 is the name of a symbolic constant, value BLOGGS;
(b) K2 is the name of a symbolic constant, value SMITHbbb;
(c) the character variable NAME is given the value FARMER;
(d) $C_{1,1}$ is given the value bbbALEXANDER;
(e) $C_{1,2}$ is given the value THOMSONbbbbb, additional blanks being inserted on the right before assignment;
(f) the character variable X is given the value A J BLOGGS;
(g) the character variable Y is given the value NEW FARMER, the value of the right-hand side being *truncated* on the right to 10 characters before assignment;
(h) $C_{2,1}$ is given the value bbbbFARQUHAR;
(i) The value of the character variable NAME changes from FARMER to FARSON, because of the statement NAME (4:6) = 'SON';
(j) $C_{2,2}$ is given the value ANDERSONbbbb, additional blanks again being inserted on the right, before assignment.

Note that if the length of the value of the character expression on the right-hand side is *less* than the length of v, the value of the character expression is padded out with blanks on the right until the two lengths are equal, before assignment to v. Similarly, if the length of the value of the character expression on the right-hand side is *greater* than the length of v, the value of the character expression is truncated from the right until the two lengths are equal, before assignment to v.

Example 15.9 No character position being *defined* in *v* may be *referenced* in the character expression on the right-hand side. For example, if C is a character variable of length 12, the character assignment statement

$$C(2:10)='ABC'//C(5:7)//'XYZ'$$

is incorrect, since character positions 5, 6, 7 are being both defined and referenced.

Example 15.10 Only as much of the value of the character expression on the right-hand side of a character assignment statement must be defined *as is needed to define* *v*. For example, if A and B are character variables of lengths 2 and 4 respectively, the character assignment statement

$$A = B$$

is meaningful if the substring $B(1:2)$ is defined, irrespective of whether or not the substring $B(3:4)$ is defined.

PARAMETER statements involving character constant expressions

Character constant expressions may occur in PARAMETER statements (see Chapter 11), a character constant expression being defined as a character expression in which each operand is a *character constant* or the *symbolic name of a character constant*. As usual, if the symbolic name of a constant occurs, it must have been defined earlier in the program unit in the same, or some other, PARAMETER statement.

Example 15.11 A FORTRAN 77 program unit might contain the following:

```
        CHARACTER*6 C1,C2,NAME*(*),PASSWD*(*)
        PARAMETER (C1='FRASER',
     +             C2='DUNLOP',
     +             NAME='JOEb'//C1,
     +             PASSWD=NAME//'bISbTHEb'//C2//'bAGENT')
```

Initialization of substrings

In addition to the initialization of character variables, arrays, and array elements, DATA statements (see Chapter 11) may also be used to initialize *substrings*.

Example 15.12 A FORTRAN 77 program unit might contain the following:

```
        CHARACTER*4 C1,C2,C3
        DATA C1(1:2),C2(2:4),C3/3*'ABCD'/
```

The effect is to initialize $C1(1:2)$ to AB, $C2(2:4)$ to ABC, and C3 to ABCD, $C1(3:4)$ and $C2(1:1)$ remaining *undefined*. Note how characters are truncated on the right, wherever necessary (cf. Example 11.7).

Input and output of character information

The edit descriptors A and Aw, where w is the field width, are used for the formatted input and output of character information. In describing their effects below, g will be used to denote the *length* of the corresponding input/output list item of type CHARACTER.

For *formatted input* of character information using the edit descriptors A and Aw there are essentially three cases to describe.

(a) *Aw with* $w \geqslant g$. In this case the *rightmost* g characters in the field specified are input and assigned to the appropriate item of type CHARACTER in the input list. Note that this is the *exact opposite* of what might be expected to happen, on the basis of what occurs when using character assignment statements.

(b) *Aw with* $w < g$. In this case the w characters in the field specified are input, padded out on the *right* with $(g - w)$ blanks, and assigned to the appropriate item of type CHARACTER in the input list.

(c) *A*. In this case a field width of g is assumed, and g characters are input and assigned to the appropriate item of type CHARACTER in the input list.

Example 15.13   Consider the record

ATOMbbMASCOTSbb+−*/bbBUMPER

Then if C1, C2, PLUS, MINUS, TIMES, DIV, and C3 are all of type CHARACTER and of length 4, the input statement

READ(*,'(A4,2X,A7,2X,4A1,2X,A)')C1,C2,PLUS,MINUS,TIMES,DIV,C3

will cause character information to be read in, and assigned to the various character variables as follows

Variable	Value assigned
C1	ATOM
C2	COTS
PLUS	+bbb
MINUS	−bbb
TIMES	*bbb
DIV	/bbb
C3	BUMP

For *formatted output* of character information using the edit descriptors A and Aw, there are also three cases to describe.

(a) *Aw with* $w \geqslant g$. In this case the value of the appropriate item of type CHARACTER in the output list is output, padded out on the *left* by $(w - g)$ blanks.

(b) *Aw with* $w < g$. In this case the *leftmost* w characters in the value of the appropriate item of type CHARACTER in the output list is output.

(c)   *A*. In this case a field width of *g* is assumed and the value of the appropriate item of type CHARACTER in the output list is output.

Example 15.14   Given that the character variables C1, C2, C3, PASSWD, and MSSAGE have the following lengths and values:

Variable	Length	Value
C1	4	PQRS
C2	5	AEIOU
C3	6	TOMCAT
PASSWD	10	EUREKAbbbb
MSSAGE	8	TOObMANY

the output statement

WRITE(*,'("b" ,2A8,2X,A,2X,A6,4X,A3)')C1,C2,C3,PASSWD,MSSAGE

will output the record

bbbbPQRSbbbAEIOUbbTOMCATbbEUREKAbbbbTOO

For *list directed input* of character information, the character information on the input record must be preceded and followed by an *apostrophe*, i.e. the character information is presented in the form of a *character constant*. Here, if *c* is defined to be the *length* of the character constant, there are two cases to consider.

(a) $c \geq g$. In this case the *leftmost g* characters of the value of the character constant are input and assigned to the appropriate item ·of type CHARACTER in the input list. Note carefully the inconsistency between this and the effect of using formatted input with $w \geq g$.

(b) $c < g$. In this case the value of the character constant is input, padded out on the right with $(g - c)$ blanks, and assigned to the appropriate item of type CHARACTER in the input list.

Note that the effect of (a) and (b) above corresponds to using a character assignment statement to assign the value of the character constant to the item in the input list. Note also that, if the character information to be read in contains an apostrophe, it must be represented, not surprisingly, in the character constant by *two consecutive* apostrophes. In addition, character information to be read in may spread over several input records, with the single proviso that consecutive apostrophes should not be split between records.

The *list directed output* of character information is not normally recommended, since the FORTRAN 77 standard permits *implementation-dependent* variations. If used, the reader is advised to consult the Standard (American National Standards Institute, 1978) for details, and also to check on the precise manner with which it has been implemented in the version of FORTRAN 77 available.

Collating sequences and character relational expressions

In many problems involving character information, it is necessary to 'order' the information in some manner. Most people, for example, if asked to put into order the words APPLE, BOAT, APE, CANDLE, DOG, DOVE, and CAN, would respond by writing APE, APPLE, BOAT, CAN, CANDLE, DOG, and DOVE, the natural reaction being to use alphabetic ordering and the assumption that a blank character 'comes before' or 'is less than' the first letter of the alphabet. In more precise terms, most people order words using the *collating sequence*

$$\text{blank} < A < B < C < D < E < \ldots\ldots\ldots < X < Y < Z$$

When 'ordering' character information, however, the above collating sequence is insufficient, in that characters other than blank and the capital letters may occur. Does, for example, /P2+5Q 'come before' −78*ZW ?

The ideal answer to this question, as far as FORTRAN 77 is concerned, is for the Standard to specify a complete collating sequence for all possible characters which may occur in character information in a FORTRAN 77 program unit. Unfortunately this cannot be done for two main reasons:

(a)   In addition to the characters in the FORTRAN 77 character set, namely

   A to Z   0 to 9   = + − * / ( ) , . $ ' : blank

   Other characters acceptable to specific implementations of FORTRAN 77 may be used.

(b)   Collating sequences for existing computer systems vary significantly, and are usually independent of the high-level languages being used.

The FORTRAN 77 Standard therefore compromises by not defining a specific collating sequence, but by insisting instead that the collating sequence for any implementation of FORTRAN 77 must possess the following properties:

(a) $0 < 1 < 2 < \ldots\ldots < 9$;
(b) $A < B < C < \ldots\ldots < Z$;
(c) $9 < A$ *or* $Z < 0$, i.e. all the digits precede A *or* follow Z;
(d)   blank $< A$ and blank < 0.

Note that this implies that, even when the standard FORTRAN 77 character set is adhered to, *different FORTRAN 77 implementations may order character information differently*, a severe restriction on the portability of some FORTRAN 77 programs.

To complicate matters even further, four additional intrinsic functions are also provided in FORTRAN 77 to facilitate the comparison of character strings using the ASCII† collating sequence. The overall position is therefore rather anomalous in that any collating sequence satisfying the above properties may be embodied in an implementation of FORTRAN 77, but at the same time four intrinsic functions exist which may be used to compare character strings on the basis of the ASCII collating sequence. The reader is referred to the next Section for details of the four intrinsic functions. The ASCII collating sequence for the standard FORTRAN 77 character set is given on page 196.

---

† American Standard Code for Information Interchange.

Example 15.15 Order the character information CAN, CAN5, CANISTER, CANDY, CAND23, CANS, and C21 using

(a) the collating sequence blank $< 0 < 1 < \ldots < 9 < A < B < \ldots < Z$;
(b) the collating sequence blank $< A < B < \ldots < Z < 0 < 1 < \ldots < 9$.

Using the first collating sequence the required order is C21, CAN, CAN5, CAND23, CANDY, CANISTER, and CANS. Using the second collating sequence the required order is CAN, CANDY, CAND23, CANISTER, CANS, CAN5, and C21.

In Chapter 9 the concept of a *relational expression* to compare the values of two *arithmetic* expressions was introduced. Relational expressions may also be used to compare the values of *character* expressions, such a relational expression taking the form

$$e_1 \; relop \; e_2$$

where

(a) e_1 and e_2 are character expressions;
(b) relop is one of the relational operators .LT., .LE., .EQ., .NE., .GT., or .GE., defined in Chapter 9.

The value of a character relational expression is once again either **true** or **false,** the comparison being carried out on the basis of the underlying collating sequence for the implementation of FORTRAN 77 being used. Not surprisingly, if the operands e_1 and e_2 are of different lengths the shorter operand is padded out with blanks on the right before the comparison is made.

Example 15.16 Given the collating sequence

$$blank < 0 < 1 < \ldots \ldots < 9 < A < B < \ldots \ldots < Z$$

evaluate the character relational expressions:

(i) 'CAN5'.GT.'CANS'
(ii) 'CANIS'//'TER'.EQ.'CANISTER'
(iii) 'C'//'21'.LE.'C'//'215'

In (i), since $5 < S$, the value of the relational expression is **false.** In (ii) both character expressions have the value CANISTER so that the value of the relational expression is **true.** In (iii) C21b and C215 are being compared, the first character expression being padded out with a blank on the right, so that, since $b < 5$, the value of the relational expression is **true.**

It is important to note that, unlike character relational expressions involving the relational operators .LT., .LE., .GT., and .GE., the values of character relational expressions involving the relational operators .EQ. and .NE. are *independent of the underlying collating sequence.*

Useful intrinsic functions

The table below lists the intrinsic functions† which are of particular interest when handling character information in a FORTRAN 77 program.

Intrinsic function	Definition	Specific name	Number of arguments	Type of	
				argument	function
Conversion to character	CHAR(i) returns ith character in collating sequence, the characters being numbered 0, 1, 2, 3, . . .	CHAR	1	INTEGER	CHARACTER
Conversion to integer	ICHAR(c) returns position of character c in collating sequence	ICHAR	1	CHARACTER	INTEGER
Length of character	LEN(c) returns length of character expression c	LEN	1	CHARACTER	INTEGER
Location of substring	If there is a substring of c_1 equal to the value of c_2, INDEX(c_1,c_2) returns the value of the starting position of that substring; otherwise INDEX(c_1,c_2) returns the value 0	INDEX	2	CHARACTER	INTEGER
Comparison of strings	LGE(c_1,c_2) compares the two character strings c_1 and c_2 using the ASCII collating sequence and returns the value **true** if $c_1 \geq c_2$, and **false** otherwise. LGT, LLE, and LLT are similarly defined (see note (e))	LGE LGT LLE LLT	2 2 2 2	CHARACTER CHARACTER CHARACTER CHARACTER	LOGICAL LOGICAL LOGICAL LOGICAL

Note:

(a)   CHAR and ICHAR provide a means of converting between the characters in the collating sequence for an implementation of FORTRAN 77 and the sequence 0, 1, 2, . . ., $(n-1)$, where n is the number of characters in the collating sequence. For example, CHAR(4) returns the *fifth* character in the collating sequence as its value, whereas ICHAR ('A') returns as its value the position of A in the collating sequence, when the positions are numbered 0, 1, 2, ...

† No *generic* names exist for these functions, for fairly obvious reasons.

(b)   The argument for CHAR must be an integer expression, the value of which must lie in the range 0 to $(n-1)$ where n is the number of characters in the collating sequence. The value returned is of type CHARACTER of length one.

(c)   The argument for ICHAR must be of type CHARACTER of length one, with value a character in the collating sequence. The value returned is an integer in the range 0 to $(n-1)$.

(d)   If there is more than one substring of C1 equal to the value of C2, then the value returned by INDEX(C1,C2) is the starting position of the *first* such substring when scanning from left to right. Remember that the character positions in a string are numbered 1, 2, 3, ...

(e)   The ASCII collating sequence for the standard FORTRAN 77 character set is:

blank	0	=	K	V
$	1	A	L	W
'	2	B	M	X
(	3	C	N	Y
)	4	D	O	Z
*	5	E	P	
+	6	F	Q	
,	7	G	R	
–	8	H	S	
.	9	I	T	
/	:	J	U	

with *ascending* collating order being obtained by reading down the columns from left to right.

Example 15.17   Given the collating sequence

blank $<$ A $<$ B $<$ . . . . . . $<$ Y $<$ Z $<$ 0 $<$ 1 $<$ 2 $<$ . . . . . . $<$ 9 $<$ . . . . . .

then

(i)   CHAR(3) returns the value C;
(ii) ICHAR('2') returns the value 29.

Example 15.18   INDEX('ABRACADABRA','ADA') returns the value 6. INDEX ('ABRACADABRA', 'BRA') returns the value 2, corresponding to the *first* occurrence of the substring BRA.

Example 15.19   Given the collating sequence

blank $<$ A $<$ B $<$ . . . . . . $<$ Y $<$ Z $<$ 0 $<$ 1 $<$ 2 $<$ . . . . . . $<$ 9

the value of the relational expression

'AB4P'.GT.'ABC'

is **true**. On the other hand, the value returned by the function reference LGT('AB4P', 'ABC') is **false**, since $4 < $ C in the ASCII collating sequence.

Variable and array dummy arguments of type CHARACTER

Dummy and actual argument association has already been fairly fully discussed in Chapters 12 and 13. There are, however, several additional points to consider when handling arguments of type CHARACTER.

A dummy argument which is a *variable* name of type CHARACTER, for example, may only be associated with an actual argument which is either a character variable, character array element, character substring, or character expression. In addition, if m is the length of the dummy argument and n is the length of the associated actual argument, m must not exceed n and, if $m < n$, only the *leftmost m* characters of the actual argument are associated with the dummy argument. Of course, if a length specification of *(*) is used for the dummy argument, as described earlier in the chapter (page 185), m is automatically set equal to n so that no problems can occur.

A dummy argument which is an *array* name of type CHARACTER, on the other hand, may only be associated with an actual argument which is either a character array, character array element, or character array element substring. The actual argument indicates the *starting point* of the association between the actual array involved and the dummy array, and the length restriction of the previous paragraph applies with m now defined as the length in characters of the *entire dummy array,* and n now defined as the length in characters of that portion of the actual array from the starting point of the association to the end of the array. In other words, *the dummy array must not extend beyond the end of the associated actual array.* It is *not* essential for the length of each dummy array element to be the same as the length of each element in the associated actual array. Furthermore, in cases where a dummy array has a length specification of *(*), the length of each element of the dummy array may be determined from the following table:

Actual argument	Length of each element of dummy array
array	length of actual array element
array element	length of actual array element
array element substring	length of actual array element substring

Example 15.20   Given the program units:

```
PROGRAM      FRED                    SUBROUTINE   JIM(C)
CHARACTER    C1*2,C2*4,C3*6          CHARACTER    C*4
   .                                    .
   .                                    .
END                                  END
```

comment on the following CALL statements which could occur in the main program FRED:

    (a)   CALL JIM(C1);
    (b)   CALL JIM(C2);
    (c)   CALL JIM(C3).

Comparison of the length of the dummy argument C, with the lengths of the actual arguments C1, C2, and C3 indicates that

    (a)   CALL JIM(C1) is *invalid*;
    (b)   CALL JIM(C2) is valid;
    (c)   CALL JIM(C3) is valid, the leftmost 4 characters of C3 being associated with C.

Note also that if the subprogram JIM had been defined thus:

$$\text{SUBROUTINE} \quad \text{JIM(C)}$$
$$\text{CHARACTER} \quad \text{C*(*)}$$

$$\vdots$$

$$\text{END}$$

then all three subroutine calls would have been valid, the length of the dummy argument C being determined on each occasion by the length of the corresponding actual argument.

Example 15.21   Given the program units:

```
PROGRAM      ALICE                    SUBROUTINE    JOAN(C,N)
 CHARACTER    C1(3)*4,C2(6)*2,         CHARACTER    C(N)*4
+             C3(0:2)*6,C4(2,3)*2

        ⋮                                    ⋮

 END                                   END
```

comment on the following CALL statements which could occur in the main program ALICE:

    (a)   CALL JOAN(C1,3);
    (b)   CALL JOAN(C2,5);
    (c)   CALL JOAN(C3,3);
    (d)   CALL JOAN(C4,3);
    (e)   CALL JOAN(C2(2)(2:2),2).

The five CALL statements may be analysed as follows.

    (a)   The length of the entire dummy array is 12 (characters), as is the length of the associated actual argument. Hence the CALL statement is valid, and the association between the characters of the dummy and actual arrays is straightforward.

    (b)   The length of the entire dummy array is 20, and the length of the associated actual argument is 12. Hence the CALL statement is invalid.

    (c)   The length of the entire dummy array is 12, and the length of the associated actual argument is 18. Hence only the *leftmost* 12 characters of the actual argument are associated with the dummy array argument as follows:

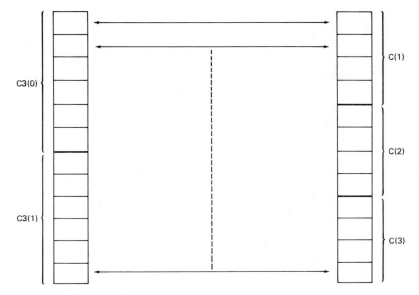

For example, C3(0)(6:6) is associated with C(2)(2:2), etc.

(d) The length of the entire dummy array is 12, and the length of the associated actual argument is also 12. Hence the CALL statement is valid and the actual argument/dummy array argument association is as follows:

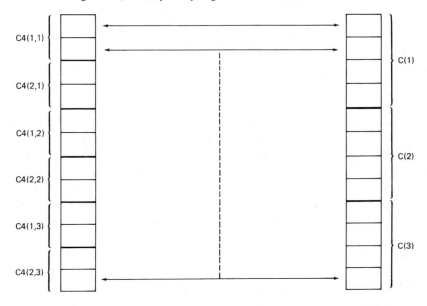

remembering that the elements of a 2-dimensional array are held in column order. For example, C4(2,3)(1:1) is associated with C(3)(3:3) etc.

(e)   The length of the entire dummy array is 8, and the actual argument/ dummy array argument association is to take place thus:

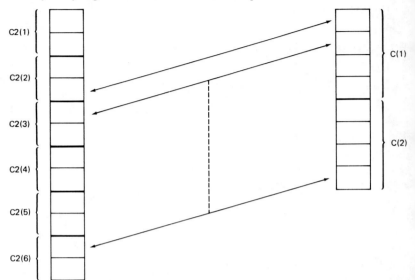

Hence the CALL statement is valid, with the length of the associated actual argument exceeding the length of the dummy array argument by 1.

The reader is left to consider (see Exercise 15.8) the effect of changing the definition of the subroutine JOAN to

> SUBROUTINE   JOAN(C,N)
> CHARACTER   C(N)*(*)
>
> .
> .
> .
>
> END

The message to be taken out of Example 15.21 and Exercise 15.8 is fairly obvious. When passing character information to a function or subroutine subprogram, keep things simple. Associating, for example, a dummy argument array of type CHARACTER with an actual argument which is an array element or an array element substring is not normally recommended. Similarly, in a dummy argument array/actual argument array association, keep the number of dimensions the same, and also the lengths of the array elements. It is very easy to create complicated FORTRAN 77 programs using some of these facilities. It is not so easy to understand what is happening, and to locate obscure bugs when they occur.

Occurrence of character information in common blocks

In FORTRAN 77, storage for character information must be kept completely separate from storage for integer, real, logical, complex, and double precision information.

Since this is the case, it follows that if a character variable or character array is in a common block *all* of the entities in that common block must be of type CHARACTER.

Some illustrative examples

In this section a number of examples are given to illustrate the use of the character handling facilities in FORTRAN 77.

Example 15.22   An input record contains, in free format, the value of a positive integer n. It is followed by n other input records, each one of which contains a piece of text. Write a FORTRAN 77 program to ascertain the number of times each letter of the alphabet occurs in the complete text. Assume that each input record is 80 characters long, and that the letters of the alphabet occupy *consecutive* positions in the collating sequence of the FORTRAN 77 implementation being used.

On the basis of the second assumption given above, the positions of the letters A, B, C, . . . within the collating sequence are given by ICHAR('A'), ICHAR('A')+1, ICHAR('A')+2, ... Hence, if C is any character in an input record, its position in the alphabet can be obtained by evaluating ICHAR(C)–ICHAR('A')+1. This forms the basis of the following simple algorithm.

> assign 0 to count$_1$, count$_2$, . . ., count$_{26}$
> assign ICHAR('A') to const
> read n
> **loop for** $i = 1, 2, 3, . . ., n$ **do**
> $\qquad$ {read characters from an input record into CH$_1$, CH$_2$, . . ., CH$_{80}$
> $\qquad$ **loop for** $j = 1, 2, 3, . . ., 80$ **do**
> $\qquad\qquad$ {assign ICHAR(CH$_j$)–const+1 to sub
> $\qquad\qquad$ **if** $0 <$ sub **and** sub < 27 **then** add 1 to count$_{sub}$
> $\qquad\qquad$ }
> $\qquad$ }
> **loop for** $k = 1, 2, 3, . . ., 26$ **do** print CHAR(k+const-1), count$_k$

This leads to the FORTRAN 77 program:

```
PROGRAM LCOUNT
INTEGER SUB,CONST,COUNT(26)
CHARACTER CH(80)*1
DATA COUNT/26*0/
CONST = ICHAR('A')
READ *,N
DO 100 I=1,N
    READ(*,'(80A1)') (CH(J),J=1,80)
    DO 200 J=1,80
        SUB=ICHAR(CH(J))-CONST+1
```

```
          IF (0.LT.SUB.AND.SUB.LT.27) THEN

                COUNT(SUB)=COUNT(SUB)+1

          END IF

200           CONTINUE

100       CONTINUE

      DO   300   K=1,26

          WRITE(*,'('' '',A1,4X,I8)') CHAR(K+CONST-1),COUNT(K)

300       CONTINUE

      END
```

Note that the algorithm depends on the existence of the functions ICHAR and CHAR. It is obvious therefore that the algorithm has been devised with the knowledge that it will be eventually implemented using FORTRAN 77. Ideally this is to be regretted, since all algorithms should be machine and language independent. In practice, however, compromises have often to be made which take into account the facilities available in the implementation language which is likely to be used.

Example 15.23 Each element except the first of the one-dimensional character array $C_0, C_1, C_2, \ldots, C_n$ contains a non-hyphenated English word, padded out on the right with blanks if necessary. Write a subroutine subprogram CSORT(C,N) to arrange the words in dictionary order using a simple insertion sort technique. Assume that the subroutine will never be called into action to operate on words containing more than 20 letters.

A simple insertion sort algorithm is as follows:

loop for $j = 2, 3, \ldots, N$ **do**
    { assign C_j to T
    assign $j - 1$ to i
    loop while $i > 0$ **and** $T < C_i$ **do**
        { assign C_i to C_{i+1}
        assign $i - 1$ to i}
    assign T to C_{i+1}
    }

leading to the FORTRAN 77 program:

```
      SUBROUTINE CSORT(C,N)

      CHARACTER C(0:N)*(*),T*20

      C(0)=' '

      DO 100 J=2,N

          T=C(J)

          I=J-1

200       IF (I.GT.0 .AND. T.LT.C(I)) THEN

                C(I+1)=C(I)
```

```
        I=I-1
        GO TO 200
      END IF
      C(I+1) = T
100   CONTINUE
      END
```

Note:

(a)   Any reader unfamiliar with the actions of an insertion sort should check the algorithm carefully by hand using sample input data.

(b)   Unless the one-dimensional array C contains an 'artificial' first element C_0, problems may arise† whenever the logical expression I.GT.0 .AND. T.LT.C(I) is evaluated with I equal to 0. It is immaterial what character string is held in C(0) provided that it has a defined value whenever the subprogram is executed.

(c)   To keep matters straightforward, whenever CSORT is called into action in another program unit, C should be replaced by the name of a one-dimensional character array with lower subscript bound *zero*, each element of which is of length $\leqslant 20$.

(d)   It is immaterial in this case whether the underlying collating sequence or the ASCII collating sequence is used, if efficiency considerations are ignored (ASCII is likely to be significantly slower if it is not the 'normal' collating sequence). To use the ASCII collating sequence is simply a matter of replacing the relational expression T.LT.C(I) by LLT(T,C(I)).

(e)   The logical operator .AND. is described in detail in Chapter 16.

Example 15.24   The following character function subprogram

```
CHARACTER *(*) FUNCTION MONTH(I)
CHARACTER M(12)*9
DATA (M(J),J=1,12)/'JANUARY','FEBRUARY',
+                  'MARCH','APRIL',
+                  'MAY','JUNE',
+                  'JULY','AUGUST',
+                  'SEPTEMBER','OCTOBER',
+                  'NOVEMBER','DECEMBER'/
MONTH = M(I)
END
```

will, when referenced, return the name of the Ith month of the year, but only the leftmost *n* characters of the name will be returned depending on what is specified in

† When using an implementation of FORTRAN 77 which is not 'smart enough' to avoid the evaluation of T.LT.C(I) whenever the value of I.GT.0 is **false**.

the referencing program unit. For example, in one program unit the type statement

CHARACTER MONTH*9

might occur, whereas in another the type statement

CHARACTER MONTH*3

might occur. In the first program unit, whenever MONTH is referenced, the name returned will contain 9 characters, whereas in the second program unit, whenever MONTH is referenced, the name returned will contain 3 characters.

Note also that

(a) the first two lines of the subprogram could also have been written thus:

FUNCTION   MONTH(I)
CHARACTER MONTH*(*),M(12)*9

(b) for clarity J has been used as the name of the implied-DO variable. I, however, could have been used, despite the fact that it is also the name of a dummy argument of type INTEGER (see Chapter 11).

Exercise 15

1 If the character variable TITLE has the value

PARIS IN THE SPRING

write down the values of TITLE(1:3), TITLE(4:8), TITLE(11:12), TITLE(:12), TITLE(16:), and TITLE(:).

2 Explain the effects of the following FORTRAN 77 statements:

```
CHARACTER*12 PW1*8,PW2*(*),X,Y,NAME*6,A*4,B*5,C(8)*30
PARAMETER(PW1='SONNET',
+          PW2='CARSON')
DATA X,Y/'CARPET TILE', 'LINOLEUM'/
NAME='ALBERT'
A=X(8:11)
B=NAME(1:2)//NAME(4:6)
C(1)=X(:11)//'S'//' ARE IN FASHION'
C(2)=NAME//' '//PW2//'IS'//C(1)(17:20)//'BED'
```

3 Order the character information† HØUSE, HUT, HØRRØR, H2SØ4, H2Ø, HALIBUT, HEAVISIDE using the collating sequence

(a) blank $< 0 < 1 < \ldots < 9 < A < B < C < \ldots < Z < \ldots$

(b) blank $< A < B < C < \ldots < Z < 0 < 1 < \ldots < 9 < \ldots$

4 Given the collating sequence (b) above, evaluate

(a) CHAR(2), CHAR(30)

(b) ICHAR('E'), ICHAR('9')

(c) 'MASCOT' .LE. 'M5'

† Ø indicates the letter O to distinguish it from the digit zero.

(d)   LLE('MASCOT', 'M5')
(e)   LGT('2+2=4', '2*2=4')

5   An input record contains, in free format, the value of a positive integer n. It is followed by n other input records, each one of which contains a piece of text. Write a FORTRAN 77 program to ascertain the number of times each of the vowels occurs in the complete text. Assume that each input record is 80 characters long.

6   Write an integer function subprogram PALIND(C) to return the value 1 if the character string C is a *palindrome* (i.e. reads the same from *right to left*, as it does from left to right), and 0 otherwise. Any blanks at the right of the character string C are to be ignored.

7   Write a character function subprogram KILL(TEXT,C) to return the character string obtained by taking the character string TEXT and deleting all occurrences of the (single) non-blank character C. Assume that TEXT will never contain more than 80 characters, and that at least one character in TEXT differs from C.

8   Repeat Example 15.21 using the amended subroutine definition:

```
SUBROUTINE JOAN(C,N)
CHARACTER  C(N)*(*)
 .
 .
 .
END
```

16 Logical facilities

> When it is not necessary to make a decision, it is necessary not to make a decision. (*Lord Falkland's Rule*)

In this chapter the logical facilities available in FORTRAN 77 are described in detail. Much of the information contained in the chapter may be skipped over lightly on a first reading since the implementation of most practical algorithms in FORTRAN 77 requires no more than a knowledge of a minimal subset of the logical facilities available. There are occasions, however, when the use of some of the more elaborate logical facilities may prove beneficial.

Logical constants

As described in Chapter 4, the two logical constants **true** and **false** are written in FORTRAN 77 as .TRUE. and .FALSE. respectively. Note once again the difference between the *representation* of a constant in FORTRAN 77, e.g. .TRUE., and its *value*, e.g. **true**.

Logical variables and arrays

The specification of variables and arrays of type LOGICAL has already been covered in Chapters 5 and 10 respectively. The following example will remind the reader of what is involved.

Example 16.1　A FORTRAN 77 program unit might contain the following statements:

LOGICAL FLAG, MARKER, SWITCH, ERROR
DIMENSION MARKER (0:10), SWITCH (5,6)

indicating that

(a)　FLAG and ERROR are variables of type LOGICAL;
(b)　$MARKER_0$, $MARKER_1$, . . ., $MARKER_{10}$ is a one-dimensional array, the elements of which are of type LOGICAL;
(c)　SWITCH is a 5×6 matrix the elements of which are also of type LOGICAL.

An alternative way of writing these statements is, of course

LOGICAL FLAG, MARKER (0:10), SWITCH (5,6), ERROR

Logical operators and expressions

A *logical expression*, i.e. an expression which has the value of either **true** or **false**, is either one of the following:

   (i)   a logical constant,
   (ii) the symbolic name of a logical constant,
  (iii) a logical variable name,
  (iv) a logical array element name,
   (v) a logical function reference,
  (vi) a relational expression (Chapter 9),

or is formed by combining together one or more of these entities using parentheses and the *logical operators* .NOT., .AND., .OR., .EQV. and .NEQV..

The logical operator .NOT. is a *unary* operator, i.e. it is applied to *one* logical entity thus:

$$.NOT. \, x_2$$

the value of .NOT. x_2 being the 'opposite' of the value of x_2. Its effect may therefore be summarized by the following 'truth table':

x_2	.NOT.x_2
true	false
false	true

Example 16.2   If the logical variable FLAG has the value **true**, then the logical expression .NOT. FLAG has the value **false**.

Example 16.3   If the real variables A and B have the values 16.8 and 18.2 respectively, the logical expression .NOT. A .GT. B has the value **true** since the relational expression A .GT. B has the value **false**. It is permissible to insert parentheses thus

$$.NOT. \, (A.GT.B)$$

for clarity, if desired.

The remaining logical operators .AND., .OR., .EQV. and .NEQV. are *binary* operators, i.e. each one is applied to *two* logical entities to produce a resulting value defined as follows:

  (a) x_1 .AND. x_2 has the value **true** if *both x_1 and x_2* have **true** as their value, and has the value **false** otherwise;
  (b) x_1 .OR. x_2 has the value **true** if *either x_1 or x_2* (or both) has the value **true**, and has the value **false** otherwise;

(c) x_1 .EQV. x_2 has the value **true** if the values of x_1 and x_2 are the *same* (i.e. both **true** or both **false**), and has the value **false** otherwise;

(d) x_1 .NEQV. x_2 has the value **true** if the values of x_1 and x_2 are *different* (i.e. one value **true** and one value **false**), and has the value **false** otherwise.

Alternatively the effects of applying .AND., .OR., .EQV., and .NEQV. may be summarized by the following truth tables:

x_1	x_2	x_1 .AND. x_2		x_1	x_2	x_1 .OR. x_2
true	true	true		true	true	true
true	false	false		true	false	true
false	true	false		false	true	true
false	false	false		false	false	false

x_1	x_2	x_1 .EQV. x_2		x_1	x_2	x_1 .NEQV. x_2
true	true	true		true	true	false
true	false	false		true	false	true
false	true	false		false	true	true
false	false	true		false	false	false

Example 16.4 If ERROR and FLAG are two logical variables with values **true** and **false** respectively, and I, J, and K are integer variables with I=−5, J=8, and K=4, then:

(a) ERROR .AND. FLAG has the value **false**;

(b) ERROR .NEQV. FLAG has the value **true**;

(c) I.GT.8 .OR. K.EQ.4 has the value **true**;

(d) K.LT.J .AND. J.LT.I has the value **false**;

(e) I.EQ.5 .EQV. FLAG has the value **true**.

Note again that parentheses could have been used in (c), (d), and (e) above to clarify what was intended, e.g. to write in the case of (c) (I.GT.8) .OR. (K.EQ.4).

More complicated logical expressions may be formed by using *several* logical operators in the one expression. Not surprisingly, an order of precedence for the various logical operators is specified in FORTRAN 77, as shown in the following table.

Operator	Precedence
.NOT.	highest
.AND.	:
.OR.	:
.EQV. or .NEQV.	lowest

Operators of equal precedence are applied from *left to right*. Wherever necessary, of course, sub-expressions in parentheses will be evaluated first, using the same order of precedence for any logical operators involved.

Example 16.5   Evaluate the following logical expressions given that B1 = **true**, B2 = **false**, B3 = **false**, X = 21.5, Y = 32.5, Z = 48.4:

(a)   B1 .OR. B2 .OR. B3;

(b)   B1 .AND. .NOT. B2 .AND. .NOT. B3;

(c)   (X .GT. Y .OR. X+Y .GT. Z) .AND. .NOT. (B1 .EQV. B2 .OR. B3).

Following the order of precedence, etc., specified above, each expression is evaluated thus:

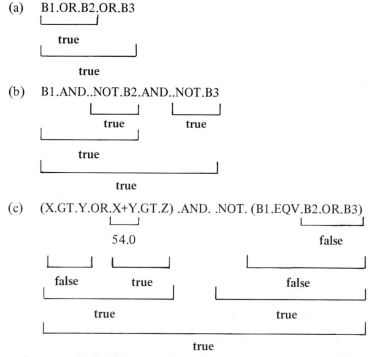

A value of **true** results in all three cases.

The discerning reader will have noted from Example 16.5, and some of the earlier examples, that there is also an order of precedence among groups of operators of *different types*, e.g. in the logical expression

$$X \text{ .GT. } Y \text{ .OR. } X+Y \text{ .GT. } Z$$

the *arithmetic operator* + is first applied, then the *relational operators* .GT., and finally the *logical operator* .OR.. The order of precedence is in fact as described in the following table:

Operator group	Precedence
Arithmetic	highest
Character	.
Relational	:
Logical	lowest

Example 16.6　　In evaluating the logical expression

$$A-B \text{ .GT. } 46.5 \text{ .OR. } I \text{ .NE. } J \text{ .AND. } C1//C2 \text{ .EQ. 'ALPHA'}$$

the arithmetic operator − is applied first; then the concatenation operator //; then the relational operators .GT., .NE., and .EQ.; then the logical operator .AND.; and finally the logical operator .OR..

Logical assignment statements

As well as their occurrence in block IF statements (Chapter 9) and logical IF statements (Chapter 23), logical expressions may also occur in *logical assignment statements* which have the form

$$v = \text{logical expression}$$

where *v* is the name of a *logical variable*, or *logical array element*. When a logical assignment statement is executed the logical expression on the right-hand side is evaluated and the resulting value (**true** or **false**) is assigned to the variable or array element whose name occurs on the left-hand side.

Example 16.7　　The following are permissible logical assignment statements.

　(a)　TEST = A .GT. B .OR. I .NE. J+17
　(b)　FLAG = (COS(X) .LT. 0.2) .AND. ((X+Y)**3 .GE. 1.6)
　(c)　MARKER = .NOT. (A+B .GT. C)
　(d)　SIGNAL = .NOT. FLAG .AND. TEST .OR. MARKER

Input and output of logical values

The edit descriptor L*w*, where *w* is the field width, is used for the formatted input and output of values for logical variables and logical array elements.

　For formatted input the appropriate field may contain optional leading blanks, optionally followed by a decimal point. The character T (for **true**) or F (for **false**) must then occur, optionally followed by other characters which have no effect on the logical value being read.

　For formatted output, on the other hand, the receiving field will consist of (*w* − 1) blanks followed by the character T or the character F as appropriate.

Example 16.8　　The following are acceptable input fields for the formatted input of logical values using the edit descriptor L8:

b.TRUE.b	bbbFALSE
.TRUE.bb	.Fbbbbbb
TRUEbbbb	b.F.bbbb
Tbbbbbbb	Fbbbbbbb
bbbbbbbT	FAULTYbb

The use of any of the fields specified in the first column would cause the corresponding logical variable to be assigned the value **true**, whereas any field in the second column would cause it to be assigned the value **false**.

For *list directed* input and output of logical values, the rules are very similar to those described above. Not surprisingly for list directed input, the optional characters after the mandatory T or F must contain neither *slashes* nor *commas*. For list directed output, on the other hand, a T or F is output as appropriate.

Simple examples involving logical facilities

In this Section several simple examples which involve the use of logical facilities are considered.

Example 16.9 Given as input data in free format are the examination results for a particular group of candidates. Each input record contains four integer values, the first being a candidate identification number, and the remaining three values being the candidate's marks in Mathematics, Physics, and Chemistry. To terminate the data, the last input record contains −1, −1, −1, −1. Write a FORTRAN 77 program which prints out

  (a) the total number of candidates;
  (b) the candidate identification number and marks of any candidate scoring more than 75 in *at least two* subjects;
  (c) the number of candidates whose marks satisfy the criterion specified in (b) above.

The following algorithm is reasonably self-explanatory:

```
assign 0 to COUNT1, COUNT2
read a record
loop while not the final record do
        {add 1 to COUNT1
        assign maths mark > 75 to the (logical) variable T1
        assign physics mark > 75 to the (logical) variable T2
        assign chemistry mark > 75 to the (logical) variable T3
        assign ((T1 and T2) or (T2 and T3) or (T3 and T1)) to GOOD
        if GOOD then
                {print candidate number and the three marks
                add 1 to COUNT2}
        read a record}
print COUNT1, COUNT2
```

It leads to the following FORTRAN 77 program:

```
PROGRAM MARKS
INTEGER COUNT1,COUNT2,CN,P,C
LOGICAL T1,T2,T3,GOOD
COUNT1=0
```

```
        COUNT2=0
        READ*,CN,M,P,C
100  IF (CN.NE.-1)THEN
            COUNT1=COUNT1+1
            T1=M.GT.75
            T2=P.GT.75
            T3=C.GT.75
            GOOD=(T1.AND.T2).OR.(T2.AND.T3).OR.(T3.AND.T1)
            IF (GOOD) THEN
                WRITE(*,'('' '',I6,3I4)') CN,M,P,C
                COUNT2=COUNT2 + 1
            END IF
            READ*,CN,M,P,C
            GO TO 100
        END IF
        WRITE(*,'('' '',2I6)')COUNT1,COUNT2
        END
```

Note that the logical variables T1, T2, T3, and GOOD are not strictly necessary, and could have been avoided by replacing the five statements from

$$T1 = M.GT.75$$

to

$$IF (GOOD) THEN$$

by

$$IF(((M.GT.75).AND.(P.GT.75)).OR.$$
$$+ \quad ((P.GT.75).AND.(C.GT.75)).OR.$$
$$+ \quad ((C.GT.75).AND.(M.GT.75))) THEN$$

The reader is left to decide which is preferable!

Example 16.10 Write a function subprogram QUAD to examine the *non-zero* coordinates of a point (x, y), and to return the value 1, 2, 3, or 4 depending on the quadrant in which the point lies, using the usual convention:

Basically the value 1 is to be returned if $x > 0$ **and** $y > 0$, the value 2 is to be returned if $x < 0$ **and** $y > 0$, etc. This leads to the program unit:

```
        INTEGER FUNCTION QUAD(X,Y)
        LOGICAL XPOS,YPOS
```

```
XPOS = X .GT. 0.0

YPOS = Y .GT. 0.0

IF (XPOS.AND.YPOS) THEN

        QUAD = 1

    ELSE IF (.NOT.XPOS.AND.YPOS) THEN

        QUAD = 2

    ELSE IF (.NOT.XPOS.AND..NOT.YPOS) THEN

        QUAD = 3

    ELSE

        QUAD = 4

END IF

END
```

Example 16.11   Write a function subprogram LEAPYR to return the value **true** if a given year Y is a leap year and to return the value **false** otherwise.

It is known that a year Y is a leap year if it is divisible by 4, *unless* Y is a century year, e.g. 1800, 1900, 2000, etc., in which case it must be divisible by 400. In logical terms this may be expressed by stating that the year Y is a leap year if *either* of the following conditions hold:

(a)   Y is divisible by 4 but not by 100;
(b)   Y is divisible by 400.

This leads to the program unit:

```
LOGICAL FUNCTION LEAPYR(Y)

INTEGER Y

LOGICAL Y4,Y100,Y400

Y4 = MOD(Y,4) .EQ. 0

Y100 = MOD(Y,100) .EQ. 0

Y400 = MOD(Y,400) .EQ. 0

LEAPYR = (Y4 .AND. .NOT. Y100) .OR. Y400

END
```

Note the use of the 'remaindering' function MOD in logical assignment statements such as Y4 = MOD(Y,4) .EQ. 0.

Exercise 16

1   Evaluate the following logical expressions given that B1 = **true**, B2 = **true**, B3 = **false**, B4 = **false**, I = $-$ 17, J = 3, and K = 20:

(a)   B1.AND.B2.AND. (I.GT.J)
(b)   .NOT.(B1.OR.B3) .OR. (B4.OR.(J$-$I).EQ.K)
(c)   ((B1.OR.B2).AND.(B1.OR.B3)).EQV.(B1.OR.(B2.AND.B3))

2   Remove unnecessary parentheses from the three logical expressions listed in question 1.

3   Given as input data in free format are the examination results for a particular group of candidates. Each input record contains five integer values, the first being a candidate identification number and the remaining four values being the candidate's marks in English, Mathematics, Physics, and Chemistry. To terminate the data, the last input record contains $-1, -1, -1, -1, -1$.

     It is required to output the candidate identification numbers and marks of all candidates whose marks satisfy *all* of the following conditions:

    (a)   there is at least one mark greater than 90;
    (b)   no mark is less than 60;
    (c)   the average mark for the four examinations is greater than 75.

Design an appropriate algorithm and write the corresponding FORTRAN 77 program.

4   With reference to Example 16.10, rewrite the function subprogram QUAD to return the value 0 if the point (x, y) lies on either axis.

5   Write a subroutine TRIANG(A,B,C,AREA,FLAG) which

    (a)   if the values of A, B, and C are the lengths of the sides of a genuine triangle sets FLAG equal to **true** and AREA equal to the area of the triangle using the formula

$$AREA = \sqrt{s(s-a)(s-b)(s-c)} \qquad \text{where } s = \tfrac{1}{2}(a+b+c)$$

    (b)   if the values of A, B, and C are not the lengths of the sides of a genuine triangle, sets FLAG to **false** and AREA equal to 0.

6   Write a function subprogram CHECK(D,M,Y) to return the value **true** if D/M/Y is a valid date in this century, and **false** otherwise. Assume the existence of the function subprogram LEAPYR (see Example 16.11).

17 Double precision facilities

An expert is a person who avoids the small errors while sweeping on to the grand fallacy. (*Weinberg's Corollary*)

This chapter contains a description of the double precision facilities provided in FORTRAN 77. The majority of programmers seldom, if ever, require to use double precision arithmetic since the precision of real arithmetic in most modern computer systems is adequate for most purposes. There are occasions, however, when results are required to a precision greater than that provided by normal real arithmetic, or when *intermediate* calculations have to be performed with greater than normal precision in order to obtain meaningful output from a program. The latter is particularly relevant in connection with the programming of *ill conditioned* problems, i.e. problems the output from which is extremely sensitive to small changes in the input data.

As has been mentioned already, most implementations of FORTRAN 77 hold the values of double precision constants, variables, and array elements with about *twice* the precision of real values. The FORTRAN 77 Standard, however, merely specifies that double precision values should be held with *greater* precision than real values. It is therefore important to ascertain, for the implementation of FORTRAN 77 that is being used, the precision of double precision values.

Double precision constants

As described in Chapter 4, a double precision constant in FORTRAN 77 may be written in one of two ways:

(a) as a basic real constant (see Chapter 4) followed by a double precision exponent;
(b) as an integer constant followed by a double precision exponent;

where, in each case, a double precision exponent is defined to be the letter D followed by an (optionally signed) integer constant, and represents a power of 10.

Example 17.1 The following table shows valid double precision constants in FORTRAN 77.

Constant	Interpretation
−6.8D−7	-6.8×10^{-7}
5D12	5×10^{12}
2.7182818284590452D0	2.7182818284590452

Note once again that it is not merely enough to write a double precision constant with a larger-than-usual number of digits. The double precision exponent *must* be present, even when, as in the last example above, the integer constant after the D is zero.

Double precision variables, arrays, and type statements

The naming and declaration of variables and arrays of type DOUBLE PRECISION has been covered already in Chapters 5 and 10. The following example will remind the reader of what is involved.

Example 17.2   A FORTRAN 77 program unit might contain the following type and DIMENSION statements:

        DOUBLE PRECISION D1,D2,D3,DVALS(−3:10),MAT,MAXVAL
        DIMENSION MAT(20,20)

indicating that

(a)   D1, D2, D3, and MAXVAL are the names of variables of type DOUBLE PRECISION;

(b) $DVALS_{-3}$, $DVALS_{-2}$, $DVALS_{-1}$, $\cdots$, $DVALS_{10}$ is a one-dimensional array, the elements of which are of type DOUBLE PRECISION;

(c)   MAT is a 20×20 matrix, the elements of which are also of type DOUBLE PRECISION.

The DIMENSION statement may, of course, be avoided by writing instead of the above:

        DOUBLE PRECISION D1,D2,D3,DVALS(−3:10),MAT(20,20),MAXVAL

Useful intrinsic functions

The following table lists those intrinsic functions which are of particular interest when handling double precision quantities in a FORTRAN 77 program unit.

Note that† :

(a)   ATAN2 (x_1, x_2) has already been defined in Chapter 12. It returns the value of $\tan^{-1}(x_1/x_2)$ in the range $-\pi <$ result $\leqslant \pi$ corresponding to the

---

† Using *generic* names whenever possible, although *specific* names could also have been used.

Intrinsic function	Definition	Generic name	Specific name	Number of arguments	Type of argument	Type of function
Square root	$\sqrt{x}\ (x \geqslant 0)$	SQRT	DSQRT	1	DOUBLE	DOUBLE
Exponential	exp (x)	EXP	DEXP	1	DOUBLE	DOUBLE
Natural logarithm	$\log_e x\ (x > 0)$	LOG	DLOG	1	DOUBLE	DOUBLE
Common logarithm	$\log_{10} x\ (x > 0)$	LOG10	DLOG10	1	DOUBLE	DOUBLE
Sine	sin x (x in radians)	SIN	DSIN	1	DOUBLE	DOUBLE
Cosine	cos x (x in radians)	COS	DCOS	1	DOUBLE	DOUBLE
Tangent	tan x (x in radians)	TAN	DTAN	1	DOUBLE	DOUBLE
Arcsine	principal value of $\sin^{-1} x$ ($|x| \leqslant 1$)	ASIN	DASIN	1	DOUBLE	DOUBLE
Arccosine	principal value of $\cos^{-1} x$ ($|x| \leqslant 1$)	ACOS	DACOS	1	DOUBLE	DOUBLE
Arctangent	principal value of $\tan^{-1} x$	ATAN	DATAN	1	DOUBLE	DOUBLE
Arctangent	See note (a) below	ATAN2	DATAN2	2	DOUBLE	DOUBLE
Hyperbolic sine	sinh x	SINH	DSINH	1	DOUBLE	DOUBLE
Hyperbolic cosine	cosh x	COSH	DCOSH	1	DOUBLE	DOUBLE
Hyperbolic tangent	tanh x	TANH	DTANH	1	DOUBLE	DOUBLE
Conversion to double precision	See note (b) below	DBLE	–	1	INTEGER	DOUBLE
			–	1	REAL	DOUBLE
			–	1	DOUBLE	DOUBLE
			–	1	COMPLEX	DOUBLE
Conversion to integer	See note (c) below	INT	IDINT	1	DOUBLE	INTEGER
Conversion to real	See note (d) below	REAL	SNGL	1	DOUBLE	REAL
Conversion to complex	See Chapter 18	CMPLX	–	1 or 2	DOUBLE	COMPLEX
Absolute value	x if $x \geqslant 0$, $-x$ if $x < 0$	ABS	DABS	1	DOUBLE	DOUBLE
Double precision product	$x_1 x_2$ evaluated to double precision	–	DPROD	2	REAL	DOUBLE
Truncation	See note (e) below	AINT	DINT	1	DOUBLE	DOUBLE
Nearest whole number	See note (f) below	ANINT	DNINT	1	DOUBLE	DOUBLE
Nearest integer	See note (f) below	NINT	IDNINT	1	DOUBLE	INTEGER
Remaindering	See Chapter 12	MOD	DMOD	2	DOUBLE	DOUBLE
Transfer of sign	$|x_1|$ if $x_2 \geqslant 0$ $-|x_1|$ if $x_2 < 0$	SIGN	DSIGN	2	DOUBLE	DOUBLE
Positive difference	$x_1 - x_2$ if $x_1 > x_2$ 0 if $x_1 \leqslant x_2$	DIM	DDIM	2	DOUBLE	DOUBLE
Largest value	max $(x_1, x_2, \ldots)$	MAX	DMAX1	2	DOUBLE	DOUBLE
Smallest value	min $(x_1, x_2, \ldots)$	MIN	DMIN1	2	DOUBLE	DOUBLE

quadrant in which the point (x_2, x_1) lies. At least one of x_1 and x_2 must be *non-zero*.

(b)   If x is of type DOUBLE PRECISION, DBLE$(x) = x$. If x is of type INTEGER or type REAL, DBLE(x) is x converted to double precision form. If x is of type COMPLEX, DBLE(x) is the *real part* of x converted to double precision form.

(c)   INT(x) is obtained by *truncating* the double precision quantity x to integer form.

(d)   REAL(x) is obtained by converting the double precision quantity x to real form, retaining in the process as much precision as possible.

(e)   AINT(x) truncates the double precision quantity x to integer form, the integer then being converted to double precision form.

(f)   ANINT(x) correctly rounds the double precision quantity x to the nearest integer and returns it in *double precision* form. NINT(x), on the other hand, correctly rounds the double precision quantity to the nearest integer and returns it in *integer* form.

The reader is advised to peruse again Examples 12.6 to 12.18 in which the actions of many of the above intrinsic functions are explained with *real* arguments. Analogous effects, of course, occur when double precision arguments are used.

Arithmetic expressions and assignment statements involving double precision quantities

Double precision constants, double precision variables, double precision array elements, etc. may be freely used as operands in arithmetic expressions (Chapter 6). Operands of different types may also be combined together using the operators $+$, $-$, $*$, $/$, and $**$ with the important exception that an operand of type DOUBLE PRECISION must never be combined with an operand of type COMPLEX.

An *implicit* type conversion usually occurs when an operand of type REAL or INTEGER is combined with an operand of type DOUBLE PRECISION using one of the operators $+$, $-$, $*$, $/$, or $**$. In the case of the first four of these operators, the conversion is always from type REAL or INTEGER to type DOUBLE PRECISION, i.e. *two operands of type DOUBLE PRECISION are eventually combined together to produce a result of type DOUBLE PRECISION*. This also applies in the case of the operator $**$, with the exception that when a double precision operand is raised to an integer power, the integer power is not converted, although the result will again be of type DOUBLE PRECISION.

Example 17.3   If D1 and D2 are of type DOUBLE PRECISION, A, B, and C of type REAL, and N of type INTEGER, the following are permissible arithmetic expressions in FORTRAN 77:

(a)   D1**3 + D2**3 − 6*D1*D2

(b)   A*SINH(2.6*D1−17.3) − D2**(B/C) + 3.654*D1

(c)   (D1/D2)**N + 1.652D2*A + EXP(D1+D2)

(d)   D1 + DPROD (B,C)

Note, for example in (b) above, that when the *generic* function name SINH is used with a double precision argument a double precision result is returned.

In *arithmetic assignment statements* (Chapter 6) of the form

$$v = \text{arithmetic expression}$$

once the arithmetic expression on the right-hand side has been evaluated its value must be assigned to the variable or array element v. If the value of the arithmetic expression is of type DOUBLE PRECISION and v is of type REAL, INTEGER, or COMPLEX an *implicit type conversion* must occur before assignment can be made. Precisely what happens is indicated in the following table:

Type of v	Value assigned to v
REAL	REAL(e)
INTEGER	INT(e)
COMPLEX	CMPLX(e)

where e is the value of the arithmetic expression, the function REAL, INT, or CMPLX being invoked as appropriate to carry out the type conversion, as described in the previous section. Note that it is permissible to assign a double precision value to a complex variable or array element, although it is not permissible to combine together a double precision operand and a complex operand using one of the operators +, −, *, /, or **.

Similarly if v is of type DOUBLE PRECISION and the value of the arithmetic expression on the right-hand side of the assignment statement

$$v = \text{arithmetic expression}$$

is of type REAL, INTEGER, or COMPLEX, the value of the right-hand side is converted to double precision form *before* assignment to v. Not surprisingly the conversion is achieved by applying the intrinsic function DBLE.

Example 17.4   If FAC, DVAL, D1, and D2 are of type DOUBLE PRECISION, U and V of type REAL, and N of type INTEGER, the following are valid arithmetic assignment statements in FORTRAN 77:

   (a)   FAC = (2.6D0*COS(D1) − 5.7*LOG(D2))/(D1−D2)
   (b)   DVAL = (D1+D2)**N + DPROD(U,V) − 16.825D−7
   (c)   V = D1**N + (D1−D2)/(D1+D2)

Example 17.5   If D is of type DOUBLE PRECISION, comment on the three statements

   (a)   D = 1/3
   (b)   D = 1.0/3.0
   (c)   D = 1D0/3D0

In (a) the right-hand side is evaluated using *integer division*, producing the result 0 which is converted to double precision form and assigned to D.

In (b) the right-hand side is evaluated using *real division*, producing the result 0.333 . . . 3 which is converted to double precision form, say 0.333 . . . 3000 . . . 0, and assigned to D.

In (c) the right hand side is evaluated to produce a double precision result, 0.333 . . . 3333 . . . 3, which is assigned to D.

Note that (c) assigns a much more *accurate* approximation of one-third to D than (b) does. This is a point often missed by inexperienced programmers who sometimes naively believe that when a real value is converted to double precision form its accuracy is somehow magically enhanced, whereas in actual fact what happens is equivalent to padding out the value with extra zeros on the right.

Example 17.6   If DPI is of type DOUBLE PRECISION, the statement

$$DPI=4*ATAN(1.0D0)$$

will give the variable DPI a value which approximates very closely to the value of π. Note that, since the generic function name ATAN has to be used with a double precision argument to return a double precision result, it is important to write 1.0D0, rather than 1.0 to obtain maximum accuracy.

Double precision operands in arithmetic relational expressions

Operands of type DOUBLE PRECISION are permitted in arithmetic relational expressions (see Chapter 9). However, an arithmetic relational expression must not contain one operand of type DOUBLE PRECISION and one of type COMPLEX.

Input and output of double precision values

Unlike FORTRAN 66 there is no special edit descriptor for the input and output of double precision values. F, E, D, and G edit descriptors may be used *as for real values,* and the reader is referred to Chapters 7 and 14 for detailed information. Essentially in both cases an input field is read in and converted to the appropriate internal form (REAL or DOUBLE PRECISION) *specified by the type of the corresponding list item.* Similarly, on output, the value of the appropriate list item of type REAL or DOUBLE precision is converted *from* internal form and output.

Real and double precision values are also handled, as described above, when *list directed* input/output is performed. The reader is therefore referred once again to Chapters 7 and 14 for detailed information.

Simple examples involving double precision facilities

In this section some simple examples are given to illustrate the use of double precision facilities in FORTRAN 77.

Example 17.7   Write a program to find, as accurately as double precision arithmetic will permit, the root near 2 of the famous† equation of Wallis, $x^3 - 2x - 5 = 0$, using the Newton–Raphson formula

$$x_{n+1} = x_n - \frac{f(x_n)}{f'(x_n)}$$

In this case

$$f(x) = x^3 - 2x - 5$$

$$f'(x) = 3x^2 - 2$$

so that the Newton–Raphson formula becomes

$$x_{n+1} = x_n - \left\{ \frac{x_n^3 - 2x_n - 5}{3x_n^2 - 2} \right\}$$

leading to the algorithm

> assign appropriate (machine dependent) tolerance to tol
> assign 2 x tol to delta
> assign 2 to x_0
> **loop while** |delta| ⩾ tol **do**
>   {assign $(x_0^3 - 2x_0 - 5)/(3x_0^2 - 2)$ to delta
>   assign x_0 – delta to x_0}
> print x_0

and hence to the FORTRAN 77 program

```
PROGRAM WALLIS

DOUBLE PRECISION X0,DELTA,TOL

PARAMETER(TOL=0.5D-20)

DELTA = 2*TOL

X0=2

100     IF (ABS(DELTA).GE.TOL)THEN

            DELTA=(X0**3-2*X0-5)/(3*X0*X0-2)

            X0=X0-DELTA

            GO TO 100

        END IF

        WRITE(*,'('' '',F25.20)') X0

        END
```

Note how the machine dependent constant 0.5D–20 has been specified in a PARAMETER statement, enabling a simple change to be made, if required, by the precision of double precision arithmetic in an implementation of FORTRAN 77. Note also that the initial value given to DELTA is unimportant, provided that it is greater in magnitude than the value of TOL.

† According to de Morgan in 1861: 'Invent a numerical method, neglect to show how it works on this equation, and you are a pilgrim who does not come in at the little wicket.'

Example 17.8   Given the elements $x_1, x_2, \ldots, x_n, y_1, y_2, \ldots, y_n$ of two vectors x and y of type REAL, the effect of round-off errors in computing the inner-product

$$x_1y_1 + x_2y_2 + x_3y_3 + \ldots + x_ny_n$$

can be reduced by evaluating the product terms as *double precision* quantities, which are added together to produce a double precision result which is *then* rounded to single precision form. Write a function subprogram XYPROD(X,Y,N) to achieve this.

A possible function subprogram is as follows:

```
FUNCTION XYPROD(X,Y,N)

REAL X(N),Y(N)

DOUBLE PRECISION SUM

SUM = 0

DO 100 I=1,N

        SUM=SUM+DPROD(X(I),Y(I))

100  CONTINUE

XYPROD=SUM

END
```

Note that it would be incorrect to initialize SUM to 0 by using a DATA statement thus

DATA SUM/0/

since SUM would have an *undefined* initial value on every reference of XYPROD after the first.

Example 17.9   A and B are two matrices, of orders $m \times n$ and $n \times p$ respectively, whose elements are of type DOUBLE PRECISION. Write a subroutine subprogram MATMUL(A,B,M,N,P,C) to evaluate the product matrix C=AB.

Since, by the usual formula

$$c_{ij} = a_{i1}b_{1j} + a_{i2}b_{2j} + \ldots + a_{in}b_{nj}$$

for $i = 1, 2, \ldots, m$ and $j = 1, 2, \ldots, p$, the following algorithm will be used:

loop for $i = 1, 2, \ldots, m$ **do**
$\quad$ {**loop for** $j = 1, 2, \ldots, p$ **do**
$\quad\quad$ {assign 0 to S
$\quad\quad$ **loop for** $k = 1, 2, \ldots, n$ **do**
$\quad\quad\quad$ {add $a_{ik}b_{kj}$ to S }
$\quad\quad$ assign S to c_{ij} }}

This leads to the subroutine:

```
SUBROUTINE MATMUL(A,B,M,N,P,C)

INTEGER P

DOUBLE PRECISION A(M,N),B(N,P),C(M,P),S

DO  100  I=1,M
```

```
      DO  100  J=1,P

         S=0

         DO  200  K=1,N

            S=S+A(I,K)*B(K,J)

200      CONTINUE

         C(I,J)=S

100   CONTINUE

      END
```

Exercise 17

1 (a)   Comment on the function references SQRT(2), SQRT(2.0), SQRT(2.0D0), DSQRT(2.0), and DSQRT(2.0D0).

   (b)   If X = 2.8D0 what are the values of AINT(X), ANINT(X), and NINT(X)?

   (c)   If X = -3.6 + 2.8i what is the value of DBLE(X)?

2 Write a FORTRAN 77 program to tabulate the double precision values of $\cosh x$, $\sinh x$, and $\cosh^2 x - \sinh^2 x - 1$ for $x = 0(0.1)10$.

3 Write a subroutine subprogram MATVEC(A,X,N,Y) to form the vector y defined by $y = Ax$ where A is an $n \times n$ matrix and x an $n \times 1$ vector, the elements of both A and x being of type **REAL**. Use the function **DPROD** to evaluate all sums of products as accurately as possible.

4 Write a FORTRAN 77 program to sum, until terms are less than 10^{-8} in magnitude, the series

$$59 + x - \frac{x^4}{4!} + \frac{x^7}{7!} - \frac{x^{10}}{10!} + \frac{x^{13}}{13!} - \ldots$$

when $x = 32.0438$, (a) using real arithmetic, and (b) using double precision arithmetic. Explain any discrepancy in your results.

5 The mathematician Gauss showed that the integral $I(k)$ defined by

$$I(k) = \int_0^1 \frac{dx}{\sqrt{(1 - x^2)(1 - k^2 x^2)}}$$

could be evaluated, for a given value of k in the range $0 \leqslant k < 1$, as follows

   (a)   let $x_0 = 1$, $y_0 = \sqrt{1 - k^2}$

   (b)   evaluate $x_1, y_1, x_2, y_2, x_3, y_3, \ldots$ using the recurrence relations

$$x_{n+1} = \tfrac{1}{2}(x_n + y_n), \quad y_{n+1} = \sqrt{x_n y_n}$$

   (c)   then

$$\lim_{n \to \infty} x_n = \lim_{n \to \infty} y_n = \frac{\pi}{2I(k)}$$

Write a function subprogram EINT(K) to return the double precision value of $I(k)$ for a given value of the real variable k in the range indicated above. Then write a main program to tabulate $I(k)$ for $k = 0(0.001)0.9$.

18 Complex number facilities

The cost of a complex system is very, very real. (*Glaser's Law*)

One of the major attractions of FORTRAN 77, as far as some practitioners of scientific computing are concerned, is that the language contains excellent, easy to use facilities for handling complex arithmetic. The purpose of this chapter is to explain these facilities in detail. The chapter may, of course, be ignored by readers whose programs are unlikely to involve the use of complex arithmetic.

Throughout this chapter it is assumed that the reader will have the necessary mathematical background required to understand the use of complex numbers and the complex intrinsic functions. Further, the mathematical convention of using i to represent $\sqrt{-1}$ has been adopted. Readers with an engineering background may be more familiar with the use of j.

Complex constants

Complex constants have already been covered in Chapter 4. To recap, a complex constant is written as two *real* or *integer constants* separated by a comma and surrounded by parentheses. The first of the two constants in the parentheses represents the *real* part of the complex number, and the second the *imaginary* part.

Example 18.1 The complex constants in the following table are valid in FORTRAN 77.

Constant	Interpretation
(3, −4)	$3-4i$
(1.763, 25)	$1.763 + 25i$
(0, −1)	$-i$
(3E4, 6.5)	$3 \times 10^4 + 6.5i$

Complex variables, arrays, and type statements

The naming and declaration of variables and arrays of type COMPLEX have been covered already in Chapters 5 and 10. The following example will remind the reader what is involved.

Example 18.2 A FORTRAN 77 program unit might contain the following type and DIMENSION statements:

        COMPLEX   Z1,Z2,CVALS(0:20),W,CTRANS
        DIMENSION CTRANS(10,15)

indicating that:

(a) Z1, Z2, and W are the names of three variables of type COMPLEX;

(b) $CVALS_0$, $CVALS_1$, $CVALS_2$, ..., $CVALS_{20}$ is a one-dimensional array, the elements of which are of type COMPLEX;

(c) CTRANS is a 10×15 matrix, the elements of which are also of type COMPLEX.

Of course, the DIMENSION statement is not strictly necessary, an equivalent form being:

        COMPLEX Z1,Z2, CVALS(0:20), W, CTRANS(10,15)

Useful intrinsic functions

The following table lists a number of intrinsic functions which are of particular interest when handling complex quantities in a FORTRAN 77 program unit.

Intrinsic function	Definition	Generic name	Specific name	Number of arguments	Type of argument	Type of function
Square root	$\sqrt{z}$ with real part of result $\geqslant 0$; if real part of result = 0 then imaginary part of result $\geqslant 0$	SQRT	CSQRT	1	COMPLEX	COMPLEX
Exponential	exp(z)	EXP	CEXP	1	COMPLEX	COMPLEX
Natural logarithm	$\log_e z$ ($z \neq 0$) with imaginary part of result in range $-\pi$ < imaginary part $\leqslant \pi$. See note (a) below	LOG	CLOG	1	COMPLEX	COMPLEX
Sine	sin z	SIN	CSIN	1	COMPLEX	COMPLEX
Cosine	cos z	COS	CCOS	1	COMPLEX	COMPLEX
Conversion to complex	See note (b) below	CMPLX	–	1 or 2	INTEGER	COMPLEX
			–	1 or 2	REAL	COMPLEX
			–	1 or 2	DOUBLE	COMPLEX
			–	1	COMPLEX	COMPLEX
Conversion to integer	See note (c) below	INT	–	1	COMPLEX	INTEGER
Conversion to real	See note (d) below	REAL	–	1	COMPLEX	REAL
Conversion to double precision	See note (e) below	DBLE	–	1	COMPLEX	DOUBLE
Modulus	$|z| = + \sqrt{x^2 + y^2}$ where $z = x + iy$	ABS	CABS	1	COMPLEX	REAL
Imaginary part	y where $z = x + iy$	–	AIMAG	1	COMPLEX	REAL
Conjugate	$x - iy$ where $z = x + iy$	–	CONJG	1	COMPLEX	COMPLEX

Note that:

(a)   In using the function LOG (or CLOG) with a complex argument, the imaginary part of the result is π only when the real part of the argument is less than 0 and the imaginary part of the argument is equal to 0.

(b)   The intrinsic function CMPLX may have one or two arguments. If it has one argument, it must be of type INTEGER, REAL, DOUBLE PRECISION, or COMPLEX. If it has two arguments, they must both be of the *same* type, INTEGER, REAL, or DOUBLE PRECISION. If a_1 is of type COMPLEX, CMPLX$(a_1) = a_1$. In all other cases, CMPLX(a_1) is the same as CMPLX(a_1, a_2) with $a_2 = 0$, and CMPLX(a_1, a_2) is defined to be the complex number whose real part is a_1 converted to *real* form and whose imaginary part is a_2 converted to *real* form.

(c)   If $z = x + iy$ then INT(z) is obtained by *truncating* x to integer form.

(d)   If $z = x + iy$ then REAL$(z) = x$. Thus REAL may not only be regarded as 'converting to real form' but also as 'obtaining the real part' (cf. AIMAG).

(e)   DBLE(z) is unlikely to be used frequently. Its effect, where $z = x + iy$, is to convert the real part x to double precision form.

Example 18.3   The following may be helpful in clarifying the effects of some of the intrinsic functions in the above table:

(a)   SQRT$((-3,-4)) = 1-2i$, since $(-3-4i)^{1/2} = \pm(1-2i)$ and sign is chosen to make real part of result $\geqslant 0$.

(b)   If Z has the value $1 + i$, then LOG(Z) returns the value $\frac{1}{2}\log_e 2 + i(\pi/4)$, since $\log_e(1 + i) = \log_e\{\sqrt{2}\exp[i((\pi/4) + 2k\pi)]\} = \frac{1}{2}\log_e 2 + i((\pi/4) + 2k\pi)$ and the value of k is chosen to make imaginary part of result lie in range $-\pi$ to π.

(c)   If A and B are of type REAL, SQRT$((A,B))$ is *invalid* since (A,B) is not an expression of type COMPLEX in FORTRAN 77. A correct version of what was intended is SQRT(CMPLX(A,B)).

Arithmetic expressions and assignment statements involving complex quantities

Complex constants, complex variables, complex array elements, etc. may be freely used as operands in *arithmetic expressions* (Chapter 6). Operands of different types may also be combined together using the operators $+$, $-$, $*$, $/$, and $**$, with the important exception that an operand of type COMPLEX must never be combined with an operand of type DOUBLE PRECISION.

Not surprisingly, an *implicit* type conversion usually occurs when an operand of type REAL or INTEGER is combined with an operand of type COMPLEX using one of the operators $+$, $-$, $*$, $/$, or $**$. In the case of the first four of these operators the conversion is always from type REAL or INTEGER to type COMPLEX, i.e. *two operands of type COMPLEX are eventually combined together to produce a result of type COMPLEX*. This also applies in the case of the operator $**$, with the exception that when a complex operand is raised to an integer power, the integer power is not converted, although the result will again be of type COMPLEX. Note also that, whenever C_1**C_2 has to be evaluated, where C_1 and C_2 are of type COMPLEX, a *principal value* is produced via the formula $C_1**C_2 = EXP(C_2*LOG(C_1))$ where EXP and LOG are as defined in the previous section on intrinsic functions.

Example 18.4   If Z is of type COMPLEX, A, B, and C of type REAL, and N of type INTEGER, the following are permissible arithmetic expressions in FORTRAN 77:

(a)   A*Z**2+B*Z+C
(b)   (2*SIN(Z)+3*COS(Z))/(Z**2+1)+(1.6,−2.4)
(c)   Z**N+1/(Z**N)
(d)   A**Z−3.654*A/Z+21.652

Note, for example in (b) above, that when the *generic* function name SIN is used with a complex argument a complex result is returned. By way of illustration (a) would be evaluated to produce a result of type COMPLEX by converting A, B, and C from type REAL to type COMPLEX, e.g. A is converted to CMPLX(A,0.0) and then combined with Z**2 using the operator *, etc.

In *arithmetic assignment statements* (Chapter 6) of the form

$$v = \text{arithmetic expression}$$

once the arithmetic expression on the right-hand side has been evaluated, its value must be assigned to the variable or array element v. Once again, if the value of the arithmetic expression is of type COMPLEX and v is of type REAL, INTEGER, or DOUBLE PRECISION, an *implicit type conversion* must occur before the assignment can be made. Precisely what happens is indicated in the following table:

Type of v	Value assigned to v
REAL	REAL (e)
INTEGER	INT (e)
DOUBLE PRECISION	DBLE (e)

e is the value of the arithmetic expression and the function REAL, INT or DBLE is invoked as appropriate to carry out the type conversion, as described in the previous section. Note that it is permissible to assign a complex value to a double precision variable or array element, although it is not permissible to combine together a complex operand and a double precision operand using one of the operators +, −, *, /, or **.

Similarly if v is of type COMPLEX and the value of the arithmetic expression on the right-hand side of the assignment statement

$$v = \text{arithmetic expression}$$

is of type REAL, INTEGER, or DOUBLE PRECISION, the value of the right-hand side is converted to complex form *before* assignment to v. Not surprisingly the conversion is achieved by applying the intrinsic function CMPLX.

Example 18.5 If W, Z, Z1, and Z2 are of type COMPLEX, U and V of type REAL, and N of type INTEGER, the following are valid arithmetic assignment statements in FORTRAN 77:

    (a)   W = (COS(Z)–(2,3))/(Z**4+Z**2+(0,1))
    (b)   Z1 = CMPLX(U+SIN(V),U–SIN(V))+EXP(Z)
    (c)   Z2 = (EXP(Z)–Z**N)/(EXP(Z)–N*Z**(N–1))
    (d)   U = Z+1/Z

In case (d), Z+1/Z is evaluated and the real part of the result assigned to U.

Complex operands in arithmetic relational expressions

Operands of type COMPLEX are permitted in arithmetic relational expressions (see Chapter 9) provided that the relational operator being used is either .EQ. or .NE.. In addition, an arithmetic relational expression must not contain one operand of type COMPLEX and one of type DOUBLE PRECISION.

Note, however, that since complex values are essentially *pairs of real values*, comparisons using .EQ. or .NE. are dangerous, because of the finite precision of real arithmetic. Thus, for example, rather than writing

$$IF (Z1.EQ.Z2) THEN$$

it is much safer to write

$$IF (ABS(Z1–Z2).LT.TOL) THEN$$

where TOL is some small positive real quantity, e.g. $\frac{1}{2} \times 10^{-6}$.

Input and output of complex values

Remembering that a complex value is merely a *pair* of real values, the formatted input/output of complex values is particularly simple. *Two* F, E, D, or G edit descriptors are required, which may be different and which may be separated by non-repeatable edit descriptors.

Example 18.6 The variables Z1 and Z2 are of type COMPLEX. Then, if the input record containing the characters

$$bbb27.27bb–215.7bbbb–7.4bbb6.572$$

is read using the READ statement

$$READ(*,'(2F8.0,4X,F4.0,2X,F6.0)')Z1,Z2$$

Z1 is assigned the value $27.27–215.7i$ and Z2 is assigned the value $-7.4+6.572i$.

Example 18.7 If Z is a variable of type COMPLEX with the value $-2.16537 + 9.14285i$ the statement

$$WRITE(*,100) Z$$
$$100 \quad FORMAT('b',F8.5,'b+b(',F7.5,')I')$$

will produce the output

$- 2.16537b+b(9.14285)I$

For *list directed input* of complex values, the appropriate information on the input record must consist of a left parenthesis, followed by a pair of numeric input fields separated by a comma, followed by a right parenthesis. The first numeric input field contains the *real* part of the complex value, and the second the *imaginary* part. Each of the numeric input fields may also be preceded or followed by zero or more blank characters. In addition, the end of a record may occur between the first numeric input field and the comma, or between the comma and the second numeric input field.

As far as *list directed output* of complex values is concerned, any value output is enclosed in parentheses with a comma separating the real and imaginary parts. Implementation-dependent embedded blanks are also permitted. The FORTRAN 77 Standard (American National Standards Institute, 1978) should be consulted for more specific information.

Example 18.8   If Z1 and Z2 are variables of type COMPLEX, the input record

bb(−2.1,5.6)bbb(21.63b,b10.94)

might be read by the input statement

READ *, Z1,Z2

to assign Z1 the value $-2.1 + 5.6i$ and Z2 the value $21.63 + 10.94i$.

Simple examples involving complex facilities

In this section several simple examples are given to illustrate the use of complex facilities in FORTRAN 77 programs.

Example 18.9   Write a subroutine subprogram CXLIN(A1,B1,C1,A2,B2,C2,Z1,Z2, FLAG) to attempt to solve for z_1 and z_2 the pair of simultaneous linear equations

$$a_1 z_1 + b_1 z_2 = c_1$$

$$a_2 z_1 + b_2 z_2 = c_2$$

with complex coefficients a_1, b_1, c_1, a_2, b_2, and c_2. If a solution exists, the logical variable FLAG is to be set to **true**; if a solution does not exist, the logical variable FLAG is to be set to **false**, and Z1 and Z2 both to zero. Then write a main program calling CXLIN to solve n different pairs of simultaneous linear equations of the above form. Assume that the first input record contains the value of n, and that each of the remaining records contains values for a set of coefficients a_1, b_1, c_1, a_2, b_2, and c_2.

The simultaneous equations are easily solved by 'school algebra' elimination to give

$$z_1 = \frac{c_1 b_2 - c_2 b_1}{a_1 b_2 - a_2 b_1} \qquad z_2 = \frac{a_1 c_2 - a_2 c_1}{a_1 b_2 - a_2 b_1}$$

provided that $|a_1 b_2 - a_2 b_1| \neq 0$. This leads to the subroutine subprogram

```
SUBROUTINE CXLIN(A1,B1,C1,A2,B2,C2,Z1,Z2,FLAG)

COMPLEX A1,B1,C1,A2,B2,C2,Z1,Z2,DENOM

LOGICAL FLAG

DENOM = A1*B2 - A2*B1

IF ( ABS(DENOM).GT.1E-6) THEN

    FLAG=.TRUE.

    Z1 = (C1*B2-C2*B1)/DENOM

    Z2 = (A1*C2-A2*C1)/DENOM

                            ELSE


    FLAG=.FALSE.

    Z1=0

    Z2=0

END IF

END
```

A main program calling CXLIN can then be written thus:

```
PROGRAM SOLVER

LOGICAL FLAG

COMPLEX A1,B1,C1,A2,B2,C2,Z1,Z2

READ *,N

DO 100 I=1,N

    READ *,A1,B1,C1,A2,B2,C2

    WRITE(*,'('' COEFFICIENTS ARE'',6F15.10)')A1,B1,C1

    WRITE(*,'(''                  '',6F15.10)')A2,B2,C2

    CALL CXLIN(A1,B1,C1,A2,B2,C2,Z1,Z2,FLAG)

    IF (FLAG) THEN

        WRITE(*,'('' SOLUTION IS Z1 ='',2F15.10)')Z1

        WRITE(*,'(''            Z2 ='',2F15.10//)')Z2

                ELSE

        WRITE(*,'('' NO UNIQUE SOLUTION''//)')

    END IF

100 CONTINUE

    END
```

Figure 18.1 shows some simple card input data for the program. The corresponding output is reproduced in Figure 18.2 on page 232.

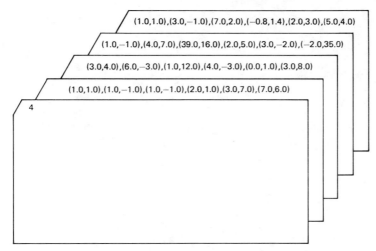

Figure 18.1   *Simple Input Data for SOLVER*

Example 18.10   The frequency-response function $G(i\omega)$ for a certain feedback system is given by the formula

$$G(i\omega) = \frac{200i(i\omega + 2)}{\omega^3(0.1i\omega + 1)(0.3i\omega + 1)(0.6i\omega + 1)(0.8i\omega + 1)}$$

where ω is the angular frequency in radians per second. Devise an algorithm and write a FORTRAN 77 program to tabulate the real and imaginary parts of G, the magnitude of G, and the amplitude of G for $\omega = \omega_0, h\omega_0, h^2\omega_0, h^3\omega_0, \ldots, \omega_1$.

A suitable algorithm is as follows:

```
print title
read ω₀, ω₁, h
print ω₀, ω₁, h
print column headings
assign ω₀ to ω
loop while ω ≤ ω₁ do
        {evaluate G, ABSG, ARGG
        print ω, real and imaginary parts of G, ABSG, ARGG
        assign hω to ω}
```

This leads to the FORTRAN 77 program:

```
PROGRAM FRTAB

COMPLEX I,G

PARAMETER (I = (0,1),PI = 3.14159265)

WRITE(*,'('' EVALUATION OF A FREQUENCY RESPONSE FUNCTION''//)')
```

```
COEFFICIENTS ARE   1.0000000000   1.0000000000   1.0000000000  -1.0000000000   1.0000000000  -1.0000000000
                   2.0000000000   1.0000000000   3.0000000000   7.0000000000   7.0000000000   6.0000000000
SOLUTION IS Z1 =   0.4470588235  -0.0117647059
            Z2 =   0.9882352941  -0.4470588235

COEFFICIENTS ARE   3.0000000000   4.0000000000   6.0000000000  -3.0000000000   1.0000000000  12.0000000000
                   4.0000000000  -3.0000000000   0.0000000000   1.0000000000   3.0000000000   8.0000000000
SOLUTION IS Z1 =  -0.1572413793   1.7268965517
            Z2 =   0.6206896552   1.5517241379

COEFFICIENTS ARE   1.0000000000  -1.0000000000   4.0000000000   7.0000000000  39.0000000000  16.0000000000
                   2.0000000000   5.0000000000   3.0000000000  -2.0000000000  -2.0000000000  35.0000000000
SOLUTION IS Z1 =   7.5227765727   4.9067245119
            Z2 =   3.6399132321  -1.7158351410

COEFFICIENTS ARE   1.0000000000   1.0000000000   3.0000000000  -1.0000000000   7.0000000000   2.0000000000
                  -0.8000000000   1.4000000000   2.0000000000   3.0000000000   5.0000000000   4.0000000000
NO UNIQUE SOLUTION
```

Figure 18.2 *Output from SOLVER*

```
      READ*,WO,W1,H
      WRITE(*,'('' WO ='',E12.4,''  W1 ='',E12.4,''  H ='',E12.4//)')
     +      WO,W1,H
      WRITE(*,'('' '',9X,''OMEGA'',11X,''GREAL'',8X,''GIMAGINARY'',7X,
     +          ''MAGNITUDE'',7X,''AMPLITUDE'')')
      W = WO
100   IF(W.LE.W1) THEN
          G = 200*I*(I*W+2)/(W**3*(0.1*I*W+1)*
     +        (0.3*I*W+1)*(0.6*I*W+1)*(0.8*I*W+1))
          ABSG = ABS(G)
          ARGG = ATAN2(AIMAG(G),REAL(G))*180/PI
          WRITE(*,'('' '',5E16.4)')W,G,ABSG,ARGG
          W=H*W
          GO TO 100
      END IF
      END
```

Note how a PARAMETER statement has been used to associate the symbolic constant name I with the complex constant i. Note also the use of the function ATAN2 to produce an amplitude in the range $-\pi$ to π, which is then converted into degrees by multiplying by $180/\pi$.

Typical output obtained by running this program is shown in Figure 18.3 on page 234.

Example 18.11   FORTRAN 77 does not contain an intrinsic function CSINH for evaluating $\sinh z$, where z is complex. Write a function subprogram CSINH(Z) to remedy this.

Since

$$\sinh z = \sinh (x + iy)$$
$$= \sinh x \cosh iy + \cosh x \sinh iy$$
$$= \sinh x \cos y + i \cosh x \sin y$$

the following function subprogram is easily obtained:

```
COMPLEX FUNCTION CSINH(Z)
COMPLEX I,Z
PARAMETER (I = (0,1))
X = REAL(Z)
Y = AIMAG(Z)
CSINH = SINH(X)*COS(Y)+I*COSH(X)*SIN(Y)
END
```

EVALUATION CF A FREQUENCY RESPONSE FUNCTION

WC =   .2000E-C1   W1 =   .1900E+03   H =   .1200E+01

CMEGA	GREAL	GIMAGINARY	MAGNITUDE	AMPLITUDE
.2000E-C1	.1300E+07	.4997E+08	.4999E+08	.8851E+02
.2400E-C1	.9023E+06	.2891E+08	.2893E+08	.8821E+02
.2880E-C1	.6265E+06	.1673E+08	.1674E+08	.8786E+02
.3456E-C1	.4349E+06	.9676E+07	.9685E+07	.8743E+02
.4147E-C1	.3019E+06	.5596E+07	.5604E+07	.8691E+02
.4977E-C1	.2095E+06	.3235E+C7	.3242E+C7	.8629E+02
.5972E-C1	.1454E+06	.1870E+07	.1875E+07	.8555E+02
.7166E-C1	.1008E+06	.1080E+07	.1084E+07	.8467E+02
.8600E-C1	.6987E+05	.6231E+06	.6270E+06	.8360E+02
.1032E+00	.4838E+05	.3591E+06	.3623E+06	.8233E+02
.1238E+00	.3346E+05	.2066E+06	.2093E+06	.8080E+02
.1486E+C0	.2310E+05	.1185E+06	.1208E+06	.7897E+02
.1783E+C0	.1591E+05	.6776E+05	.6960E+05	.7679E+02
.214CE+C0	.1092E+05	.3853E+05	.4005E+05	.7418E+02
.2568E+00	.7455E+04	.2174E+05	.2298E+05	.7107E+02
.3081E+00	.5054E+04	.1213E+05	.1314E+05	.6739E+02
.3698E+00	.3392E+04	.6608E+04	.7481E+04	.6304E+02
.4437E+00	.2245E+04	.3584E+04	.4229E+04	.5793E+02
.5325E+00	.1459E+04	.1867E+04	.2369E+04	.5199E+02
.6390E+C0	.9249E+03	.9301E+03	.1312E+04	.4516E+02
.7668E+00	.5680E+03	.4344E+03	.7151E+03	.3741E+02
.9201E+C0	.3354E+03	.1841E+03	.3825E+03	.2876E+02
.1104E+C1	.1889E+03	.6613E+02	.2001E+03	.1930E+02
.1325E+C1	.1008E+03	.1623E+C2	.1021E+03	.9148E+01
.1590E+C1	.5066E+02	-.1350E+01	.5068E+02	-.1527E+01
.1908E+01	.2388E+02	-.5323E+C1	.2446E+02	-.1257E+02
.2290E+C1	.1050E+02	-.4639E+01	.1148E+02	-.2383E+02
.2747E+C1	.4280E+01	-.3020E+C1	.5238E+01	-.3521E+02
.3297E+C1	.1597E+01	-.1689E+01	.2324E+01	-.4659E+02
.3956E+C1	.5331E+00	-.8501E+00	.1003E+01	-.5791E+02
.4748E+C1	.1506E+00	-.3937E+00	.4216E+00	-.6907E+02
.5697E+C1	.2994E-01	-.1698E+00	.1724E+00	-.8000E+02
.6836E+C1	-.7308E-03	-.6872E-01	.6872E-01	-.9061E+02
.8204E+C1	-.5005E-02	-.2622E-01	.2670E-01	-.1008E+03
.9844E+01	-.3541E-02	-.9480E-02	.1012E-01	-.1105E+03
.1181E+C2	-.1848E-02	-.3262E-C2	.3749E-02	-.1195E+03
.1418E+02	-.8346E-03	-.1074E-C2	.1360E-02	-.1279E+03
.1701E+02	-.3449E-03	-.3404E-03	.4846E-03	-.1354E+03
.2041E+02	-.1341E-03	-.1046E-03	.1700E-03	-.1421E+03
.2450E+C2	-.4994E-04	-.3133E-04	.5895E-04	-.1479E+03
.2940E+C2	-.1803E-04	-.9206E-05	.2025E-04	-.1530E+03
.3527E+C2	-.6369E-05	-.2666E-05	.6904E-05	-.1573E+03
.4233E+C2	-.2214E-05	-.7639E-C6	.2342E-05	-.1610E+03
.508CE+C2	-.7612E-06	-.2172E-C6	.7916E-06	-.1641E+03
.6C95E+C2	-.2596E-06	-.6142E-07	.2668E-06	-.1667E+03
.7315E+C2	-.8807E-07	-.1730E-07	.8976E-07	-.1689E+03
.8777E+C2	-.2976E-07	-.4859E-08	.3015E-07	-.1707E+03
.1053E+C3	-.1003E-07	-.1362E-08	.1012E-07	-.1723E+03
.1264E+C3	-.3373E-08	-.3813E-09	.3395E-08	-.1736E+03
.1517E+C3	-.1133E-08	-.1067E-09	.1138E-08	-.1746E+03
.1820E+C3	-.3802E-09	-.2981E-1C	.3814E-C9	-.1755E+03

Figure 18.3   *Output from FRTAB*

Exercise 18

1 By choosing a number of arbitrary points inside the unit circle, write a FORTRAN 77 program to demonstrate that the transformation

$$w = \log \frac{1 + z}{1 - z}$$

maps z into the infinite horizontal strip with

$$-\frac{\pi}{2} \leqslant v \leqslant \frac{\pi}{2}$$

where $w = u + iv$.

2   Write a FORTRAN 77 program to tabulate the complex potential ψ given by

$$\psi = \frac{200}{\pi} \log_e \left\{ \frac{\sinh y + i \sin x}{\cosh y - \cos x} \right\}$$

for $x = 0.1(0.1)3.0$, $y = 0(2)10$.

3   The frequency-response function $G(i\omega)$ for a certain feedback system is given by the formula

$$G(i\omega) = \frac{-15(i\omega + 20)(i\omega + 30)(i\omega - 40)(i\omega - 10)}{\omega^2 (i\omega + 5)(i\omega + 8)(i\omega + 50)(i\omega + 60)}$$

Write a FORTRAN 77 program to tabulate the real and imaginary parts of G, the magnitude of G, and the amplitude of G for $\omega = \omega_0$, $h\omega_0$, $h^2\omega_0$, $h^3\omega_0, \ldots, \omega_1$.

4   FORTRAN 77 does not contain an intrinsic function CCOSH for evaluating $\cosh z$, where z is complex. Write a function subprogram CCOSH(Z) to remedy this.

5   Write a FORTRAN 77 program, based on the Newton–Raphson formula, to find the root near 3 of the equation $e^{iz} + 1 = 0$.

19 The use of files

Interchangeable tapes wont. (*Troutman's Fourth Programming Postulate*)

The facilities provided for the input and output of data in FORTRAN 77 are sufficiently flexible to allow for data to be associated with a variety of units, e.g. card readers, line printers, magnetic tapes, magnetic discs, timesharing terminals, etc. Throughout this book, the input/output facilities have been discussed independently of the actual unit which may be involved. While this may be satisfactory for relatively small amounts of data, it is inappropriate when processing large amounts of data.

Successful and efficient data handling depends upon the methods of storage and access of the data in addition to a well designed and carefully coded program. To take an extreme example, a large card file is less easily handled than the same information on magnetic tape due to the larger bulk of the cards and the inability of the card reader to skip back and re-read a record. In addition, the use to be made of the data will determine the detailed structure of the records within the file and the best method of access. Thus while a *tape* file might be preferable to a *card* file, a *disc* file is likely to be an even more satisfactory solution if the records are to be accessed in a fairly random fashion.

FORTRAN 77 allows a programmer to access records in a file stored on any of a variety of media. In this chapter files are considered in more depth with particular reference to the characteristics and the use of files stored on magnetic media (such as tape or disc).

File properties

A given computer system will contain a number of files. From a specific FORTRAN 77 program, some of these files will be inaccessible for reasons of security. Such files therefore do not exist for this program. To access files that do exist for the program, they must be connected to an external unit.

Each file has a set of properties which are specified at the time of its connection to a unit. These properties are

1. Name
2. Method of access (either *sequential* or *direct*)

3.   Form of data (either *formatted* or *unformatted*)
4.   Length of record

The computer system being used may restrict the properties allowed by a particular file (for example, a magnetic tape file may be restricted to sequential access only). In particular, the form of a *file name* will be determined by each computer system. It should be noted that a file need not have a name. In addition, the properties may be restricted by the storage medium or the unit being used. For example, a file held on cards will only be able to be accessed sequentially and its record length will probably be fixed at 80 characters. Similarly not all operations are possible on all files. For example, WRITE, PRINT, BACKSPACE, and REWIND statements cannot be applied to a file connected to a card reader.

The properties of a *preconnected* file will be outside the control of the programmer. However, by using the various specifiers in the OPEN statement (Chapter 14), a programmer may specify the properties of the other files to be accessed.

Example 19.1   The statement

OPEN(17,FILE='DHMDAT',STATUS='NEW',FORM='UNFORMATTED')

will create a new file (i.e. one that currently does not exist for this program) and connect it to the external unit 17. The file is given the name DHMDAT. Its records will be unformatted and will be accessed sequentially (the default value). Remember that for sequentially accessed files, the record length is not specified.

Example 19.2   The statement

OPEN(51,FILE='ABINFO',ACCESS='DIRECT',FORM='FORMATTED',
+   RECL=1024)

will connect the file named 'ABINFO' to unit 51. Direct access will be used to access the formatted records of length 1024 characters. Note that the file status is unknown but if the file exists, that file will be used; otherwise a new file will be created.

File position
Certain input/output statements affect the position of a file. If an error condition occurs the file position becomes indeterminate.

The *initial point* of a file is the position immediately preceding the first record. The *terminal point* is immediately after the last record.

If a file is positioned

(a)   within a record, that record is the *current record*.
(b)   within the ith record or between the $(i-1)$th and ith records, the $(i-1)$th record is the *preceding record*. Clearly, if $i = 1$, there is no preceding record.
(c)   within the ith record or between the ith and $(i+1)$th records, the $(i+1)$th record is the *next record*. Clearly if the ith record is the last record in the file, there is no next record.

The following diagrams illustrate the above terminology:

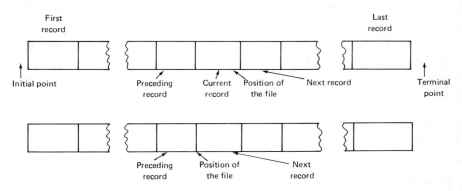

Note that if the file is positioned between records, there is no current record.

The data transfer statements cause the next record to be read or written if using sequential access and cause a specified record to be read or written if using direct access. After an ENDFILE statement, the file is positioned after the endfile record. The OPEN, CLOSE, and INQUIRE statements do not affect the position of a file. The BACKSPACE and REWIND statements are discussed later.

Methods of access

The records of a file will be ordered in sequence often according to some key. For example, a master file containing information on bank accounts may be held in ascending order of account numbers. In this case the key is the account number. Assuming that the details of an individual account may only be identified by means of the account number, consider two tasks which are performed on such a file.

1 Each account record must be updated by the transactions (debits and credits) which have taken place on this account since the previous update. A common technique used to effect this is to sort the transaction records into ascending order of account number. A *sequential* search is made through the master file until an account number matches with the first record in the transaction file. The master record is then updated. Since the records of both files are held in the same order, the next master record to be updated will be further down the file, therefore the search is continued sequentially with the next master record and so on until all the specified accounts have been updated. Normally, this method creates a new master file containing the up-to-date information on all accounts. Thus the old master file and the transaction file are read sequentially and the new master file is written sequentially (see Example 19.15).

2 The bank manager is provided with a printed list of bad debtors which contains the account number, the name of the account holder, and the outstanding debt. In order to determine what action to take, the manager may require the details of at least some of these accounts. Accordingly, a list of account numbers is prepared. However, this list is likely to be very short compared with the total number of accounts. Therefore the appropriate record in the master file is

accessed *directly*, that is, using the account number the filing system will go directly to that record without reading all the preceding records (as with sequential access) (see Example 19.16).

Alternatively, the file of accounts might be held in alphabetic order of the names of the account holders. In this case, it would be convenient to use an account holder's name as the key when searching the file. The use of the account number as a search key is not precluded but the search would probably be slower and less efficient.

Remember that some files may be accessed by one method only (e.g. a card file may only be accessed sequentially).

Sequential access

When a file is accessed sequentially, a data transfer statement causes the *next* record to be read or written. A file is connected for sequential access

(a) by preconnection — for example, the designated input and output units;

(b) by including the access specifier ACCESS = 'SEQUENTIAL' in the OPEN statement referring to the connection;

(c) by omitting the access specifier in the OPEN statement since its default value is 'SEQUENTIAL' (see Chapter 14).

Example 19.3 The following OPEN statements cause connection for sequential access

(a) OPEN(10)

(b) OPEN(25,ACCESS='SEQUENTIAL')

(c) OPEN(19,BLANK='NULL',STATUS='OLD',FILE='ACCOUNTS')

It should be noted that even if the computer system allows the file to be accessed both sequentially and directly, once the records have been connected for sequential access they must not be read or written by direct access input/output statements.

In addition to data records, a sequential access file may be terminated by an endfile record.

A limited amount of manipulation is possible on a sequential access file by means of the BACKSPACE and REWIND statements.

The BACKSPACE statement

The BACKSPACE statement causes the file to be positioned before the preceding record. If the file is at its initial point, the statement has no effect. The BACKSPACE statement has the following forms:

BACKSPACE   unit

BACKSPACE(speclist)

where

(a) unit is an external unit identifier

(b)   speclist is a list of specifiers as follows:

Specifier	Form	
Unit	UNIT = external unit identifier	as defined for the
I/O status	IOSTAT = integer variable or integer array element	OPEN statement
Error	ERR = statement label	(Chapter 14)

Note that the unit specifier is obligatory while the other two are optional.

Example 19.4   The following are valid BACKSPACE statements

(a)   BACKSPACE 25
(b)   BACKSPACE (37)
(c)   BACKSPACE (UNIT=52)
(d)   BACKSPACE(78, IOSTAT=IOERR,ERR=50)

Example 19.5   What is the effect of the statement

BACKSPACE 19

on the file connected to unit 19 if the file is positioned

(a)   at its initial point;
(b)   between records 12 and 13;
(c)   at its terminal point?

(a)   The statement has no effect.

(b)   The file is positioned between records 11 and 12.

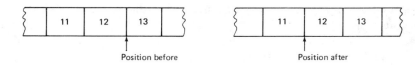

(c)   The file is positioned between the second last and the last records.

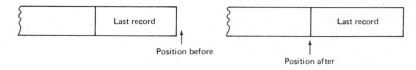

The REWIND statement
The REWIND statement causes the file to be positioned at its initial point. If the file is at its initial point the statement has no effect. The REWIND statement has the

following forms:

$$\text{REWIND} \quad \text{unit}$$
$$\text{REWIND(speclist)}$$

where unit and speclist are as defined for the BACKSPACE statement.

Example 19.6 The following are valid REWIND statements.

  (a)   REWIND 95
  (b)   REWIND (84,ERR=952)
  (c)   REWIND (UNIT=75, IOSTAT=ISPEC)

Direct access
When a file is connected for direct access its individual records must be uniquely identified. In FORTRAN 77 a record is identified by a positive integer called the *record number*. Thus when reading from or writing to a direct access file a record number must be specified in the data transfer statement.
  A file is connected for direct access

  (a)   by preconnection;
  (b)   by including the access specifier ACCESS='DIRECT' in the OPEN statement referring to the connection.

Example 19.7 Write FORTRAN 77 statements to read 3 real values from record 25 and to write them to record 149 of the file connected to unit 21.

$$\text{READ (21,REC=25)X,Y,Z}$$
$$\text{WRITE (21,REC=149)X,Y,Z}$$

Notice that, unlike sequential access files, there is no need to skip through the first 24 records before arriving at record 25, i.e. access is *direct*.
  The required record number is given in the *record specifier* in the control information list of a READ or WRITE statement (see Chapter 14). The record specifier has the form:

$$\text{REC} = \text{recno}$$

where recno is an integer expression with a positive value. A data transfer statement containing a record specifier is a *direct access input/output statement*.
  In a FORTRAN 77 direct access file, all records must have the same length. This length must be specified when the file is connected (see Chapter 14 and 'Record length' below).

Example 19.8 The following OPEN statements cause connection for direct access

  (a)   OPEN(12,ACCESS='DIRECT',RECL=512)
  (b)   OPEN(91,FILE='RANDAT',ACCESS='DIRECT',RECL=4500)

Other points concerning files connected for direct access are:

(a) Records may not be read or written by sequential access input/output statements or using list-directed formatting.

(b) The file must not contain an endfile record (unless the file may also be connected for sequential access in which case the endfile record, if any, is not considered to be part of the file).

Files using both access methods

It is perfectly permissible in FORTRAN 77 for a file to be connected for sequential access at one time and for direct access at another time provided, of course, that the computer system allows it for this file. When the file is connected for sequential access the order of records is the order of the record numbers used for direct access. When connected for direct access, the endfile record (if any) is considered not to be part of the file.

Form of data

Data in a record may be *formatted* or *unformatted*. In general terms, a formatted record contains character information and an unformatted record contains binary information.

Formatted records

A formatted record consists of a sequence of characters. A file is connected for formatted records

(a) by preconnection – for example the designated input and output units;

(b) by including the form specifier FORM='FORMATTED' in the OPEN statement referring to the connection;

(c) by omitting the form specifier from the OPEN statement if the file is being connected for *sequential access* since in this case the default value is 'FORMATTED' (see Chapter 14).

Example 19.9 The following OPEN statements cause connections for formatted data

(a)   OPEN (98)

(b)   OPEN (84,FORM='FORMATTED',ACCESS='DIRECT',RECL=750)

(c)   OPEN (88,ACCESS='SEQUENTIAL')

Once connected for formatted data, a file may not be accessed using unformatted data transfer statements.

A formatted data transfer statement must refer to a format specification giving the precise format of the data in the record or records being accessed. If the file is connected for direct access and a further record is required, the record number is increased by one. Remember that direct access records are of a fixed size and so the number of characters read or written must not exceed this size.

Example 19.10   The statement

READ(6, '(3I3/4F10.0)',REC=4)I1,I2,I3,A,B,C,D

will cause three integers to be read from record 4 and assigned to I1, I2, and I3 respectively, followed by four real values to be read from record 5 and assigned to A, B, C, and D respectively.

Unformatted records
A unformatted record consists of a sequence of values in some form determined by the computer system being used. The data in a record may, of course, contain characters. A file is connected for unformatted records

(a)   by preconnection;
(b)   by including the form specifier FORM='UNFORMATTED' in the OPEN statement referring to this connection;
(c)   by omitting the form specifier from the OPEN statement if the file is being connected for *direct access*, since in this case the default value is 'UNFORMATTED'.

Example 19.11   The following OPEN statements cause connection for unformatted records:

(a)   OPEN(61,FORM='UNFORMATTED')
(b)   OPEN(31,ACCESS='DIRECT',RECL=512)

Once connected for unformatted records, a file may not be accessed using formatted data transfer statements.

Unformatted data is in a machine readable form only and would have to be edited for printing. However, unformatted data is read and written more efficiently than formatted data because there is no editing involved in transferring it between the computer memory and the external storage medium.

Example 19.12   The elements of a 10 x 10 matrix are stored in an unformatted record in column order in a sequential access file connected to unit 28. Print them, one row per line, on the designated output unit. (Assume the input file is positioned before the record.)

REAL A(10,10)
.
.
.
READ(28)A
PRINT'("b",10F10.4)', ((A(I,J),J=1,10),I=1,10)

Clearly unformatted data transfer statements make no reference to a format specification. Therefore, data are transferred, without editing, from one record only. It is important to ensure that the number of values required on input does not exceed the number of values in the record being read. Further the type of each value in the record must agree with the type of the corresponding item in the input list (except that one complex value may correspond to two real items or two real values may correspond to one complex item). The length of a character item in the input list must agree with the length of the character value.

Record length

The length of a record depends on the output list when the record is written as well as on the computer system and the storage medium. Records in a direct access file are of a fixed length but need not be filled. Records in a sequential access file may be of any length which may be restricted by the computer system or storage medium.

Formatted records are measured in characters. Unformatted records are measured in units specified by the computer system being used. Typically, these units will be words, bytes, or even bits.

When a file is connected for direct access the record length must be specified, the length being an integer expression with a positive value.

Example 19.13   The statement

```
    OPEN(UNIT=33,FILE='MINE',STATUS='OLD',ACCESS='DIRECT',
  +      FORM='FORMATTED',RECL=512)
```

will connect the existing file named MINE to unit 33 for formatted direct access with records of length 512 characters.

Example 19.14   The statement

```
    OPEN(51,STATUS='SCRATCH',ACCESS='DIRECT',RECL=1024)
```

will create a scratch file on unit 51 for unformatted direct access with records of length 1024 units. Note that the unit length is installation dependent.

The handling of large amounts of data

As can be seen from the foregoing discussion, the input/output facilities are powerful and flexible. However, they are perhaps shown to the best advantage when dealing with large amounts of data held on a suitable storage medium, typically magnetic tape or disc.

The organization of the data, including the best method of storage (that is, record contents, format, and length), the storage medium, and the data structures to handle it within the program, is an integral part of program design. While this is outside the scope of this book, the reader is recommended to consult an appropriate text on the subject (for example Dodd, 1969) as part of the problem analysis phase of the program design (see Chapter 2).

Magnetic tape

A magnetic tape stores its data in a serial manner and is therefore best suited for the storage of sequential access files. It is, of course, possible to effect direct access on a magnetic tape, but as this may well involve skipping up and down the tape it is likely to be slow and inefficient.

However, blocks of data may be of any length. While there will be an economic minimum length and a technical maximum length for each computer system, files containing records of different sizes will be well-suited to magnetic tape. It is important to note that in many systems the way in which data is written to (and hence read from) magnetic tape may be different from that apparent in the FORTRAN 77 program. This is due to the operating system attempting to optimize the use of the tape and may involve such aspects as writing two or more records in one tape block. While this is hidden from the programmer and need not affect the program (and data) design, it is essential to investigate this feature of the operating system when handling large data files.

Magnetic disc

A magnetic disc stores data in directly addressable sectors on the disc and is therefore suited for the storage of direct access files. A disc can equally well be used for sequential access files, though if large amounts of data are involved where little or no direct access is required then magnetic tapes may prove to be more efficient and more economic.

A disc sector is a fixed size. This is unlikely to limit the record size since two or more sectors can usually be read (or written) in one operation. However, the record size would normally have to be a multiple of the sector size. As stated in the section on magnetic tape, it is important to note that the operating system may, for example, block records to optimize disc usage.

Simple examples involving large data files

This section consists of two simple examples illustrating the use of a sequential access file and a direct access file, based on the illustration in the section 'Methods of access'.

Example 19.15   A magnetic disc file, ACOUNT, contains information on a bank's customer accounts. Each record of the file contains an account number, a customer's name, his or her bank balance, and the customer's permitted overdraft; the account number is an integer, the name is 30 characters long, and the balance and permitted overdraft are real values.

A magnetic tape file, TRANS, contains changes (debits and credits) to some of the above accounts. Each record of this file contains an integer account number and the net (real) value of the change in the account; that is a positive value for a net credit and a negative value for a net debit.

Assuming that

(a)   the account records in both files are held in ascending account number order;
(b)   both files are sequential and unformatted;
(c)   both files are terminated by an endfile record;

(d)   ACOUNT is to be connected to unit 12;

(e)   TRANS is to be connected to unit 39;

(f)   all accounts in TRANS are unique and appear in ACOUNT;

write a FORTRAN 77 program

(i)   to create a new disc file, BCOUNT, connected to unit 13, containing the records of ACOUNT updated by TRANS;

(ii) to print on the designated output unit the customer records which have been updated and in which the permitted overdraft has been exceeded.

Algorithm

```
read a transaction record (from TRANS)
loop while not end-of-file (TRANS) do
        {read a master record (from ACOUNT)
        loop while master account no ≠ transaction account no do
                {write the master record (to BCOUNT)
                  read a master record (from ACOUNT)}
        (a match has been found)
        update the balance
        if permitted overdraft has been exceeded then print the updated record
        write the updated record (to BCOUNT)
        read a transaction record (from TRANS)}
read a master record (from ACOUNT)
loop while not end-of-file (ACOUNT) do
        {write the master record (to BCOUNT)
          read a master record (from ACOUNT)}
```

```
      PROGRAM UPDTAC
******THIS  PROGRAM UPDATES RECORDS OF BANK ACCOUNTS AND PRINTS THOSE
******            UPDATED BALANCES EXCEEDING OVERDRAFT LIMIT
      INTEGER MACNUM,TACNUM,MSTUNT,TRNUNT,NEWUNT
      REAL BALANC,OVRDFT,CHANGE
      CHARACTER*30 NAME
      CHARACTER*6 MASTER,TRANS,NEWMST
      PARAMETER(MASTER='ACOUNT',MSTUNT = 12,
     +          TRANS='TRANS',TRNUNT = 39,
     +          NEWMST='BCOUNT',NEWUNT = 13)

      OPEN(MSTUNT,FILE=MASTER,FORM='UNFORMATTED',STATUS='OLD')
      OPEN(TRNUNT,FILE=TRANS,FORM='UNFORMATTED',STATUS='OLD',)
      OPEN(NEWUNT,FILE=NEWMST,FORM='UNFORMATTED',STATUS='NEW')
      PRINT 10
10    FORMAT('1 ACC NO',3X,'NAME',30X,'BALANCE',4X,'OVERDRAFT')
```

```
81      READ(TRNUNT,END=90)TACNUM,CHANGE

******LOOP WHILE NOT EOF

        READ(MSTUNT,END=96)MACNUM,NAME,BALANC,OVRDFT

80      IF(MACNUM.NE.TACNUM)THEN

******          RECORD NOT TO BE UPDATED

        WRITE(NEWUNT)MACNUM,NAME,BALANC,OVRDFT

        READ(MSTUNT,END=96)MACNUM,NAME,BALANC,OVRDFT

        GO TO 80

        END IF

******  MATCH FOUND

        BALANC=BALANC+CHANGE

        IF(BALANC.LT.OVRDFT)THEN

            PRINT'('' '',I7,3X,A30,2(3X,F9.2))',MACNUM,NAME,BALANC,OVRDFT

        END IF

        WRITE(NEWUNT)MACNUM,NAME,BALANC,OVRDFT

    GO TO 81

******  ALL TRANSACTIONS HAVE BEEN COMPLETED

90  READ(MSTUNT,END=91)MACNUM,NAME,BALANC,OVRDFT

******  COPY OVER ANY REMAINING MASTER RECORDS

        WRITE(NEWUNT) MACNUM,NAME,BALANC,OVRDFT

    GO TO 90

******TIDY UP FILES

91  ENDFILE(NEWUNT)

    CLOSE(NEWUNT)

    CLOSE(MSTUNT)

    REWIND(TRNUNT)

    CLOSE(TRNUNT)

    STOP

******INVALID EOF ON THE MASTER FILE

96      PRINT'(//'' ***UNEXPECTED EOF DETECTED IN FILE '',A6)',MASTER

    END
```

Note the following points.

(a) The PARAMETER statement is used to keep the program as general as possible. Thus for the next update the master file will be BCOUNT and so the PARAMETER statement could be changed to, say:

```
    PARAMETER(MASTER='BCOUNT ,MSTUNT=13,
   +           TRANS='TRANS',TRNUNT=39,
   +           NEWMST='CCOUNT',NEWUNT=14)
```

(b)   Advantage is taken of the default values in the OPEN and CLOSE statements. In particular, when closed, all three files are saved (i.e. STATUS= KEEP').

(c)   The program would work equally well if the files ACOUNT and BCOUNT were tape files or the file TRANS were a disc file.

(d)   The problem has been simplified to assume that the master file will contain all accounts mentioned in the transaction file. In practice this must be checked.

(e)   No programmed action is taken if an error is detected in any of the files.

Example 19.16   Consider the file ACOUNT specified in the last example. Assume that it may also be connected for direct access (on unit 12) and that all records are of length 36 units. (Assume the unit to be a byte in this case; hence the account number = 2 bytes, the name = 30 bytes, the balance = 2 bytes, and the overdraft limit = 2 bytes).

The bank manager, having read the list of accounts whose balance exceeds the permitted overdraft, wishes to consult the balance of certain of these accounts prior to their being updated. Therefore, a set of account numbers terminated by a negative number is prepared for input through the designated input unit.

Assuming that the record number of each account in the file ACOUNT is the same as the account number, write a FORTRAN 77 program to print out the account number, name and balance for each of the prepared account numbers.

Algorithm

```
read an account number
loop while the account number > 0 do
        {read the record (account no) (from ACOUNT)
         print the account number, name and balance
         read an account number}
```

```
      PROGRAM BLKLST
******THIS PROGRAM PRINTS THE RECORD, PRIOR TO UPDATING, FOR SPECIFIED ACCOUNTS
      INTEGER ACCNUM,MACNUM,MSTUNT
      REAL  BALANC
      CHARACTER NAME*30, MASTER*6
      PARAMETER(MASTER='ACOUNT',MSTUNT=12)
      OPEN(MSTUNT,FILE=MASTER,FORM='UNFORMATTED',STATUS='OLD',RECL=36,ACCESS='DIRECT')
      PRINT 10
10    FORMAT('1 LIST OF POOR ACCOUNTS PRIOR TO UPDATING'//
     +       '  ACC NO',3X,'NAME',30X,'BALANCE')
      READ*,ACCNUM
1     IF(ACCNUM.GT.0)THEN
******    LOOP WHILE THERE ARE STILL ACCOUNTS REQUIRED
          READ(MSTUNT,REC=ACCNUM)MACNUM,NAME,BALANC
```

```
        PRINT'('' '',I7,3X,A30,3X,F9.2)',MACNUM,NAME,BALANC

        READ*,ACCNUM

        GO TO 1

     END IF

  END
```

Note that in practice it is likely to be a gross oversimplification to assume that the record number will be the same as the account number.

Exercise 19

1   With reference to Example 19.15, no check is made that the account number in the transaction file exists in the master file. Since the records of both files are stored in ascending order of account number, this check is straightforward.
    Amend the program, UPDTAC, in Example 19.15

(a)   to make the above check, taking appropriate action on failure;
(b)   to take appropriate action if an error is detected in any of the files.

2   Write a FORTRAN 77 program to print the file ACOUNT (specified in Example 19.15).

3   With reference to Example 19.15, the transaction file contains the net credit or debit to an account. Consider a different transaction file CREDEB, which contains the individual transactions on a file, each record comprising an account number and a single credit (positive value) or debit (negative value) to the account. Thus the file might contain more than one record for a specified account. For example, if a customer (account no. 147) credits his account with £425.52 and makes payments of £62.47, £18.25, and £34.92, the transaction file will contain 4 records for this account as follows:

147	+ 425.52
147	− 62.47
147	− 18.25
147	− 34.92

Assuming that

(i)   the transaction records are held in ascending account number order;
(ii)   for each account, the credits will precede the debits;
(iii) all other information is as specified in Example 19.15;

write a FORTRAN 77 program

(a)   to update the account records in file ACOUNT by the transactions CREDEB, creating the new file BCOUNT;
(b)   to print the updated record and each transaction for an account which, when updated, exceeds its permitted overdraft.

4   Write a FORTRAN 77 program to update the records of the file ACOUNT (by overwriting using direct access) with the transactions in a file DEBCRE which is not sorted (i.e. the records will be in a random order). The specification of ACOUNT is given in Example 19.16.

20 Case studies

In this chapter four 'case studies' are presented which bring together much of the material described in earlier chapters. Various aspects of 'real life' programming are also illustrated by one or more of these case studies, including

(a)   taking advantage of algorithms which have been developed by others, often in the dim and distant past;

(b)   top down design of algorithms;

(c)   the creation of almost trivial subprograms which are then used collectively to perform a far from trivial task;

(d)   the copious use of comments to explain the actions of a program unit;

(e)   the importance of lay-out in making a program unit understandable to others;

(f)   the necessity for program units not only to perform correctly with valid data but also to detect and handle *erroneous* data.

Each case study is of a non-specialist nature in that it can be understood without a background of knowledge from some specific area of study.

Case study 1: League tables

This example was considered in Chapter 2, where the algorithms were developed. A brief statement of the problem is:

'For many team games competition is organized into leagues with the position of each team in the league being recorded in a table. This league table is updated after every match between two teams.

Given a league table and a set of match results as data, write a FORTRAN 77 program to update the table and print it.'

The algorithm designed in Example 2.3 was

```
read the current table
print the table
loop while there is a match result to process do
        {read a result
```

> print it
> update the home team entry
> update the visiting team entry }
> sort the updated table
> print it

Before this algorithm can be further refined more information is required about the data held in the table and the form of the results. This information will vary according to the game being considered. For this case study a league table for Association Football (Soccer) will be updated.

In Association Football the team scoring the greater number of goals wins the match. If both teams score the same number of goals the match is drawn. The result of a match will have the form

Name of home team	Goals scored by home team	Name of visiting team	Goals scored by visiting team

Typical results are:

Aberdeen	3	Rangers	0
Manchester United	2	Manchester City	2
Stirling Albion	1	Hearts	2

Assume the results are stored on a file connected to the designated input unit. Each record holds the result of one match in the form (A20, I4, 3X, A20, I4) and the results are terminated with a negative value as the home team goals.

An entry in the league table comprises eight items, namely the team name; the number of matches played, won, drawn, and lost; the total number of goals scored for and against the team; and the total number of points awarded to the team in the competition. Two points are awarded for a win, one for a draw, and zero for a loss. Position in the league table is determined by the total points gained in the competition; the greater the number of points, the higher the position. If two (or more) teams have the same points total, their relative position is determined by *goal difference*, that is (goals for − goals against). The team with the greater goal difference obtains the higher position. A typical league table showing the position of teams at some point during the football season is shown on page 252.

Assume that the current league table is stored in an unformatted sequential file, LEAGUE, connected to unit 19 and that the updated table is to be stored in an unformatted sequential file LEAGUF connected to unit 58. Each file consists of one record containing a value giving the number of teams in the league, followed by the entry for each team in position order. It is reasonable to assume that a league table is small (no more than 30 teams, say) and so can be read into and accessed in the main store of the computer.

The data structure used to store the table within the computer affects the way in which the program is written. Since each table entry consists of one character value and seven integer values, one possible data structure is a one-dimensional character array, NAME, and a two-dimensional integer array, INFO. Thus the entry of the

A FOOTBALL LEAGUE TABLE

Team	Matches				Goals		Points
	Played	Won	Drawn	Lost	For	Against	
Dundee	31	20	5	6	71	36	45
Hearts	30	18	7	5	62	35	43
Morton	28	18	5	5	60	32	41
Dumbarton	29	11	13	5	48	37	35
Stirling Albion	30	12	9	9	46	39	33
Kilmarnock	30	10	10	10	39	36	30
Arbroath	30	9	12	9	36	44	30
Hamilton	30	9	10	11	45	43	28
St Johnstone	29	11	6	12	42	48	28
Airdrieonians	30	8	9	13	37	49	25
Queen of the South	29	7	10	12	37	52	24
Montrose	29	8	6	15	44	52	22
Alloa	31	6	7	18	32	69	19
East Fife	30	3	7	20	34	61	13

team in the ith position in the league will be stored in NAME(I) and in the ith row of INFO, as follows:

the number of matches played	in INFO(I,1)
the number of matches won	in INFO(I,2)
the number of matches drawn	in INFO(I,3)
the number of matches lost	in INFO(I,4)
the number of goals scored for	in INFO(I,5)
the number of goals scored against	in INFO(I,6)
the points total	in INFO(I,7)

The main program is coded from the above algorithm.

```
      PROGRAM LGTBL
******THIS PROGRAM UPDATES A FOOTBALL LEAGUE TABLE WITH A SET OF MATCH RESULTS
      INTEGER INFO(30,7),OUT,N,HMGLS,VSTGLS
      CHARACTER*20 NAME(30),HOME,VISIT,OUTNAM*6
      PARAMETER(OUT=58,OUTNAM='LEAGUF')

      CALL READLT(NAME,INFO,N)

      CALL PRNTLT(NAME,INFO,N)
******PRINT HEADING FOR THE RESULTS
      PRINT 50
50    FORMAT(///' RESULTS OF MATCHES'/
     +          ' ------- -- -------')
      READ 51,HOME,HMGLS,VISIT,VSTGLS
51    FORMAT(A20,I4,3X,A20,I4)
1     IF(HMGLS.GE.0)THEN
```

```
        PRINT 52,HOME,HMGLS,VISIT,VSTGLS
52      FORMAT(' ',A20,I4,3X,A20,I4)
        CALL UPDATE(HOME,HMGLS,VSTGLS,NAME,INFO,N)
        CALL UPDATE(VISIT,VSTGLS,HMGLS,NAME,INFO,N)
        READ 51,HOME,HMGLS,VISIT,VSTGLS
        GO TO 1
     END IF
     CALL SORT(NAME,INFO,N)
     CALL PRNTLT(NAME,INFO,N)
******WRITE OUT THE NEW TABLE TO A NEW FILE (LEAGUF)
     OPEN(OUT,FILE=OUTNAM,FORM='UNFORMATTED',STATUS='NEW',ERR=99)
     WRITE(OUT,ERR=99)N,(NAME(I),(INFO(I,J),J=1,7),I=1,N)
     CLOSE(OUT,ERR=99)
     STOP
99   PRINT'('' ***ERROR IN FILE '',A6)',OUTNAM
     END
```

Four subprograms are required in the program to read, print, update, and sort the league table. The read and print subroutines are straightforward.

```
     SUBROUTINE READLT(NAME,INFO,N)
******THIS SUBROUTINE READS IN A LEAGUE TABLE FROM A FILE
     INTEGER INFO(30,7),N,IN
     CHARACTER NAME(30)*20,INNAME*6
     PARAMETER(IN=19,INNAME='LEAGUE')

     OPEN(IN,FILE=INNAME,FORM='UNFORMATTED',STATUS='OLD',ERR=99)
     READ(IN,ERR=99)N,(NAME(I),(INFO(I,J),J=1,7),I=1,N)
     CLOSE(IN,ERR=99)
     RETURN
99   PRINT'('' ***ERROR IN FILE '',A6)',INNAME
     STOP
     END
     SUBROUTINE PRNTLT(NAME,INFO,N)
******THIS SUBROUTINE PRINTS A LEAGUE TABLE
     INTEGER INFO(30,7),N
     CHARACTER NAME(30)*20

     PRINT 5
5    FORMAT('1',22X,'LEAGUE TABLE'/
```

```
    +             23X,'------ -----'//
    +         6X,'TEAM',19X,'MATCHES',9X,'GOALS',5X,'PTS'/
    +         24X,'PL  WON  DREW LOST FOR AGNST')
      PRINT 6,(NAME(I),(INFO(I,J),J=1,7),I=1,N)
6     FORMAT(' ',A20,6I5,4X,I3)
      END
```

The update module requires as parameters, the team name and the number of goals scored for and against. The algorithm refined slightly from Example 2.3 is:

search the league table for this team, stopping if the name cannot be found
update the number of matches played
if the match was won **then** { update number of matches won
                       add two to the points total }
       else if the match was drawn **then**   update the number of matches drawn
                                 add one to the points total
                      else   update the number of matches lost
update the goals for and the goals against.

```
      SUBROUTINE UPDATE(TEAM,GLSFOR,GLSAG,NAME,INFO,N)
******THIS SUBROUTINE UPDATES THE ENTRY FOR THE GIVEN TEAM IN THE TABLE
      INTEGER INFO(30,7),N,PLD,WON,LOST,DRAWN,GLF,GLA,PTS,GLSFOR,GLSAG
      CHARACTER*20 NAME(30),TEAM
      PARAMETER(PLD=1,WON=2,DRAWN=3,LOST=4,GLF=5,GLA=6,PTS=7)
      I=1
      IF(NAME(I).NE.TEAM)THEN
          IF(I.EQ.N)THEN
******            TEAM NOT FOUND
                  PRINT 15,TEAM
15                FORMAT(' ***ERROR,TEAM -',A20,'- NOT FOUND')
                  STOP
          END IF
          I=I+1
          GO TO 1
      END IF
******TEAM FOUND, I IS THE INDEX OF THE ENTRY
      INFO(I,PLD)=INFO(I,PLD)+1
      IF(GLSFOR.GT.GLSAG)THEN
          INFO(I,WON)=INFO(I,WON)+1
          INFO(I,PTS)=INFO(I,PTS)+2
              ELSE IF(GLSFOR.EQ.GLSAG)THEN
```

```
              INFO(I,DRAWN)=INFO(I,DRAWN)+1

              INFO(I,PTS)=INFO(I,PTS)+1

                            ELSE

              INFO(I,LOST)=INFO(I,LOST)+1

     END IF

     INFO(I,GLF)=INFO(I,GLF)+GLSFOR

     INFO(I,GLA)=INFO(I,GLA)+GLSAG

     END
```

Note the use of the symbolic constants PLD, WON, DRAWN, LOST, GLF, GLA, and PTS to make the code more readable.

The results of the matches played are unlikely to lead to a large change in the position of teams and so a simple bubble sort can be used to sort the updated entries. The algorithm is:

> assume at least one exchange of entries
> **loop while** at least one exchange occurred during the last loop **do**
> > **loop for** $i = 1, 2, \ldots, n-1$ **do**
> > > **if** points for team$_i$ < the points for team$_{i+1}$ **or**
> > > (points for team$_i$ = points for team$_{i+1}$ **and**
> > > > goal difference for team$_i$ < goal difference for team$_{i+1}$)
> > > > > **then** exchange the team entries

```
      SUBROUTINE SORT(NAME,INFO,N)

******THIS SUBROUTINE SORTS THE ENTRIES INTO DESCENDING ORDER OF POINTS

******           AND DESCENDING GOAL DIFFERENCE WITHIN POINTS

      INTEGER INFO(30,7),TEMP,GLF,GLA,PTS

      CHARACTER*20 NAME(30),TEMPNM

      LOGICAL EXCHNG

      PARAMETER(PTS=7,GLF=5,GLA=6)

      EXCHNG=.TRUE.

15    IF(EXCHNG)THEN

          EXCHNG=.FALSE.

          DO 10 I=1,N-1

              IF(INFO(I,PTS).LT.INFO(I+1,PTS).OR.INFO(I,PTS).EQ.INFO(I+1,PTS)

     +           .AND.(INFO(I,GLF)-INFO(I,GLA)).LT.(INFO(I+1,GLF)-INFO(I+1,GLA)))

     +               THEN

              TEMPNM=NAME(I)

              NAME(I)=NAME(I+1)

              NAME(I+1)=TEMPNM

              DO 11 J=1,7

                  TEMP=INFO(I,J)
```

```
                    INFO(I,J)=INFO(I+1,J)

                    INFO(I+1,J)=TEMP

11              CONTINUE

                    EXCHNG=.TRUE.

            END IF

10          CONTINUE

        GO TO 15

    END IF

    END
```

Case study 2: Some aspects of the calendar

Easter Sunday does not occur on a *fixed* day each year since the date is determined by the occurrence of the first full moon on or after the vernal equinox. In addition, many days of religious significance in each year are definable in terms of Easter Sunday, as illustrated in the following table:

Day	Relationship to Easter Sunday (ES)
Ash Wednesday	ES − 46
First Sunday in Lent	ES − 42
Fifth Sunday in Lent	ES − 14
Palm Sunday	ES − 7
Maundy Thursday	ES − 3
Good Friday	ES − 2
Rogation Sunday	ES + 35
Ascension Day (Holy Thursday)	ES + 39
Whit Sunday (Pentecost)	ES + 49
Trinity Sunday	ES + 56
Corpus Christi	ES + 60

The objective of this case study is to tabulate, for a period of years, the dates of these various days of special significance.

Fortunately an algorithm for the calculation of the date of Easter Sunday itself is very straightforward, thanks to a formula devised by the celebrated mathematician Gauss. Gauss' formula, valid for the Gregorian calendar until the year 4200, is as follows:

(a) let a, b, and c be the remainders on dividing the year y respectively by 4, 7, and 19

(b) let d be the remainder on dividing by 30 the expression

$$19c + 15 + [y/100] - [y/400] - [y/300]$$

(c) let e be the remainder on dividing by 7 the expression

$$2a + 4b + 6d + 4 + [y/100] - [y/400]$$

(d)   If *either* (i) $d = 29$ *and* $e = 6$ or (ii) $d = 28$ *and* $e = 6$ *and* $c > 10$ then set e equal to -1

(e)   Easter Sunday is $(d + e + 1)$ days after March 21.

Note that [ ] indicates that remainders are ignored after division operations, i.e. *integer* division is performed.

Using this approach a subroutine subprogram EASTER may be created without difficulty (see page 258). To check the validity of the year y, a more general subroutine CHECK(D,M,Y), which will check the validity of *any* Gregorian date $d/m/y$ between 1/1/1583 and 31/12/4200, has been called into action. This subroutine is self-explanatory and is given on page 259. Note that it calls in turn two other subprograms, namely

(a)   the logical function subprogram LEAPYR(Y) which returns the value **true** if the year y is a leap year, and the value **false** otherwise. The reader is referred to Example 16.11 (page 213) for the specification of LEAPYR.

(b)   the subroutine subprogram ERROR(I) which, depending on the value of I, prints out an appropriate error message and then *causes execution to terminate*. A policy of gathering together all error messages into one subprogram has been adopted in this case study, and the reader is referred to page 260 for a listing of the subroutine ERROR.

Having obtained the date of Easter Sunday in a particular year y, the next problem is to calculate the dates of related religious events, which may be reduced to a repetition of the simpler problem of finding the date x days before or after Easter Sunday, a positive value for x indicating an event *after* Easter Sunday and a negative value for x indicating an event *before* Easter Sunday. Once again, various approaches are possible, but the following systematic method has much to commend it.

It is based on the fact that the days in a year may be identified, not only by specifying for each one a *month* and a *day count* within the month, e.g. May 23, but alternatively by numbering them 1, 2, 3, 4, . . ., 365 (or 366 in a leap year). Thus, for example, 10 March in 1978 corresponds to day 69, since $31 + 28 + 10 = 69$, and 69 is said to be the *Julian number* for 10 March in 1978.

It immediately follows that a general approach to the problem of finding the date x days before or after a given date is to convert the given date to Julian number form, add x, and then convert the Julian number obtained back to the equivalent day and month form. Two subprograms are therefore indicated, one to convert from day and month form to Julian number form, and one to achieve the reverse conversion.

The function subprogram JULIAN(D,M,Y), given on page 260, takes a date $d/m/y$ and, having checked its validity, returns the Julian number corresponding to that date. The subprogram is based on the simple approach of adding to d the number of days in each of the months 1, 2, 3, . . ., $(m - 1)$. Note that LEAPYR(Y) is called once again in order to determine the number of days in February in the year y.

Similarly the subroutine subprogram UNJUL(JULNUM,Y,D,M), given on page 261, takes a Julian number, JULNUM, and a year y and, having checked the validity of both JULNUM and y, converts back to normal day d and month m form. Briefly the reverse process to that described in the previous paragraph is employed, i.e. the numbers of days in January, February, March, ... are subtracted from the Julian number until a zero or negative result is obtained from which d and m are easily calculated. Note that LEAPYR(Y) is also called in this subprogram to determine the number of days, 365 or 366, in the year y against which JULNUM must be checked.

Finally a program DAYTAB to achieve the original objective is given on page 262. The main program is surprisingly short if comments and heading specifications are removed. Note how the x-values to be added to the Julian number form of the date of Easter Sunday in a year y are held in a one-dimensional integer array x, which is initialized by means of a DATA statement. The inner loop of the program simply adds an x-value to the Julian number for Easter Sunday, converts the resulting value back into day d and month m form, and stores these values in the one-dimensional integer arrays D and M for subsequent output.

```
      SUBROUTINE EASTER(Y,D,M)
*
******GIVEN A YEAR Y, THE SUBROUTINE EASTER CALCULATES
*     THE DAY D AND THE MONTH M ON WHICH EASTER
*     SUNDAY FALLS IN THAT YEAR.   THE METHOD USED
******IS DUE TO GAUSS.
*
      INTEGER Y,D,A,B,C,DD,E,TEMP
*
******CHECK VALIDITY OF Y
*
      CALL CHECK(1,1,Y)
*
******NOW APPLY METHOD OF GAUSS.
*
      A=MOD(Y,4)
      B=MOD(Y,7)
      C=MOD(Y,19)
      DD=MOD(19*C+15+Y/100-Y/400-Y/300,30)
*
******DD HAS BEEN USED TO AVOID A NAME CLASH
*
      E=MOD(2*A+4*B+6*DD+4+Y/100-Y/400,7)
      IF((DD.EQ.29.AND.E.EQ.6).OR.(DD.EQ.28.AND.E.EQ.6
     +      .AND.C.GT.10)) THEN
            E=-1
```

```
      END IF

      TEMP=DD+E+1

      IF(TEMP.GT.10) THEN

            M=4

            D=TEMP-10

                        ELSE

            M=3

            D=21+TEMP

      END IF

      END


      SUBROUTINE CHECK(D,M,Y)
*
******THE SUBROUTINE CHECK CHECKS THE VALIDITY
*     OF A GREGORIAN DATE D/M/Y.   IF THE DATE
*     IS VALID, CONTROL IS RETURNED TO THE CALLING
*     PROGRAM UNIT;   IF INVALID, A SUBROUTINE WITH THE NAME ERROR
*     IS CALLED TO OUTPUT AN APPROPRIATE MESSAGE AND
*     TO TERMINATE EXECUTION.   A PARAMETER STATEMENT
*     IS USED TO DEFINE THE RANGE WITHIN WHICH
*     Y MUST LIE.   NOTE ALSO THAT A CALL OF
*     CHECK OF THE FORM 'CALL CHECK(1,1,Y)' MAY
******BE USED TO CHECK THE VALIDITY OF A YEAR Y.
*
      INTEGER  D,Y,YLOW,YHIGH,MONTH(12)
      LOGICAL LEAPYR
      PARAMETER(YLOW=1583,YHIGH=4200)
      DATA MONTH(1),(MONTH(I),I=3,12)/2*31,30,31,30,2*31,30,31,30,31/
*
******CHECK VALIDITY OF Y
*
      IF(Y.LT.YLOW.OR.Y.GT.YHIGH) THEN
         CALL ERROR(1)
      END IF
*
******SET MONTH(2) EQUAL TO 28 OR 29
*
      IF (LEAPYR(Y)) THEN
         MONTH(2)=29
```

```
                      ELSE
          MONTH(2)=28
      END IF
*
******CHECK VALIDITY OF M
*
      IF(M.LT.1.OR.M.GT.12) THEN
          CALL ERROR(3)
      END IF
*
******CHECK VALIDITY OF D
*
      IF(D.LT.1.OR.D.GT.MONTH(M)) THEN
          CALL ERROR(4)
      END IF
      END

      SUBROUTINE ERROR(I)
      INTEGER SUB
      PARAMETER (SUB=4)
      CHARACTER TEXT(SUB+1)*80
      DATA (TEXT(I),I=1,SUB+1)/
     +' IMPERMISSIBLE YEAR VALUE',
     +' INVALID JULIAN NUMBER',
     +' .IMPERMISSIBLE MONTH VALUE',
     +' IMPERMISSIBLE DAY VALUE',
     +' SUBROUTINE ERROR(I) CALLED WITH INVALID I'/
      IF (I.GE.1.AND.I.LE.SUB) THEN
          WRITE(*,10) TEXT(I)
                              ELSE
          WRITE(*,10) TEXT(SUB+1)
      END IF
10    FORMAT(A80)
      STOP
      END
      FUNCTION JULIAN(D,M,Y)
*
******GIVEN A DATE D/M/Y, THE INTEGER FUNCTION
*     JULIAN RETURNS AS ITS VALUE THE JULIAN
```

```
*      NUMBER CORRESPONDING TO DAY D AND MONTH M
******IN THE YEAR Y
*
       INTEGER D,Y,SUM,MONTH(12)
       LOGICAL LEAPYR
       DATA MONTH(1),(MONTH(I),I=3,12)/2*31,30,31,30,2*31,30,31,30,31/
*
******CHECK VALIDITY OF DATE D/M/Y
*
       CALL CHECK(D,M,Y)
*
******SET MONTH(2) EQUAL TO 28 OR 29.
*
       IF (LEAPYR(Y)) THEN
           MONTH(2)=29
                      ELSE
           MONTH(2)=28
       END IF
*
******CALCULATE JULIAN NUMBER
*
       SUM=D
       DO 100 I=1, M-1
           SUM=SUM+MONTH(I)
100    CONTINUE
       JULIAN=SUM
       END
       SUBROUTINE UNJUL(JULNUM,Y,D,M)
*
******GIVEN THE JULIAN NUMBER, JULNUM, FOR A DAY
*      WITHIN A YEAR Y, THE SUBROUTINE UNJUL
*      WILL CONVERT IT TO NORMAL DAY D AND
******MONTH M FORM.
*
       INTEGER Y,D,MONTH(12),YDAYS,TEMP
       LOGICAL LEAPYR
       DATA MONTH(1),(MONTH(I),I=3,12)/2*31,30,31,30,2*31,30,31,30,31/
*
```

```
******CHECK VALIDITY OF Y
*
      CALL CHECK(1,1,Y)
*
******SET MONTH(2) EQUAL TO 28 OR 29 AND YDAYS EQUAL
******TO 365 OR 366.
*
      IF (LEAPYR(Y)) THEN
          MONTH(2)=29
          YDAYS=366
                      ELSE
          MONTH(2)=28
          YDAYS=365
      END IF
*
******CHECK VALIDITY OF JULNUM
*
      IF (JULNUM.LT.1.OR.JULNUM.GT.YDAYS) THEN
            CALL ERROR(2)
      END IF
*
******CALCULATE D AND M
*
      I=1
      TEMP=JULNUM
100   IF (TEMP.GT.0) THEN
            TEMP=TEMP-MONTH(I)
            I=I+1
            GO TO 100
      END IF
      D=TEMP+MONTH(I-1)
      M=I-1
      END

      PROGRAM DAYTAB
      INTEGER Y,YLOW,YHIGH,ESD,ESM,EJN,D(12),M(12),X(12)
      CHARACTER MNAME(12)*3
      DATA (MNAME(I),I=1,12)/'JAN','FEB','MAR','APR','MAY','JUN',
     +                       'JUL','AUG','SEP','OCT','NOV','DEC'/,
```

```
     +        (X(I),I=1,12)/-46,-42,-14,-7,-3,-2,0,35,39,49,56,60/
*
******OUTPUT HEADINGS
*
     WRITE(*,20)
20   FORMAT(' RELIGOUS FESTIVALS'//
     +        ' YEAR',4X,'ASH',5X,'1ST SUN',4X,'5TH SUN',4X,'PALM',5X,
     +        'MAUNDY',5X,'GOOD',5X,'EASTER',3X,'ROGATION',1X,'ASCENSION',4X,
     +        'WHIT',5X,'TRINITY',1X,'CORPUS'/
     +        7X,'WEDNESDAY',2X,'IN LENT',4X,'IN LENT',3X,'SUNDAY',3X,
     +        'THURSDAY',3X,'FRIDAY',4X,'SUNDAY',4X,'SUNDAY',5X,'DAY',6X,
     +        'SUNDAY',4X,'SUNDAY',2X,'CHRISTI'//)
*
******INPUT LOWER AND UPPER LIMITS FOR Y
*
     READ *,YLOW,YHIGH
*
******MAIN PART
*
     DO 100 Y=YLOW,YHIGH
          CALL EASTER(Y,ESD,ESM)
          EJN=JULIAN(ESD,ESM,Y)
          DO 200 I=1,12
               JULNUM=EJN+X(I)
               CALL UNJUL(JULNUM,Y,D(I),M(I))
200       CONTINUE
          WRITE(*,'('' '',I4,12(4X,A3,1X,I2))')
     +                    Y,(MNAME(M(I)),D(I),I=1,12)
100  CONTINUE
     END
```

Case study 3: Processing exam marks

Marks obtained by candidates in examinations are used for many purposes and as a result are processed in many different ways. In this case study, a master file of marks is available and may be connected for either sequential or direct access.

Two programs are developed using this file. The first processes the marks sequentially to compute the average mark obtained in each exam and to create a file consisting of Computer Science marks only. The second program scans this new file (sequentially) for 'good' candidates (that is, those scoring 75% or over in Computer Science) all of whose marks are obtained from the master file (directly) and printed.

The master file, called EXMLST, is a disc file containing a directory of classes followed by the exam marks for each of these classes. The data for each class is held in the following form:

first record	: the name of the class
second record	: the number of exam candidates in the class (n)
	: the number of exams taken by the class (m)
	: the name of each subject examined (i.e. m names in all)
third and subsequent records	: the candidate number
(i.e. n records in all)	: the name of the candidate
	: the mark obtained in each exam (i.e. m marks in all)

Therefore the data for each class takes up ($n + 2$) records.

The directory is held in the first two records of the file. Each directory entry contains the name of a class followed by the record number of the first record (the class name) of the data in the file for that class. For example, the first two entries in the directory might be:

ACCOUNTING AND COMP SCI YEAR 1   3
MECHANICAL ENGINEERING YEAR 3   55

That is the data for the first class starts at record 3 and the data for the second class starts at record 55. The following diagram illustrates the layout of the file EXMLST, assuming the above directory entries.

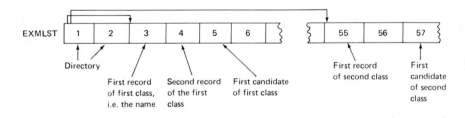

Other information about the master file follows:

(a)   Its records are unformatted and of length 320 bytes.
(b)   It should be connected to unit 24.
(c)   It is terminated by an endfile record.
(d)   The record containing an individual candidate's marks has the record number ($CL + CN + 1$) where CL is the class record number given in the directory and CN is the candidate number; e.g. the first candidate in the second class has marks in record 57 (i.e. $55 + 1 + 1$)

start of second class   candidate number

(e)   All names are 30 characters long.
(f)   All other values are integers.

(g)   The number of exams taken by a class is never more than 10 (i.e. $m \leqslant 10$).

(h)   If a candidate is absent from an exam, his or her mark for that exam is -1.

(i)   Each record of the directory contains entries for 10 classes.

The new file (to hold the Computer Science marks) will be a tape file with the name CMPSCI and, should have the same form as the master file but without a directory. Thus the second record of each class will contain

the number of candidates in the class (n)
the value 1 (being the number of exams taken) (m)
the value 'COMPUTER SCIENCE' (being the name of the exam)

If, however, there is no Computer Science exam for this class, the class will contain only two records, namely, the class name and a record with two zero values (n and m).

Other information about the new file follows:

(a)   It will be accessed sequentially and so no record length is specified.

(b)   It should be connected to unit 34.

First program
In the first program, the master file is processed for two reasons:

(a)   to print, on the designated output unit, for each exam in each class
    (i)   the average mark obtained,
    (ii)   the number of candidates sitting the exam,
    (iii)   the number of absentees;

(b)   to create a new file consisting of Computer Science marks only.

Since the data for each list will be processed, the master file will be accessed sequentially. Therefore the directory may be skipped. There are no obvious self-contained modules (except perhaps for the error conditions) and so the program consists of a single main program.

Algorithm

    skip the directory (on EXMLST)
    read class name (from EXMLST)
    loop while not end-of-file **do**
        {read number of candidates (total), number of exams (exams) and names
                                of exams (from EXMLST)
        initialize counts for average (sumex) and number of candidates present
                                  (present)
        write class name (to CMPSCI)
        if one of the exam names is 'COMPUTER SCIENCE' **then** write total, 1,
                            'COMPUTER SCIENCE' (to CMPSCI)
           else write 0,0 (to CMPSCI)

> **loop for** i = 1, 2, . . . , total **do**
>> {read candidate number, name and marks (from EXMLST)
>> **loop for** j = 1, 2, . . . , exams **do**
>>> {**if** candidate present **then** {add marks$_j$ to sumex$_j$
>>>> add one to present$_j$} }
>>> **if** there is a computer science exam **then** write candidate number,
>>>> name, and mark (to CMPSCI)}
>> print list heading
>> **loop for** j = 1, 2, . . . , exams **do**
>>> {print exam heading
>>> print average mark, number present and number absent}
>> read class name (from EXMLST)}

```
      PROGRAM FILES
******THIS PROGRAM PRINTS STATISTICS ON THE LISTS OF EXAM MARKS IN THE
******    FILE EXMLST AND FORMS A NEW FILE FOR COMP SCI MARKS
      INTEGER SUMEX(10), PRESNT(10), MARK(10)
      INTEGER OLDFIL,NEWFIL,TOTAL,EXAMS,CHINDX,CANDNO,PRES,ABSENT
      CHARACTER*30 EXAM(10), CLASS,CHOSEN,NAME,CHNAME*6,MSTNAM*6
      LOGICAL CHOOSE
      PARAMETER ( CHOSEN='COMPUTER SCIENCE',
     +          CHNAME='CMPSCI', NEWFIL=34,
     +          MSTNAM='EXMLST', OLDFIL=24)
      OPEN(OLDFIL, FILE=MSTNAM,FORM='UNFORMATTED',STATUS='OLD',ERR=98)
      OPEN(NEWFIL, FILE=CHNAME,FORM='UNFORMATTED',STATUS='NEW',ERR=99)
******SKIP THE DIRECTORY
      READ(OLDFIL,END=97,ERR=98)
      READ(OLDFIL,END=97,ERR=98)
20    READ(OLDFIL,END=90,ERR=98) CLASS
******LOOP WHILE NOT EOF
        READ(OLDFIL,END=97,ERR=98)TOTAL,EXAMS,(EXAM(J),J=1,EXAMS)
        CHOOSE=.FALSE.
        DO 10 J=1,EXAMS
******    INITIALISE COUNTS
          SUMEX(J)=0
          PRESNT(J)=0
******    SEARCH FOR CHOSEN EXAM
          IF(.NOT.CHOOSE.AND.EXAM(J).EQ.CHOSEN) THEN
******        CHOSEN EXAM FOUND
              CHINDX=J
              CHOOSE=.TRUE.
```

```
              END IF
10        CONTINUE
******    INITIALISE THE NEW FILE
          WRITE(NEWFIL,ERR=99)CLASS
          IF(CHOOSE) THEN
              WRITE(NEWFIL,ERR=99)TOTAL,1,CHOSEN
                      ELSE
              WRITE(NEWFIL,ERR=99) 0,0
          END IF
          DO 11 I=1, TOTAL
******        PROCESS A CANDIDATE
          READ(OLDFIL,END=97,ERR=98)CANDNO,NAME,(MARK(J),J=1,EXAMS)
          DO 12 J=1, EXAMS
******        PROCESS EACH MARK
              IF(MARK(J).GE.0) THEN
                  SUMEX(J) = SUMEX(J)+MARK(J)
                  PRESNT(J) = PRESNT(J)+1
              END IF
12        CONTINUE
******    WRITE CHOSEN MARK TO NEW FILE
          IF(CHOOSE) THEN
              WRITE(NEWFIL,ERR=99)CANDNO,NAME,MARK(CHINDX)
          END IF
11        CONTINUE
          PRINT'(''1STATISTICS FOR CLASS '',A30///)',CLASS
          DO 13 J=1, EXAMS
******        PRINT STATS FOR EACH EXAM
          PRES=PRESNT(J)
          AVERAG=SUMEX(J)/REAL(PRES)
          PRINT 9, EXAM(J),AVERAG,PRES
9         FORMAT(' EXAM IN ',A30//
     +            ' AVERAGE MARK = ',F6.2/
     +            ' NO. OF CANDIDATES SITTING = ',I5)
          ABSENT=TOTAL-PRES
          IF(ABSENT.EQ.0) THEN
              PRINT'('' ZERO ABSENTEES'')'
                      ELSE
              PRINT'('' NO. OF ABSENTEES = '',I5)',ABSENT
          END IF
```

```
13       CONTINUE

         GO TO 20

******VALID EOF LANDS HERE

******TIDY UP FILES

90       ENDFILE(NEWFIL,ERR=99)

         REWIND(NEWFIL,ERR=99)

         CLOSE(NEWFIL,ERR=99)

         CLOSE(OLDFIL,ERR=98)

         STOP

******   ERROR CONDITIONS IN THE FILES

97       PRINT'(///'' *** UNEXPECTED EOF DETECTED IN FILE '',A6)',MSTNAM

         STOP

98       PRINT'(///'' *** ERROR DETECTED IN FILE '',A6)',MSTNAM
         STOP
99       PRINT'(///'' *** ERROR DETECTED IN FILE '',A6)',CHNAME

         END
```

Second program

The second program searches through the file CMPSCI looking for candidates who scored at least 75% in Computer Science and prints out his or her marks in the other exams which he or she sat.

In this case, the master file is used to obtain individual records and so is accessed directly. Therefore the directory is used to locate the start of data for a given class. In contrast to the first program, the error messages are grouped together and printed from a subroutine.

Algorithm

> read the directory (from EXMLST)
> read the class name (from CMPSCI)
> **loop while not** end-of-file (CMPSCI) **do**
>> {print heading for this list
>> read no. of candidates (total) (from CMPSCI)
>> **if** there are no candidates **then print** 'no Computer Science exam for this class'
>>> **else**
>>> {read the number of exams (exams) and their names for this class (from EXMLST)
>>> **loop for** $i = 1, 2, \ldots$, total **do**
>>>> {read candidate no, name and mark (from CMPSCI)
>>>> **if** mark $\geqslant$ 75 **then** {read the rest of the candidates marks (from EXMLST)
>>>>> print the name and marks under a heading }}

if none scored $\geqslant 75$ **then** print 'no candidate in this class scored
$\geqslant 75$ in Computer Science'}

read class name from CMPSCI}

```
      PROGRAM FILES2
******THIS PROGRAM PRINTS THE EXAM RECORDS OF A CANDIDATE WHO SCORED AT
******          LEAST 75 IN COMPUTER SCIENCE
      INTEGER MARK(10), RECNO(20)
      INTEGER CLSNDX, CLSREC, EXAMS, CANDNO, MRK, T1, CHFIL, TOTAL
      CHARACTER*30 LIST(20), EXAM(10)
      CHARACTER *30 CLASS, CHOSEN, NAME, C1, CHNAME *6, MSTNAM*6
      LOGICAL NONE
      PARAMETER (CHOSEN='COMPUTER SCIENCE',
     +           CHNAME='CMPSCI',CHFIL=34,
     +           MSTNAM='EXMLST',MASTER=24)
      OPEN(MASTER,FILE=MSTNAM,STATUS='OLD',ACCESS='DIRECT',RECL=320,
     +          ERR=98)
      OPEN(CHFIL, FILE=CHNAME, STATUS='OLD', FORM='UNFORMATTED', ERR=99)
******READ THE DIRECTORY OF CLASS NAMES AND RECORD NUMBERS
      READ(MASTER,REC=1,ERR=98)(LIST(I),RECNO(I),I=1,10)
      READ(MASTER,REC=2,ERR=98)(LIST(I),RECNO(I),I=11,20)
      CLSNDX=0
20    READ(CHFIL,END=90,ERR=99) CLASS
******LOOP WHILE NOT EOF
         CLSNDX=CLSNDX+1
******   FIRST CHECK THAT THE CLASS NAMES MATCH
         IF(CLASS.NE.LIST(CLSNDX))THEN
             CALL ERROR(4)
         END IF
         PRINT'(''1LIST OF TOP CANDIDATES IN CLASS '',A30///)',CLASS
         READ(CHFIL,END=97,ERR=99)TOTAL
         IF(TOTAL.EQ.0) THEN
             PRINT'('' NO '',A30,'' EXAM IN THIS CLASS''),CHOSEN
                 ELSE
******       THE CHOSEN EXAM WAS SAT BY THIS CLASS
******       READ THE EXAM NAMES FROM THE MASTER FILE
             CLSREC=RECNO(CLSNDX)
             READ(MASTER,REC=CLSREC+1,ERR=98)T1,EXAMS,(EXAM(J),J=1,EXAMS)
             NONE=.TRUE.
```

```
              DO 10 I=1,TOTAL
******            PROCESS MARKS
              READ(CHFIL,END=97,ERR=99)CANDNO,NAME,MRK
              IF(MRK.GE.75) THEN
                  IF(NONE) THEN
                      NONE=.FALSE.
                      PRINT'('' '',A4,23X,10(3X,A7)/)','NAME',(EXAM(J),J=1,EXAMS)
******                    ONLY FIRST 7 CHARS OF EXAM NAME PRINTED
                  END IF
                  READ(MASTER,REC=CLSREC+CANDNO+1,ERR=98) T1,C1,
     +                        (MARK(J), J=1,EXAMS)
                  PRINT'('' '',A30,10I10)',NAME,(MARK(J),J=1,EXAMS)
              END IF
10            CONTINUE
              IF(NONE) THEN
                  PRINT'('' NO CANDIDATE SCORED 75 OR MORE IN '',A30)',CHOSEN
              END IF
          END IF
      GO TO 20
******VALID EOF LANDS HERE
90    REWIND(CHFIL,ERR=98)
      CLOSE(CHFIL,ERR=98)
      CLOSE(MASTER,ERR=99)
      STOP
******    ERROR CONDITIONS IN THE FILES
*         EOF IN CHOSEN FILE
97        CALL ERROR(1)
*         MASTER FILE ERROR
98        CALL ERROR(2)
*         CHOSEN FILE ERROR
99        CALL ERROR(3)
      END

      SUBROUTINE ERROR(I)
******THIS SUBROUTINE PRINTS OUT THE ERROR REQUESTED BY THE ARGUMENT I.
      INTEGER TOT
      PARAMETER(TOT=4)
      CHARACTER ERR(TOT+1)*60
      DATA(ERR(I),I=1,TOT+1)/
```

```
+               ' *** UNEXPECTED EOF IN CHOSEN FILE',

+               ' *** ERROR DETECTED IN MASTER FILE',

+               ' *** ERROR DETECTED IN CHOSEN FILE',

+               ' *** CLASS NAMES  DO NOT MATCH, FILES OUT OF STEP',

+               ' *** SUBROUTINE ERROR CALLED WITH INVALID ARGUMENT'/
      IF(I.GE.1.AND.I.LE.TOT) THEN

          PRINT 25, ERR(I)

                              ELSE

          PRINT 25, ERR(TOT+1)

      END IF

      STOP
25    FORMAT(A60)

      END
```

Note that:

(a) by comparing the class names in each file, a check is made that the files have not got out of step;

(b) in this program the errors are handled by a subroutine.

Case study 4: Poetic riddles

The following type of riddle is well-known:

My first is in boot and also in shoe,
My second is in putty but not in glue,
My third is in water and also in tap,
My fourth is in panic but not in flap,
My fifth is in choice and also in choose,
My sixth is in drink but not in booze,
What am I?

The aim of this case study is to analyse such poems and print out information which will be helpful in attempting to solve the riddle. The authors are grateful to one of their colleagues, Dr R. H. Davis, for bringing this type of problem to their attention.

To simplify matters the following assumptions will be made:

(a) each input record is structured as in the poem above, and contains a maximum of 80 characters including blanks;

(b) each line of a poem commences in column 1 of an input record, and is terminated on the right hand side by at least one blank character;

(c) the words in each line are separated by *single* blank characters;

(d) no word contains more than 20 characters;

(e) no punctuation occurs;

(f) the input data is correct.

The final assumption is, of course, incredibly naive, and Exercise 20.5 invites the reader to consider the data validation aspect of this problem in more detail.

An initial attempt at an algorithm is fairly easy to produce along the following lines:

> read a line
> print it
> **loop while not** the last line **do**
> > {analyse line to ascertain word 1, type-of-line, word 2
> > find letters in word 1
> > find letters in word 2
> > depending on type-of-line, find and print out letters which are either in
> > > (a) word 1 **and** word 2, **or**
> > > (b) word 1 **and not** word 2
> > read a line
> > print it}

Here word 1 and word 2 are the two words in each line the letters of which are to be used, and type-of-line is either 'and also' or 'but not'.

The analysis of a line to ascertain word 1, type-of-line, and word 2 is reasonably straightforward, *on the assumption that the input data is correct.* Note that, for example

(a) the start of word 1 occurs immediately after the string 'is in ', i.e. 6 character positions after the first '*i*'. It is insufficient to search merely for the first occurrence of the string 'in' since, for example, the word 'ninth' might occur in a line of a poem.

(b) the end of word 1 occurs immediately before the next blank character.

(c) 'and also' or 'but not ' may be picked up as the eight characters after the blank character referred to in (b).

(d) the start of word 2 occurs immediately after the next string 'in ', i.e. 3 character positions after the '*i*'.

A subroutine DECODE may therefore be created along the following lines to analyse each line of text:

```
      SUBROUTINE DECODE(TEXT,WORD1,WORD2,TYPE)

      CHARACTER TEXT*80,WORD1*20,WORD2*20,TYPE*8

      INTEGER L,R
*
******FIND FIRST WORD
*
      L=INDEX(TEXT,'IS IN ')+6

      R=(L-1)+INDEX(TEXT(L:),' ')-1

      WORD1=TEXT(L:R)
*
******FIND TYPE OF LINE
```

```
*
      TYPE=TEXT(R+2:R+9)
*
******FIND SECOND WORD
*
      L=(R-1)+INDEX(TEXT(R:),'IN')+3
      WORD2=TEXT(L:)
*
      END
```

Moving on to the next part of the algorithm, a method must be devised for finding, and holding in an appropriate manner, the letters in each of WORD1 and WORD2. Here the problem is not in finding the letters in each word, which is straightforward, but in deciding how to hold the information in order that the *next* part of the algorithm is as simple and efficient as possible. Various approaches may be adopted and the one used here is to create for each word a one dimensional logical array with 26 elements (corresponding to the letters of the alphabet), and to set to **true** the elements of these two arrays corresponding to the letters in the two words. Note that

(a) if the underlying collating sequence for the implementation of FORTRAN 77 being used contains characters other than letters between A and Z, more than 26 elements will have to be allocated to each array. A PARAMETER statement in the main program unit will be used to specify the appropriate value.

(b) the elements of each array must be initialized to **false** at an appropriate point in the algorithm. A subroutine VFALSE may be created for this task thus:

```
      SUBROUTINE VFALSE(A,N)
      LOGICAL A(N)
      DO 100 I=1,N
         A(I)=.FALSE.
100   CONTINUE
      END
```

Not surprisingly a subroutine SET is also created for finding the letters in a word and holding them as described above:

```
      SUBROUTINE SET(A,N,WORD)
      LOGICAL A(N)
      CHARACTER WORD*20
      INTEGER FAC,SUB
      FAC=ICHAR('A')
      DO 100 I=1,20
```

```
      SUB=ICHAR(WORD(I:I))-FAC+1
      IF (1.LE.SUB.AND.SUB.LE.N) THEN
            A(SUB)=.TRUE.
      END IF
100   CONTINUE
      END
```

The main program may now be written without difficulty. COUNT is an integer variable taking the values 1, 2, 3, . . ., corresponding to the lines of the poem being processed.

```
      PROGRAM RIDDLE
      INTEGER COUNT,FAC
      CHARACTER TEXT*80,WORD1*20,WORD2*20,TYPE*8
      PARAMETER(N=26)
      LOGICAL X(N),Y(N),Z
      DATA COUNT/1/
      FAC=ICHAR('A')
*
******READ AND PRINT A LINE
*
      READ(*,'(A80)')TEXT
      WRITE(*,'('' '',A80)')TEXT
*
******PROCESS EACH LINE IN TURN
*
100   IF(TEXT(1:4).NE.'WHAT') THEN
*
******      INITIALISE ARRAYS X,Y
*
            CALL VFALSE(X,N)
            CALL VFALSE(Y,N)
*
******      ANALYSE LINE
*
            CALL DECODE(TEXT,WORD1,WORD2,TYPE)
*
******      FIND AND STORE LETTERS
*
            CALL SET(X,N,WORD1)
```

```
           CALL  SET(Y,N,WORD2)
*
******     OUTPUT  EXPLANATORY  TEXT
*
           WRITE(*,'(85X,''LETTER'',I3)')COUNT
*
******     OUTPUT  POSSIBLE  LETTERS
*
           DO 200 I=1,N
               IF (TYPE.EQ.'AND ALSO') THEN
                    Z=X(I).AND.Y(I)
                                      ELSE
                    Z=X(I).AND..NOT.Y(I)
               END IF
               IF(Z) THEN
                    WRITE(*,'(110X,A1)')CHAR(I+FAC-1)
               END IF
200        CONTINUE
*
******     WRITE A LINE OF BLANKS AND INCREMENT COUNT
*
           WRITE(*,'( )')
           COUNT=COUNT+1
*
******     READ AND PRINT NEXT LINE
*
           READ(*,'(A80)')TEXT
           WRITE(*,'('' '',A80)')TEXT
*
               GO TO 100
       END IF
*
       END
```

Note finally that the program as given above merely indicates the possible choices for *each letter* in the answer to the riddle. Even more helpful would be a list of *all possible answers* to the riddle. The reader is invited to extend the program in this direction.

Exercise 20

1   With reference to Case study 1:

It is an important aspect of data handling to ensure that the data is correct and self consistent. For example, in the league table, the following relationships hold:

(a)   for each entry
  (i)   the points total = number of matches won x 2 + number of matches drawn
  (ii) number of matches played = number of matches won + number of matches drawn + number of matches lost
(b)   for the whole table
  (i)   the sum of all games won = the sum of all games lost
  (ii) the sum of all goals scored for = the sum of all goals scored against

Write a FORTRAN 77 subroutine subprogram CHECK(NAME,INFO,N) to check that all the above relationships hold with respect to the league table. Indicate where the reference or references to CHECK should be made.

2   With reference to Case study 2:

(a)   The astronomer Zeller devised the following method for calculating the day of the week corresponding to a given date $d/m/y$ in the Gregorian calendar:

  (i)   if $m = 1$ or 2, add 12 to m and subtract 1 from y;
  (ii) let r be the remainder on dividing by 7 the expression

$$d + 2m + 2 + [(3m + 3)/5] + y + [y/4] - [y/100] + [y/400]$$

  where [ ] indicates that remainders are ignored after division operations;
  (iii) if $r = 0$ then day is a Saturday, if $r = 1$ then day is a Sunday, if $r = 2$ then day is a Monday, . . ., if $r = 6$ then day is a Friday.

Write a subroutine subprogram ZELLER(D,M,Y,R,DNAME) to set R equal to the value specified by Zeller's method, and DNAME equal to the name (abbreviated to 3 characters) of the corresponding day of the week.

(b)   Given the following definitions for *Golden Number, Dominical Letter, Epiphany*, and *Advent Sunday* extend the program DAYTAB to tabulate also for each year Y its Golden Number, Dominical letter(s), the day of the week on which Epiphany falls, and the date of Advent Sunday.

  (i)   *Golden Number:* (the remainder on dividing Y by 19) + 1.
  (ii) *Dominical Letter:* A, B, C, D, E, F, or G depending on whether 1 January is a Sunday, or 2 January is a Sunday, or 3 January is a Sunday, . . ., or 7 January is a Sunday. A leap year has *two* Dominical letters, the first calculated as above, and the second its predecessor in the alphabet (G is regarded as the 'predecessor' of A).
  (iii) *Epiphany:* 6 January.
  (iv) *Advent Sunday:* The Sunday such that there are precisely three Sundays between it and Christmas Day.

3   With reference to Case study 3:

(a)   No check is made in the second program to ensure that the master record read is that for the required candidate. What amendments are needed to add this validation?

(b)   It will be noted that with fixed size blocks of 320 bytes, most of the blocks will be only partly filled. For example, a candidate record is a maximum of 52 bytes (candidate number = 2, name = 30, marks = 2 each, say). It would therefore be worth packing data for several candidates into one record.

What amendments would be necessary to the first program if data on six candidates were packed into a record? That is, each class list has the format

first and second records   : unchanged
third and subsequent records : candidate number, name and (m) marks
for six candidates

Each list therefore contains $\text{INT}(n/6) + 3$ records if n is not a multiple of 6 and $\text{INT}(n/6) + 2$ records otherwise.

4   A sequential unformatted file, PHONEX, contains the names, addresses, and telephone numbers of all students and employees in a University. The information is grouped into the departments of the University and ordered alphabetically on the name field within departments. The format of records in a department is:

first record: department name (character *50) and total number of people
in the department

second and subsequent records:

(i)   person's name   (character *35)
(ii)   address   (character *80)
(iii) telephone number   (integer – 10 digits)
(iv)   category code   (integer – 1 digit)

The category codes are as follows:

0   an employee
1   first year undergraduate
2   second year undergraduate
3   third year undergraduate
4   fourth year undergraduate
9   postgraduate

Each year student records on the file must be updated with first, second, and third year students becoming second, third, and fourth year students respectively, the old fourth year students being removed and a new set of first year students being added.

If the information about new first year students is held on a sequential formatted card file on the designated input unit, write a FORTRAN 77 program to update the student records as specified, creating a new file PHONEY, and print on the designated output unit, the name, address, and telephone number for each fourth year student record being deleted. The new data for each department is in the form:

(i)   the first card contains department name;
(ii)   a group of three cards for each student containing the students name, address, and telephone number respectively in the format (A35/A80/I10);
(iii) the final group of three cards comprise a card containing the character Z in each of the first 6 columns followed by two blank cards.

Assume the order of departments in both files is the same.

5   With reference to Case study 4:

(a)   consider whether it is possible, without complicating program logic too much, to permit a less rigidly specified format for each input line;

(b)   write a subroutine to validate each line of the poem being input.

6   Devise an algorithm and write a FORTRAN 77 program to output a complete calendar for a given year y. Use the subroutine ZELLER (see Question 2) to ascertain the day of the week on which 1 January falls.

7   (a)   Integer solutions of the equation $x^3 + y^3 = a^3 + b^3$ (and other similar equations) may be found by the following method:

(i)   For all possible values of x and y in some range $1 \leqslant x \leqslant y \leqslant N$ fill up a matrix A thus:

$$A = \begin{bmatrix} 1^3 & 1^3 & 1^3 + 1^3 \\ 1^3 & 2^3 & 1^3 + 2^3 \\ \cdot & \cdot & \cdot \\ \cdot & \cdot & \cdot \\ 1^3 & N^3 & 1^3 + N^3 \\ 2^3 & 2^3 & 2^3 + 2^3 \\ 2^3 & 3^3 & 2^3 + 3^3 \\ \cdot & \cdot & \cdot \\ \cdot & \cdot & \cdot \\ \cdot & \cdot & \cdot \\ 2^3 & N^3 & 2^3 + N^3 \\ 3^3 & 3^3 & 3^3 + 3^3 \\ \cdot & \cdot & \cdot \\ \cdot & \cdot & \cdot \\ \cdot & \cdot & \cdot \\ N^3 & N^3 & N^3 + N^3 \end{bmatrix}$$

(ii)   Sort the rows into order using the values in the third column as key values.

(iii)   Scan down the third column looking for *identical* values. Each pair of such values generates a solution of the original equation.

Write a FORTRAN 77 program, based on this approach, to output all integer solutions of the equation $x^3 + y^3 = a^3 + b^3$ with x, y, a, $b \leqslant 50$.

(b)   Modify the program to eliminate solutions which are simple multiples of other solutions, i.e. eliminate any solution such that the highest common factor of x, y, a, and b is greater than unity.

21 Program portability

Everything put together falls apart sooner or later. (*Simon's Law*)

The main objective of this chapter is to offer helpful advice about minimizing the problems of moving FORTRAN 77 program units from machine to machine. Many of the points covered have already been discussed in earlier chapters. Nevertheless there are sound reasons for gathering them together into an integrated description for the benefit of the reader.

Beyond the scope of this chapter is consideration of the methods of recording information on magnetic media and the problems associated with the portability of *data* files. Transferring, for example, an unformatted magnetic tape file containing the internal representations of real values is a far from trivial task.

Adherence to the Standard

When writing FORTRAN 77 program units, *adhere to the Standard*. Avoid, even at the loss of some efficiency, non-standard enhancements provided by manufacturers.

On rare occasions, however, it may be necessary to use non-standard FORTRAN 77 facilities, in order to avoid *gross* inefficiencies. When such non-standard facilities are used in a program unit, their presence should be clearly indicated.

Checking programs for adherence to the Standard

Ideally any FORTRAN 77 compiler provided by a computer manufacturer should be able to flag, both at compile-time and at run-time, any departures from the Standard detected in a FORTRAN 77 program unit. In addition, enhancements to FORTRAN 77 provided by a manufacturer should be clearly indicated in the manufacturer's documentation.

Unfortunately not all manufacturers are sufficiently user-orientated to provide such facilities, and indeed it may appear to be in their interests to encourage customers to use highly *non-standard* features, in order that the transfer of programs to some other manufacturer's machine is as awkward as possible. Under such circumstances, the use of a preprocessor or verifier, if available, to check for syntactical adherence to the Standard, is recommended, particularly for large FORTRAN 77 programs.

Planning with portability in mind

Always design and write FORTRAN 77 programs on the assumption that they are going to be moved from machine to machine, even although such a prospect may seem unlikely at the time. With this in mind

(a)   use structured design and programming techniques;
(b)   insert copious explanatory comments;
(c)   maintain adequate documentation;
(d)   pay attention to program layout;
(e)   isolate machine-dependent constants by using, for example, PARAM-ETER statements, and confine, if possible, machine dependent and non-standard features to a few *subprograms*, for easy replacement;
(f)   highlight all non-standard features used, if any;
(g)   keep the program simple and straightforward, e.g. avoid subtle effects created by the interaction of COMMON blocks and EQUIVALENCE statements.

All of the above are examples of good programming style, which make it easier to carry out alterations to an existing program to enable it to run on another machine.

Precision of arithmetic

Many portability problems encountered by scientists and engineers may be traced to the fact that the precision of real arithmetic in the machine *from* which a program is being transferred, is sometimes *much greater* than the precision of real arithmetic in the machine *to* which the program is being transferred. For example, moving a scientific FORTRAN program from a Burroughs B6800 system to an IBM 370 system is not without problems in this respect, the precision of real arithmetic in the two machines being 39 bits and 24 bits respectively. As a result, the output from a transferred program may be suspect, if not totally meaningless, particularly if the problem being solved is *ill-conditioned*, i.e. sensitive to small changes in the input data.

There is no simple way of guarding against such difficulties when writing a FORTRAN 77 program for the first time. A judicious use of *double precision* arithmetic, when moving the program to a machine whose precision is inadequate, should improve matters considerably. The advice of an expert in numerical analysis will often be helpful in this respect. Remember, for example, that the indiscriminate use of double precision arithmetic will increase execution times significantly, by a factor of about 3 if double precision operations are performed by *hardware*, and by a factor much greater than 3 if double precision operations are performed by *software*.

It is also worth mentioning in this section that subprograms for generating random numbers are notoriously difficult to move from machine to machine. Do not assume that a random number generator, which performs admirably on one machine, will produce equally good pseudo-random number sequences on another. *Portable* random number generators are surprisingly difficult to construct.

Internal representations and collating sequences

Although FORTRAN 77 program units involving the manipulation of character information should be much more portable than the equivalent FORTRAN 66 program units, there remain potential areas of difficulty. The most obvious of these is the fact that the character collating sequence is not *completely* specified, although comparisons of character strings on the basis of the ASCII collating sequence may be carried out.

Great care is therefore required in writing FORTRAN 77 program units involving the use of character facilities. In particular, the explicit use of the *internal* values of characters is not recommended, nor are non-standard characters in a local character set.

Similarly avoid the use of properties of the internal representations of integer values, real values, etc. Do not, for example, write FORTRAN 77 statements based on the assumption that the sign bit for an integer may be found at the extreme left of its internal representation. What applies to one machine may not necessarily apply to another.

Local limits and restrictions

When planning to move a FORTRAN 77 program to another machine, it is important to obtain information concerning local limits and restrictions. The following is by no means a complete check list, but indicates the nature of the information to be ascertained.

(a) What are the ranges for integer, real, and double precision values?
(b) What is the precision of real arithmetic and the precision of double precision arithmetic?
(c) What are the smallest positive real and double precision values which have internal representations?
(d) What is the collating sequence?
(e) How are overflow and underflow handled? Is an error signalled, or does execution continue with the 'out of range' value replaced by the nearest 'in range' value?
(f) What restrictions, if any, are imposed by the FORTRAN 77 compiler, e.g. lengths of character constants, array dimension sizes, maximum number of subprograms in an executable program?
(g) What are the restrictions on file names?
(h) Which file access methods are available?
(i) Which input/output units are available, and what are the standard external unit identifiers?
(j) Is there a maximum size for records on disc and magnetic tape?
(k) Is the machine a virtual memory machine?

Note that the answer to the last question above can have a significant effect on the performance of FORTRAN 77 programs involving the manipulation of large arrays, particularly if the elements are accessed in 'row' rather than 'column' order. A detailed discussion, however, is beyond the scope of this book.

Further reading

Much of the literature on the portability of software has been contributed by members of implementation teams for libraries of mathematical and statistical software, and many useful ideas can be gleaned from their experiences, although the solutions adopted are not always relevant to the individual programmer wishing to improve the portability of his or her FORTRAN programs. Of particular interest is the work of the implementation teams for the IMSL library in the United States (Aird *et al.*, 1977; International Mathematical and Statistics Libraries, 1975) and the NAG library in the United Kingdom (Ford *et al.*, 1973).

Bell Laboratories staff have also made significant contributions in the area of portability in recent years. The creation of PFORT, a 'safe' subset of FORTRAN 66, and a PFORT verifier (Ryder, 1974) are particularly noteworthy. More recently, the development of PORT (Fox *et al.*, 1977), a portable mathematical subroutine library, has stimulated much interest. PORT incorporates the simple idea of using *comment cards* to hold the values of machine-dependent constants for a wide variety of computer systems. To activate the machine-dependent constants for a particular system is merely a matter of blanking out the C in column 1 of the appropriate cards.

Finally attention is drawn to the excellent survey report by Muxworthy (1976) covering many aspects of program portability.

22 Programming style

An ounce of image is worth a pound of performance. (*Peter's Placebo*)

Throughout this book suggestions and recommendations have been made on aspects of problem analysis and programming practice. These follow the general principles of structured programming which, if obeyed thoughtfully and carefully, will lead to more reliable programs. Having discussed FORTRAN 77 in some detail it seems appropriate to consider in this chapter those aspects which should lead to 'good' FORTRAN 77 programs; that is, how to develop a good programming style.

Good programming style is developed with years of experimenting and experience and to some extent is a matter of personal preference. However there are certain guidelines which are generally accepted to lead to programs which are efficient, reliable and easy to maintain. The following points could be described as some of the objectives of a program:

(a)   it should produce the correct results using valid data;
(b)   it should trap invalid data;
(c)   it should work efficiently in terms of the resources it requires including time, memory, file access, etc.;
(d)   the people who use it should have a high level of confidence in it;
(e)   it should be easy to maintain.

These objectives cannot be met without a great deal of thought and care. Developing a style of program design and coding to meet *all* the objectives is part of the development of a good programmer.

Programming style starts with the design of the algorithm and the splitting up of the problem into its constituent modules. Then comes the discipline of implementing the algorithmic structures in a consistent manner, the careful design of the module interfaces and the apparently trivial but important points of the choice of variable names, the sensible layout of the program and the annotation of the coding by use of comments. Of course, no program should be released for use without sensible user documentation and comprehensive maintenance documentation but these aspects are beyond the scope of this book.

Algorithmic structures

As explained in Chapter 2, it is generally recognized that three structures only are required to design any algorithm. These are

(a)   the processing statement,
(b)   the decision structure,
(c)   the looping structure.

Therefore, to convert an algorithm into a program it is necessary to decide which structures in the chosen programming language are best suited to implementing the algorithmic structures. In some languages, the conversion is simple since there are language statements which are directly equivalent to the algorithmic structures. This is not true of FORTRAN 77, as was demonstrated in Chapter 9. Indeed this is one of the failings of the new Standard. However, this cannot be used as an excuse for poor programming style since the algorithmic structures can be implemented easily if a little inelegantly.

Notice, however, that the use of only three algorithmic structures results in a self-imposed *restriction* in the use of FORTRAN 77. It is an important discipline of programming that these restrictions are not ignored; hence no 'trick' coding (which usually ends up confusing everyone) and no short-cuts (at least initially). The resultant program should be an obvious FORTRAN 77 copy of the algorithm and consist of combinations of:

(a)   *processing statements* – assignment and input/output statements, CALL, RETURN, STOP, and END statements;
(b)   *decision structures* – block IF, END IF, ELSE, and ELSE IF statements with the associated IF-block, ELSE-block, and ELSE IF-block;
(c)   *looping structures* – a block IF statement with a GO TO statement as the last statement of the IF-block, a DO statement with the associated DO-loop, and, when the loop termination is the recognition of an endfile record, a READ statement which contains an end-of-file specifier.

Example 22.1   Typical processing statements used in the book have been

(a)   Y = 2*SIN(X)+3.165*X*X*EXP(X)
(b)   READ (24,END=97,ERR=98)
(c)   WRITE (14,92,IOSTAT=IOERR)((X(I,J),J=1,N),I=1,N)
(d)   CALL CHECK(EMPNO,RATE,TIME,THALF,DT)

Example 22.2   Typical decision structures used in the book have been

(a)   IF(BALANC .LT. 0) THEN
                          PRINT *, BALANC
                  END IF

(b)   IF(MONTH .EQ. 12) THEN
                          MONTH = 1

```
        YEAR = YEAR+1
                ELSE
        MONTH = MONTH + 1
    END IF
```

Example 22.3   Typical looping structures used in the book have been

(a)
```
        10    IF(X .GE. 0) THEN
                SUM = SUM+X
                READ *,X
                GO TO 10
              END IF
```

which implements **loop while** $x \geqslant 0$ **do** { add x to the sum

read another value of x }

(b)
```
              DO 25 J=1, N−1
                X(INDX,J+1) = T(J)
        25    CONTINUE
```

which implements **loop for** $j = 1, 2, \ldots, n - 1$ **do** assign T_j to $x_{\text{indx.}j+1}$

No other structures have been used in the book. It is therefore strongly recommended that a programmer choose a small set of structures together with their implementations in FORTRAN 77 and then *use no other structure.*

Use of the GO TO statement
The GO TO statement is often blamed as a manifestation of bad programming practice. This is, of course, a gross oversimplification. However, misuse of the GO TO statement is a sign of poor design and muddled thinking. The trouble is that it is an easy statement to use, and is often a convenient and fast means of overcoming a tricky piece of coding. Never fall into the trap of using any statement, far less the GO TO statement, merely as a convenience. It must form part of the overall design.

In FORTRAN 77 it is difficult to avoid using the GO TO statement. The following is a list of occasions when it may be used sensibly:

(a)   in implementing a **loop while** statement;
(b)   in error situations where control must pass from the main algorithm to a special terminating or recovery sequence;
(c)   in circumstances where it is necessary to jump out of a loop for abnormal reasons.

Example 22.4   The character array LIST contains 30 names. Determine whether or not the name contained in the variable NAME is in this array.

Algorithm

```
        assign 1 to i
        loop while list_i ≠ name do
```

{**if** i = 30 **then goto** exit
increment i}
(name found)

.

.

.

exit: (name not found)

Code

```
            I = 1
24          IF(LIST(I).NE.NAME)THEN
               IF(I.EQ.30)THEN
                  GO TO 55
               END IF
               I = I+1
               GO TO 24
            END IF
******NAME FOUND
```

.

.

.

```
******NAME NOT FOUND
55          .
```

.

.

Note that if the name is found, the variable I will be $\leqslant 30$ and be the index of the name in LIST.

For a detailed discussion on the use of GO TO statements in programming the reader should consult Knuth's excellent paper (1974).

Modules

An important task in the design of an algorithm is the identification and specification of its modules. There are no specific rules to assist in the identification of modules and different programmers will often split up the same problem in different ways. However, a module should be a logically distinct entity designed to do a specific task within the algorithm. Therefore the specification should be clear, and the interface between the module and the rest of the algorithm simple and unambiguous.

Usually a module is implemented either as a function subprogram or a subroutine subprogram with the arguments or common blocks acting as the data interface. In Chapter 13 it was recommended that arguments should be used in preference to COMMON because the subprogram is then completely self-contained and does not depend on common blocks being declared in other program units. The subprogram can therefore be used in different programs with very little difficulty. Also the use of COMMON can produce unexpected side-effects with the consequent difficulties of debugging and maintenance.

Since a module is defined to do a specific task, it is difficult to see what function is served by having multiple entry points to the module. This can only make a module more complex and hence more error prone and more difficult to use. The possible gains in efficiency are far outweighed by the poor structure and the danger of misuse. Therefore, the reader is strongly urged never to use the ENTRY statement (see Chapter 23).

One advantage of using a module is that a possibly major task is effectively executed by a single statement (the subprogram reference). This allows the overall design structure to remain clear at the program level. However, the assumption is made that the module will return control to where it was referenced and nowhere else. If alternative return points are permitted, the structure cannot be seen clearly (even with well commented programs) and again debugging and maintenance are made more difficult. A good programmer should *never* use the alternate return facility in FORTRAN 77 (see Chapter 23) since this leads to a 'spaghetti-like' structure which is next to impossible to understand. Different conditions which arise inside the module can be communicated through arguments if necessary and acted on *at the point of reference.*

To summarize, a subprogram should have one entry point and one place of return with all necessary communication taking place through the arguments.

Coding

Most modern programming languages have sufficient scope to allow the programmer to reflect the algorithmic structure and hence the design plan in the program. Apart from the points of implementation touched on above, this includes points such as choosing meaningful names for variables, laying out the program statements sensibly and annotating the code by well-chosen comments.

It should be noted, however, that most modern programming languages have sufficient scope also to allow the programmer to do almost anything else instead! Because various facilities are available in a programming language does not mean that they have to be used.

Variables

The choice of meaningful variable names is a very important aspect. For example it may be quicker and more convenient to use X where YEAR would be better, but it makes the code significantly less readable. Similarly, it may be amusing to use names like FRED and R2D2 but if they represent pressure and volume in the program, they will not aid the programmer in the long run.

Example 22.5   Which coding sequence is the more understandable?

```
IF(MONTH.EQ.12) THEN            IF(I.EQ.12) THEN
        MONTH = 1                       I = 1
        YEAR = YEAR+1                   J = J+1
                ELSE                            ELSE
        MONTH = MONTH+1                 I = I+1
END IF                          END IF
```

Another aspect of variable names arises when the same name is used for different purposes in different program units. While it is probably harmless to use names like I and J for loop counts or T and TEMP for storing intermediate results in different program units or different parts of the same program unit, it would not be sensible to use TEMP to hold an intermediate result in one part of the program and a value of temperature in another part. This can only lead to confusion.

FORTRAN 77 is not very helpful when choosing variable names since they are restricted to not more than six letters and digits. It can be very frustrating trying to think of a meaningful name which fits into six characters, but that is no reason not to try — and succeed. Comments can be used to describe the more obscure names.

The implicit naming convention is a well-known feature of FORTRAN and it enables variables to be used without being declared explicitly. Few FORTRAN programmers would include the name I in a type statement

$$\text{INTEGER I}$$

On the other hand, this convenience can lead to slovenly programming and the use of names such as IYEAR instead of YEAR to avoid the simple declaration

$$\text{INTEGER YEAR}$$

It is worth considering declaring all variable names explicitly (even I) as required in other programming languages. Such a self-imposed restriction can be a small aid in clarifying the code.

Layout

Throughout the book the sensible layout of program statements has been emphasized. With judicious use of spacing in a line and of blank lines, a program can be converted from a mass of (almost) indistinguishable statements to a readable structured algorithm (provided the design effort has been made). The difference this makes to debugging and maintenance far outweighs the initial effort involved.

A typical example of sensible layout is the indenting of IF-blocks, etc., and DO-loops to show clearly where these groups of statements end.

Comments

Programmers are regularly being urged to comment their programs. However, as with the choice of sensible variable names, the thought required seems counter-productive in the 'white-heat' of coding and, somehow, promises to insert comments later are rarely kept.

Comments are only of value if they are relevant, understandable, and not superfluous. A comment such as

```
*                    INCREMENT I
```

to annotate the statement

$$\text{I} = \text{I}+1$$

is superfluous, adds nothing to the understanding of the program and merely clutters up the code. A few well-chosen comments are more important than a mass of irrelevant comments inserted to give the appearance of a well annotated program.

Comments should clarify the code and illuminate the implementation of the algorithmic structures. The following is a list of places where, in general, comments are useful.

(a)   At the beginning of a program unit to explain the purpose of the unit.
(b)   At the beginning of loops and decisions to explain their purpose.
(c)   With portions of complex coding to clarify and explain the complexities.
(d)   With the declarations to explain the purpose of the variables being declared.
(e)   At the beginning of a subprogram to explain the purpose of the arguments.
(f)   Where coding has been 'further refined' to eliminate inefficiencies (Knuth, 1974).

While it is undoubtedly a chore, the thoughtful programmer will insert helpful comments.

Conclusion

The points discussed briefly in this chapter are merely initial guidelines to good programming style. A fuller exploration has been made by Kernighan and Plauger (1974).

A program must communicate not only with a computer system, but also with the original programmer and the maintenance programmer. Therefore, a good programmer develops a style to meet the objectives mentioned at the start of the chapter and to communicate with other programmers.

23 Other facilities

> Once you open a can of worms, the only way to recan them is to use a larger can. (*Zymurgy's First Law of Evolving Systems Dynamics*)

The purpose of this chapter is to describe a number of other facilities available in FORTRAN 77. In the opinion of the authors, many of these facilities are *undesirable* features of the language, and should therefore not be used. Included in this category are:

> arithmetic IF statements
> assigned GO TO statements
> ASSIGN statements
> IMPLICIT statements
> ENTRY statements
> 'alternate' RETURN statements
> EQUIVALENCE statements

Some of these are relics of earlier versions of FORTRAN, e.g. arithmetic IF statements. Others contradict principles of structured programming, e.g. ENTRY and 'alternate' RETURN statements.

On the other hand, many existing FORTRAN programs will contain instances of these facilities, and it is therefore helpful in understanding such programs to have some knowledge of their effects. During a first reading of this chapter, however, the asterisked sections may be conveniently ignored.

The logical IF statement

The logical IF statement has the form:

$$\text{IF (lexp) S}$$

where

> (a) lexp is a logical expression as described in Chapter 16.
> (b) S is any executable FORTRAN 77 statement except a DO, block IF, ELSE IF, ELSE, END IF, END, or another logical IF statement.

Briefly the effect of a logical IF statement is that the statement S is executed if and only if the value of the logical expression lexp is **true**.

Example 23.1   The following are examples of logical IF statements:

   (a)   IF (I.NE.0) S=S+X(I)
   (b)   IF (J.LE.N) READ*,X,Y
   (c)   IF(I.LT.1.OR. I.GT.N) GO TO 100

Example 23.2   The logical IF statement

$$IF\ (R.LE.0)\ R=R+7$$

has the same effect as the block IF statement

$$IF\ (R.LE.0)\ THEN$$
$$R=R+7$$
$$END\ IF$$

Note from Example 23.2 above that there is some convenience in using a logical IF statement instead of a block IF statement whose IF-block consists of a *single* statement. On the other hand, whenever a block IF statement is followed by an IF-block containing *several* statements, there is no elegant way of achieving the same effect using logical IF statements. For this reason, logical IF statements were deliberately avoided in earlier chapters, although they provide a convenient mechanism in circumstances similar to those described in the example above.

Example 23.3   The FORTRAN 77 program lines

$$IF\ (R.LE.0)$$
$$R=R+7$$

are *invalid*, a continuation character being required in column 6 of the second line.

*The arithmetic IF statement

The arithmetic IF statement is a *dangerous* statement, since its use tends to be coupled with the occurrence of numerous GO TO statements in the same program unit. These in turn cause the logic of the program unit to be difficult to follow, and even more difficult to debug.

The arithmetic IF statement has the form

$$IF\ (arithmetic\ expression)\ s_1,\ s_2,\ s_3$$

where s_1, s_2, and s_3 are statement labels attached to *executable* statements in the same program unit. The effect of an arithmetic IF statement is that the arithmetic expression† is evaluated, and control is transferred to the statement with label s_1 if the value of the arithmetic expression is *less than* zero, to the statement with label s_2 if the value of the arithmetic expression is *equal to* zero, and to the statement with label s_3 if the value of the arithmetic expression is *greater than* zero.

† It must not be of type COMPLEX.

Example 23.4   The arithmetic IF statement

$$IF(I+J)\ 20,30,5$$

causes control to be transferred to the statement with statement label 20 if $I+J<0$, to the statement with statement label 30 if $I+J=0$, and to the statement with statement label 5 if $I+J>0$.

Example 23.5   The statement labels s_1, s_2, and s_3 need not be all different. For example, the arithmetic IF statement

$$IF\ (K)\ 10,20,10$$

causes control to be transferred to the statement with statement label 10 if $K \neq 0$, and to the statement with statement label 20 if $K=0$.

The computed GO TO statement

The computed GO TO statement has the form

$$GO\ TO\ (s_1, s_2, s_3, s_4, \ldots, s_n)\ i$$

where

(a) s_1, s_2, s_3, $\ldots$, s_n are statement labels (which need not be all different) attached to *executable* statements in the same program unit.

(b) i is an integer expression.†

The effect of the statement is as follows:

if value of $i = 1$ transfer control to the statement with statement label s_1
if value of $i = 2$ transfer control to the statement with statement label s_2

.   .   .   .
.   .   .   .
.   .   .   .

if value of $i = n$ transfer control to the statement with statement label s_n

Note also that if the value of i is less than 1 or greater than n, no action is performed, i.e. the computed GO TO statement has the same effect as a CONTINUE statement.

Example 23.6   The following is an example of a computed GO TO statement:

$$GO\ TO\ (10,30,10,40,50,30)\ KAPPA$$

The computed GO TO statement can be useful, particularly when one of several sections of program is to be executed, depending on the value of some integer variable.

---

† i may be preceded by an optional comma.

Example 23.7   An input record contains values for an integer *i* and a real variable *x*. Depending on the value of *i*, write a program to evaluate, for the given value of *x*, the indicated expression in the following list:

$$i = 1, x^3 - 3x^2 + 2x - 1$$
$$i = 2, \sin x - 2 \cos x$$
$$i = 3, e^x - 7x^2 + 11$$
$$i = 4, x^2 \sin x - e^x \cos x$$

One solution is to use a computed GO TO statement thus:

```
      PROGRAM FUNC
      READ*,I,X
      GO TO (100,200,300,400)I
      WRITE(*,10)I,X
10    FORMAT(' ',I3,F10.4,5X,'INVALID VALUE FOR I')
      STOP
100   Y=X**3-3*X*X+2*X-1
      GO TO 500
200   Y=SIN(X)-2*COS(X)
      GO TO 500
300   Y=EXP(X)-7*X*X+11
      GO TO 500
400   Y=X*X*SIN(X)-EXP(X)*COS(X)
500   WRITE(*,20)I,X,Y
20    FORMAT(' ',I3,F10.4,5X,F10.4)
      END
```

Alternatively nested ELSE IF statements may be used thus:

```
      PROGRAM FUNC
      READ*,I,X
      IF (I.EQ.1) THEN
          Y=X**3-3*X*X+2*X-1
          ELSE IF (I.EQ.2) THEN
                Y=SIN(X)-2*COS(X)
              ELSE IF (I.EQ.3) THEN
                  Y=EXP(X)-7*X*X+11
                  ELSE IF (I.EQ.4) THEN
                      Y=X*X*SIN(X)-EXP(X)*COS(X)
                      ELSE
                      WRITE(*,10)I,X
```

```
10              FORMAT(' ',I3,F10.4,5X,'INVALID VALUE FOR I')

                STOP

        END IF

        WRITE(*,20)I,X,Y
20      FORMAT(' ',I3,F10.4,5X,F10.4)

        END
```

Essentially one of the above approaches must be adopted, since FORTRAN 77 does not possess a 'case' statement (cf. PASCAL). The reader is left to decide which is preferable.

*The assigned GO TO statement and the ASSIGN statement

The assigned GO TO statement is contrary to the principles of structured programming, and is also a statement for which it is difficult to envisage where it would be of real benefit. It may be used in the simple form

$$GO\ TO\ i$$

where i is the name of an integer variable. At the time of execution of such an assigned GO TO statement, i must have as its value the value of a *statement label* attached to some *executable* statement in the same program unit. Control is then transferred to that executable statement.

A more complicated form of assigned GO TO statement is also permissible, namely

$$GO\ TO\ i, (s_1, s_2, \ldots, s_n)$$

where $s_1, s_2, \ldots, s_n$ are statement labels attached to *executable* statements in the same program unit, and the comma after the i is *optional*. The effect in this case is similar to that described above, except that at the time of execution of the assigned GO TO statement the statement label value of i must be the value of one of the statement labels in the parentheses.

In order to assign an appropriate statement label value to i, a special *statement label assignment statement* must be used. This statement, often called an ASSIGN statement, has the form

$$ASSIGN\ s\ TO\ i$$

where s is a statement label attached to some executable or FORMAT statement in the same program unit.

Example 23.8   A FORTRAN 77 program unit might contain the following statements:

.

.

.

ASSIGN 30 TO K

.
.
.

$$\text{GO TO K } (30,100)$$

.
.
.

100      $Y = X - 7.6$

.
.
.

30      $I = I + 1$

.
.
.

Execution of the assigned GO TO statement would cause a transfer of control to the statement with statement label 30, i.e. the statement $I = I + 1$ would be executed immediately after the execution of the assigned GO TO statement. Note that the statement

$$\text{ASSIGN 30 TO K}$$

cannot be replaced by the arithmetic assignment statement

$$K = 30$$

since only an ASSIGN statement may be used to give a *statement label value* to K. Later in the program, however, K may be given a normal integer value (by means of, for example, an arithmetic assignment statement), or another statement label value (by means of another ASSIGN statement).

As mentioned earlier, an ASSIGN statement may also be used to assign to an integer variable the value of a statement label attached to some FORMAT statement in the same program unit. Such an ASSIGN statement is used in conjunction with an input or output statement containing the integer variable as a *format identifier*.

Example 23.9   A FORTRAN 77 program unit might contain the following statements:

.
.
.

$$\text{ASSIGN 50 TO J}$$

.
.

$$\text{WRITE } (*,J) \text{ X,Y}$$

.
.
.

$$50 \qquad \text{FORMAT('b',2F15.5)}$$

.
.
.

Note finally that, while an integer variable has a statement label value as the result of the execution of some ASSIGN statement, the variable must not be *referenced* in any way other than those described above, i.e. in an assigned GO TO statement or as a format identifier in an input/output statement.

*The IMPLICIT statement

The normal FORTRAN 77 implicit naming convention states that, if the symbolic name of a constant, variable, array, external function, or statement function in a program unit commences with one of the letters I, J, K, L, M, or N, the data type associated with that name in the program unit is INTEGER; if, on the other hand, the symbolic name begins with some other letter, the data type associated with that name in the program unit is REAL.

The normal implicit naming convention may be changed within a program unit by means of IMPLICIT statements. Such statements, however, can be fraught with difficulties since it is all too easy to forget the *new* implicit naming convention when creating a name for a particular entity in that program unit. In addition, the types associated with the names of external functions referenced in the program unit, may also be affected.

By way of illustrating IMPLICIT statements, a program unit might, for example, contain the IMPLICIT statement:

```
        IMPLICIT COMPLEX(W,Z),
      +          DOUBLE PRECISION (D,S–V,X,Y),
      +          LOGICAL (B,K–M),
      +          INTEGER (P–R),
      +          CHARACTER*6 (C)
```

establishing new implicit naming conventions thus:

First letter of name	Associated type
W,Z	COMPLEX
D,S,T,U,V,X,Y	DOUBLE PRECISION
B,K,L,M	LOGICAL
P,Q,R	INTEGER
C	CHARACTER*6
I,J,N	INTEGER
A,E,F,G,H,O	REAL

Note how

(a)   writing, for example, S–V implies a *range* of initial letters S, T, U, and V;

(b)   the last two lines of the above table are remnants from the normal implicit naming convention, names beginning with one of the letters A, E, F, G, H, I, J, N, O being unaffected by the IMPLICIT statement above.

An IMPLICIT statement specifies a type for any constant, variable, array, external function, or statement function whose name begins with any letter specified in the IMPLICIT statement, either as a *single* letter or as part of a *range* of letters. An IMPLICIT statement applies only within the program unit in which it occurs, and has no effect on the type of any *intrinsic* function.

Not surprisingly the type implied by an IMPLICIT statement for any constant, variable, array, external function or statement function, may be overridden (or confirmed) by the appearance of the appropriate name in a *type statement*. Similarly the presence of an explicit type specification in a FUNCTION statement overrides (or confirms) the type implied for that function subprogram name by any IMPLICIT statement.

Example 23.10   A function subprogram definition might commence thus:

```
COMPLEX   FUNCTION  FRED(A,B,N,C)
IMPLICIT   INTEGER (A,B,D–G),
+                  CHARACTER*4(C)
CHARACTER C*8
       .
       .
       .
```

Note that, despite the IMPLICIT statement:

(a)   FRED is the name of a function subprogram returning a value of type COMPLEX;

(b)   C is a dummy variable argument of type CHARACTER and of length *8*.

Within the specification statements of a program unit, IMPLICIT statements must precede all other specification statements except PARAMETER statements, which may be interspered with IMPLICIT and other specification statements. If, however, the initial letter of any symbolic constant name occurs either explicitly or implicitly in an IMPLICIT statement, the IMPLICIT statement must *precede* the PARAMETER statement defining the symbolic constant.

Example 23.11   A FORTRAN 77 main program might commence thus:

```
PROGRAM ALBERT
PARAMETER (N=2)
IMPLICIT CHARACTER *(N) (X)
PARAMETER (X='ABC')
```

with the following effects:

(a)   N is the symbolic name of a constant of type INTEGER, value 2;

(b)   names in the program unit commencing with the letter X are no longer of type REAL by default, but are now of type CHARACTER and length 2 by default;

(c)   X is the symbolic name of a constant of type CHARACTER and length 2, value AB.

Note that the statements must occur in the above order. In particular, the first PARAMETER statement must *define* the symbolic constant N before it is *used* in the IMPLICIT statement, and the IMPLICIT statement must in turn precede the second PARAMETER statement, because the symbolic constant name X commences with a letter which occurs in the IMPLICIT statement.

Note finally that a program unit may contain more than one IMPLICIT statement. Fairly reasonably, however, the same initial letter must not appear as a single letter, or be included in a range of letters, more than once in *all* the IMPLICIT statements in a program unit.

Statement functions

A statement function statement may be used to define a new function in FORTRAN 77 provided that:

(a)   the function is so simple that it can be defined using a *single* statement;

(b)   the function is going to be referenced from *one* program unit only.

The following example illustrates the definition and use of a statement function.

Example 23.12   A FORTRAN 77 program unit might commence thus:

```
PROGRAM RCALC
REAL MASS,LENGTH,P,Q
COMPLEX W,Z
QUAD(X,Y)=A*X**2+B*X*Y+C*Y**2
```

The fourth line is a statement function statement defining a function QUAD with two arguments X, Y. When called into action later in the program unit by writing, for example,

$$T=2*QUAD(P,3.6)-7.8 \tag{1}$$

the actual arguments P,3.6 are associated with the dummy arguments X,Y; then the right-hand side of the statement function statement is evaluated; and finally the resulting value is returned to be used as an operand in the arithmetic expression on the right-hand side of (1). Note that a *real* value is returned, since the name QUAD of the statement function implies type REAL by the implicit naming convention. Note also that the right-hand side of the statement function statement not only involves the dummy arguments X,Y but also the actual real variables A, B, and C. Not surprisingly, whenever QUAD is called into action A, B, and C must have *defined* values.

In general, a statement function is *defined* by writing a statement function statement of the form:

$$\text{fname}(x_1, x_2, x_3, \ldots, x_n) = \text{expression}$$

where

(a)   *fname* is the name of the statement function, created according to the usual rules. If the type to be associated with the function name (i.e. the type of the value to be returned when the function is referenced) is not implied by the implicit naming convention in operation in the program unit, the name of the statement function must also appear in a *prior type statement*.

(b) $x_1, x_2, \ldots, x_n$ are the *dummy variable arguments* (*n* may be zero) of the statement function. Once again, if the type of a dummy variable argument is not correctly implied by the first letter of its name, the name must appear in a prior type statement. In addition, each name must not occur more than once in the list $x_1, x_2, \ldots, x_n$.

(c)   *expression* is the expression (arithmetic, logical, or character) whose value is to be returned whenever the function is referenced. Each operand in the expression on the right-hand side must be one of the following:

(i) a constant; (ii) the symbolic name of a constant; (iii) a variable name; (iv) an array element name; (v) an intrinsic function reference; (vi) a reference to *another* statement function defined *earlier* in the program unit; (vii) an external function reference; (viii) a dummy procedure reference; (ix) an expression, in parentheses, satisfying the same criteria.

Note that each variable reference may be either a reference to a dummy argument or to a variable in the same program unit as the statement function statement.

Example 23.13   A FORTRAN 77 program unit might contain

```
            .
            .
            .


      INTEGER  SUMSQ
      SUMSQ(N)=N*(N+1)*(2*N+1)/6
```

Note the appearance of SUMSQ in a type statement to over-ride the implicit naming convention.

Example 23.14   A FORTRAN 77 program unit might contain

```
            .
            .
            .


      INTEGER  APSUM,A,D
      APSUM(A,D,N)=N*(2*A+(N-1)*D)/2
```

In this case both the statement function name, APSUM, and two of the dummy variable arguments of the statement function, A and D, appear in a prior type statement.

Example 23.15   A FORTRAN 77 program unit might contain

.

.

.

```
COMPLEX  Z,CSINH,CCOSH,CFUNC
CSINH(Z)=0.5*(EXP(Z)−EXP(−Z))
CCOSH(Z)=0.5*(EXP(Z)+EXP(−Z))
CFUNC(Z)=(A*CSINH(Z)−B*CCOSH(Z))/(A*CSINH(Z)+B*CCOSH(Z))
```

Here three statement functions, CSINH, CCOSH and CFUNC, are defined, and the definition of CFUNC involves references of CSINH and CCOSH.

It is also important to note, with regard to Example 23.15, that the symbolic name Z is being used for several *different* entities. Each statement function has a dummy variable argument, *local* to the statement function statement, and the name Z has been given to that dummy variable argument in all three cases. In addition, elsewhere in the program unit, the name Z may be attached to a variable of type COMPLEX.

Example 23.16   An example of a character statement function definition is:

.

.

```
CHARACTER*6  PASSWD*20,C1,C2,C3,CH
PASSWD(C1,C2,C3)='*'//C1//C2//C3//'*'
```

To reference a statement function it is used as an operand in an expression by writing the name of the statement function followed by, in parentheses, a list of actual arguments. The actual arguments must agree, of course, in *order, number,* and *type* with the corresponding dummy arguments.

Execution of a statement function reference results in the following:

(a)   evaluation of actual arguments which are expressions;

(b)   association of actual arguments with the corresponding dummy arguments;

(c)   evaluation of the expression on the right-hand side of the statement function statement;

(d)   conversion, if necessary, of the resulting value to the type of the statement function according to the usual arithmetic assignment rules; or a change, if necessary, in the length of a character expression value according to the usual character assignment rules.

Example 23.17   With reference to Examples 23.12 to 23.16, the following are examples of references to the various statement functions:

- (a)   TVAL = QUAD(X1,X2) − QUAD(SIN(P),COS(Q))
- (b)   KONS = 3*SUMSQ(M+5) + 2
- (c)   SUM1 = APSUM(ISTART,INC,50)
- (d)   W = 3*CSINH(Z)+(0,1)*CFUNC(Z+1/Z)
- (e)   CHWORD = PASSWD(CH,'SECRET',CH)

Note finally, with regard to statement functions, that:

- (a)   An actual argument in a statement function reference may be any expression except a character expression involving concatenation of a variable or dummy argument whose length specification is *(*).
- (b)   The length specification of a character statement function or statement function dummy argument of type CHARACTER must be of the form * followed by an integer constant expression.
- (c)   statement function statements in a program unit must come after the specification statements (if any) and before the first executable statement.

There are a number of other restrictions of relatively little practical importance.

*The ENTRY statement

ENTRY statements may be used to specify *alternative entry points* into a function or subroutine subprogram. In the opinion of the authors, this is a thoroughly bad facility the use of which is to be strongly discouraged since one of the principles of structured programming is that each 'module' should have exactly *one* point of entry. For this reason, the treatment of ENTRY statements is deliberately superficial.

Example 23.18   Consider the following function subprogram:

```
FUNCTION AREA(A,B,C)
PARAMETER (PI=3.14159265,
+            FAC=PI/180)
*
S=0.5*(A+B+C)
AREA=SQRT(S*(S-A)*(S-B)*(S-C))
RETURN
*
ENTRY AREA1(A,ANGA,ANGB,ANGC)
X=A*SIN(FAC*ANGB)/SIN(FAC*ANGA)
AREA1  =  0.5*A*X*SIN(FAC*ANGC)
RETURN
```

```
*

     ENTRY  AREA2(A,B,ANGC)

     AREA2=0.5*A*B*SIN(FAC*ANGC)

     RETURN

*

     ENTRY  AREA3(X1,Y1,X2,Y2,X3,Y3)

     AREA3=0.5*ABS(X1*(Y2-Y3)+X2*(Y3-Y1)+X3*(Y1-Y2))

*

     END
```

In another program unit the following references to this function might occur:

(a) AREA(P,Q,R). This causes an association between the actual arguments P,Q,R, and the dummy arguments A,B,C, followed by the execution of the statements:

$$S=0.5*(A+B+C)$$
$$AREA=SQRT(S*(S-A)*(S-B)*(S-C))$$
$$RETURN$$

(b) AREA1(X,THETA1,THETA2,THETA3). This causes an association between the actual arguments X,THETA1,THETA2,THETA3, and the dummy arguments A,ANGA,ANGB,ANGC, followed by the execution of the statements:

$$X=A*SIN(FAC*ANGB)/SIN(FAC*ANGA)$$
$$AREA1=0.5*A*X*SIN(FAC*ANGC)$$
$$RETURN$$

Note how execution commences with the first executable statement after the ENTRY statement containing the name AREA1.

(c) AREA2(S1,S2,PHI). This causes an association between the actual arguments S1,S2,PHI, and the dummy arguments A,B,ANGC, followed by the execution of the statements:

$$AREA2=0.5*A*B*SIN(FAC*ANGC)$$
$$RETURN$$

(d) AREA3(1.6,2.4,3.0,-1.5,2.0,3.0). This causes an association between the actual arguments 1.6,2.4,3.0,-1.5,2.0,3.0, and the dummy arguments X1,Y1,X2,Y2,X3,Y3, followed by the execution of the statements:

$$AREA3=0.5*ABS(X1*(Y2-Y3)+X2*(Y3-Y1)+X3*(Y1-Y2))$$
$$END$$

Essentially therefore, by choosing different entry points to the function subprogram, it is possible to evaluate the area of a triangle given one of the following sets of information:

(i)   three sides,
(ii)   one side and three angles,
(iii)   two sides and the contained angle,
(iv)   the Cartesian coordinates of the three vertices.

Note that each ENTRY statement specifies an *entry name* and the associated dummy arguments. The dummy arguments associated with different ENTRY statements need not agree in order, number, type, or name, nor do they have to agree in order, number, type, or name with the dummy arguments in the initial FUNCTION or SUBROUTINE statement of the subprogram. When a function or subroutine is referenced via an entry name, execution commences with the first executable statement following the ENTRY statement containing that entry name.

*Alternative RETURN points

RETURN statements of the form

$$\text{RETURN } e$$

where *e* is an integer expression, may be used to return from a *subroutine subprogram* to one of several alternative points in a program unit containing a call of that subroutine. As with ENTRY statements, the authors are of the opinion that the use of alternative return points is to be strongly discouraged, since structured programming principles are again being contravened. The description in this Section is, therefore, by no means comprehensive.

Example 23.19   Consider the following FORTRAN 77 subroutine TRIANG and main program unit TPROG:

```
SUBROUTINE TRIANG(A,B,C,AREA,*,*)
LOGICAL TEST
TEST=(A+B.GT.C.AND.B+C.GT.A.AND.C+A.GT.B)
IF (TEST) THEN
     S=0.5*(A+B+C)
     AREA=SQRT(S*(S-A)*(S-B)*(S-C))
     RETURN 1
             ELSE
     AREA=0
     RETURN 2
END IF
END
```

```
      PROGRAM TPROG
          ⋮
          ⋮
          ⋮
      CALL TRIANG(X,Y,Z,AVAL,*100,*200)
          ⋮
          ⋮
100   WRITE(*,10) AVAL
          ⋮
          ⋮
200   WRITE(*,20)
20    FORMAT(' SIDES OF TRIANGLE ARE INVALID')
          ⋮
          ⋮
      END
```

Three aspects are worth noting:

(a)   In the SUBROUTINE statement two dummy arguments have been specified as *asterisks*. Dummy arguments in an ENTRY statement may be similarly specified.

(b)   In the CALL statement each of the 'asterisk' dummy arguments has been replaced by an *alternate return specifier* of the form '* statement label', the various statement labels being statement labels attached to *executable* statements in the program unit containing the CALL statement.

(c)   The subroutine subprogram contains two RETURN statements, namely RETURN 1 and RETURN 2. The effect of executing such a RETURN statement is as follows:

(i)   the integer expression e after the keyword RETURN is evaluated;

(ii)   if the value of e is less than 1 or greater than the number of asterisks in the SUBROUTINE (or ENTRY) statement, a 'normal' RETURN statement is executed as described in Chapter 12;

(iii) if, on the other hand, the value of e is such that $1 \leqslant e \leqslant n$, where n is the number of asterisks in the SUBROUTINE (or ENTRY) statement, control is returned to the (executable) statement in the calling program unit identified by the alternate return specifier in the CALL statement *associated with the eth asterisk*.

In the case above, therefore, after the execution of the subroutine, control is returned to either the statement with statement label 100, or to the statement with statement label 200, depending on which of the RETURN statements was executed.

*The EQUIVALENCE statement

An EQUIVALENCE statement is used to specify that two or more entities in the *same program unit* are to share storage units, a facility of dubious value. It has the form:

$$\text{EQUIVALENCE }(a_1,a_2,\ldots,a_m),(b_1,b_2,\ldots,b_n),\ldots$$

where

(a)   each pair of matching parentheses contains a list of entities which are to share storage units;

(b)   each entity is either a *variable name, array element name, array name,* or *character substring name.*

Precisely what is meant by 'sharing storage units' is best illustrated by example.

Example 23.20   Consider the following EQUIVALENCE statement:

$$\text{EQUIVALENCE }(I,J,K),(X,Y,A,B),(Z1,Z2)$$

where I, J, and K are variables of type INTEGER, X, Y, A, and B are variables of type REAL, and Z1 and Z2 are variables of type COMPLEX. Then numeric storage units might be allocated for the values of these variables as follows:

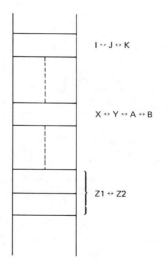

Thus the names I, J, K may be used interchangeably in the program unit in which the EQUIVALENCE statement occurs, similarly the names X, Y, A and B, and the names Z1 and Z2. Note, in passing, that a *complex* value in FORTRAN 77 occupies 2 numeric storage units (as does a *double precision* value).

Example 23.21   Consider a program unit containing the following statements:

$$\text{INTEGER }A(2,3),B(3),C(5),\text{SUB}$$
$$\text{EQUIVALENCE }(\text{SUB},A(1,2),B(2),C(3))$$

Remembering that the elements of arrays are held in consecutive storage units, the EQUIVALENCE statement establishes an association not only among SUB, A(1,2),

B(2), and C(3), but also among various other entities, as can be seen from the following diagram:

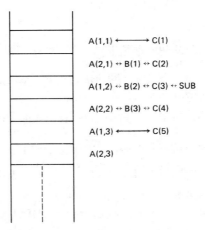

Thus, for example, A(2,1), B(1), and C(2) may also be used interchangeably in the program unit containing the above statements.

Example 23.22   The statements

$$\text{REAL A(2,3),B(3),C(0:5)}$$
$$\text{EQUIVALENCE (A,B(2),C)}$$

have the same effect as the statements

$$\text{REAL A(2,3),B(3),C(0:5)}$$
$$\text{EQUIVALENCE (A(1,1),B(2),C(0))}$$

That is, when an array name without a 'subscript'† occurs in an EQUIVALENCE statement it has the same effect as using the array element name identifying the *first* element of that array.

There are seldom good reasons for using EQUIVALENCE statements, and devious bugs may be introduced by using EQUIVALENCE statements in ways which are not completely straightforward. In particular:

- (a)   Do not mix *data types* within a list in an EQUIVALENCE statement. The FORTRAN 77 Standard only prohibits the equivalencing of entities of type CHARACTER with entities of other types. It is good programming practice, however, not to equivalence entities of different types.
- (b)   Avoid using entities in EQUIVALENCE statements which reside in *common blocks*. Although FORTRAN 77 permits this, with a few minor restrictions, it is once again good programming practice not to take advantage of the fact.

---

† In the FORTRAN 77 sense.

Note finally that dummy argument names must not appear in a list in an EQUIVALENCE statement.

*The PAUSE statement

In its simplest form, a PAUSE statement may be written thus

PAUSE

and, when executed, causes the execution of the executable program in which it occurs to be *suspended*. Execution may only be resumed by intervention from *external* sources, e.g. by action on the part of a Computer Operator. The PAUSE statement is therefore unlikely to be used when a FORTRAN 77 program is being executed under the control of a modern operating system.

Appendix 1
FORTRAN 66 v
FORTRAN 77

One of the criteria used in developing the FORTRAN 77 Standard was compatibility with the 1966 Standard (American National Standards Institute, 1966) (called FORTRAN 66 in this book). An interesting aspect of the 1966 Standard is that few FORTRAN 66 programmers seem to be fully aware of its restrictions since so many compilers provide 'additional facilities' (often without acknowledging them as such). Also many textbooks on FORTRAN 66 describe the additional features supplied by the more popular implementations. It will therefore come as a surprise to some programmers that facilities such as the IMPLICIT statement and T format are new to *Standard* FORTRAN. It is to be hoped that the same fate will not befall the 1977 Standard.

Complete compatibility between FORTRAN 77 and FORTRAN 66 has not been achieved. However, the conflicts which do exist are mainly due to the closer specification of facilities, the correction of errors in the 1966 Standard, or additions to the power of the language.

As for the future, the revision of the 1977 Standard started as soon as work on that Standard was completed. While this revision will undoubtedly mean additional facilities such as a 'while' statement, it may also remove some of the historical and anachronistic features of the current language. For example, it has already been stated that some specific function names will be deleted in a future standard.

Conflicts with FORTRAN 66

Twenty-four conflicts between FORTRAN 77 and FORTRAN 66 are listed in Appendix A of the Standard (American National Standards Institute, 1978). The most important of these are:

(a)   Hollerith constants and Hollerith data are not part of FORTRAN 77. Their place has been taken by the data type CHARACTER. In FORTRAN 66, Hollerith constants are permitted in DATA and CALL statements, and character data can be read into numeric variables using A-format.

(b)   Subscript checking is done on each dimension in a subscripted variable.

In FORTRAN 66, provided the subscript value does not exceed the size of the array, the reference is valid. In the example

$$REAL\ X(10, 10)$$

.

.

.

$$Y=X(15,2)$$

the reference to X(15,2) is not permitted in FORTRAN 77 but is permitted in FORTRAN 66.

(c)   FORTRAN 77 does not permit a transfer of control into a DO-loop from outside the DO-loop. In FORTRAN 66, it is permitted under certain conditions. The concept is known as 'the extended range of a DO'.

(d)   The FORTRAN 66 supplied functions are in two categories called 'intrinsic functions' and 'basic external functions'. The names of the 'intrinsic functions' are not permitted to be used as actual arguments. If the name of a 'basic external function' is used as an actual argument, the name must appear in an EXTERNAL statement. In FORTRAN 77 all supplied functions are called intrinsic functions and only the type conversion, string comparison, choosing largest value, and choosing smallest value function names may not be used as actual arguments. If any other intrinsic function name is used as an actual argument, it must appear in an INTRINSIC statement not an EXTERNAL statement.

(e)   More supplied functions have been added and their names may clash with other names used in FORTRAN 66 programs.

(f)   The units and range of the arguments and results of intrinsic functions are specified for FORTRAN 77 but are not for FORTRAN 66. Thus the specifications used in some FORTRAN 66 implementations may differ from the 1977 Standard.

(g)   The 1966 Standard does not prohibit a (sequential) file from containing both formatted and unformatted records. The 1977 Standard does.

Conflicts with dialects of FORTRAN 66

Many 'FORTRAN 66' compilers offer facilities additional to the 1966 Standard. Some of these facilities are incorporated into the 1977 Standard. However the precise form and meaning of these facilities may not be the same. Great care should therefore be taken when first running a non-standard FORTRAN 66 program under a FORTRAN 77 system.

Additional facilities

FORTRAN 77 has many facilities not provided in FORTRAN 66. These range from the addition of major features (such as direct access files) to the removal of restrictions (such as that on the form of subscript expressions).

The most important additions are:

(a)   type CHARACTER, the use of substrings and the concatenation operator;

(b)   the PARAMETER statement;
(c)   the block IF, ELSE, ELSE IF, and END IF statements;
(d)   direct access files;
(e)   the OPEN and CLOSE statements;
(f)   the error and end specifiers in input/output statements;
(g)   apostrophe, positional, sign, and blank editing;
(h)   list-directed input/output.

Important changes to features already included in FORTRAN 66 are:

(a)   the ability to specify the lower bound of an array dimension;
(b)   a subscript expression may be any integer expression;
(c)   most restrictions on the mixing of entities of different types in an expression have been relaxed;
(d)   the initial, terminal, and incrementation parameters in a DO statement may be numeric expressions taking any value;
(e)   an implied DO loop may be used in a DATA statement;
(f)   expressions may appear in an output list;
(g)   the reading of an endfile record is defined.

An important change to the execution of a DO-loop is that under appropriate conditions (the iteration count = 0), the DO-loop will not be executed. This is known as a 'zero trip' DO-loop. Most implementations of FORTRAN 66 will execute the DO-loop once regardless of the values of the DO statement parameters, although this is not standard FORTRAN 66.

Type CHARACTER

The introduction of type CHARACTER has not only replaced Hollerith constants and data but has also been accompanied by the definition of storage units for numeric data and character data. More precisely:

(a)   an integer, real, or logical datum is contained in one numeric storage unit;
(b)   a double precision or complex datum is contained in two numeric storage units;
(c)   a character datum comprises one character storage unit for each character in the datum.

The 1977 Standard does not specify a relationship between a numeric storage unit and a character storage unit. For this reason

(a)   numeric data and character data cannot be held in the same common block;
(b)   a numeric entity cannot be equivalenced to a character entity and *vice versa*.

In FORTRAN 66 character data are stored in numeric entities and so the above restrictions do not apply.

Conclusion

While FORTRAN 77 is an extension of FORTRAN 66 and most of the conflicts are small, difficulties may be encountered when trying to use a FORTRAN 77 compiler to compile a FORTRAN 66 program. It is recommended that the precautions taken are similar to those suggested under program portability (see Chapter 21), in particular, the program should be tested thoroughly.

Appendix 2
Summary of executable and non-executable statements

Each statement in FORTRAN 77 is classified as *executable* or *non-executable*. To quote the FORTRAN 77 Standard, 'Executable statements specify actions. Non-executable statements describe the characteristics, arrangement, and initial values of data; contain editing information; specify statement functions, and classify program units.' For convenience, the various types of executable and non-executable statements in FORTRAN 77 are summarized and listed in this section.

Executable statements

		Chapter references
Assignment statements	Arithmetic assignment statements	6, 17, 18
	Logical assignment statements	16
	Character assignment statements	15
	Statement label assignment (ASSIGN) statements	23
Control statements	Unconditional GO TO statements	9
	Computed GO TO statements	23
	Assigned GO TO statements	23
	Block IF statements	9
	ELSE IF statements	9
	ELSE statements	9
	END IF statements	9
	Logical IF statements	23
	Arithmetic IF statements	23
	DO statements	9
	CONTINUE statements	9
	STOP statements	8
	PAUSE statements	23
	END statements	8
	CALL statements	12
	RETURN statements	12, 23

	READ statements	7, 14
	WRITE statements	7, 14
	PRINT statements	7
	OPEN statements	14
Input/output statements	CLOSE statements	14
	INQUIRE statements	14
	BACKSPACE statements	19
	ENDFILE statements	14
	REWIND statements	19

Non-executable statements

	Type statements	4, 10, 15, 16, 17, 18
	DIMENSION statements	10
	COMMON statements	13
	PARAMETER statements	11
Specification statements	INTRINSIC statements	13
	EXTERNAL statements	13
	SAVE statements	12, 13
	IMPLICIT statements	23
	EQUIVALENCE statements	23
	PROGRAM statements	8
	FUNCTION statements	12
Program unit statements	SUBROUTINE statements	12
	BLOCK DATA statements	13
	ENTRY statements	23

DATA statements	11
FORMAT statements	14
Statement function statements	23

Appendix 3
Order of statements
and comment lines
in a program unit

The following table, taken from the FORTRAN 77 Standard, indicates the required order of statements of various types and comment lines in a program unit.

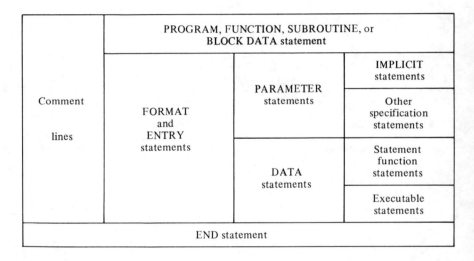

	PROGRAM, FUNCTION, SUBROUTINE, or BLOCK DATA statement		
Comment lines	FORMAT and ENTRY statements	PARAMETER statements	IMPLICIT statements
			Other specification statements
		DATA statements	Statement function statements
			Executable statements
END statement			

Roughly speaking, vertical lines in the table separate categories of statement which may be *interspersed*. Horizontal lines, on the other hand, indicate 'an order of occurrence' of various categories of statement within a program unit. More precisely:

(a)   the *first* statement in a program unit is either a PROGRAM, FUNCTION, SUBROUTINE, or BLOCK DATA statement;

(b)   specification statements (including PARAMETER statements) precede DATA statements and statement function statements;

(c)   IMPLICIT statements precede all other specification statements except PARAMETER statements, which may be interspersed with IMPLICIT and other specification statements, subject to the restrictions described in Chapter 23;

(d)   statement function statements precede executable statements;

(e)   DATA statements may be freely interspersed with statement function statements and executable statements;

(f)   FORMAT statements may occur anywhere *within* a program unit;

(g)   ENTRY statements may also occur anywhere *within* a subprogram unit, except, not surprisingly, between a block IF statement and the corresponding END IF statement, or between a DO statement and the terminal statement of its DO-loop;

(h)   the *last* statement in a program unit must be an END statement;

(i)   comment lines may occur anywhere in a program unit (even before the first statement) up to the END statement.

Appendix 4
Syntax diagrams
for FORTRAN 77

The charts in this appendix describe the syntax of FORTRAN 77 and are copied from the Standard (American National Standards Institution, 1978). It should be noted that certain syntactic features are not represented in the charts. These include the use of blanks, the layout of statements, comment lines, certain context dependent features, etc. Some clarification is contained in footnotes where appropriate.

A syntactic entity is written in lower case letters, e.g. symbolic_name, and it is described in a numbered chart, e.g. symbolic_name is described in chart 99.

The charts are in the form of a 'railway track'.

A junction in the 'track' specifies alternative paths.

A number, n, in a *semi-circle* indicates that this 'track' may be traversed *at most* n times.

A number, n, in a *circle* indicates that this 'track' must be traversed *exactly* n times.

For example, a symbolic name has the form of from one to six letters or digits starting with a letter. Its syntax chart is:

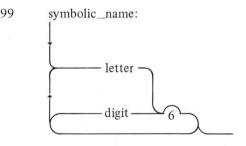

99   symbolic_name:

(letter and digit are described in charts 116 and 115 respectively).

The following diagrams and index are reproduced, with permission, from American National Standard FORTRAN, X3.9, 1978 by the American National Standards Institute, copies of which may be purchased from the American National Standards Institute, 1430 Broadway, New York, New York 10018.

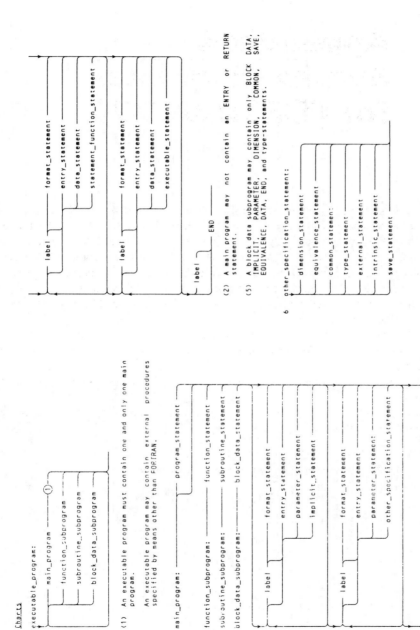

F2 Charts

1 executable_program:

    main_program
    function_subprogram
    subroutine_subprogram
    block_data_subprogram

(1) An executable program must contain one and only one main
    program.

    An executable program may contain external procedures
    specified by means other than FORTRAN.

2 main_program:

    program_statement

3 function_subprogram: function_statement

4 subroutine_subprogram: subroutine_statement

5 block_data_subprogram: block_data_statement

    label   format_statement
            entry_statement
            parameter_statement
            implicit_statement

    label   format_statement
            entry_statement
            parameter_statement
            other_specification_statement

    label   format_statement
            entry_statement
            data_statement
            statement_function_statement

    label   format_statement
            entry_statement
            data_statement
            executable_statement

    label   END

(2) A main program may not contain an ENTRY or RETURN
    statement.

(5) A block data subprogram may contain only BLOCK DATA,
    IMPLICIT, PARAMETER, DIMENSION, COMMON, SAVE,
    EQUIVALENCE, DATA, END, and type-statements.

6 other_specification_statement:

    dimension_statement
    equivalence_statement
    common_statement
    type_statement
    external_statement
    intrinsic_statement
    save_statement

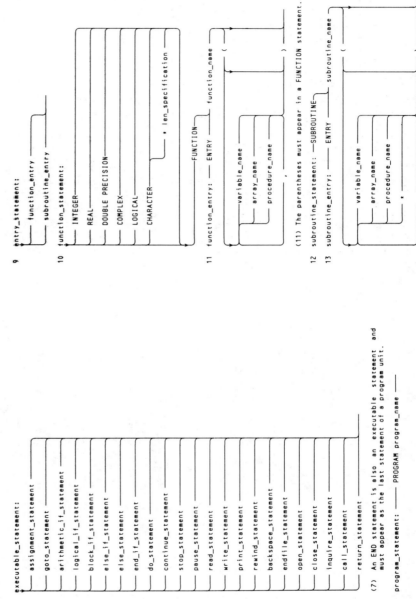

7 executable_statement:
- assignment_statement
- goto_statement
- arithmetic_if_statement
- logical_if_statement
- block_if_statement
- else_if_statement
- else_statement
- end_if_statement
- do_statement
- continue_statement
- stop_statement
- pause_statement
- read_statement
- write_statement
- print_statement
- rewind_statement
- backspace_statement
- endfile_statement
- open_statement
- close_statement
- inquire_statement
- call_statement
- return_statement

(7) An END statement is also an executable statement and must appear as the last statement of a program unit.

8 program_statement: —— PROGRAM program_name ——

9 entry_statement:
- function_entry
- subroutine_entry

10 function_statement:
- INTEGER
- REAL
- DOUBLE PRECISION
- COMPLEX
- LOGICAL
- CHARACTER —— * len_specification

—— FUNCTION ——

11 function_entry: —— ENTRY —— function_name ——
(—— variable_name
array_name
procedure_name ,)

(11) The parentheses must appear in a FUNCTION statement.

12 subroutine_statement: ——SUBROUTINE—— subroutine_name

13 subroutine_entry: —— ENTRY —— subroutine_name
(—— variable_name
array_name
procedure_name ,)

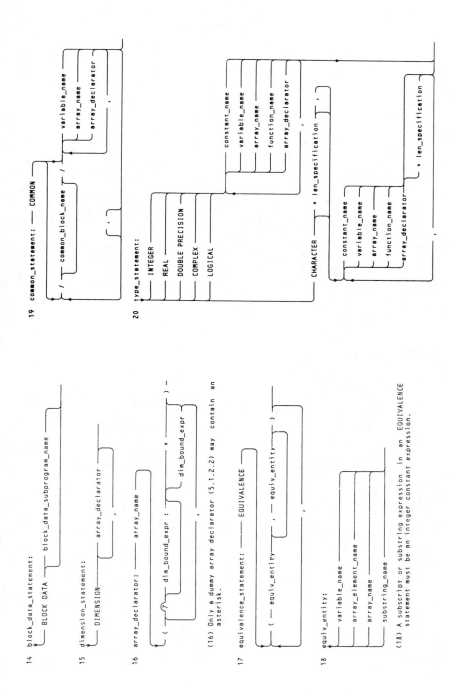

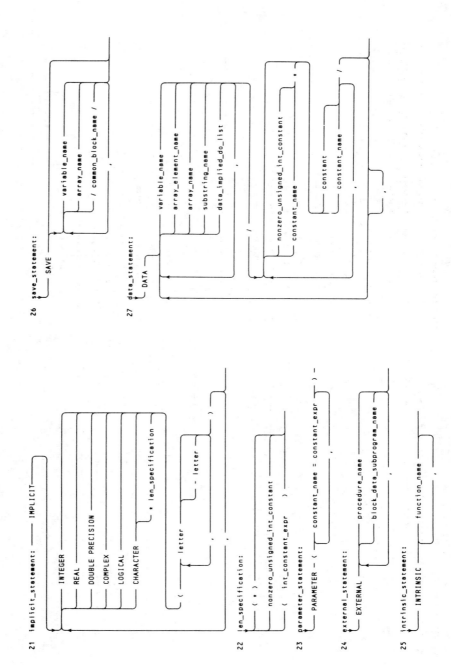

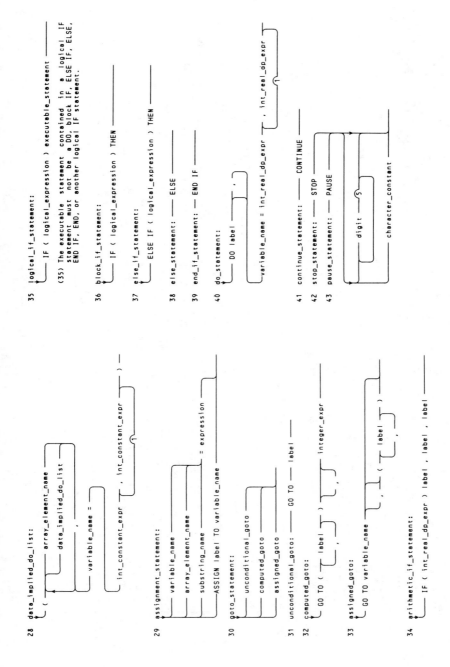

28 data_implied_do_list:

array_element_name

data_implied_do_list

variable_name =

int_constant_expr , int_constant_expr)

29 assignment_statement:

variable_name

array_element_name

substring_name

ASSIGN label TO variable_name

= expression

30 goto_statement:

unconditional_goto

computed_goto

assigned_goto

31 unconditional_goto: GO TO — label

32 computed_goto:

GO TO (label) integer_expr

33 assigned_goto:

GO TO variable_name

(label , label , label)

34 arithmetic_if_statement:

IF (int_real_dp_expr) label , label , label

35 logical_if_statement:

IF (logical_expression) executable_statement

(35) The executable statement contained in a logical IF
statement must not be a DO, block IF, ELSE IF, ELSE,
END IF, END, or another logical IF statement.

36 block_if_statement:

IF (logical_expression) THEN

37 else_if_statement:

ELSE IF (logical_expression) THEN

38 else_statement: ELSE

39 end_if_statement: END IF

40 do_statement:

DO label

variable_name = int_real_dp_expr , int_real_dp_expr

41 continue_statement: CONTINUE

42 stop_statement: STOP

43 pause_statement: PAUSE

digit

character_constant

44 write_statement: WRITE

45 read_statement: READ

46 print_statement: PRINT

(control_info_list)
format_identifier , io_list

47 control_info_list:
unit_identifier
FMT = format_identifier
UNIT = unit_identifier
REC = integer_expr
END = label
ERR = label
IOSTAT = variable_name / array_element_name

(47) A control_info_list must contain exactly one unit_identifier. An END= specifier must not appear in a WRITE statement.

48 io_list:
expression
array_name
io_implied_do_list

(48) In a READ statement, an input/output list expression must be a variable name, array element name, or substring name.

49 io_implied_do_list:
(io_list , variable_name = int_real_dp_expr , int_real_dp_expr , int_real_dp_expr)

50 open_statement:
OPEN (
UNIT = unit_identifier
ERR = label
FILE = character_expression
STATUS = character_expression
ACCESS = character_expression
FORM = character_expression
RECL = integer_expr
BLANK = character_expression
IOSTAT = variable_name / array_element_name
)

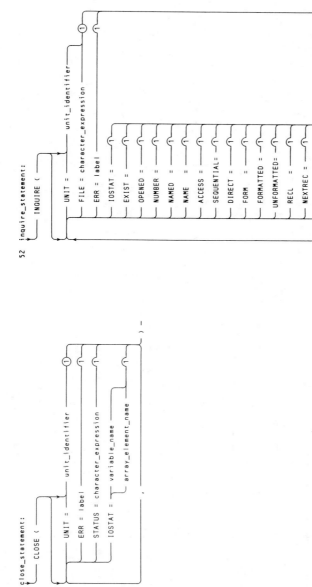

51 close_statement:

52 inquire_statement:

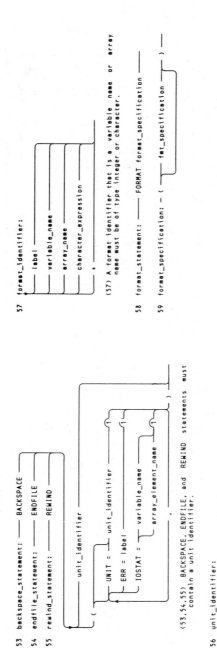

53 backspace_statement: ── BACKSPACE

54 endfile_statement: ── ENDFILE

55 rewind_statement: ── REWIND

unit_identifier

(UNIT = unit_identifier
ERR = label
IOSTAT = variable_name / array_element_name)

(53,54,55) BACKSPACE, ENDFILE, and REWIND statements must contain a unit identifier.

56 unit_identifier:
integer_expr
variable_name
array_name
array_element_name
substring_name

(56) An unit identifier must be of type integer or character, or be an asterisk.

57 format_identifier:
label
variable_name
array_name
character_expression
*

(57) A format identifier that is a variable name or array name must be of type integer or character.

58 format_statement: ──── FORMAT format_specification

59 format_specification: ── (fmt_specification)

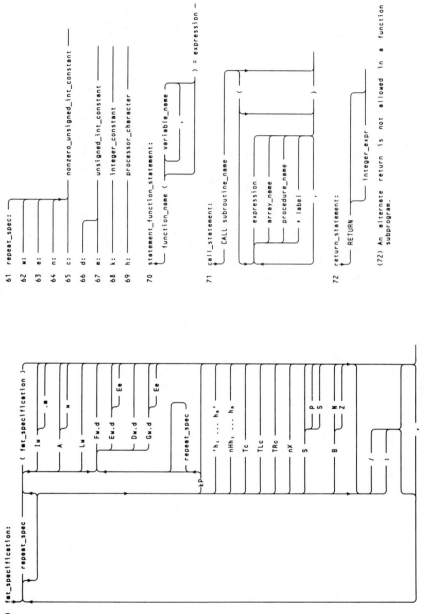

60 fmt_specification:

61 repeat_spec:

62 w:

63 e:

64 n:

65 c: nonzero_unsigned_int_constant

66 d: unsigned_int_constant

67 m: integer_constant

68 k: integer_constant

69 h: processor_character

70 statement_function_statement:
    function_name (variable_name ,) = expression

71 call_statement:
    CALL subroutine_name (expression array_name procedure_name * label)

72 return_statement:
    RETURN integer_expr

(72) An alternate return is not allowed in a function subprogram.

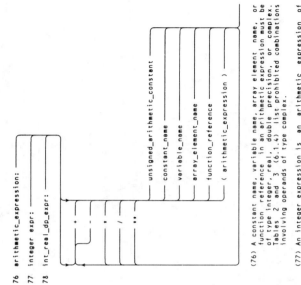

73 function_reference:

function_name (expression
array_name
procedure_name ,)

74 expression:

arithmetic_expression
character_expression
logical_expression

75 constant_expr:

arithmetic_const_expr
character_const_expr
logical_const_expr

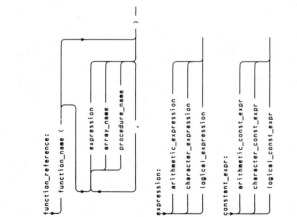

76 arithmetic_expression:
77 integer expr:
78 int_real_dp_expr:

+
-
*
/
**

unsigned_arithmetic_constant
constant_name
variable_name
array_element_name
function_reference
(arithmetic_expression)

(76) A constant name, variable name, array element name, or function reference in an arithmetic expression must be of type integer, real, double precision, or complex. Tables 2 and 3 (6.1.4) list prohibited combinations involving operands of type complex.

(77) An integer expression is an arithmetic expression of type integer.

(78) An int_real_dp_expression is an arithmetic expression of type integer, real, or double precision.

79 arithmetic_const_expr:

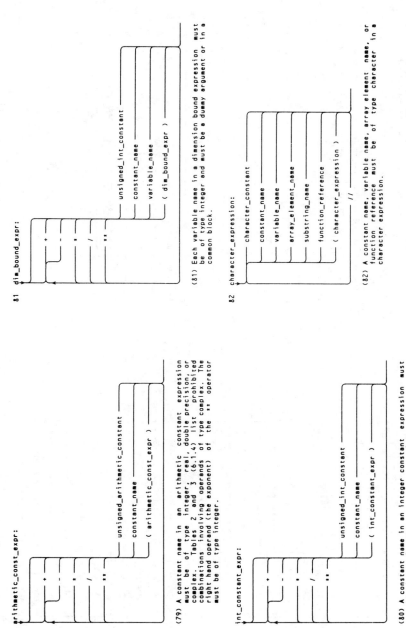

(79) A constant name in an arithmetic constant expression must be of type integer, real, double precision, or complex. Tables 2 and 3 (6.1.4) list prohibited combinations involving operands of type complex. The right hand operand (the exponent) of the ** operator must be of type integer.

80 int_constant_expr:

(80) A constant name in an integer constant expression must be of type integer.

81 dim_bound_expr:

(81) Each variable name in a dimension bound expression must be of type integer and must be a dummy argument or in a common block.

82 character_expression:

(82) A constant name, variable name, array element name, or function reference must be of type character in a character expression.

83 character_const_expr:

- character_constant
- constant_name
- (character_const_expr)
- //

(83) A constant name must be of type character in a character constant expression.

84 logical_expression:

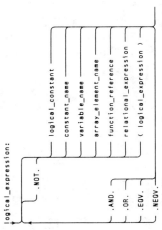

- .NOT.
- logical_constant
- constant_name
- variable_name
- array_element_name
- function_reference
- relational_expression
- (logical_expression)
- .AND.
- .OR.
- .EQV.
- .NEQV.

(84) A constant name, variable name, array element name, or function reference must be of type logical in a logical expression.

85 logical_const_expr:

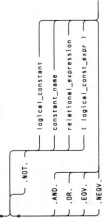

- .NOT.
- logical_constant
- constant_name
- relational_expression
- (logical_const_expr)
- .AND.
- .OR.
- .EQV.
- .NEQV.

(85) A constant name must be of type logical in a logical constant expression. Also, each primary in the relational expression must be a constant expression.

86 relational_expression:

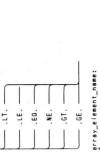

- arithmetic_expression rel_op arithmetic_expression
- character_expression rel_op character_expression

(86) An arithmetic expression of type complex is permitted only when the relational operator is .EQ. or .NE.

87 rel_op:

- .LT.
- .LE.
- .EQ.
- .NE.
- .GT.
- .GE.

88 array_element_name:

array_name (integer_expr ,)

89 substring_name:

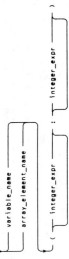

- variable_name
- array_element_name

(integer_expr : integer_expr)

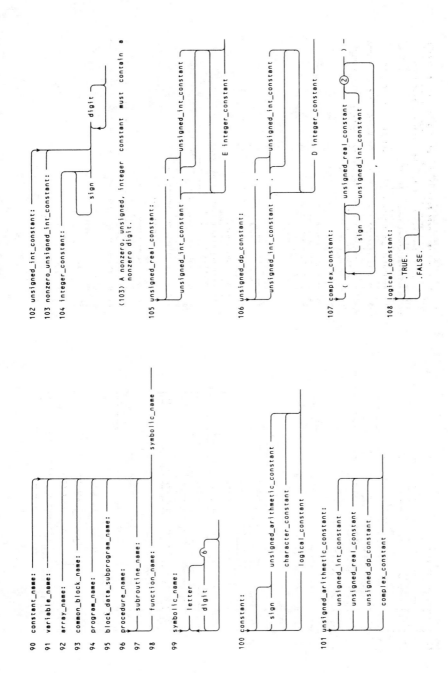

90 constant_name:

91 variable_name:

92 array_name:

93 common_block_name:

94 program_name:

95 block_data_subprogram_name:

96 procedure_name:

97 subroutine_name:

98 function_name:

99 symbolic_name:
    letter
    digit

100 constant:
    sign   unsigned_arithmetic_constant
    character_constant
    logical_constant

101 unsigned_arithmetic_constant:
    unsigned_int_constant
    unsigned_real_constant
    unsigned_dp_constant
    complex_constant

102 unsigned_int_constant:

103 nonzero_unsigned_int_constant:

104 integer_constant:
    sign   digit

(103) A nonzero, unsigned, integer constant must contain a nonzero digit.

105 unsigned_real_constant:
    unsigned_int_constant   .   unsigned_int_constant
    E integer_constant

106 unsigned_dp_constant:
    unsigned_int_constant   .   unsigned_int_constant
    D integer_constant

107 complex_constant:
    (unsigned_real_constant   )
         sign   unsigned_int_constant

108 logical_constant:
    .TRUE.
    .FALSE.

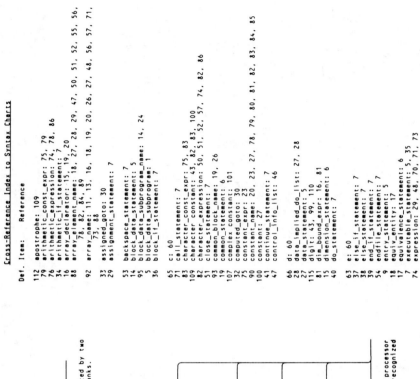

109 character_constant:

(109) An apostrophe within a data string is represented by two consecutive apostrophes with no intervening blanks.

110 label:

(110) A label must contain a nonzero digit.

111 processor_character:

112 apostrophe:

113 nonapostrophe_character:

114 sign:

115 digit:

116 letter:

(111) A blank is a processor character. The set of processor characters may include additional characters recognized by the processor.

References

T. J. Aird, E. L. Battiste, and W. C. Gregory, 'Portability of Mathematical Software Coded in Fortran', *ACM Transactions on Mathematical Software* (1977), **3** (2), 113–27.

American National Standards Institute, *American National Standard FORTRAN, X3.9–1966* (FORTRAN 66). This Standard has been superseded by *X3.9–1978*.

American National Standards Institute, *American National Standard Basic FORTRAN, X3.10–1966*. This Standard has been withdrawn.

American National Standards Institute, *American National Standard FORTRAN, X3.9–1978* (FORTRAN 77). This Standard is available from the American National Standards Institute, 1430 Broadway, New York, NY 10018, USA.

D. W. Barron, *An Introduction to the Study of Programming Languages* (Cambridge: Cambridge University Press, 1977).

E. W. Dijkstra, 'The Humble Programmer', *CACM* (1972), **15** (10), 859–66.

G. G. Dodd, 'Elements of Data Management Systems', *ACM Computing Surveys,* (1969), **1** (2), 117–33.

B. Ford, S. J. Hague, J. A. Prentice, and D. B. Taylor, 'The Development and Maintenance of Multi-Machine Software in the NAG Project', in *Proceedings of the Conference on Software for Numerical Mathematics,* edited by D. Evans (New York: Academic Press, 1973), pp. 383–91.

P. A. Fox, A. D. Hall, and H. L. Schryer, 'The PORT Mathematical Subroutine Library', *Bell Laboratories Computing Science Technical Report* # 47 (1977).

P. E. Gill, W. Murray, S. M. Picken, and M. H. Wright, 'The Design and Structure of a FORTRAN Program Library for Optimization', *National Physical Laboratory Report NAC82* (1977).

International Mathematical and Statistical Libraries, *The IMSL Library* (1975).

B. W. Kernighan and P. J. Plauger, *The Elements of Programming Style* (New York: McGraw-Hill, 1974).

D. E. Knuth, 'Structured Programming with GO TO Statements', *ACM Computing Surveys* (1974), **6** (4), 261–301.

D. T. Muxworthy, 'A Review of Program Portability and Fortran Conventions', *European Computer Program Institute Technical Papers Series Report No. 1* (1976).

National Computer Centre, 'Standard FORTRAN Programming Manual' (1970).

B. G. Ryder, 'The PFORT Verifier', *Software Practice and Experience* (1974), **4** (4), 359–77.

J. E. Sammet, *Programming Languages, History and Fundamentals* (New Jersey: Prentice-Hall, 1969).

E. Yourdon, *Techniques of Program Structure and Design* (New Jersey: Prentice-Hall, 1975).

Solutions to exercises

Exercise 2 (page 13)

1 and 2. The first Case Study in Chapter 20 deals with the League Table problem concerning Association Football. Many games use league tables in a similar fashion.

3. *First refinement*

```
            increment day
            if day overflows then  { set day to 1
                                     increment month
                                     if month overflows then   {set month to 1
                                                                increment year}}
            print day, month, year
```

Second refinement

```
            expand 'day overflows' and 'month overflows' (remember the date
            input is valid)
```

Day overflows: day = 32 or (day = 31 and month = 4, 6, 9 or 11)
                  or (day = 30 and month = 2 and year is a leap year)
                  or (day = 29 and month = 2 and year is not a leap year)

Month overflows: month = 13.

Year is a leap year: the 20th century runs from 1901 through 2000 and so all year numbers divisible by 4 indicate a leap year.

Algorithm

```
        increment day
        if day = 32  or (day = 31 and month = 4, 6, 9 or 11)
                    or (day = 30 and month = 2 and year is divisible by 4)
                    or (day = 29 and month = 2 and year is not divisible by 4)
                then{ set day to 1
                      increment month
                      if month = 13 then { set month to 1
                                           increment year}}
        print day, month, year
```

4. *First refinement*

```
            if year is out of range then fail
                else if month is out of range then fail
                    else if day is out of range then fail
```

Second refinement

Year range is	$1950 \leqslant \text{year} \leqslant 2050$
Month range is	$1 \leqslant \text{month} \leqslant 12$
Day range is	$1 \leqslant \text{day} \leqslant 31$ (for month = 1, 3, 5, 7, 8, 10, 12)
	$1 \leqslant \text{day} \leqslant 30$ (for month = 4, 6, 9, 11)
	$1 \leqslant \text{day} \leqslant 29$ (for month = 2 **and** year is a leap year)
	$1 \leqslant \text{day} \leqslant 28$ (for month = 2 **and** year is not a leap year)

Algorithm
if year < 1950 **or** year > 2050 **then** print 'year number error'
    else if month < 1 **or** month > 12 **then** print 'month number error'
        else if day < 1 **or** day > 31 **or** (day > 30 **and** month = 4, 6, 9, or 11)
                or (day > 29 **and** month = 2 **and** year is divisible by 4)
                or (day > 28 **and** month = 2 **and** year is not divisible by 4)
        then print 'day number error'.

5. Let the elements of vector A be $a_1, a_2, \ldots, a_m$, the elements of vector B be $b_1, b_2, \ldots, b_n$, and the elements of vector C be $c_1, c_2, \ldots$.

Algorithm
    initialize i, j, and k to 1
    loop while $i \leqslant m$ **and** $j \leqslant n$ **do**
              { **if** $a_i < b_j$ **then** { copy a_i to c_k
                                increment i }
                        else { copy b_j to c_k
                                if $a_i = b_j$ **then** increment i
                                increment j }
                increment k }
    if $i \leqslant m$ **then loop for** $i = i, i + 1, \ldots, m$ **do** { copy a_i to c_k
                                            increment k }
        else if $j \leqslant n$ **then loop for** $j = j, j + 1, \ldots, n$ **do** { copy b_j to c_k
                                            increment k }

Exercise 3 (page 18)

1. (a) +, −, ∗ and /
   (b) (i) *main program* FLAG,A,B,C,S,AREA,ANGA,ANGB,ANGC
       (ii) *subprogram* X,Y,Z,PI,TEMP,ANGVAL
   (c) PROGRAM,LOGICAL,READ,PRINT,IF,THEN,SQRT,ELSE,END,
      FUNCTION,ACOS
   (d) *valid input data:* printout would consist of angle values and area value,
      followed by message "INVALID INPUT DATA".
      invalid input data: no printout.
   (e) yes − ANGC = ANGVAL(A,B,C) for example
   (f) 'less than' − .LT.
      'not equal' − .NE.
      'or' − .OR.
   (g) PI = 3.14159265
      TEMP = (B∗B+C∗C−A∗A)/(2∗B∗C)
      ANGA = (180/PI)∗ACOS(TEMP)
      TEMP = (C∗C+A∗A−B∗B)/(2∗C∗A)
      ANGB = (180/PI)∗ACOS(TEMP)

Exercise 4 (page 24)

1. real, real, integer, real, invalid, real, invalid, logical, logical, double precision, double precision, complex, double precision, invalid, character, character, character, invalid, invalid, invalid, complex, character.

2.

Character constant	Length
'TRUE'	4
'EVE''S PUDDING'	13
'4+3=6'	5
'2.25D−1.6'	9

4. (a) The range of valid integer constants is machine dependent.
   (b) The precision of real constants and of double precision constants is machine dependent.
   (c) The ranges of valid real and double precision constants are machine dependent.
   (d) 'Double precision' does not necessarily imply twice the precision of real arithmetic.
   (e) 'Underflow' is machine dependent, i.e. the replacement by the system of small non-zero real values by zero.
   (f) Characters outwith the FORTRAN 77 character set are implementation dependent.

Exercise 5 (page 28)

1. Valid names are

FVALUE	FRED
APT26	COLOUR
XBAR	EMC2
PI	X15P26

2. INTEGER X5,WEIGHT,COUNT
   REAL L,KAPPA
   COMPLEX Z1,Z2,Z3

3. VOL,X,Y,KAPPA, and LEVEL could be removed.

4. (a) L,M, and N are of lengths 2,6, and 4 respectively.
   (b) ANAME,BNAME,X,Y, and VAL are of lengths 8,8,6,6, and 8 respectively.
   (c) CHAR,C1,C2,P,Q, and CNEW are of lengths 1,1,1,6,8, and 1 respectively.

5. Real variables are subject to range restrictions and precision limitations which vary from implementation to implementation. These restrictions and limitations are normally identical to those for real constants. Similar remarks apply to integer and double precision variables.

6. According to the Standard, the character sequence REAL is interpreted as a keyword or variable name depending on the *context* in which it occurs. Unless you have a weird sense of humour, this is something you should not do deliberately in a FORTRAN 77 program unit.

Exercise 6 (page 38)

1. (a) A=P*(1+R/100)**N
   (b) Y=3.65*X**3−2.73*X**2+X−17.5
   (c) V=4.0/3.0*3.14159265*R**3
   (d) Y=(A+B)/(C+D*(F+G))
   (e) EPROX=1+X+X**2/2+X**3/6+X**4/24
   (f) ALPHA=A*B+C**D−16*X
   (g) S=U*T+0.5*F*T**2
   (h) Y=(1/A)**2*(R/12.3)**3*(S/23.4)**4
   (i) Z=((A+B)/(C−D))**(−1.73)
   (j) VAL=2**2**N

2. (a) Missing right parenthesis.
   (b) Missing operator (probably *).
   (c) Missing operator (probably *).
   (d) Two operators side by side.
   (e) Incorrect form for arithmetic assignment statement (two = signs);
       two missing operators (probably * in each case).
   (f) Variable name containing more than six characters;
       missing operator if RT is intended to be R*T.

3. (a) 15.5   (b) 20   (c) 23.0
   (d) 9   (e) 1.0   (f) 3.333 ... 33
   (g) 0.0

4. (a) R=SQRT(X**2+Y**2+Z**2)
   (b) Y=ALOG(X+SQRT(X**2+A**2))
   (c) Z=ALOG10(ALPHA)
   (d) B=3.14159265/2*(A**2+B**2)**1.5/(A*B)
   (e) A=4*3.14159265*ALOG(3*(1+SQRT(2.0))/(1+SQRT(10.0)))
   (f) X=2*3.14159265*A/TAN(THETA)
   (g) S=ATAN(X/(Y+A*X))
   (h) V=SQRT(REAL(M+N))
   (i) T=SIN(SQRT(A*A+B*B)*COS(2.537*Y*Z)**5)

Exercise 7 (page 55)

1. (a) Valid.
   (b) Invalid − no unit identifier.
   (c) Valid.
   (d) Invalid − expressions may not appear in the input list.
   (e) Invalid − the format specification, *fs*, must be enclosed in apostrophes, '*fs*'.

2. (e) is the only invalid statement and it has no unit identifier.

3. (a) I = 38, J = 976, X = 21.30, K = 4, L = 876, Y = 302.9781.
   (b) I = 3, J = 897, K = 621, FRED = 0.304, JIM = 876, IAN = 302, HARRY = 0.978, NUM = 1.

4. (a) bb−10bb5248
       b−1.50bb49.00
       87296.37512.
   (b) THE NUMBER OF APPLES IN BARRELb5248IS**
       THE AVERAGE PER BARREL ISbb−1.5bWITH STANDARD
       DEVIATIONbb48.996

5. (a) X=3897621.304, I=876, Z=302.9781
   (b) Assuming only one record per PRINT statement:
   bbbbbbb−10bbbbbbb5248
   bbbb−1.50000bbbbb48.99600bb87296.37512

6. The PRINT statement in each case would be

   PRINT f,TEMP1,TEMP2,TEMP3,TEMP4,TEMP5,TEMP6,TEMP7,TEMP8,
   +   TEMP9,TEMP10,TEMP11,TEMP12

   where, if each value is to be printed using the edit specification F10.2,

   in (a) f is '("b",12F10.2)'
   in (b) f is '("b",F10.2)'
   in (c) f is '("b",3F10.2)'

Exercise 8 (page 64)

1.

```
      PROGRAM CTOF
******THIS PROGRAM CONVERTS A TEMPERATURE IN DEGREES CENTIGRADE
******                   TO A TEMPERATURE IN DEGREES FAHRENHEIT
      READ *, CENT
      FAHREN = 9*CENT/5 + 32
      PRINT'('' TEMPERATURE'',F7.2,'' DEG C ='',F7.2,'' DEG F'')',
     +        CENT,FAHREN
      END
```

2.

```
      PROGRAM SIMPTX
******THIS PROGRAM CALCULATES TAX DUE ON AN INCOME OVER 700
      REAL INCOME, TAX
      READ *, INCOME
      TAX = 0.2*300 + 0.3*(INCOME-700)
      PRINT'('' TAX DUE ON'',F9.2,'' IS'',F8.2)',INCOME,TAX
      END
```

3.

```
      PROGRAM TAXSMP
******THIS PROGRAM CALCULATES TAX DUE ON ANY INCOME
      REAL INCOME,TAX
      READ *,INCOME
      TAX=0.2*MIN(DIM(INCOME,400.0),300.0)+0.3*DIM(INCOME,700.0)
      PRINT'('' TAX DUE ON'',F9.2,'' IS'',F8.2)',INCOME,TAX
      END
```

4.

```
      PROGRAM TRINGL
******THIS PROGRAM READS TWO SIDES AND ENCLOSED ANGLE OF A TRIANGLE
******               CALCULATES THIRD SIDE AND AREA
      READ *,X,Y,ANGZ
******TO CONVERT FROM DEGREES TO RADIANS MULTIPLY BY DTOR=PI/180
      DTOR=3.14159265/180
      Z=SQRT(X*X+Y*Y-2*X*Y*COS(DTOR*ANGZ))
      AREA=0.5*X*Y*SIN(DTOR*ANGZ)
      PRINT'('' TWO SIDES ARE'',2F7.2,'' ANGLE IS'',F7.2,'' DEGREES''/
     +        '' THIRD SIDE IS'',F7.2,'' AND AREA IS'',F9.2)',X,Y,ANGZ,
     +        Z,AREA
      END
```

5.

```
      PROGRAM SATLIT
******THIS PROGRAM CALCULATES THE CIRCULAR VELOCITY, ESCAPE VELOCITY AND TIME
******               FOR ONE ORBIT FOR A GIVEN ALTITUDE (IN FEET)
      R=20.904E+6
      READ *, H
      VCIRC = 25830*SQRT(R)/SQRT(H+R)
      VESCAP = VCIRC*SQRT(2.0)
******CIRCUMFERENCE OF ORBIT IS 2*PI*(H+R)
      CIRCUM = 2*3.14159265*(H+R)
      TIME = CIRCUM/VCIRC
******UNITS ARE FT/SEC AND SEC
      C = 3600.0/5280.0
      VCIRC = VCIRC*C
      VESCAP = VESCAP*C
      TIME = TIME/60
      PRINT'('' AT ALTITUDE'',F12.1,'' FEET''/'' VC='',F9.2,'' MPH'',
     +        '' VE='',F9.2,'' MPH''/'' ORBIT TIME ='',F6.2,'' MINS'')',
     +        H,VCIRC,VESCAP,TIME
      END
```

6.

```
      PROGRAM HEAT
******THIS PROGRAM CALCULATES HEAT TO RAISE TEMP FROM T1 TO T2 DEG K
      READ *,A,B,C,D,T1C,T2C
******CONVERT TEMPS TO DEG K
```

```
T1K = T1C+273.2

T2K = T2C+273.2

REQHT = A*(T2K-T1K) + 0.5*B*(T2K**2 - T1K**2)

+          + C*(T2K**3-T1K**3)/3 + 0.25*D*(T2K**4-T1K**4)

PRINT'('' HEAT REQUIRED TO RAISE TEMPERATURE FROM'',F6.1,'' TO'',

+         F6.1,'' DEG C IS'',F9.3)',T1C,T2C,REQHT

END
```

Exercise 9 (page 83)

1. (a) I.EQ.0
   (b) J+K.LE.2*M+N−12*K*N
   (c) A.GE.B
   (d) C*C+D*D.LE.G*G
   (e) COS(X+Y).LT.SIN(A+B)
   (f) EXP(3*U+4*W)−ALOG(X−Y).GT.EXP(G/F)

2. (a) IF(PERIOD.LT.1) THEN
                   RATE=0.2
        END IF
   (b) IF(INCOME.LE.400)THEN
                TAX=0
                          ELSE
                TAX=0.2*(INCOME−400)
        END IF
   (c) IF(DAY.NE.31)THEN
             DAY=DAY+1
                      ELSE IF(MONTH.EQ.12)THEN
                          PRINT'('' YEAR ENDS'')'
                          STOP
                                        ELSE
                          DAY=1
                          MONTH=MONTH+1
        END IF

3. Number the statements consecutively from 1 to 12.

   (a) The IF-block for statement 1 is statements 2 to 9.
        The IF-block for statement 2 is statement 3.
        The ELSE IF-block for statement 4 is statements 5 and 6.
        The ELSE block for statement 7 is statement 8.
        The ELSE block for statement 10 is statement 11.
   (b) year = 2000: execute statement 2
                    month ≠ 2: execute statements 3, 9, and 12
                    month = 2: execute statement 4
                                day = 29: execute statements 5, 6, 9, 12
                                day ≠ 29: execute statements 7, 8, 9, 12
        year ≠ 2000: execute statements 10, 11, and 12.

(c) IF(YEAR.EQ.2000)THEN
    IF(MONTH.NE.2)THEN
        PRINT*,'MONTH NOT FEBRUARY'
            ELSE IF(DAY.EQ.29) THEN
                MONTH=3
                DAY=1
                      ELSE
                DAY=DAY+1
    END IF
            ELSE
      PRINT*,'YEAR NOT 2000'
    END IF

4. (a) 25   IF(X.GT.0)THEN
              SUMX=SUMX+X
              SUMX2=SUMX2+X*X
              READ*,X
              GO TO 25
              END IF
(b)   DO 10 N=1,99,2
                SUM=SUM+X*X*T/(N*(N+1))
10   CONTINUE

5. (a) 20
   (b) $(29-64-7)/(-7) = 6$
   (c) $(2j+15-(i-10)+m^2)/m^2 = 1+(2j-i+25)/m^2$

6.

```
      PROGRAM SQROOT

******THIS PROGRAM CALCULATES THE SQUARE ROOT USING NEWTON-RAPHSON

      READ *,X

******FIRST APPROXIMATION = X, SECOND APPROX = X/2

      ROOT1=X

      ROOT2=0.5*X

15    IF(ABS(ROOT2-ROOT1).GT.1E-6)THEN

          ROOT1=ROOT2

          ROOT2=0.5*(ROOT2+X/ROOT2)

          GO TO 15

      END IF

      PRINT'('' SQUARE ROOT OF'',F12.4,'' IS'',F12.6)',X,ROOT2

      END
```

7.

```
      PROGRAM KTOR

******THIS PROGRAM TABULATES RANKINE TEMPERATURES FOR KELVIN TEMPERATURES

******            BETWEEN 200 AND 800 IN INTERVALS OF 5

      PRINT'('' TABLE OF RANKINE TEMPERATURES''/'' DEG K     DEG R'')'
```

```
      DO 50 K=200,800,5

          C=K-273

          F=9*C/5+32

          R=F+460

          PRINT'('' '',I5,F10.2)',K,R
50    CONTINUE

      END
```

Exercise 10 (page 97)

1. (a)   D=SQRT((X(2)−X(1))∗∗2+(Y(2)−Y(1))∗∗2+(Z(2)−Z(1))∗∗2)
  (b)   X=(U(1)+U(3)+U(5)+U(7)+U(9))∗∗3
  (c)   C=A(1,5)+A(2,4)+A(3,3)+A(4,2)+A(5,1)
  (d)   W=X(I+1)∗Y(J+1)−2∗X(I)∗Y(J)+X(I−1)∗Y(J−1)
  (e)   X(N+2)=X(N+1)−(X(N+1)−X(N))∗∗2/(X(N+1)−2∗X(N)+X(N−1))

2. (a)

```
      PROGRAM MAXVAL

      REAL MAX

      READ *,N

      MAX=0.0

      DO 100 J=1,N

          READ *,X

          IF(X.GT.MAX) THEN

                MAX=X

          END IF

100   CONTINUE

      WRITE(*,'('' '',F12.4)')MAX

      END
```

  (b)

```
      PROGRAM MAXVAL

      REAL MAX,X(1000)

      READ *,N,(X(I),I=1,N)

      MAX=0.0

      DO 100 J=1,N

          IF(X(J).GT.MAX)THEN

                MAX=X(J)

          END IF

100   CONTINUE

      WRITE(*,'('' '',F12.4)')MAX

      END
```

3.

```
PROGRAM REORD
REAL X(500),Y(500)
N=0
READ *,A,B
100    IF(A.GT.0)THEN
          N=N+1
          X(N)=A
          Y(N)=B
          READ *,A,B
          GO TO 100
       END IF
       WRITE(*,'('' X-VALUES ARE'')')
       WRITE(*,'('' '',6F10.4)')(X(I),I=1,N)
       WRITE(*,'('' Y-VALUES ARE'')')
       WRITE(*,'('' '',6F10.4)')(Y(I),I=1,N)
       END
```

4.

```
PROGRAM SPROD
REAL X(100),Y(100)
READ *,N,(X(I),I=1,N),(Y(I),I=1,N)
S=0.0
DO 100 I=1,N
   S=S+X(I)*Y(I)
100    CONTINUE
WRITE(*,'('' VALUE OF SCALAR PRODUCT IS'',F12.6)')S
END
```

5.

```
PROGRAM MATMUL
INTEGER P
REAL A(20,20),B(20,20),C(20,20)
READ *,M,N,P,((A(I,J),J=1,N),I=1,M),
+             ((B(I,J),J=1,P),I=1,N)
DO 100 I=1,M
DO 100 J=1,P
   S=0.0
****** CALCULATE C(I,J) AS A SUM OF PRODUCTS
   DO 200 K=1,N
          S=S+A(I,K)*B(K,J)
```

```
200         CONTINUE

            C(I,J)=S

100    CONTINUE

       WRITE(*,'('' ELEMENTS OF AB ARE ROW BY ROW'')')

       WRITE(*,'('' '',6F10.5)')((C(I,J),J=1,P),I=1,M)

       END
```

6. (a)
```
               MAX=A(1,1)
               DO 100 I=1,10
               DO 100 J=1,20
                   IF(A(I,J).GT.MAX) THEN
                           MAX=A(I,J)
                   END IF
       100     CONTINUE
```

   (b)
```
               NUMNEG=0
               DO 100 I=1,10
               DO 100 J=1,20
                   IF(A(I,J).LT.0.0) THEN
                           NUMNEG=NUMNEG+1
                   END IF
       100     CONTINUE
```

   (c)
```
               SUMPOS=0.0
               DO 100 I=1,10
               DO 100 J=1,20
                   IF(A(I,J).GT.0.0)THEN
                        SUMPOS=SUMPOS+A(I,J)
                   END IF
       100     CONTINUE
```

   (d)
```
               S1=0.0
               DO 100 J=1,20
                   S1=S1+A(1,J)
       100     CONTINUE
               DO 200 I=2,10
                   S2=0.0
                   DO 300 J=1,20
                       S2=S2+A(I,J)
       300         CONTINUE
                   IF(S2.GT.S1)THEN
                           S1=S2
                   END IF
       200     CONTINUE
```

Exercise 11 (page 104)

1.
```
    DOUBLE PRECISION DPI
    COMPLEX ZSTART
    CHARACTER*6 PWORD,OPS
    PARAMETER (PI=3.14159265,
   +            ABZERO=-273.2,
```

```
+                    C=2.9978E10,
+                    DPI=3.14159265388979324D0,
+                    FAC=1760.0,
+                    ZSTART=(2,-3),
+                    PWORD='KILROY',
+                    CSQ=C*C,
+                    PIBY6=PI/6,
+                    IMAX=2**39-1,
+                    OPS='+-*/**')
```

2.   INTEGER COUNT
     DOUBLE PRECISION D1,D2
     COMPLEX Z
     LOGICAL L1,L2,L3
     REAL X(0:20),A(10,15)
     CHARACTER CVAL*8
     DATA P,Q,COUNT,D1,D2,Z,L1,L2,L3,X,A,CVAL
     +   /-1963.57,2.164E-8,0,2*-1.57D-4,(-5,-3),
     +   3*.TRUE.,21*0.0,150*1.0,'CODEWORD'/

3. (a) Elements of array X initialized to 1.0 and −1.0 alternately.
   (b) A initialized to DAVID
        B initialized to BOBbb
        C initialized to FREDE
   (c) Diagonal elements of matrix A initialized to 0.0.
   (d) All elements K_{ij} with $j \geqslant i$ of matrix K initialized to -1.

Exercise 12 (page 129)

1. (a)

```
      FUNCTION DIST(X,Y)

******THIS FUNCTION CALCULATES THE DISTANCE FROM (0,0) TO (X,Y)

      DIST=SQRT(X*X+Y*Y)

      END
```

   (b)

```
      FUNCTION DIST2(X1,Y1,X2,Y2)

******THIS FUNCTION CALCULATES THE DISTANCE FROM (X1,Y1) TO (X2,Y2)

      DIST2=SQRT((X2-X1)**2+(Y2-Y1)**2)

      END
```

2.

```
      FUNCTION AREA(A,B,C)

******THIS FUNCTION CALCULATES THE AREA OF TRIANGLE ABC CHECKING

******               THAT THE SIDES A,B AND C FORM A TRIANGLE

      IF((A+B-C)*(B+C-A)*(C+A-B).GT.0) THEN

            S=0.5*(A+B+C)

            AREA=SQRT(S*(S-A)*(S-B)*(S-C))

                              ELSE
```

```
          PRINT'('' SIDES'',3F6.2,'' DO NOT FORM A TRIANGLE'')',
     +              A,B,C
          STOP
       END IF
       END
```

3.

```
     FUNCTION SUMGEO(A,R)
******THIS FUNCTION CALCULATES THE SUM TO INFINITY OF
******            A+AR+AR**2+....+AR**N
     IF(ABS(R).LT.1)THEN
          SUMGEO=A/(1-R)
                    ELSE
          PRINT'('' R OUT OF RANGE'',F6.2)',R
          STOP
     END IF
     END
```

4.

```
     INTEGER FUNCTION FIB(N)
******THIS FUNCTION CALCULATES THE NTH FIBONACCI NUMBER
     INTEGER F1,F2
     IF(N.LT.1)THEN
          PRINT'('' N LESS THAN 1'',I6)',N
          STOP
            ELSE IF((N-1)*(N-2).EQ.0)THEN
                    FIB=1
                    RETURN
                              ELSE
                    F1=1
                    F2=1
                    DO 10 I=3,N
                       FIB=F1+F2
                       F1=F2
                       F2=FIB
10                  CONTINUE
     END IF
     END
```

5.

```
     SUBROUTINE LIMITS(X,N,TOP,BOTTOM)
******THIS SUBROUTINE FINDS THE LARGEST AND SMALLEST VALUES IN VECTOR X
```

```
      REAL X(N)

      TOP=X(1)

      BOTTOM=X(1)

      DO 15 I=2,N

         T=X(I)

         IF(T.GT.TOP)THEN

              TOP=T

                       ELSE IF(T.LT.BOTTOM) THEN

                                 BOTTOM=T

         END IF

15    CONTINUE

      END
```

Exercise 13 (page 151)

1.

```
      FUNCTION TAX(INCOME)

******THIS FUNCTION CALCULATES THE TAX DUE ON INCOME

      REAL INCOME

      IF(INCOME.LT.2500)THEN

              TAX=0

         ELSE IF(INCOME.LT.5000)THEN

                    TAX=(INCOME-2500)*0.1

              ELSE IF(INCOME.LT.7500)THEN

                    TAX=250+(INCOME-5000)*0.2

                 ELSE IF(INCOME.LT.10000) THEN

                         TAX=750+(INCOME-7500)*0.3

                    ELSE

                         TAX=1500+(INCOME-10000)*0.4

      END IF

      END
```

2.

```
      REAL FUNCTION MEDIAN(X,N)

******THIS FUNCTION CALCULATES THE MEDIAN OF THE VALUES IN VECTOR X

      REAL X(N)

      REAL Y(1000)

******MOVE X VALUES TO Y AND SORT Y

      DO 10 I=1,N

         Y(I)=X(I)
```

```
10      CONTINUE

        CALL SORT(Y,N)

        IF(MOD(N,2).EQ.0)THEN

            MEDIAN=(Y(N/2)+Y(N/2+1))/2.0

                          ELSE

            MEDIAN=Y(N/2+1)

        END IF

        END
```

3. calculate the mean
move the values to a local vector y
sort y
calculate the median
assign zero to count
assign 1 to i
loop while $i \leqslant N$ **do**
       {assign 1 to maxcount and y_i to tempmode
       assign $i + 1$ to j
       loop while $j \leqslant N$ **and** tempmode $= y_j$ **do**
           {increment maxcount and j}
       if maxcount $>$ count **then** {assign maxcount to count
                                 assign tempmode to mode}
       assign j to i}

```
        SUBROUTINE MIDDLE(X,N,MEAN,MEDIAN,MODE)

******THIS SUBROUTINE CALCULATES THE MEAN, MEDIAN AND MODE OF THE

******                   VALUES IN VECTOR X

        REAL X(N),MEAN,MEDIAN,MODE

        REAL Y(1000),TMODE

        INTEGER COUNT, MAXCNT

******CALCULATE THE MEAN AND MOVE X TO Y FOR SORTING LATER

        MEAN=0

        DO 30 I=1,N

            MEAN = MEAN + X(I)

            Y(I) = X(I)

30      CONTINUE

        MEAN=MEAN/N

******CALCULATE THE MEDIAN

        CALL SORT(Y,N)

        IF(MOD(N,2).EQ.0)THEN

            MEDIAN=(Y(N/2)+Y(N/2+1))/2.0

                          ELSE

            MEDIAN=Y(N/2+1)

        END IF
```

```
******CALCULATE THE MODE
      COUNT=0
      I=1
32    IF(I.LE.N)THEN
             MAXCNT=1
             TMODE=Y(I)
             J=I+1
******       COUNT OCCURRENCES OF Y(I)
31           IF(J.LE.N)THEN
                  IF(ABS(TMODE-Y(J)).LE.1E-6)THEN
                     MAXCNT=MAXCNT+1
                     J=J+1
                     GO TO 31
                  END IF
             END IF
******       IF THERE ARE MORE OCCURRENCES OF THIS VALUE REPLACE CURRENT MODE
             IF(MAXCNT.GT.COUNT)THEN
                  COUNT=MAXCNT
                  MODE=TMODE
             END IF
******       MOVE TO NEXT VALUE
             I=J
             GO TO 32
      END IF
      END
```

4. (a) *Subroutine using arguments*

```
      SUBROUTINE SORTMK(CANDNO,MATHS,PHYSIC,CMPSCI,N)
******THIS SUBROUTINE SORTS EXAM MARKS INTO DESCENDING ORDER OF COMPUTER
******              SCIENCE MARKS
      INTEGER CANDNO(N),MATHS(N),PHYSIC(N),CMPSCI(N)
      INTEGER EXCHNG
      EXCHNG=1
20    IF(EXCHNG.EQ.1)THEN
         EXCHNG=0
         DO 10 J=1,N-1
             IF(CMPSCI(J).LT.CMPSCI(J+1))THEN
                  CALL SWAP(CMPSCI(J),CMPSCI(J+1))
                  CALL SWAP(CANDNO(J),CANDNO(J+1))
```

```
              CALL SWAP(MATHS(J),MATHS(J+1))

              CALL SWAP(PHYSIC(J),PHYSIC(J+1))

              EXCHNG=1

         END IF

10       CONTINUE

       GO TO 20

     END IF

   END
```

It will be noted that this algorithm requires that elements in all four vectors be swapped. A convenient method for implementing this is a subroutine SWAP.

```
SUBROUTINE SWAP(A,B)

******THIS SUBROUTINE EXCHANGES THE VALUES OF A AND B

   INTEGER A,B,T

   T=A

   A=B

   B=T

   END
```

(b) *Subroutine using common storage*
This subroutine is the same as the one above except that the SUBROUTINE statement is replaced by

SUBROUTINE SORTMK

and the first two INTEGER type statements are replaced by

COMMON/MARK/CANDNO(1000),MATHS(1000),PHYSIC(1000),
+   CMPSCI(1000),N
INTEGER CANDNO, PHYSIC, CMPSCI, EXCHNG

(c) *Comparison*
Since the differences are concerned with passing information between program units, it is not surprising that the main bodies of the subroutines are the same. Three points should be noted:
(i) In (a), the argument list is quite long at five entities. Thus each reference to the subroutine must contain a five entity argument list. Whereas in (b), there is no argument list.
(ii) In (a), the actual number of elements to be sorted is made available through N and so the dummy arrays are adjustable. In (b), although N is in common storage, the arrays must be given a fixed size since adjustable arrays may not appear in a common block. Thus any change in this size must affect directly all program units using this common block, whereas in (a) such a change should be made in one place only.
(iii) The subroutine SWAP must use arguments.

5. (a)

```
   FUNCTION TIME(HRS,MINS,HRSF,MINF)

******THIS FUNCTION CALCULATES THE TIME BETWEEN START (HRS,MINS) AND FINISH
```

```
******              (HRSF,MINF) IN HOURS
      INTEGER HRS,MINS,HRF,MINF
      TIME = HRSF-HRS+REAL(MINF-MINS)/60
      END
```

(b)

```
      FUNCTION BASIC(STHRS,STMIN,FINHRS,FINMIN)
******THIS FUNCTION CALCULATES THE TOTAL TIME WORKED AT THE BASIC RATE
      INTEGER STHRS(7),STMIN(7),FINHRS(7),FINMIN(7)
      INTEGER SH,SM,FH,FM
******BASIC RATE IS 8.00 TO 16.00 MON TO FRI
      BASIC=0
      DO 5 I=2,6
         SH=STHRS(I)
         IF(SH.LT.16)THEN
            FH=FINHRS(I)
            IF(FH.GE.8)THEN
               SM=STMIN(I)
               FM=FINMIN(I)
               IF(SH.LT.8)THEN
                  SH=8
                  SM=0
               END IF
               IF(FH.GE.16)THEN
                  FH=16
                  FM=0
               END IF
               BASIC=BASIC+TIME(SH,SM,FH,FM)
            END IF
         END IF
5     CONTINUE
      END
      FUNCTION BASHLF(STHRS,STMIN,FINHRS,FINMIN)
******THIS FUNCTION CALCULATES THE TOTAL TIME WORKED AT TIME AND ONE HALF
      INTEGER STHRS(7),STMIN(7),FINHRS(7),FINMIN(7)
      INTEGER S,F,SH,SM,FH,FM
 *****TIME AND ONE HALF IS PAID 16.00 to 24.00 MON TO FRI, 8.00 to 16.00 SAT
      BASHLF=0
      S=16
```

```
      F=24
      DO 5 I=2,7
         IF(I.EQ.7) THEN
            S=8
            F=16
         END IF
         SH=STHRS(I)
         IF(SH.LT.F)THEN
            FH=FINHRS(I)
            IF(FH.GE.S)THEN
               SM=STMIN(I)
               FM=FINMIN(I)
               IF(SH.LT.S)THEN
                  SH=S
                  SM=0
               END IF
               IF(FH.GE.F)THEN
                  FH=F
                  FM=0
               END IF
               BASHLF=BASHLF+TIME(SH,SM,FH,FM)
            END IF
         END IF
5     CONTINUE
      END
      FUNCTION DOUBLE(STHRS,STMIN,FINHRS,FINMIN)
******THIS FUNCTION CALCULATES THE TOTAL TIME WORKED AT DOUBLE TIME
      INTEGER STHRS(7),STMIN(7),FINHRS(7),FINMIN(7)
      INTEGER H,M
******DOUBLE TIME IS PAID 0.00 TO 8.00 MON TO SAT, 16.00 TO 24.00 SAT, ALL SUN
      DOUBLE=TIME(STHRS(1),STMIN(1),FINHRS(1),FINMIN(1))
      DO 5 I=2,7
         IF(STHRS(I).LT.8)THEN
            H=FINHRS(I)
            M=FINMIN(I)
            IF(H.GE.8)THEN
               H=8
               M=0
            END IF
```

```
                 DOUBLE=DOUBLE+TIME(STHRS(I),STMIN(I),H,M)

          END IF
5     CONTINUE
******SAT 16.00 TO 24.00
      IF(FINHRS(7).GE.16)THEN

          H=STHRS(7)

          M=STMIN(7)

          IF(H.LT.16)THEN

             H=16

             M=0

          END IF

          DOUBLE=DOUBLE+TIME(H,M,FINHRS(7),FINMIN(7))

      END IF

      END

      PROGRAM WAGES
******THIS PROGRAM CALCULATES EMPLOYEES WAGES
      INTEGER STHRS(7),STMIN(7),FINHRS(7),FINMIN(7),EMPNO,SH,SM,FH,FM
      READ'(F10.0,I6)',RATE,NUMEMP
      PRINT'('' BASIC RATE IS '',F7.2)',RATE
      DO 100 I=1,NUMEMP
          READ'(I10,2X,28I2)',EMPNO,(STHRS(J),STMIN(J),FINHRS(J),
     +                         FINMIN(J),J=1,7)
******    CHECK DATA
          DO 101 J=1,7
             SH=STHRS(J)
             SM=STMIN(J)
             FH=FINHRS(J)
             FM=FINMIN(J)
             IF(SH.LT.0.OR.SH.GT.24.OR.FH.LT.0.OR.FH.GT.24.OR.
     +          SM.LT.0.OR.SM.GT.59.OR.FM.LT.0.OR.FM.GT.59.OR.
     +          (SH.EQ.24.AND.SM.GT.0).OR.(FH.EQ.24.AND.FM.GT.0).OR.
     +          SH.GT.FH.OR.(SH.EQ.FH.AND.SM.GT.FM))THEN
                   GO TO 999
             END IF
101       CONTINUE
          WAGE=RATE*BASIC(STHRS,STMIN,FINHRS,FINMIN)
     +         + 1.5*RATE*BASHLF(STHRS,STMIN,FINHRS,FINMIN)
     +          +2*RATE*DOUBLE(STHRS,STMIN,FINHRS,FINMIN)
          PRINT'('' '',I10,4X,F7.2)',EMPNO,WAGE
```

```
          GO TO 100
******    INVALID DATA
999       PRINT'('' DATA INVALID FOR EMPLOYEE '',I10)',EMPNO
100   CONTINUE
      END
```

Note that the code used to check the data uses the logical operators .OR. and .AND. which are covered in Chapter 16.

Exercise 14 (page 183)

1. (a) b1576, bbb1576, bbb01576, ***
   (b) b−0.0162, b−0.02, b−0.1620E−01, bbb−0.162E−1, b−0.0

2. X=1234.6, Y=9875.0, I=−4, Z=2.5, J=70, K=83, L1=0, L2=12, L3=34, L4=60, A=34.6, K4=75, M1=57, M2=0, M3=83

3.

```
      PROGRAM FORM
      INTEGER F(1000)
      REAL    X(1000)
      READ 12, N,(F(I),X(I),I=1,N)
12    FORMAT(I5/(I5,F12.0))
      PRINT 13,N,(F(I),X(I),I=1,N)
13    FORMAT( ' ',I5/5(' ',I5,F12.3))
      END
```

4.

```
      PROGRAM CALLS
******THIS PROGRAM PRINTS A FILE OF PHONE CALL UNITS USED BY CUSTOMERS
      INTEGER CUST,PEAK,STNDRD,CHEAP
      PRINT 15
15    FORMAT('1 CUSTOMER',5X,'PEAK',2X,'STNDRD',3X,'CHEAP')
21    READ(UNIT=24,FMT=16,ERR=99,END=20)CUST,PEAK,STNDRD,CHEAP
16    FORMAT(I10,3I5)
          PRINT 17,CUST,PEAK,STNDRD,CHEAP
17        FORMAT(' ',I10,3(3X,I5))
          GO TO 21
20    STOP
99    PRINT 98
98    FORMAT(' ***ERROR DETECTED IN FILE ON UNIT 24')
      END
```

5.   OPEN(24,FILE='PHONE ,STATUS='OLD',ERR=99)

Insert this OPEN statement immediately before the statement labelled 21. Replace statement 20 by

20   CLOSE(24,ERR=99)
            STOP

6.

```
      PROGRAM EXPENS
******THIS PROGRAM CREATES A FILE OF CUSTOMERS WHO USE MORE THAN
******             25 PER CENT OF THEIR UNITS AT THE PEAK RATE
      INTEGER CUST,PEAK,STNDRD,CHEAP,TOTAL
      OPEN(24,FILE='PHONE',STATUS='OLD',ERR=99)
      OPEN(25,FILE='QPEAK',STATUS='NEW',ERR=97)
50    READ(24,16,ERR=99,END=60)CUST,PEAK,STNDRD,CHEAP
16    FORMAT(I10,3I5)
         TOTAL=PEAK+STNDRD+CHEAP
         IF(PEAK.GT.0.25*TOTAL) THEN
             WRITE(25,16,ERR=97) CUST, PEAK, STNDRD, CHEAP
         END IF
         GO TO 50
60    CLOSE(24,ERR=99)
      ENDFILE(25,ERR=97)
      CLOSE(25,ERR=97)
      STOP
******ERRORS
99    PRINT 98
98    FORMAT(' ***ERROR DETECTED IN FILE ON UNIT 24')
      STOP
97    PRINT 96
96    FORMAT(' ***ERROR DETECTED IN FILE ON UNIT 25')
      END
```

Exercise 15 (page 204)

1. PAR,IS IN,HE,PARIS IN THE,RING,
   PARIS IN THE SPRING

2.

Character variable or array element	Length	Value
PW1	8	SONNETbb
PW2	6	CARSON
X	12	CARPETbTILEb
Y	12	LINOLEUMbbbb
NAME	6	ALBERT
A	4	TILE
B	5	ALERT
C(1)	30	CARPETbTILESbAREbINbFASHIONbbb
C(2)	30	ALBERTbCARSONbISbINbBEDbbbbbbbb

3. (a) H2∅,H2S∅4,HALIBUT,HEAVISIDE,H∅RR∅R,H∅USE,HUT
   (b) HALIBUT,HEAVISIDE,H∅RR∅R,H∅USE,HUT,H2∅,H2S∅4

4. (a) B,3
   (b) 5,36
   (c) **true**
   (d) **false**
   (e) **true**

5.

```
PROGRAM VCOUNT
INTEGER COUNT1,COUNT2,COUNT3,COUNT4,COUNT5
DATA COUNT1,COUNT2,COUNT3,COUNT4,COUNT5/5*0/
CHARACTER CH(80)*1
READ*,N
DO 100 I=1,N
    READ(*,'(80A1)')(CH(J),J=1,80)
    DO 200 J=1,80
        IF(CH(J).EQ.'A')THEN
            COUNT1 = COUNT1+1
        ELSE IF (CH(J).EQ.'E') THEN
            COUNT2 = COUNT2+1
        ELSE IF (CH(J).EQ. 'I') THEN
            COUNT3 = COUNT3+1
        ELSE IF (CH(J).EQ.'O') THEN
            COUNT4 = COUNT4+1
        ELSE IF (CH(J).EQ.'U') THEN
            COUNT5 = COUNT5+1
        END IF
200     CONTINUE
```

```
100    CONTINUE
       WRITE(*,20)COUNT1,COUNT2,COUNT3,COUNT4,COUNT5
20     FORMAT('bAbbb',I6,10X,'Ebbb',I6,10X,'Ibbb',I6,10X,'Obbb',I6,10X,
     +         'Ubbb',I6)
       END
```

6.

```
       INTEGER FUNCTION PALIND(C)
       CHARACTER C*(*)
       PALIND=1
******SEARCH FROM THE RIGHT FOR FIRST NON-BLANK CHARACTER
       L=LEN(C)
100    IF((C(L:L).EQ.' ').AND.(L.NE.1)) THEN
            L=L-1
            GO TO 100
       END IF
******IF L IS GREATER THAN 1, COMPARE CORRESPONDING
******CHARACTERS WORKING IN FROM ENDS TOWARDS MIDDLE
       IF (L.NE.1) THEN
            I=1
            J=L
200         IF((C(I:I).EQ.C(J:J)).AND.(I.LT.J))THEN
                 I=I+1
                 J=J-1
                 GO TO 200
            END IF
******      IF I IS LESS THAN J AT THIS POINT,
******      2 CHARACTERS HAVE FAILED TO MATCH.
            IF(I.LT.J)THEN
                 PALIND=0
            END IF
       END IF
       END
```

7.

```
       CHARACTER*80 FUNCTION KILL(TEXT,C)
       CHARACTER TEXT*(*),C,X,S*82,T*81
       INTEGER COUNT
       L=LEN(TEXT)
******TO AVOID PROBLEMS WHEN C OCCURS AT ONE OF THE
```

```
******EXTREMITIES OF TEXT, ADD A CHARACTER, OTHER THAN C,
******AT EACH END.
     X='*'
     IF (X.EQ.C) THEN
        X='+'
     END IF
     S=X//TEXT//X
******NOW LOCATE EACH OCCURRENCE OF C AND CONCATENATE
******PORTIONS ON EACH SIDE. COUNT REGISTERS THE
******NUMBER OF OCCURRENCES.
     COUNT=0
     I=INDEX(S,C)
100  IF (I.NE.0) THEN
           COUNT=COUNT+1
           T=S(1:I-1)//S(I+1:)
           S=T
           I=INDEX(S,C)
           GO TO 100
     END IF
******NOW REMOVE CHARACTER X AT EACH END.
     KILL=S(2:L-COUNT+1)
     END
```

8. All five calls are valid, the actual argument/dummy argument association being as follows:

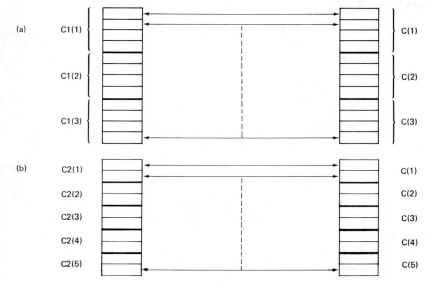

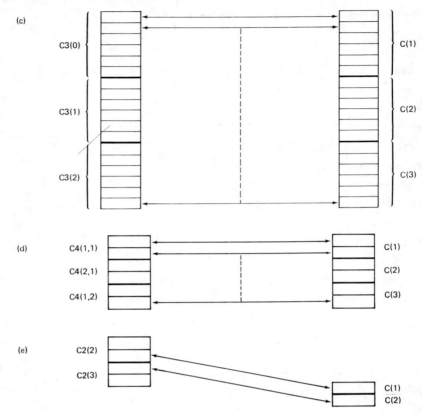

Exercise 16 (page 213)

1. (a) B1.AND.B2.AND.(I.GT.J)

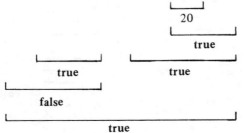

(c) ((B1.OR.B2).AND.(B1.OR.B3)).EQV.(B1.OR.(B2.AND.B3))

2. (a) B1.AND.B2.AND.I.GT.J
   (b) .NOT.(B1.OR.B3).OR.B4.OR.J−I.EQ.K
   (c) (B1.OR.B2).AND.(B1.OR.B3).EQV.B1.OR.B2.AND.B3

3. read a record
   loop while CN≠−1 **do**
       {assign (E>90)**or**(M>90)**or**(P>90)**or**(C>90) to L1
        assign (E≥60)**and**(M≥60)**and**(P≥60)**and**(C≥60) to L2
        assign ¼(E+M+P+C)>75 to L3
        assign L1 **and** L2 **and** L3 to GOOD
        if GOOD **then** print CN,E,M,P,C
        read a record}

```
       PROGRAM MARKS2

       INTEGER CN,E,P,C

       LOGICAL L1,L2,L3,GOOD

       READ *,CN,E,M,P,C

100    IF (CN.NE.-1) THEN

           L1=(E.GT.90).OR.(M.GT.90).OR.(P.GT.90).OR.(C.GT.90)

           L2=(E.GE.60).AND.(M.GE.60).AND.(P.GE.60).AND.(C.GE.60)

           L3=0.25*(E+M+P+C).GT.75.0

           GOOD=L1.AND.L2.AND.L3

           IF (GOOD) THEN

                   WRITE(*,'('' '',I6,4I4)')CN,E,M,P,C

           END IF

           READ *,CN,E,M,P,C

           GO TO 100

       END IF

       END
```

4.

```
       INTEGER FUNCTION QUAD(X,Y)

       LOGICAL AXIS,XPOS,YPOS,XNEG,YNEG

       PARAMETER (TOL=1E-6)

       AXIS=(ABS(X).LT.TOL).OR.(ABS(Y).LT.TOL)

       XPOS=X.GT.0.0

       YPOS=Y.GT.0.0

       XNEG=X.LT.0.0
```

```
      YNEG=Y.LT.0.0

      IF (AXIS) THEN

            QUAD=0

         ELSE IF (XPOS.AND.YPOS)THEN

               QUAD=1

            ELSE IF (XNEG.AND.YPOS)THEN

                  QUAD=2

               ELSE IF (XNEG.AND.YNEG)THEN

                     QUAD=3

                  ELSE

                        QUAD=4

      END IF

      END
```

5.

```
      SUBROUTINE TRIANG(A,B,C,AREA,FLAG)

      LOGICAL FLAG

      FLAG=(A+B.GT.C).AND.(B+C.GT.A).AND.(C+A.GT.B)

      IF (FLAG) THEN

            S=0.5*(A+B+C)

            AREA=SQRT(S*(S-A)*(S-B)*(S-C))

               ELSE

            AREA=0.0

      END IF

      END
```

6.

```
      LOGICAL FUNCTION CHECK(D,M,Y)

      INTEGER D,Y,MONTH(12)

      LOGICAL DTEST,MTEST,YTEST,LEAPYR

      DATA MONTH(1),(MONTH(I),I=3,12)/2*31,30,31,30,2*31,30,31,30,31/

      YTEST=(1901.LE.Y).AND.(Y.LE.2000)

      MTEST=(1.LE.M).AND.(M.LE.12)

      DTEST=.FALSE.

      IF(YTEST.AND.MTEST)THEN

         IF(LEAPYR(Y))THEN

            MONTH(2)=29

                  ELSE

            MONTH(2)=28

         END IF
```

```
        DTEST=(1.LE.D).AND.(D.LE.MONTH(M))

    END IF

    CHECK=YTEST.AND.MTEST.AND.DTEST

    END
```

Exercise 17 (page 223)

1. (a) SQRT(2)   invalid
        SQRT(2.0)   returns real (single precision) value of $\sqrt{2}$
        SQRT(2.0D0)   returns double precision value of $\sqrt{2}$
        DSQRT(2.0)   invalid
        DSQRT(2.0D0)   returns double precision value of $\sqrt{2}$
   (b) AINT(X)   2D0
        ANINT(X)   3D0
        NINT(X)   3
   (c) $-3.6D0$

2.
```
    PROGRAM HYPER

    DOUBLE PRECISION X,U,V,W

    DO 200 I=0,100

        X=DBLE(I)/10

        U=COSH(X)

        V=SINH(X)

        W=U*U-V*V-1

        WRITE(*,'('' '',F5.1,2E30.20,E15.5)')X,U,V,W

200 CONTINUE

    END
```

3.
```
    SUBROUTINE MATVEC(A,X,N,Y)

    REAL A(N,N),X(N),Y(N)

    DOUBLE PRECISION S

    DO 100 J=1,N

        S=0

        DO 200 K=1,N

            S=S+DPROD(A(J,K),X(K))

200     CONTINUE

        Y(J)=S

100 CONTINUE

    END
```

4.
```
    PROGRAM SERSUM

    INTEGER DENOM
```

```
      DOUBLE PRECISION DX,DXCUBE,DSUM,DTERM
      PARAMETER(X=32.0438,
     +          DX=X,
     +          XCUBE=X*X*X,
     +          DXCUBE=DX*DX*DX)
      SUM=59.0+X
      TERM=X
      DSUM=59.0D0+DX
      DTERM=DX
      N=4
100   IF (ABS(DTERM).GE.1D-8) THEN
          DENOM=N*(N-1)*(N-2)
          TERM=-TERM*XCUBE/DENOM
          SUM=SUM+TERM
          DTERM=-DTERM*DXCUBE/DENOM
          DSUM=DSUM+DTERM
          N=N+3
          GO TO 100
      END IF
      WRITE(*,'('' SUM ='',F15.7/'' DSUM ='',F15.7)')SUM,DSUM
      END
```

Simple algebra shows that, when $x = 32.0438$, the terms increase in magnitude up to the term $x^{31}/31!$ and then start to decrease again, eventually becoming very small. The largest term, therefore, when $x = 32.0438$ is $(32.0438)^{31}/31! \simeq 5.79 \times 10^{12}$, so that, to produce a result accurate say to 7 decimal places, intermediate arithmetic has to be performed to about 20 significant figures. Most modern computer systems do not perform real arithmetic to this precision. Hence the first result output is likely to be highly inaccurate, unlike the second which should be approximately $0.1001896\ldots$.

5.

```
      DOUBLE PRECISION FUNCTION EINT(K)
      REAL K
      DOUBLE PRECISION TOL,X,Y,XNEW,YNEW,PI
      PARAMETER(TOL=1D-20)
      PI=4*ATAN(1D0)
      X=1
      Y=SQRT(1-DPROD(K,K))
100   IF(ABS(X-Y).GE.TOL) THEN
          XNEW=0.5D0*(X+Y)
          YNEW=SQRT(X*Y)
```

```
        X=XNEW

        Y=YNEW

        GO TO 100

    END IF

    EINT=0.5D0*PI/X

    END



    PROGRAM ELLIP

    REAL K

    DOUBLE PRECISION EINT

    DO 100 I=0,900

        K=I/1000.0

        WRITE(*,'('' '',F5.3,F25.20)')K,EINT(K)

100 CONTINUE

    END
```

Exercise 18 (page 234)

1.

```
    PROGRAM CXTRANS

    COMPLEX Z,W

    WRITE(*,10)

10  FORMAT(8X,'Z',21X,'W')

    READ *,Z

100 IF (ABS(Z).LT.1) THEN

        W=LOG((1+Z)/(1-Z))

        WRITE(*,'('' '',2F8.5,5X,2F8.5)')Z,W

        READ *,Z

        GO TO 100

    END IF

    END
```

2.

```
    PROGRAM TABPOT

    COMPLEX I,CXPOT(6)

    PARAMETER(PI=3.1416,

   +          CONST=200/PI,

   +          I=(0,1))

    WRITE(*,10)

10  FORMAT(15X,'Y=0',18X,'Y=2',18X,'Y=4',18X,'Y=6',18X,'Y=8',18X

   +    'Y=10'//)
```

```
      DO 100 L=1,30
         X=L/10.0
         U=SIN(X)
         V=COS(X)
         J=1
         DO 200 IY=0,10,2
            Y=IY
            CXPOT(J)=CONST*LOG((SINH(Y)+I*U)/(COSH(Y)-V))
            J=J+1
200      CONTINUE
         WRITE(*,20)X,(CXPOT(K),K=1,6)
20       FORMAT(' ',F3.1,2X,6(E9.2,',',E9.2,2X))
100   CONTINUE
      END
```

3. The required program is identical to that given in Example 18.10, except that the arithmetic assignment statement for G is now:

$$G=-15*(I*W+20)*(I*W+30)*(I*W-40)*(I*W-10)/$$
$$+\qquad (W*W*(I*W+5)*(I*W+8)*(I*W+50)*(I*W+60))$$

4. $\cosh z = \cosh(x + iy)$
$$= \cosh x \cosh iy + \sinh x \sinh iy$$
$$= \cosh x \cos y + i \sinh x \sin y$$

Hence:

```
      COMPLEX FUNCTION CCOSH(Z)
      COMPLEX I,Z
      PARAMETER (I=(0,1))
      X=REAL(Z)
      Y=AIMAG(Z)
      CCOSH=COSH(X)*COS(Y)+I*SINH(X)*SIN(Y)
      END
```

5. $f(z) = e^{iz} + 1$, $f'(z) = i\,e^{iz}$

```
      PROGRAM PICALC
      COMPLEX Z0,DELTA
      PARAMETER(TOL=0.5E-6,
     +          I=(0,1))
      DELTA=(1,1)
      Z0=(3,0)
100   IF(ABS(DELTA).GE.TOL) THEN
         DELTA=(EXP(I*Z0)+1)/(I*EXP(I*Z0))
```

```
        Z0=Z0-DELTA

        GO TO 100

     END IF

     WRITE(*,'('' '',2F8.5)')Z0

     END
```

Exercise 19 (page 249)

1. Since the files are held in ascending order of account number, the account number from the master file will be less than or equal to the account number from the transaction file, unless the transaction record refers to an account which does not exist in the master file. While simple amendments *could* be made to the program in Example 19.15, this would lead to a badly structured program. It is, therefore, more sensible to redesign the algorithm.

read a master record (from ACOUNT)
read a transaction record (from TRANS)
loop while neither file has completed **do**
    {**if** master account no < transaction account no **then**
        {write the master record (to BCOUNT)
        read a master record (from ACOUNT)}
      else if master account no = transaction account no **then**
        {update the balance
        if permitted overdraft has been exceeded **then** print the updated record
        write the updated record (to BCOUNT)
        read a master record (from ACOUNT)
        read a transaction record (from TRANS)}
        else { print 'transaction account does not exist'
        read a transaction record (from TRANS)}}
if transaction file has completed **then**
    loop while master file has not completed **do**
      {write the master record (to BCOUNT)
      read a master record (from ACOUNT)}
    else print 'unexpected end of master file'

Apart from inserting the type statement

                INTEGER MSTEND, TRNSND

the program statements of Example 19.15 remain unchanged down to and including statement 10. Thereafter the coding is

```
     READ(MSTUNT,IOSTAT=MSTEND,ERR=99)MACNUM,NAME,BALANC,OVRDFT

     READ(TRNUNT,IOSTAT=TRNSND,ERR=98)TACNUM,CHANGE

******LOOP WHILE NEITHER EOF

81   IF(MSTEND.EQ.0.AND.TRNSND.EQ.0) THEN

        IF(MACNUM.LT.TACNUM) THEN

           WRITE(NEWUNT,ERR=97)MACNUM,NAME,BALANC,OVRDFT

           READ(MSTUNT,IOSTAT=MSTEND,ERR=99)MACNUM,NAME,BALANC,OVRDFT

        ELSE IF(MACNUM.EQ.TACNUM) THEN
```

```
                              BALANC=BALANC+CHANGE

                              IF(BALANC.LT.OVRDFT) THEN

                                  PRINT15,MACNUM,NAME,BALANC,OVRDFT
15
                                  FORMAT(' ',I7,3X,A30,2(3X,F9.2))

                              END IF

                              WRITE(NEWUNT,ERR=97)MACNUM,NAME,BALANC,OVRDFT

                              READ(MSTUNT,IOSTAT=MSTEND,ERR=99)MACNUM,NAME,BALANC,OVRDFT

                              READ(TRNUNT,IOSTAT=TRNSND,ERR=98)TACNUM,CHANGE

                                          ELSE

                              PRINT 11, TACNUM
11
                                  FORMAT(' TRANSACTION ACCOUNT ',I7,' DOES NOT EXIST')

                              READ(TRNUNT,IOSTAT=TRNSND,ERR=98)TACNUM,CHANGE

                     END IF

                     GO TO 81

                 END IF

                 IF(TRNSND.LT.0)THEN
90
                     IF(MSTEND.EQ.0 )THEN

                         WRITE(NEWUNT,ERR=97)MACNUM,NAME,BALANC,OVRDFT

                         READ(MSTUNT,IOSTAT=MSTEND,ERR=99)MACNUM,NAME,BALANC,OVRDFT

                         GO TO 90

                     END IF

                                ELSE

                     PRINT'(//'' ***UNEXPECTED EOF DETECTED IN FILE '',A6)',MASTER

                 END IF

                 ENDFILE(NEWUNT,ERR=97)

                 CLOSE(NEWUNT,ERR=97)

                 CLOSE(MSTUNT,ERR=99)

                 REWIND(TRNUNT,ERR=98)

                 CLOSE(TRNUNT,ERR=98)

                 STOP

******ERRORS

99       PRINT 95,MASTER

         STOP

98       PRINT 95,TRANS

         STOP

97       PRINT 95,NEWMST

95       FORMAT(//' ***ERROR DETECTED IN FILE ',A6)

         END
```

2.

```
      PROGRAM PRNTFL

******THIS PROGRAM PRINTS THE DETAILS OF CUSTOMERS ACCOUNTS

      CHARACTER MASTER*6,NAME*30

      PARAMETER(MASTER='ACOUNT',MSTUNT=12)

      OPEN(MSTUNT,FILE=MASTER,FORM='UNFORMATTED',STATUS='OLD')

      PRINT 10

10    FORMAT('1 ACC NO',3X,'NAME',30X,'BALANCE',4X,'OVERDRAFT')

20    READ(MSTUNT,END=99)MACNUM,NAME,BALANC,OVRDFT

         PRINT'('' '',I7,3X,A30,2(3X,F9.2))',MACNUM,NAME,BALANC,OVRDFT

         GO TO 20

99    END
```

3. The variable numtran counts the number of transactions made on an account.

```
read a master record
read a transaction record
set numtran to zero
loop while neither file completed do
  { if master account number < transaction account number then
       { if numtran ≠ 0 then
            { if overdraft has been exceeded then
                 { print the current record
                   print the transaction records for this account }
              set numtran to zero }
         write the record
         read the next master record }
    else if master account number = transaction account number then
                     { increment numtran
                       update balance
                       read a transaction record }
       else          { print 'transaction account does not exist'
                       read a transaction record }}
if numtran ≠ 0 then
  { if overdraft has been exceeded then
       { print the current record
         print the transaction records for this account }}
copy remaining master records to the new file
```

```
      PROGRAM TRANS

******THIS PROGRAM UPDATES A MASTER ACCOUNT FILE WITH INDIVIDUAL TRANSACTIONS

      INTEGER MACNUM,TACNUM,MSTUNT,TRNUNT,NEWUNT,NUMTRN,MSTEND,TRNSND

      REAL BALANC,OVRDFT,CHANGE

      CHARACTER*30 NAME

      CHARACTER*6  MASTER,TRANS,NEWMST

      PARAMETER(MASTER='ACOUNT',MSTUNT=12,
     +          TRANS='CREDEB',TRNUNT=39,
     +          NEWMST='BCOUNT',NEWUNT=13)
```

```
        OPEN(MSTUNT,FILE=MASTER,FORM='UNFORMATTED',STATUS='OLD')

        OPEN(TRNUNT,FILE=TRANS,FORM='UNFORMATTED',STATUS='OLD')

        OPEN(NEWUNT,FILE=NEWMST,FORM='UNFORMATTED',STATUS='NEW')
******NUMTRN IS THE NO. OF TRANSACTION FILES FOR THE ACCOUNT

        NUMTRN=0

        READ(MSTUNT,IOSTAT=MSTEND,ERR=99)MACNUM,NAME,BALANC,OVRDFT

        READ(TRNUNT,IOSTAT=TRNSND,ERR=98)TACNUM,CHANGE

81      IF(MSTEND.EQ.0.AND.TRNSND.EQ.0)THEN

            IF(MACNUM.LT.TACNUM)THEN

                IF(NUMTRN.NE.0)THEN

                    IF(BALANC.LT.OVRDFT)THEN

                        PRINT 100,MACNUM,NAME,BALANC,OVRDFT

                        CALL PTRANS(TRNUNT,NUMTRN)

                        READ(TRNUNT,IOSTAT=TRNSND,ERR=98)TACNUM,CHANGE

                    END IF

                    NUMTRN=0

                END IF

                WRITE(NEWUNT,ERR=97)MACNUM,NAME,BALANC,OVRDFT

                READ(MSTUNT,IOSTAT=MSTEND,ERR=99)MACNUM,NAME,BALANC,OVRDFT

            ELSE IF(MACNUM.EQ.TACNUM)THEN

                NUMTRN=NUMTRN+1

                BALANC=BALANC+CHANGE

                READ(TRNUNT,IOSTAT=TRNSND,ERR=98)TACNUM,CHANGE

            ELSE

                PRINT 11,TACNUM

11              FORMAT(//' TRANSACTION ACCOUNT ',I7,' DOES NOT EXIST')

                READ(TRNUNT,IOSTAT=TRNSND,ERR=98)TACNUM,CHANGE

            END IF

            GO TO 81

        END IF

******EOF DETECTED - CHECK LAST UPDATE

        IF(NUMTRN.NE.0)THEN

            IF(BALANC.LT.OVRDFT)THEN

                PRINT 100,MACNUM,NAME,BALANC,OVRDFT

100             FORMAT(//' ACCOUNT ',I7,3X,A30/10X,'HAS A BALANCE ',F9.2,3X,
     +               'WHICH EXCEEDS THE OVERDRAFT LIMIT ',F9.2)

                CALL PTRANS(TRNUNT,NUMTRN)

                READ(TRNUNT,IOSTAT=TRNSND,ERR=98)TACNUM,CHANGE
```

```
          END IF

        END IF

        IF(TRNSND.LT.0)THEN
90      (from this point the code is identical with that of Exercise 19.1

          from statement 90 to the end).

        SUBROUTINE PTRANS(UNIT,NUMTRN)
******THIS SUBROUTINE PRINTS THE LAST NUMTRN TRANSACTION RECORDS
******SINCE FILE IS POSITIONED ONE RECORD TOO FAR, NUMTRN+1 BACKSKIPS ARE MADE
        INTEGER UNIT
        DO 50 I=1,NUMTRN+1
            BACKSPACE(UNIT,ERR=98)
50      CONTINUE
        PRINT 60
60      FORMAT(' THE TRANSACTIONS FORMING THIS UPDATE RUN ARE')
        DO 51 I=1,NUMTRN
            READ(UNIT,ERR=98)IGNORE,CHANGE
            PRINT'(20X,F9.2)',CHANGE
51      CONTINUE
        RETURN
98      PRINT'(//'' ***ERROR DETECTED IN UNIT '',I4)',UNIT
        STOP
        END
```

4.

```
        PROGRAM TRANS2
******THIS PROGRAM UPDATES THE MASTER FILE USING DIRECT ACCESS
        INTEGER MACNUM,TACNUM,MSTUNT,TRNUNT
        REAL BALANC,OVRDFT,CHANGE
        CHARACTER*30 NAME
        CHARACTER*6 MASTER,TRANS
        PARAMETER(MASTER='ACOUNT',MSTUNT=12,
      +          TRANS='DEBCRE',TRNUNT=39)
        OPEN(MSTUNT,FILE=MASTER,FORM='UNFORMATTED',ACCESS='DIRECT',RECL=36,STATUS='OLD')
        OPEN(TRNUNT,FILE=TRANS,FORM='UNFORMATTED',STATUS='OLD')
70      READ(TRNUNT,END=75)TACNUM,CHANGE
            READ(MSTUNT,REC=TACNUM)MACNUM,NAME,BALANC,OVRDFT
            BALANC=BALANC+CHANGE
            WRITE(MSTUNT,REC=TACNUM)MACNUM,NAME,BALANC,OVRDFT
            GO TO 70
```

```
75      REWIND(TRNUNT)

        CLOSE (TRNUNT)

        CLOSE (MSTUNT)

        END
```

Note that error conditions are ignored in this solution.

Exercise 20 (page 276)

1.

```
        SUBROUTINE CHECK(NAME,INFO,N)
******THIS SUBROUTINE CHECKS THAT THE LEAGUE TABLE IS SELF-CONSISTENT
        INTEGER INFO(30,7),N

        CHARACTER NAME(30)*20

        INTEGER PLD,WON,DRAWN,LOST,GLF,GLA,PTS,SUMWON,SUMLST,SUMGLF,SUMGLA,
     +          P,W,D,L,NTS
        PARAMETER(PLD=1,WON=2,DRAWN=3,LOST=4,GLF=5,GLA=6,PTS=7)

        SUMWON=0

        SUMLST=0

        SUMGLF=0

        SUMGLA=0

        DO 25 I=1,N

            P=INFO(I,PLD)

            W=INFO(I,WON)

            D=INFO(I,DRAWN)

            L=INFO(I,LOST)

            NTS=INFO(I,PTS)

            IF(P.NE.W+D+L)THEN

                PRINT 10,NAME(I)

10              FORMAT(' ***ERROR IN ENTRY FOR ',A20)

                PRINT 11,P,W,D,L

11              FORMAT(' PLAYED',I4,' NOT=WON',I4,' +DRAWN',I4,' +LOST',I4)

            END IF

            IF(NTS.NE.2*W+D)THEN

                PRINT 10,NAME(I)

                PRINT 12,NTS,W,D

12              FORMAT(' POINTS',I4,' NOT=2*WON',I4,' +DRAWN',I4)

            END IF

            SUMWON=SUMWON+W

            SUMLST=SUMLST+L

            SUMGLF=SUMGLF+INFO(I,GLF)
```

```
           SUMGLA=SUMGLA+INFO(I,GLA)
25     CONTINUE
       IF(SUMWON.NE.SUMLST)THEN
           PRINT 13
13         FORMAT(' ***ERROR-TABLE INCONSISTENT')
           PRINT 14,SUMWON,SUMLST
14         FORMAT(' TOTAL WON',I4,' NOT=TOTAL LOST',I4)
       END IF
       IF(SUMGLF.NE.SUMGLA)THEN
           PRINT 13
           PRINT 15,SUMGLF,SUMGLA
15         FORMAT(' TOTAL GOALS FOR',I5,' NOT=TOTAL GOALS AGAINST',I5)
       END IF
       END
```

References to CHECK should be made immediately after the table has been printed.

2. (a)

```
       SUBROUTINE ZELLER(D,M,Y,R,DNAME)
*
******THE SUBROUTINE ZELLER CALCULATES THE DAY
*     OF THE WEEK CORRESPONDING TO A GIVEN
*     GREGORIAN DATE D/M/Y USING ZELLER'S METHOD
*     IF A SATURDAY, R IS SET TO 0; IF A SUNDAY,
*     R IS SET TO 1;  IF A MONDAY R IS SET
*     TO 2 ETC. DNAME IS SET EQUAL TO THE FIRST
******THREE CHARACTERS OF THE NAME OF THE DAY
*
       INTEGER D,Y,R
       CHARACTER*3 DNAME,NAME(0:6)
       DATA(NAME(I),I=0,6)/'SAT','SUN','MON','TUE','WED','THU','FRI'/
*
******CHECK VALIDITY OF DATE D/M/Y
*
       CALL CHECK(D,M,Y)
*
******NOW APPLY ZELLER'S METHOD
*
       NM=M
```

```
      NY=Y
      IF (M.EQ.1.OR.M.EQ.2)THEN
            NM=NM+12
            NY=NY-1
      END IF
      R=MOD(D+2*NM+2+(3*NM+3)/5+NY+NY/4-NY/100+NY/400,7)
      DNAME=NAME(R)
      END
```

The subroutine subprogram CHECK is given on page 259.

(b) Insert after the line with statement label 200:

```
*
******    GOLDEN NUMBER
*
          GNUM=MOD(Y,19)+1
*
******    DOMINICAL LETTER
*
          CALL ZELLER(1,1,Y,R,DNAME)
          IF(R.EQ.O.OR.R.EQ.1)THEN
                  R=R+7
          END IF
          R=9-R
          LETTR1=CHAR(ICHAR('A')+R-1)
          IF(LETTR1.EQ.'A')THEN
                  LETTR2='G'
                      ELSE
                  LETTR2=CHAR(ICHAR(LETTR1)-1)
          END IF
          IF (LEAPYR(Y)) THEN
              DLETTR=LETTR1//','//LETTR2
                      ELSE
              DLETTR=LETTR1
          END IF
*
******    EPIPHANY
*
          CALL ZELLER(6,1,Y,R,EPFNY)
```

```
*
******    ADVENT SUNDAY
*
          CALL ZELLER(25,12,Y,R,DNAME)

          JULNUM=JULIAN(25,12,Y)

          R=R-1

          IF(R.LE.0)THEN

                  R=R+7

          END IF

          CALL UNJUL(JULNUM-R-21,Y,ADDAY,ADMNTH)
```

In addition the following type statements are required:

> INTEGER GNUM,R,ADDAY,ADMNTH
> CHARACTER DNAME*3,LETTR1,LETTR2,DLETTR*3,EPFNY*3
> LOGICAL LEAPYR

and the FORMAT statement and the second WRITE statement must also be modified.

3. (a) To verify that the master record read is the correct one, insert before the PRINT statement two lines before statement 10

> IF(C1.NE.NAME)THEN
>   CALL ERROR(5)
> END IF

In subroutine ERROR, an extra error message should be inserted and the value of TOT increased to 5.

(b) The list contains either INT($n/6$)+1 or INT($n/6$) records of candidate information. Therefore the loop in which all candidates in a class are processed should be executed either TOTAL/6+1 or TOTAL/6 times respectively.

Information on up to six candidates will have to be read and so CANDNO and NAME will be 6 element vectors and MARK will be a 6x10 two dimensional array. The declarations for these three entities will be

> INTEGER CANDNO(6), MARK(6,10)
> CHARACTER*30 NAME(6)

The statements from

> DO 11 I=1, TOTAL

to

> 11   CONTINUE

become

```
IF(MOD(TOTAL,6).EQ.0)THEN

    LF=TOTAL/6

                ELSE

    LF=TOTAL/6+1

END IF

L=6
```

```
      DO 11 I=1,LF
         IF(6*I.GT.TOTAL)THEN
            L=TOTAL-6*(I-1)
         END IF
         READ(OLDFIL,END=97,ERR=98)(CANDNO(K),NAME(K),(MARK(K,J),
     +                                 J=1,EXAMS),K=1,L)
         DO 12 K=1,L
         DO 12 J=1,EXAMS
            IF(MARK(K,J).GE.0)THEN
               SUMEX(J)=SUMEX(J)+MARK(K,J)
               PRESNT(J)=PRESNT(J)+1
            END IF
12       CONTINUE
         IF(CHOOSE)THEN
            WRITE(NEWFIL,ERR=99)(CANDNO(K),NAME(K),MARK(K,CHINDX),K=1,L)
         END IF
11    CONTINUE
```

4. Since it is not known how many fourth-year students will be deleted and how many new first-year students will be added, the new first record for each department cannot be written until all that department's records have been processed. In the sample solution, these records are stored temporarily on a scratch file and sorted before being written to the new file PHONEY. It is assumed that a subroutine is available to sort the records appropriately.

read the department name and number of people (total) from PHONEX
loop while not end of file **do**
  { read department name from cards
  if these names are not the same **then** print an error message and stop
  initialize count for deleted students
  loop for $i = 1, 2, \ldots,$ total **do**
    { read a record from PHONEX
      if category code = 0 or 9 **then** write the record to SCRATCH
        else if category code = 1, 2, or 3 **then** write the record to SCRATCH
        with the category code incremented
        else if category code = 4 **then**
          { increment no of deleted students
            print name, address and phone no.}
        else print an error message and stop}
  initialize count for new students
  read a record from cards
  loop while name $\neq$ **'ZZZZZ' do**
    { increment no. of new students
     write record to SCRATCH with a category code of 1
     read a record from cards}
  skip the two blank cards
  set new total to old total + no. of new students − no. of deleted students
  write department name and new total to PHONEY

sort the records on **SCRATCH**
copy records on **SCRATCH** to **PHONEY**}

```
      PROGRAM PHONE
******THIS PROGRAM UPDATES A FILE OF RECORDS CONTAINING PHONE NUMBERS
      INTEGER OUTFLE,SCRFLE,TOTAL,DELETE,TELEPH,CAT
      CHARACTER INNAME*6,OUTNME*6,DEPTF*50,DEPTC*50,NAME*35,ADDRES*80
      PARAMETER(INFILE=12,INNAME='PHONEX',
     +          OUTFLE=22,OUTNME='PHONEY',
     +          SCRFLE=19)
      OPEN(INFILE,FILE=INNAME,FORM='UNFORMATTED',STATUS='OLD',ERR=99)
      OPEN(OUTFLE,FILE=OUTNME,FORM='UNFORMATTED',STATUS='NEW',ERR=98)
      OPEN(SCRFLE,FORM='UNFORMATTED',STATUS='SCRATCH',ERR=97)
1     READ(INFILE,END=90,ERR=99)DEPTF,TOTAL
******LOOP WHILE NOT EOF DO
          READ'(A50)',DEPTC
          IF(DEPTF.NE.DEPTC)THEN
              PRINT 199,DEPTF,DEPTC
199           FORMAT(//' ***ERROR - DEPT NAMES NOT THE SAME'/A50/A50)
              GO TO 90
          END IF
          PRINT 10,DEPTF
10        FORMAT(//' LIST OF STUDENTS DELETED FROM ',A50)
          DELETE=0
          DO 50 I=1,TOTAL
              READ(INFILE,END=96,ERR=99)NAME,ADDRES,TELEPH,CAT
              IF(CAT.EQ.0.OR.CAT.EQ.9)THEN
                  WRITE(SCRFLE,ERR=97)NAME,ADDRES,TELEPH,CAT
                ELSE IF(CAT.EQ.1.OR.CAT.EQ.2.OR.CAT.EQ.3)THEN
                    WRITE(SCRFLE,ERR=97)NAME,ADDRES,TELEPH,CAT+1
                  ELSE IF(CAT.EQ.4)THEN
                      DELETE=DELETE+1
                      PRINT 11,NAME,ADDRES,TELEPH
11                    FORMAT(' ',A35,5X,A80/41X,I10)
                    ELSE
                      PRINT 198,CAT
198                   FORMAT(//' ***ERROR-INVALID CATEGORY ',I5)
                      GOTO 90
                END IF
50        CONTINUE
```

```
******    ADD THE NEW STUDENTS
          NEW=0
          READ 12,NAME,ADDRES,TELEPH
12        FORMAT(A35/A80/I10)
******    LOOP WHILE NOT EOF
51        IF(NAME.NE.'ZZZZZZ')THEN
                  NEW=NEW+1
                  WRITE(SCRFLE,ERR=97)NAME,ADDRES,TELEPH,1
                  READ 12,NAME,ADDRES,TELEPH
                  GO TO 51
          END IF
          REWIND(SCRFLE, ERR=97)
          TOTAL=TOTAL+NEW-DELETE
          WRITE(OUTFLE,ERR=98)DEPTF,TOTAL
          CALL SORT(SCRFLE,TOTAL)
          DO 52 I=1,TOTAL
                  READ(SCRFLE,END=95,ERR=97)NAME,ADDRES,TELEPH,CAT
                  WRITE(OUTFLE,ERR=98)NAME,ADDRES,TELEPH,CAT
52        CONTINUE
          REWIND(SCRFLE, ERR=97)
          GO TO 1
******END OF MAIN LOOP
90    CLOSE(INFILE,ERR=99)
      ENDFILE(OUTFLE, ERR=98)
      CLOSE(OUTFLE,ERR=98)
      CLOSE(SCRFLE,ERR=97)
      STOP
******ERROR CONDITIONS
99    PRINT 150,INNAME
150   FORMAT(//' ***ERROR DETECTED IN FILE ',A6)
      STOP
98    PRINT 150,OUTNME
      STOP
97    PRINT 150,'SCRTCH'
      STOP
96    PRINT 151,INNAME
151   FORMAT(//' ***UNEXPECTED EOF IN FILE ',A6)
      STOP
95    PRINT 151,'SCRTCH'
      END
```

5. (a) One possibility is to allow more than one blank between words. This does not affect the main program unit RIDDLE, but the subroutine DECODE must be amended along the following lines:

```
      SUBROUTINE DECODE(TEXT,WORD1,WORD2,TYPE)
      CHARACTER TEXT*80,WORD1*20,WORD2*20,TYPE*8
      INTEGER L,R
*
******FIND FIRST OCCURRENCE OF 'IN'.
*
      L=INDEX(TEXT,'IN')
*
******IF NOT FOLLOWED BY A BLANK (E.G. AS IN 'NINTH') FIND
******NEXT OCCURRENCE. IN EITHER CASE ADD 2 FOR POSITION OF BLANK
*
      IF(TEXT(L+2:L+2).NE.' ')THEN
            L=(L+1)+INDEX(TEXT(L+2:),'IN')
      END IF
      L=L+2
*
******SKIP OVER BLANKS TO FIND START OF WORD1.
*
100   IF(TEXT(L:L).EQ.' ')THEN
            L=L+1
            GO TO 100
      END IF
*
******FIND NEXT BLANK, AND MOVE BACK 1 CHARACTER TO FIND
******END OF WORD1.
*
      R=(L-1)+INDEX(TEXT(L:),' ')-1
*
      WORD1=TEXT(L:R)
*
******SKIP OVER BLANKS TO FIND START OF 'AND ALSO' OR
******'BUT NOT'
*
      L=R+1
200   IF(TEXT(L:L).EQ.' ')THEN
            L=L+1
```

```
            GO TO 200
      END IF
*
******OBTAIN TYPE-OF-LINE
*
      IF(TEXT(L:L+2).EQ.'AND')THEN
            TYPE='AND ALSO'
                        ELSE
            TYPE='BUT NOT'
      END IF
*
******FIND NEXT 'IN', AND ADD 2 FOR POSITION OF SUBSEQUENT
******BLANK.
*
      L=(L-1)+INDEX(TEXT(L:),'IN')+2
*
******SKIP OVER BLANKS TO FIND START OF WORD2
*
300   IF(TEXT(L:L).EQ.' ')THEN
            L=L+1
            GO TO 300
      END IF
*
******OBTAIN WORD2
*
      WORD2=TEXT(L:)
*
      END
```

(b) Validation routines can range from the trivial to the extremely complex depending on how much validation is considered essential. A 'reasonable' validation subroutine subprogram VLDATE is listed below. For clarity it has been constructed as a separate subroutine. If efficiency is of paramount importance it would be more sensible to rewrite DECODE to include validation tests in order to avoid the double scanning of each card.

```
SUBROUTINE VLDATE(TEXT,COUNT)
INTEGER COUNT,L(9),R(9)
CHARACTER TEXT*80,PREVCH,WORD(16)*10
LOGICAL T1,T2,T3,T4,T5,T6,T7,T8
DATA(WORD(I),I=1,16)/'FIRST','SECOND',
   +              'THIRD','FOURTH',
```

```
     +                       'FIFTH','SIXTH',
     +                       'SEVENTH','EIGHTH',
     +                       'NINTH','TENTH',
     +                       'ELEVENTH','TWELFTH',
     +                       'THIRTEENTH','FOURTEENTH',
     +                       'FIFTEENTH','SIXTEENTH'/
*
******FIND POSITIONS OF START AND FINISH OF EACH WORD
******AND STORE AS L(1),R(1),L(2),R(2),L(3),R(3),---------.
*
      PREVCH=' '
      J=1
      DO 100 I=1,80
          IF(TEXT(I:I).NE.' '.AND.PREVCH.EQ.' ')THEN
              L(J)=I
          ELSE IF (TEXT(I:I).EQ.' '.AND.PREVCH.NE.' ')THEN
              R(J)=I-1
              J=J+1
              IF(J.GT.9.AND.TEXT(I:).NE.' ')THEN
                  GO TO 200
              END IF
          END IF
          PREVCH=TEXT(I:I)
100   CONTINUE
*
******PERFORM VALIDITY TESTS
*
      FLAG=.FALSE.
      T1=L(1).EQ.1
      IF(J.EQ.10)THEN
        T2=TEXT(L(1):R(1)).EQ.'MY'
        T3=TEXT(L(2):R(2)).EQ.WORD(COUNT)
        T4=TEXT(L(3):R(3)).EQ.'IS'
        T5=TEXT(L(4):R(4)).EQ.'IN'
        T6=(TEXT(L(6):R(6)).EQ.'AND').AND.(TEXT(L(7):R(7)).EQ.'ALSO')
        T7=(TEXT(L(6):R(6)).EQ.'BUT').AND.(TEXT(L(7):R(7)).EQ.'NOT')
        T8=TEXT(L(8):R(8)).EQ.'IN'
        FLAG=T1.AND.T2.AND.T3.AND.T4.AND.T5.AND.(T6.OR.T7).AND.T8
      ELSE IF(J.EQ.4)
```

```
          T2=TEXT(L(1):R(1)).EQ.'WHAT'

          T3=TEXT(L(2):R(2)).EQ.'AM'

          T4=TEXT(L(3):R(3)).EQ.'I'

          FLAG=T1.AND.T2.AND.T3.AND.T4

       END IF

*

******IF FLAG IS TRUE, RETURN TO CALLING PROGRAM UNIT;

******OTHERWISE OUTPUT ERROR MESSAGE AND STOP.

*      IF(FLAG)THEN

            RETURN

       END IF

200    WRITE(*,'('' INVALID DATA CARD'')')

       STOP

       END
```

Note that the error message merely indicates the detection of an invalid data card, not the *nature* of the error. The subroutine could be adapted to provide more helpful information.

6. The following program is based on the idea of filling up a matrix with the information for 3 months, outputting it, filling up the matrix with the information for the next 3 months, outputting it, etc. Since a month can never spread over more than 6 weeks (look at a calendar!) a 7x18 matrix is appropriate.

```
       PROGRAM CLNDR

       INTEGER DAYVAL,QRTR,MONTH(12),R,Y,A(7,18)

       LOGICAL LEAPYR

       CHARACTER DNAME*3,HDING(4)*90

       DATA(MONTH(I),I=1,12)/31,28,31,30,31,30,2*31,30,31,30,31/,

      +         (HDING(I),I=1,4)/

      +'(13X,''JANUARY'',21X,''FEBRUARY'',22X,''MARCH'')',

      +'(14X,''APRIL'',24X,''MAY'',25X,''JUNE'')',

      +'(14X,''JULY'',24X,''AUGUST'',21X,''SEPTEMBER'')',

      +'(13X,''OCTOBER'',21X,''NOVEMBER'',20X,''DECEMBER'')'/


*

       READ*,Y

       WRITE(*,'(''1'',''CALENDAR FOR '',I4//)')Y

*

       IF(LEAPYR(Y))THEN

          MONTH(2)=29

       END IF

*
```

```
        CALL ZELLER(1,1,Y,R,DNAME)

        IF(R.EQ.O)THEN

                R=R+7

        END IF
*

        M=1

        DAYVAL=1

        I=R
*

        DO 100 QRTR=1,4

                WRITE(*,HDING(QRTR))

                CALL ZERO(A,7,18)

                J=1

200             IF(J.NE.19)THEN

                        IF(I.LE.7.AND.DAYVAL.LE.MONTH(M))THEN
*

                                A(I,J)=DAYVAL

                                I=I+1

                                DAYVAL=DAYVAL+1

                        END IF
*

                        IF(I.GT.7)THEN

                                I=1

                                J=J+1

                        END IF
*

                        IF(DAYVAL.GT.MONTH(M))THEN

                                M=M+1

                                DAYVAL=1

                                IF(J.LT.7)THEN

                                        J=7

                                ELSE IF(J.LT.13)THEN

                                        J=13

                                ELSE IF(J.GT.13)THEN

                                        J=19

                                        CALL PRNTUP(A)

                                END IF

                        END IF
```

```
                    GO TO 200

                END IF

100     CONTINUE

        END

        SUBROUTINE ZERO(A,M,N)

        INTEGER A(M,N)

        DO 100 I=1,M

        DO 100 J=1,N

            A(I,J)=0

100     CONTINUE

        END

        SUBROUTINE PRNTUP(A)

        INTEGER A(7,18)

        CHARACTER NAME(7)*3

        DATA (NAME(I),I=1,7)/'SUN','MON','TUE','WED','THU','FRI','SAT'/

        DO 100 I=1,7

            WRITE(*,10) NAME(I),(A(I,J),J=1,18)

10          FORMAT(' ',A3,2X,6(I3.0,1X),4X,6(I3.0,1X),4X,(I3.0,1X))

100     CONTINUE

        WRITE(*,'( )')

        WRITE(*,'( )')

        END
```

Note the use of a character array element as a format identifier in the statement
WRITE(*,HDING(QRTR))

7. (a)

```
        PROGRAM SOLVE

        INTEGER SUB,X,Y

        PARAMETER (N=50,

     +              M=N*(N+1)/2)

        INTEGER A(M,3)

        DATA SUB/0/

*

        DO 100 X=1,N

        DO 100 Y=X,N

            SUB=SUB+1

            A(SUB,1)=X**3

            A(SUB,2)=Y**3
```

```
         A(SUB,3)=X**3+Y**3
100   CONTINUE
*

      CALL RSORT(A,M,3,3)
*

      DO 200 I=1,M-1
        IF(A(I,3).EQ.A(I+1,3))THEN
           WRITE(*,10)A(I,1),A(I,2),A(I+1,1),A(I+1,2)
10         FORMAT(' ',4I4)
        END IF
200   CONTINUE
*

      END

      SUBROUTINE RSORT(A,M,N,K)
*
******RSORT SORTS THE ROWS OF THE M*N
******MATRIX A INTO ORDER, USING THE ELEMENTS IN
******THE KTH COLUMN AS KEYS.   A SIMPLE BUBBLE
******SORTING TECHNIQUE IS USED.
*

      INTEGER A(M,N),T
      LOGICAL FLAG
*

      I=1
      FLAG=.TRUE.
*

100   IF(I.LT.M.AND.FLAG)
         FLAG=.FALSE.
         DO 200 L=1,M-I
           IF(A(L,K).GT.A(L+1,K))THEN
              DO 300 J=1,N
                 T=A(L,J)
                 A(L,J)=A(L+1,J)
                 A(L+1,J)=T
300           CONTINUE
              FLAG=.TRUE.
           END IF
200      CONTINUE
```

```
     I=I+1

     GO TO 100

     END IF

     END
```

(b) Change integer type specification in main program unit to

INTEGER SUB,X,Y,U,V,HCF

and replace WRITE statement by:

```
     U=HCF(A(I,1),A(I,2))
     V=HCF(A(I+1,1),A(I+1,2))
     IF(HCF(U,V).EQ.1)THEN
         WRITE(*,10)A(I,1),A(I,2),A(I+1,1),A(I+1,2)
     END IF
```

where HCF(X,Y) is an integer function subprogram which returns the *highest common factor* of the integers X and Y. It may be based on the usual Euclidean algorithm thus:

```
     INTEGER FUNCTION HCF(X,Y)

     INTEGER X,Y,REM,A,B,

     A=X

     B=Y

     REM=1

100  IF (REM.NE.0) THEN

         REM=MOD(A,B)

         A=B

         B=REM

         GO TO 100

     END IF

     HCF=A

     END
```

Index